DUE PROCESS AND VICTIMS' RIGHTS:
THE NEW LAW AND POLITICS OF CRIMINAL JUSTICE

In the last two decades courts have been increasingly concerned about the rights of those accused of crime, while legislatures have been devoting more attention to the rights of crime victims and groups, such as women and children, who are disproportionately subject to some crimes. In *Due Process and Victims' Rights* Kent Roach argues that these concerns have transformed debates about criminal justice. He examines recent cases in which due process and victims' rights have clashed and concludes that, in most instances, victims' rights claims have ultimately prevailed. He concludes that the future of criminal justice will depend on whether victims' rights continue to develop in a punitive fashion or whether they inspire increased emphasis on crime prevention and restorative justice.

This is the first full-length study of the law and politics of criminal justice in the era of the Charter and victims' rights. It examines changing discourse in the courts, legislatures, and the media, and the role of women, young people, various minorities, Aboriginal people, and crime victims in criminal justice reform. It builds new models of criminal justice based on victims' rights as alternatives to Herbert Packer's famous due-process and crime-control models. As a compendium of key legal decisions and important critical works, this book will be a valuable resource for both scholars and practitioners.

KENT ROACH is Dean and Professor of Law at the University of Saskatchewan. He is author of *Constitutional Remedies in Canada*, which was awarded the Walter Owen Prize for the best Canadian law book of 1994/5.

KENT ROACH

Due Process and Victims' Rights: The New Law and Politics of Criminal Justice

UNIVERSITY OF TORONTO PRESS
Toronto Buffalo London

© University of Toronto Press 1999
Toronto Buffalo London
Printed in the U.S.A.

Reprinted 2015

ISBN 0-8020-0931-X (cloth)
ISBN 0-8020-7901-6 (paper)

Printed on acid-free paper

Canadian Cataloguing in Publication Data

Roach, Kent, 1961–
    Due process and victims' rights : the new law and
    politics of criminal justice

    Includes bibliographical references and index.
    ISBN 0-8020-0931-X (bound)   ISBN 0-8020-7901-6 (pbk.)

    1. Victims of crimes – Legal status, laws, etc. – Canada.
    2. Due process of law – Canada.   3. Criminal justice,
    Administration of – Canada.   I. Title.

    KE9443.R62 1999   344.713'03288   C98-932664-0
    KF9763.R62 1999

University of Toronto Press acknowledges the financial assistance to its
publishing program of the Canada Council for the Arts and the Ontario Arts
Council.

This book has been published with the help of a grant from the Humanities
and Social Sciences Federation of Canada, using funds provided by the Social
Sciences and Humanities Research Council of Canada.

Contents

For my family

Acknowledgments

Research for this book was made possible by grants from the Foundation for Legal Research and the Caesar Wright Foundation for Legal Research. I am most grateful for this valuable financial support.

The University of Toronto's Centre of Criminology provided me with a home during my 1996–7 sabbatical year, when much of this book was researched and drafted. I thank Bill Bateman of Woodsworth College, Ron Daniels, Dean of the Faculty of Law, and Clifford Shearing, Director of the Centre of Criminology, for allowing me to shape my teaching and leave schedule to facilitate this research. The graduate and undergraduate criminology students in my Criminal Process seminars at the Centre of Criminology and Woodsworth College deserve special thanks for being sounding boards for my ideas and convincing me that non-lawyers would be interested in the subject matter of this book.

I was fortunate enough to be asked to talk about my research at the University of Victoria's Faculty of Law, at Green College of the University of British Columbia, at the Native Law Centre at the University of Saskatchewan, and at the Department of Justice in Ottawa. Thanks to Don Galloway, Richard Ericson, Ruth Thompson, and Catherine Kane for coordinating these talks which provided an opportunity to have my ideas vigorously challenged.

Thanks also to Virgil Duff and the staff at the University of Toronto Press for their valuable assistance in helping prepare the manuscript for publication.

I was also fortunate enough to have excellent research assistance. Chris de Sa, a recent graduate of the University of Toronto Faculty of Law, spent a summer cheerfully tracking down often vague research requests. Rob Centa, now a third-year student at the University of Toronto Faculty of Law, spent another summer and part of the subsequent year exceeding all my research expectations. Both were a pleasure to work with and improved the book immensely. I have attempted to include relevant events as of 1 January 1998. Parts of Chapter 1 appeared in volume 89 of the *Journal of Criminal Law and Criminology*.

My intellectual debts in writing this book are numerous. In particular I would like to thank Nick Bala, John Braithwaite, Kathy Brock, Christine Boyle, Alan Cairns, Stephen Cheesman, Tony Doob, David Dyzenhaus, Richard Ericson, Marty Friedland, John Hagan, Michael Mandel, Janet Mosher, Jonathan Rudin, Peter Russell, Martha Shaffer, Clifford Shearing, Don Stuart, and the anonymous reviewers for their valuable input. Their responses reaffirmed my faith in a scholarly community which listens and respects while not necessarily agreeing. Given the distinctive voices of my consultants, I believe the usually trite disclaimer about my own responsibility for the errors and shortcomings of the book is in order.

My greatest debt is to my family for their cheerful and loving support. My parents, Howard and Grace Roach, and my in-laws, Sharon and Cecil Cox, provided encouragement and babysitting. My daughters, Carey and Erin Roach, always greeted me with enthusiasm when I emerged from the basement after yet another lengthy struggle with the book. Most of all, my wife, Jan Cox, provided support, constructive criticism, and gentle reminders of past frustrations when writing. I dedicate this book to my family.

Kent Roach
September 1998

DUE PROCESS AND VICTIMS' RIGHTS

Introduction

The way that Canadians think and talk about criminal justice has changed dramatically in the last two decades. This book attempts to make sense of these developments and provide a new framework for the choices to be made in the future.

Before 1980, the courts and legislatures were reluctant to recognize the rights of the accused or the crime victim. Parliament had supreme authority for enacting criminal laws, which were then enforced through the largely unfettered discretion of police and prosecutors. The system functioned and thought of itself as a smooth and efficient crime-control assembly line (Packer 1968: 159). The 1982 enactment of the Canadian Charter of Rights and Freedoms (the Charter) and the 1984 enactment of the Young Offenders Act (YOA) gave the accused new rights. In the late 1980s, the Supreme Court interpreted these rights so that they equalled and sometimes exceeded American due-process rights. *Miranda* warnings, the exclusionary rule, and warrant, disclosure, and speedy-trial requirements came north of the border. These changes created the impression, and, at times, the reality that the criminal justice system had turned into a due-process obstacle course (ibid: 163) in which defence lawyers and the Supreme Court blocked the efforts of police, prosecutors, and Parliament to find and convict the guilty. The effect of the due-process revolution was dramatic and enough for one generation to absorb. It was, however, less than half the story.

The accused had more rights, but more frequently landed in jail. Between 1980–1 and 1994–5, there was a 50 per cent increase in the population of Canada's prisons. From 1986–7 to 1994–5, there was a 26 per cent increase in the numbers of young people imprisoned even while the YOA was becoming infamous for its leniency and concern about due process (Canadian Centre for Criminal Justice Statistics [CCCJS] 1996b: 14–16). Clearly, due process was not inconsistent with increased punishment, and some commentators argued that it legitimated increased crime control (Ericson 1983; Mandel 1994, 1996). However, this view ignored the emergence of victims' rights, which more directly enabled and legitimated the criminal sanction.

'Victims' rights' are defined broadly in this book to include not only the claims made by crime victims that they were inadequately protected from crime and/or mistreated during the investigation and prosecution of crime, but also similar claims by disadvantaged groups disproportionately subject to some crimes. Victims' rights advocates did not march under the same banner, and included those on the right, who traditionally sided with the state and the police, and those on the left, who sought equality for disadvantaged groups. They all agreed, however, that criminal justice could no longer be defined as a matter between the accused and the state.

In the 1980s and the 1990s, legislatures frequently turned to criminal justice reforms in an attempt to better protect victims and potential victims of crimes, including women, children, and various minorities. This process intensified as governments tightened their belts and responded to the due-process decisions of the courts. The result has been criticized as legalized politics (Mandel 1994, 1996) and as politicized law (Knopff and Morton 1992; Morton 1992a), but included a more comprehensive criminalization of politics. This process of criminalization began when legislatures, courts, and the media focused on criminal justice issues that were symptoms of social, economic, political, and cultural problems. The courts played a role in this process, but not the dominant role that most commentators suggested. My 'criminalization of politics' thesis can explain why the reform of sexual-assault laws became the focus of much feminist energy and how the treatment of young people was dominated by issues concerning sexual abuse of children and the YOA. It can explain how the prosecution of police shootings and Robert Latimer came to symbolize the treatment of racial minorities and the disabled, respectively, and how criminal justice issues dominated other aspects of justice for Aboriginal peoples. It can also explain how attempts to deny 'faint hope' hearings to a small number of murderers dominated the victims' rights movement. Criminalized politics was often symbolic, punitive, and divisive, but relatively inexpensive compared with other reforms.

The emergence of due process and victims' rights produced a new kind of political case in the 1990s. The old political case set off the accused's claims to liberty against the state's interest in crime control. The new one pitted the accused's due-process and free-expression claims against the security and equality rights of crime victims and potential victims. It was fought in cases involving what in the 1960s were called 'victimless crimes,' such as pornography, hate propaganda, euthanasia, prostitution, and abortion (Packer 1968). The criminal sanction was no longer defended as a manifestation of community morality, but as a means to recognize the rights of disadvantaged groups, to respond to the risks they faced, and to provide them with a symbol of the state's care and recognition. The new political case was also fought in cases involving due-process challenges to laws and prosecutions targeting sexual assault and abuse, hate crimes, war crimes, police shootings of minorities, and publication bans. Consistent with Canadian political traditions, the new political case was often resolved by court decisions upholding the criminal sanction or by parliamentary replies to due-process decisions and not, as in the United States, in riots after jury acquittals (Fletcher 1995). Much of this book examines the struggles between due process and victims' rights that were fought in the courts, the media, and the legislatures over the last decade.

The traditional models of crime control and due process can no longer explain the law and politics of criminal justice as a matter of positive description. They are also impoverished normative guides for future reform. Given the increases in prison populations during the Charter era, it can no longer be assumed that respect for due-process rights will increase liberty or encourage decriminalization. Given the levels of widespread and often unreported crime revealed by victimization studies, it can no longer be assumed that prosecutions and punishment will control crime. Crime victims are not included in the traditional models, but they can no longer be ignored. Victims and potential victims must be included in new frameworks, and the future of criminal justice will largely depend on how victims' rights evolve. The dominant direction so far has been a punitive one which merged with crime control and opposed due-process claims. The focus was on the criminal sanction and its promise of safety and security. A punitive model of victims' rights promoted the power of the traditional agents of crime control – legislatures, police, and prosecutors – while not necessarily empowering crime victims and potential victims. Victims' rights became the new means to legitimate crime control and to counter due-process claims.

Taking seriously the failure of the criminal law to protect and respect victims, however, also led some away from reliance on the criminal sanction and towards crime prevention and restorative justice. Corporations and advantaged individuals learned that traditional crime-control responses did not control crime, and invested in private policing, security systems, and insurance. It was the disadvantaged who were left to rely on the criminal sanction and to fight the new political case. A greater emphasis on crime prevention, including social development (Canada 1993a), could protect potential victims of crime and counter the tendency to criminalize social and economic problems. When crime does occur and is reported, some social response is required, but not always a punitive one. There are limits to how much the adversarial criminal trial process can be made victim-sensitive and avoid revictimization. Family conferences, Aboriginal justice, victim–offender reconciliation programs – all included victims, but did not rely on adversarial legal procedures or punishment. These interventions had the potential to empower crime victims, offenders, their families and communities, to the detriment of crime-control professionals. A non-punitive model of victims' rights based on crime prevention and restorative justice presented a far more radical challenge to the criminal justice system than due-process or punitive forms of victims' rights.

The choice between punitive and non-punitive versions of victims' rights is not zero-sum. We may be moving towards crime prevention and restorative justice at the individual, corporate, and local levels while focusing on more punitive victims' rights issues at the level of public culture and discourse. Although this approach will allow genuine alternatives to crime control and due process to grow, they will not flourish if public discourse continues to focus on more punitive approaches and the due-process challenges that they inspire.

Methodology

This book is primarily concerned with understanding changes in the way we think and talk about criminal justice – what some scholars would call the ideology, discourse, public culture, or symbolic order of criminal justice (McBarnet 1981; Gusfield 1981). At this level, the change has been profound and controversial. My analysis attempts to take into account obvious operational changes such as increased prison populations, but is primarily concerned with how public actors such as legislators, judges, interest groups, and the media have defined criminal justice issues.

This book is written from a legal-process perspective that is concerned with legislative, administrative, judicial, and private ordering, and their interactions (Roach 1996c, 1997). The legal-process approach can accommodate legal pluralism, which assumes that all forms of ordering have a legitimate role in various contexts. Most critics and defenders of due process have focused too much on the courts. The courts frequently did not have the last word, and media, legislative, and administrative responses to their rulings were not studied enough. Critics and defenders of victims' rights examined both the courts and the legislatures, but sometimes ignored the important role of non-adjudicative forms of dispute resolution. Some crime victims may have good reasons for not reporting crime and may have engaged in their own forms of healing, shaming, and prevention. Restorative justice and Aboriginal justice are promising alternatives to criminal prosecutions.

The legal-process approach is also rooted in a pragmatic approach to politics which attempts, as best it can, to understand competing perspectives and achieve some reconciliation between them. A pragmatist is wary about the type of principled yet divisive battles that pit principles and people irreconcilably against each other. It is not a coincidence that my favoured non-punitive victims' rights model attempts to avoid conflict through crime prevention and to heal it through restorative justice. Moreover, my pragmatic approach explains my scepticism about the symbolic confrontations between due process and victims' rights discussed throughout this book. Both sides in the new political cases had valid points and perspectives, and it was unfortunate that there were so many zero-sum confrontations wherein some legitimate concern lost and, worse for a pragmatist, was ignored or discredited.

A pragmatist is vulnerable to claims that he or she is not only unprincipled, but arrogant in attempting to understand perspectives different from his or her own. The idea that an observer can have some partial success in understanding diverse viewpoints is a controversial one (Cairns 1995: 125), especially in a book such as this, which examines and draws connections among the incredibly diverse worlds of crime victims and potential victims of crime, many of whom do not want to be connected and disclaim membership in any wider victims' movement (Rock 1986). Nevertheless, at various times, their disproportionate victimization by crime and/or victimization by the operation of the criminal process affected criminal justice debates and for that reason cannot be ignored.

This book cannot tell the full story of the diverse and frequently disadvantaged groups mentioned in it. As a consequence of the criminalization of politics, it would not be surprising that many of the episodes discussed here were divisive and defensive distractions. Women's groups might have preferred national day care, equal pay, employment equity, better social services, and equality-based education, but what they got in the 1980s and 1990s were new laws and policies targeting sexual and wife assault, prostitution, and pornography. Criminal laws targeting the sexual abuse of children, and hate and war crimes against minorities, were easier to obtain than the more expensive and radical interventions required to come to grips with the causes of these ugly problems. Aboriginal people might have preferred self-government, but they got numerous public inquiries into criminal justice matters. Crime victims might have preferred less crime and a more fundamental restructuring of justice, but they received victim-impact statements, victims' bills of rights, and the partial repeal of 'faint hope' hearings. Many of the interventions examined in this book were relatively cheap and symbolic. They reflected a politics that was criminalized in the sense that criminal justice reform was offered as the primary response to broader problems. My hope is that better appreciation of the limits of punitive policies and of symbolic struggles between due process and victims' rights can be a prelude to a more holistic integration of criminal justice with social, political, cultural, and economic justice.

The Organization of This Book

Chapter 1 outlines competing models of the criminal process. The starting point is Herbert Packer's famous crime-control and due-process models. The claims of Packer's many critics are examined, and alternative models based on punitive and non-punitive forms of victims' rights are developed. This chapter also describes how Packer's crime-control model captured the operation and ideology of the Canadian criminal justice system before the 1980s, and the fragile and contingent place of due process in the Charter.

The next two chapters examine Canada's due-process revolution with respect to police powers and criminal trials. The courts actively enforced an expanded right against self-incrimination and required the state to obtain warrants, provide disclosure, and satisfy speedy-trial standards. At the same time, however, these chapters also reveal significant support for the critical thesis that due-process decisions produced crime-control responses from legislatures and administrators. The intervention of victims and other third parties in the criminal trial is also examined, as is the use of victims' rights as a new justification for crime-control measures.

Chapter 4 deals with how what Packer believed were victimless and consensual crimes vulnerable to due-process challenges were relegitimated in the 1990s as crimes which protected equality rights and responded to the risk of violence against disadvantaged groups. The new political cases described in this chapter would be unrecognizable to Packer because they pitted the accused's rights, not against the state's attempt to enforce morality, but against the equality and security rights of victims and groups of potential victims. This chapter also explores how legislators and others defended the criminal sanction in the name of victims and potential victims even when some in the target groups wanted decriminalization. The new defence of the criminal sanction in the name of victims' rights focused on the symbolic value of criminal law and reproduced the crime-control assumption that the criminal law could control crime.

The remaining chapters consider how the concerns of various groups were projected onto due-process, crime-control, and punitive and non-punitive forms of victims' rights. Chapter 5 focuses on women, who were the most influential group of crime victims and potential victims of crime. Due-process strategies, such as the use of battered women's syndrome to support self-defence claims, and crime-control strategies, such as mandatory charge and prosecution policies for wife abuse, are examined. This chapter also provides detailed case studies of three mega-political cases in which due-process decisions affecting sexual-assault laws and prosecutions were met with legislative replies emphasizing the rights of women and children as victims and potential victims of sexual violence.

Chapter 6 explores the changing understandings of young people in the criminal justice system and reflects many of the themes discussed throughout the book. The discovery of child sexual abuse through victimization studies and subsequent attempts to increase reporting by making the prosecution process more victim-sensitive has many parallels to the sexual- and wife-assault reforms discussed in chapter 5. This chapter also discusses the YOA as a due-process reform while also considering the critical thesis that due process was for crime control, as measured by the increasing number of youths punished. Finally, crime prevention and family conferencing are examined as alternative and non-punitive responses that do not rely on either crime control or due process.

The seventh and eighth chapters, on minorities and Aboriginal people, respectively, follow a similar pattern. They examine, first, how due process was offered as a solution to the racist exercise of discretion in the criminal process and overrepresentation in prison, and, then, how crime control was offered as a response to disproportionate victimization among these groups. These strategies not only invited due-process challenges, but relied on the dubious assumption that the criminal law controlled crime. Finally, both chapters explore alternatives to due process and crime control, including crime prevention, restorative justice, and Aboriginal justice.

Chapter 9 discusses crime victims who were not members of the groups considered in previous chapters. Increased concern about crime victims is traced through victimization surveys, victims' bills of rights, and new political cases pitting victims' rights against due process and freedom of expression. Next, victims' rights reforms such as victim-impact statements and attempts to repeal 'faint hope' hearings are examined. These reforms assumed that increasing the punishment of the offender would control crime and respect victims. Finally, non-punitive alternatives, including victim compensation, victim–offender reconciliation programs, and crime prevention are explored.

The final chapter outlines the main themes explored in this book. The future of criminal justice will and should include victims and potential victims of crime. Much will depend on how much concerns about victims are channelled into increased reliance on the criminal sanction and combat with due process, and how much they inspire increased emphasis on crime prevention and restorative justice.

1

Models of the Criminal Process

This chapter outlines models of the criminal process and places them in theoretical and historical context. The crime-control model represents many of the traditional values of the Canadian criminal justice system and was entrenched in the law and operation of the criminal justice as late as 1980. It assumes that the criminal law, enacted by Parliament and enforced by police and prosecutors, can control crime. The due-process model best describes the values that the Supreme Court of Canada embraced in many, but not all, of its early decisions under the Charter. Its main goal is the protection of the rights of the accused, which, it is assumed, will protect the rights of all Canadians. Models based on victims'[1] rights[2] can develop in a punitive direction that merges with the crime-control model or they can introduce new concerns about crime prevention and restorative justice.

The Criminal Process

'The criminal process' refers to the wide range of activities and actors which respond to crime. It can be charted as an orderly progression, but it is not. About a quarter of adult Canadians are victimized by crime in a year, but most do not report the crime to the police. Of the more than 3 million crimes reported to the police in a year, most are not cleared by the laying of a charge. Only a small percentage of charges actually result in a trial. Most cases result in a guilty plea and/or a withdrawal of charges by the prosecutor. When a trial is held, allegations that police or prosecutors have violated the accused's Charter rights may lead to a focus on the accused's rights and remedies, not guilt or innocence. Governments spend about $10 billion on the criminal process each year, with about 60 per cent being devoted to policing; 25 per cent to corrections; 9 per cent to courts; and 6 per cent to legal aid for accused who cannot afford a defence lawyer (Canadian Centre for Criminal Justice Statistics [CCCJS] 1995). This accounts for only 3 per cent of all government expenditures, but criminal justice matters attract a disproportionate amount of attention from the media and legislatures – attention that produces conditions conducive to the criminalization of politics.

Models of the Criminal Process

A useful way to cope with the complexity of the criminal process is to employ models which simplify the details of the process and highlight common themes and trends. 'As in the physical and social sciences, [models present] a hypothetical but coherent scheme for testing the evidence' produced by decisions made by thousands of people every day (King 1981: 12). Unlike in the sciences, however, it is not possible or desirable to reduce the discretionary and humanistic systems of criminal justice to a single truth. For this reason, multiple models are helpful because 'multiple versions of what is going on, existing side by side, may legitimately account in different ways for various aspects of the system's operation' (ibid: 122). None of the models presented in this chapter was intended to operate to the exclusion of others or to be accepted as the only legitimate positive or normative guide to the criminal process. It is, however, valuable to identify the areas where each model is dominant and to have a sense of the overall trends. It can also be liberating to appreciate the different values found in the criminal process and the contingency of which model dominates.

Because they are abstract and value-laden, models of the criminal process are useful in describing not only the operation of the process, but the ideologies and discourses which surround criminal justice (Foucault 1991: 54). The most successful models have become terms of art, so that people now debate and advocate the crime-control and due-process values that Herbert Packer (1964, 1968) identified. Victims' rights also promises to become a rallying point for various reform strategies and ideologies. In short, the construction of models provides an accessible language to discuss the values of criminal justice, the actual operation of criminal justice, and the discourses that surround criminal justice.

Packer's Two Models of Criminal Justice

The most successful attempt to construct models of the criminal process was achieved by the American legal scholar Herbert Packer. His due-process and crime-control models set the standard for more than a generation of observers (Goldstein 1974; Sanders and Young 1994: 13). Many have attempted to replace or add to Packer's models (Griffiths 1970; Feeley 1973; Goldstein 1974; Damaska 1973; Arnella 1983), but none of these efforts has enjoyed his success and durability. However, some critics (McBarnet 1981; Ericson and Baranek 1982) have had a measure of success in deconstructing his models.

The essence of each of Packer's two models is captured by an evocative metaphor. The criminal process in the crime-control model resembles a high-speed 'assembly-line conveyor belt' (Packer 1968: 159) operated by the police and prosecutors. The end product of the assembly-line is a guilty plea. In contrast, the due-process model is an 'obstacle course' (ibid: 163) in which defence lawyers argue before judges that the prosecution should be rejected because the accused's rights have been violated. The assembly line of the crime-control model is primarily concerned with efficiency, while the due-process model is concerned with fairness to the accused and 'quality control' (ibid: 165). What follows are descriptions of the two abstract and dichotomized models as Packer understood them.

The Crime-Control Model

The crime-control model looks to the legislature, as opposed to the courts, as its 'validating authority' (Packer 1968: 173) and accepts the extensive reliance that legislatures place on the criminal sanction. The criminal sanction is assumed to be 'a positive guarantor of social freedom' and necessary for the maintenance of 'public order' (ibid: 158). It is employed both for the liberal purpose of protecting people and their property from harm and for the conservative purpose of promoting order and social stability (Hagan 1991: ch.5; Bogart 1994: 194–5). Given the reality of limited law enforcement resources (*contra* Ashworth 1994: 26), the criminal process must place 'a premium on speed and finality' (Packer 1968: 159). This is achieved by allowing its expert administrators, the police and prosecutors, to screen out the innocent and secure 'as expeditiously as possible, the conviction of the rest, with a minimum of occasions for challenge, let alone post-audit' (ibid: 160).

Most fact-finding in the crime-control model is conducted by the police in the streets and station-houses, not by lawyers and judges in the courts. The police, as well as the public (*contra* Arnella 1983), are concerned with 'factual guilt,' in the sense that the accused probably committed the criminal act. They are not overly concerned with 'legal guilt' that could be established beyond a reasonable doubt through admissible evidence and after considering all the accused's rights and defences.

The police are given broad investigative powers to arrest people for questioning, and this is often the quickest means by which to establish if the suspect is factually guilty (Packer 1968: 177). The only limitations on police interrogations are those designed to ensure the reliability of the suspect's statements. The 'evil of a coerced confession is that it may result in the conviction of an innocent man ... It is a factual question in each case whether the accused's confession is unreliable' (ibid: 189). Detained people are not allowed to contact a lawyer because this will slow down the process and only benefit the guilty, who will follow their lawyer's advice not to say anything. 'A lawyer's place is in court. He should not enter a criminal case until it is in court' (ibid: 203). The police should also have wide powers to conduct searches because only the factually guilty have something to hide (ibid: 196). Illegally seized evidence should be admissible at trial. Unlike coerced confessions, guns, drugs, and stolen property reveal the truth, no matter how the police obtained them (ibid: 199).

It would be a mistake to dismiss the crime-control model as thuggish and unconcerned with police abuse. Police misconduct should be taken seriously in disciplinary, civil, and even criminal proceedings. In this respect the crime-control model embraces Dicey's (1959) idea that the rule of law is based on the ability to impose the ordinary law on state officials. What the crime-control model rejects is allowing 'the criminal ... to go free because the constable has blundered' (*Defore* 1926: 587). The criminal trial of a factually guilty accused is an inappropriate and indirect vehicle for addressing police and prosecutorial misconduct.

The trial is not that important in the crime-control model because its 'center of gravity lies in the early, administrative fact-finding stages' (Packer 1968: 162). The prosecutor, as opposed to a judge at a preliminary hearing, 'is in the best possible position to evaluate the evidence amassed by the police and decide whether it warrants holding the suspect for a determination of guilt' (ibid: 206). Prosecutors, like police, can be trusted not to waste their limited time and resources on the innocent. Pre-trial detention is the rule not only to ensure the accused's presence at trial, but to prevent future crime and to persuade the accused to plead guilty at the first opportunity (ibid: 211–14). Under these conditions, 'it is in the interest of all – the prosecutor, the judge, the defendant – to terminate without trial every case in which there is no genuine doubt about the factual guilt of the defendant' (ibid: 222). Trial judges should happily accept guilty pleas and not inquire into the factual accuracy of the plea or whether the accused had any defences. They should also give the accused a sentencing discount for saving resources by pleading guilty at the earliest opportunity (ibid: 223).

Because of the ability of the police and prosecutors to screen out the factually innocent, judges and jurors should not be 'haunted by the ghost of the innocent man convicted. It is an unreal dream. What we need to fear is the archaic formalism and the watery sentiment that obstructs, delays, and defeats the prosecution of crime' (*Garsson* 1923: 649). Appeals should not be encouraged and allowed only if the accused establishes that 'no reasonable trier of fact could have convicted on the evidence presented' (Packer 1968: 230). The prosecutor should also be allowed to appeal because the acquittal of a guilty person is as harmful as and more likely to occur than the conviction of an innocent person.

The Due-Process Model

The due-process model starts with 'skepticism about the morality and utility of the criminal sanction' (Packer 1968: 170), especially in relation to 'victimless crimes' based on consensual transactions (ibid: 151). This scepticism is based on the liberal values of 'the primacy of the individual and the complementary concept of limitation on official power' (ibid: 165) and concerns about the intrusive policing required to enforce drug, obscenity, and prostitution laws. Many police abuses could be prevented if the legislature did not insist on criminalizing such activities. Decriminalization would also reduce the workload of the criminal justice system and allow more time to be devoted to respecting the rights of those accused of more serious crimes. The due-process model places much less emphasis on efficiency and guilty pleas than does the crime-control model (ibid: 179). Its 'validating authority' (ibid: 173) is the Supreme Court and the restrictions that courts interpreting the constitution place on the state's creation and pursuit of crime.

The due-process model is also concerned with equality in the sense that all accused, regardless of wealth or social status, should receive equal treatment by, for example, being represented by a lawyer (ibid: 168). Minorities and the poor bear the brunt of police abuse and prosecutions (ibid: 180). It is assumed that protecting the due-process rights of all accused will protect the rights of the most disadvantaged. Perhaps because he wrote before victimization studies and feminist and critical realist scholarship documented disproportionate victimization among the disadvantaged, Packer did not consider that crime victims are also frequently from the same disadvantaged groups. He could only see the criminal case as a bipolar matter between the state and the accused.

The due-process model imposes numerous restraints on the police in order to protect the rights of suspects and minimize informal fact-finding in the streets and station-houses. The police should not arrest or detain a person in order to develop their case. If there is any communication between the police and the accused, the accused should be carefully informed about the right to be silent and the right to contact counsel. 'There is no moment in the criminal process when the disparity in resources between the state and the accused is greater than at the moment of arrest' (ibid: 203). Any statements taken absent a clear and voluntary waiver by the accused of his or her rights should be excluded from a subsequent criminal trial in order to protect the accused from unfair self-incrimination. 'The rationale of exclusion is not that the confession is untrustworthy, but that it is at odds with the postulates of an accusatory system of criminal justice in which it is up to the state to make its case against a defendant without forcing him to co-operate in the process, and without capitalizing on his ignorance of his legal rights' (ibid: 191).

The criminal trial of factually guilty accused must address violations of their rights because those subject to police abuse -'the poor, the ignorant, the illiterate, the unpopular' (ibid 180) – will not, as required by the crime-control model, be able to bring separate civil, disciplinary, or criminal actions (ibid: 200). Because police and prosecutors are so concerned with short cuts, it is also necessary to 'penalize, and thus label as inefficient' (ibid: 180) within the trial, violations of the accused's rights. Strong 'prophylactic and deterrent' (ibid: 168) exclusionary rules are necessary because much police abuse will never be remedied.

Judges at preliminary hearings must be satisfied that a *prima facie* case exists. 'The prosecutor cannot be trusted to do this screening job any more than the police can' (ibid: 207). Because of the presumption of innocence and the harmful effects of pre-trial detention on the preparation of a defence, an accused should be detained awaiting trial only when absolutely necessary to ensure attendance at trial. Alternatives to cash bail should be used because 'a system that makes pre-trial freedom conditional on financial ability is discriminatory' (ibid: 217). Neither the prosecutor nor the judge should encourage guilty pleas by offering deals to an accused who pleads guilty. 'A criminal trial should be viewed not as an undesirable burden but rather as the logical and proper culmination of the process' (ibid: 224). The criminal trial is concerned not with factual guilt, but with whether the prosecutor can establish legal guilt beyond a reasonable doubt on the basis of legally obtained evidence. Only defence lawyers and appointed judges can be relied upon to appreciate the importance of legal guilt (ibid: 167).

Because of the concern about even minor risks of convicting the innocent, the accused should have wide rights of appeal. Appellate courts should reverse convictions whenever trial judges fail to protect the accused's rights. 'The reversal of a criminal conviction is a small price to pay for an affirmation of proper values and a deterrent example of what will happen when those values are slighted' (ibid: 231–2). Just as the legislature sets the tone by criminalizing much conduct in the crime-control model, the Supreme Court is the most important institution in the due-process model because it defines the legal rights and remedies of the accused (ibid: 173).

The Context of Packer's Models

Although Packer's models have had remarkable durability, they are a product of the time and place in which they were conceived. Writing in the 1960s in the United States, Packer believed that the criminal process 'is being turned from an assembly line into an obstacle course' (ibid: 239). The most important factor was the activism of the U.S. Supreme Court under the leadership of Chief Justice Earl Warren (Graham 1970; Baker 1983; Bradley 1993). As will be seen in chapters 2 and 3, the Supreme Court of Canada under the leadership of Chief Justices Brian Dickson and Antonio Lamer in the late 1980s and early 1990s moved the Canadian system in the same direction, and sometimes further.

In 1961, the Warren Court imposed on the states the exclusionary rule, which rendered unconstitutionally seized evidence inadmissible in criminal trials (*Mapp* 1961). The exclusionary rule was intended to deter constitutional violations by removing the incentive for police to disregard the constitution (*Elkins* 1960: 217). Involuntary confessions were excluded, not on the crime-control ground that they might be unreliable, but because they infringed the accused's rights and were obtained through police misconduct. The Warren Court also regulated the ability of police to conduct searches incident to arrest; obtain search warrants; and engage in electronic surveillance and investigative stops.

Defence counsel play a key role in the due-process model, and Packer (1968: 236–7) believed the Warren Court's most significant decision was

Gideon v Wainwright (1963), which required the states to provide defence counsel to those charged with felonies who could not afford to hire their own lawyer. The famous *Miranda* (1966) rules required the police to inform suspects of their right to counsel, including publicly funded counsel. Failure to provide these warnings or allow an accused to obtain a lawyer would result in the exclusion of even trustworthy confessions. The *Miranda* rules were designed to protect the right against self-incrimination, which was extended from the courthouse to the station-house. *Miranda* was so controversial that Congress unsuccessfully attempted to overrule it (Baker 1983).

The Warren Court affected criminal trials by imposing speedy trial obligations on the states (*Klopfer* 1967); requiring prosecutors to disclose exculpatory evidence to the accused (*Brady* 1963); and holding that the accused's silence at trial could not be used as evidence of guilt (*Griffin* 1965). Proceedings designed to discover the best interests of juvenile delinquents were affected by rulings that young people had the same due-process rights as adults. This included protection against self-incrimination, the right to be represented by counsel, the right to confront and cross-examine witnesses (*Gault* 1967), and the right to have guilt proved beyond a reasonable doubt (*Winship* 1970). The Warren Court was concerned with protecting the accused from the state's power in the streets, station-houses, and courthouses.

Packer recognized that the due process promoted by the U.S. Supreme Court was fragile. It required 'constant attention' (Packer 1968: 240) from the courts, and even minor changes in judicial personnel or attitudes would make a difference. Legislatures would not support due process because 'reform in the criminal process has very little political appeal' and 'every significant move in the Due Process direction' would be 'greeted with dire predictions about an imminent breakdown in the criminal process.' Packer was confident, however, that because they were based on the 'high ground of the Constitution,' due-process decisions could not be overruled by the legislature (ibid: 241–2).

The year that Packer's major work was published, Congress enacted the aptly named Omnibus Crime Control and Safe Streets Act that attempted to overrule *Miranda* and was 'designed more to chastise the Supreme Court than to improve the law' (Graham 1970: 319; Bradley 1993: 30). Courts largely ignored this law. As will be seen in chapters 2 and 5, some of the due-process decisions of the Dickson/Lamer Court have also attracted legislative replies, but they have been taken much more seriously. This difference is related to the less absolutist structure of the

Canadian constitution, which allows the legislature to place reasonable limits on rights, and even contemplates that legislatures can win their arguments with courts by opting out of due-process rights. It may also be related to the more pluralistic nature of Canadian constitutional values, which include respect for social order and the equality rights of disadvantaged groups who may be adversely affected by due-process decisions (Roach 1993b).

Shortly before his death in 1972, Packer conceded that the due-process revolution in the United States had failed. He recognized that empirical studies suggested that even the robust exclusionary rules created in *Mapp* and *Miranda* 'change nothing.' To the end, however, he maintained his faith in decriminalization and argued that 'we can never effect changes in the criminal process until we limit and thereby decrease the case load that afflicts all the instruments of the criminal process' (Packer 1973: 13). Packer hoped that due process would encourage legislatures to place less reliance on the criminal sanction, especially with respect to 'victimless' crimes such as abortion, incest, bigamy, gambling, public drunkenness, homosexuality, narcotics, pornography, and prostitution. Because these crimes involved 'consensual transactions' (Packer 1968: 151), they required the police to engage in entrapment, electronic surveillance, searches, and interrogations. The police were the most intrusive and visible, 'when they are doing their least important' work (ibid: 284). In advocating decriminalization of such crimes, Packer reflected much liberal thought of the time (Schur 1965). In Canada, the LeDain Commission recommended the partial decriminalization of marijuana, in part because 'the use of special methods of search, undercover agents and informers, and police encouragement of offences' to enforce drug laws 'tends to bring the law and police into some disrepute' (Canada 1972: 297–8). Pierre Trudeau justified partial decriminalization of abortion and homosexuality by arguing that 'the state had no place in the bedrooms of the nation' (Viau 1996: 98). As will be seen in chapter 4, most of Packer's arguments for decriminalization did not win the day and today seem dated and insensitive in light of new understandings of harms and risks and scepticism about whether disadvantaged individuals genuinely consent to such activities.

Packer's models also seem outdated today because they ignore crime victims (Ashworth 1994: 28). Packer wrote before victimization studies revealed high levels of unreported crime, and he assumed that efficiency in processing the minority of cases reported to the police would actually control crime. Of all the crime victims that Packer neglected, the most influential have been women (Elias 1986: 20; Rock, 1986). Packer failed to include women in more important ways than his constant and now irritating use of the masculine pronoun. He wrote at a time when sexual and domestic violence against women and children was publicly ignored and seen as a private matter. Feminism emerged as a powerful intellectual and political force only after Packer had articulated his models.

Packer's Critics

Packer's work has attracted significant criticism. His due-process model appears to be empirically irrelevant in most cases and critical theorists argue that instead of restraining the state, the illusion of due process enables and legitimates crime control. Others have suggested that due process is all too real and, by hindering crime control, harms the disadvantaged. Some critics have argued that Packer's two models are united by liberal, adversarial assumptions which limit creative thinking about criminal justice. The models also fail to take account of new knowledges about crime victimization and new concerns about crime victims.

The Empirical Irrelevance of Due Process: The Process Is the Punishment

Empirical researchers are suspicious of attempts to reduce the complexities of the criminal process to rational goals such as crime control or due process. Feeley (1973: 415) has argued that 'any analysis of organizational behaviour must be open-ended enough to identify and deal with the multiplicity of goals, values and incentives of the various actors comprising the system. To do otherwise is likely to lead into the trap of reification and away from social theory' (ibid: 415). Many empirical studies have illustrated that police, prosecutors, judges, and defence counsel share common organizational interests that defy the contrasting ideologies of crime control and due process. These professionals are bureaucrats who habitually cooperate to maximize their own organizational interests, not warriors for crime control or due process. This does not make the fact that we think they are such warriors insignificant.

Due process is irrelevant in minor cases because 'the cost of invoking one's rights is frequently greater than the loss of the rights themselves, which is why so many defendants accept a guilty plea without a battle' (Feeley 1979: 277). Due-process rights 'function largely as hollow symbols of fairness or at best as luxuries or reserves to be called upon only in big, intense, or particularly difficult cases' (ibid: 290). Defence lawyers frequently recommend guilty pleas in order to secure the most efficient and lenient disposition for their clients (Bottoms and McClean 1976; McConville and Baldwin 1977, 1981). Organizationally, they are agents of crime control who only rarely challenge the admissibility of evidence and launch appeals (Ericson and Baranek 1982).

These empirical accounts of the operation of the criminal process confirm Packer's sense that, in most cases, the criminal process operates as a crime-control assembly line culminating in the guilty plea. What would have surprised Packer is that defence lawyers, judges, and the accused, his agents of due process, all find guilty pleas to be in their own interests. This empirical research suggests that, at best, there are 'two tiers of justice' (McBarnet 1981: ch.7). Packer's models retain their utility, but due process begins to look like a thin, rich layer of whipped cream that adorns a thick, tough, and less costly pudding of crime control.

The Ideological Significance of Due Process: Due Process Is for Crime Control

If due process appears irrelevant to so many empirical researchers, this begs the question of its ideological or political function. For many critics, the answer is that 'due process is for crime control' (McBarnet 1981: 156; Carlen 1976: 42; Ericson 1982: 15; Ericson and Baranek 1982: 223; Ericson and Haggerty 1997: 65). This is a catchy slogan, but one that must be carefully unpacked because it means different things at different times to even the same people.[3]

Due process can be for crime control because the formal law created by legislatures and courts enable police and prosecutors to exercise broad and discretionary powers. Doreen McBarnet (1981) found that the procedural law of England and Scotland did not embrace the due-process values articulated by Packer, but rather authorized the police and prosecutorial discretion associated with crime control. Richard Ericson (1981, 1982) drew similar conclusions in his pre-Charter study of the formal and informal powers of patrol officers and detectives. The law was expansive, vague, or silent about the limits of police power and 'even in the rare instances where the police introduce evidence in court which is judged to have been obtained as a result of an illegal search, the evidence is still admissible because of the lack of an exclusionary rule' (Ericson 1981: 15). Law was 'enabling' and 'explicitly for crime control' because it gave police and detectives great discretion and was formulated for their 'pragmatic use and benefit' (ibid: 11, 219, 1982: 13).

These conclusions about the operational content of the law would not surprise or threaten Packer. The United Kingdom and pre-Charter Canada did not have an entrenched bill of rights or a tradition of judicial activism, both key elements of the due-process model. Packer would expect that Canada's adoption of the Charter in 1982 would allow the courts to infuse the operational content of the law with due process, but would recognize that legislatures would still pass laws to enable police and prosecutors to pursue crime control. The discovery of crime-control values in the formal law is not, however, trivial, and Packer can be criticized for ahistorically ignoring that, before the Warren Court, many American courts embraced crime control (Goldstein 1974: 1010). As Mike McConville (1991: 189–90) notes, both due process and crime control are embedded in fundamental legal principles. This means that troubling police practices can be legitimated by 'a legal rhetoric' that is 'expressive of crime control values.' Crime control is an ideology that appeals to legislators and some judges, as well as a description of how the police and courts operate.

Due process is also said to be for crime control because it helps legitimate the imposition of the criminal sanction. 'Due process' refers here not so much to the operational content of the law, but to the 'rhetoric of justice' (McBarnet 1981: 6)[4] or the 'rhetoric of reform' (Ericson and Baranek 1982: 230).[5] This idealized and publicly consumed version of the law supports crime control by creating the illusion that accused are treated fairly and have every opportunity to exercise their rights in the due-process obstacle course. In reality, however, the passive and dependent accused is processed along the assembly line of crime control. Packer would have been surprised and threatened by this purported relation between due process and crime control. He believed that due process would, however imperfectly, restrain crime control, not legitimate it.

The critical conclusion that due process is for crime control discounts the idea that due process can develop an internal dynamic that is not easily controlled. A year after the Charter was introduced, Richard Ericson (1983: 20) concluded that it contained many fictive aspects and should be more honestly called 'The Canadian Charter for the Restriction of Rights and Freedoms.' It was 'not a tool to control the discretion of government and legal agents, but a means to enable, justify and legitimate their discretionary power' (ibid: 14). The law, even the Charter, remained enabling: 'there more to restrict than liberate, more to regulate than to provide relief, more to deny the rights of the many and grant privileges to a few' (ibid: 53). Due process is for crime control because it is not really due process. There is a competing hypothesis, however – namely,

E.P. Thompson's idea that 'the law may be rhetoric but it need not be empty rhetoric' and that rulers could become 'prisoners of their own rhetoric' (Thompson 1975: 263). The development of the Charter may help to illuminate this debate about the enabling and autonomous features of the law.

Michael Mandel (1989, 1994, 1996) has argued that the Charter is fictive, enabling, and legitimating. This combination is difficult to refute (Russell 1989: 192). If nothing about crime control changes under the Charter, this will be evidence of its fictive and enabling function. On the other hand, if defence lawyers' 'dreams come true' (Gold and Fuerst 1992) and accused gain dramatically more rights and remedies, this will affirm the elaborate nature of the Charter's legitimating role. Drawing on realist criminology (Lowman and MacLean 1992), Mandel (1994: 230–40) and other Charter critics (Petter 1986; Monahan 1987; Bakan 1997) have also argued that due process has been used by powerful interests and corporations to exploit disadvantaged crime victims. This line of argument is in some tension with the primary argument that the Charter will enable and legitimate crime control.

Mandel is persuasive when he argues that due process has not restrained crime control. As the courts recognized more and more due-process rights in the 1980s and 1990s, prison populations continued to expand (Mandel 1996: 376–80).[6] The only reservation is that we do not know whether there would have been even more repression in the absence of due process. Don Stuart (1996a: vi) has argued that repression would have been worse without the Charter because politicians would 'have been unable to resist the political expediency of pandering to the perceived need to toughen penal responses.' Prison capacities, however, limit how much worse it could have been, and the Canadian experience suggests that at the very least due process was not inconsistent with increased crime control.

Mandel's further claim that the Charter has legitimated increased crime control is more problematic. It is one thing to accept that due process will not empty the jails or even restrain prison growth, but it is quite another to suggest that the crime-control business would not have boomed in the absence of due process. The media imperfectly transmits due-process decisions for public consumption. As will be seen, some important due-process decisions never made the front page, while those that did tended to offend public sensibilities by creating the impression that the courts were allowing the factually guilty to go unpunished and were frustrating the prosecution of sexual assault cases. Due-process decisions constitute an indirect and somewhat strange way to legitimate the criminal sanction to the public.

Mandel's analysis ignores the role that victims' rights, including the equality rights of disadvantaged groups, played in legitimating the criminal sanction and giving crime control a new human and rights-bearing face. Because he defines the disadvantaged in class terms, Mandel does not emphasize the ability of politicized, post-materialist groups[7] such as feminists and crime victims to lobby for and legitimate increased crime control. Mandel also did not explain why, before 1980 and during times of other prison growth (Chan and Ericson 1981), Canadian courts celebrated crime-control values without provoking a legitimation crisis (Habermas 1976: 70). The contingency, fragility, and controversial nature of due process makes it difficult to see it as an elaborate legitimation technique.

The Limited Liberal and Adversarial Vision of Packer's Models

Packer's due-process and crime-control models have been criticized for their procedural and political assumptions. They were designed to operate 'within the framework of contemporary American society' (Packer 1968: 154) and assumed an adversarial system, even though most of the world employs inquisitorial procedures (Goldstein 1974: 1015). This has political as well as procedural implications. The adversarial system is based on a vision of a reactive state that is concerned only with settling disputes, as opposed to an activist state which attempts to 'manage the lives of people and steer society' (Damaska 1986: 11). Packer's models may be unable to capture the ambitions of the activist state, including tory and socialist aspects of Canada's political culture (Lipset 1990; Bogart 1994; Greshner 1994).

Packer (1968: 156) conceived rights in a traditional liberal manner as a negative check on government. They protected the individual from the state, and remedies were limited to the 'sanction of nullity' (ibid: 240–1), in which evidence was excluded and prosecutions rejected. He did not imagine rights as a positive guarantee of safety, security, or equality, or conceive the criminal sanction as a remedy required to respect the rights of victims and potential victims of crime. The limited vision of Packer's models did not go unnoticed at the time he wrote. John Griffiths (1970: 359) criticized Packer for operating within the 'prevailing ideology' of liberal, American legal thought. Packer's models were united in their assumption that individuals had interests opposed to those of the state and the community. They differed only in terms of whether the individual or the state had the upper hand.

Griffiths presented a third 'family' model which assumed that the state and the accused, like a parent and child, had common interests if only because they continued to live together after punishment. The needs of the accused would be more important than his or her rights, and the state should be assumed to act in good faith. The closest example of this 'family' model was the 1908 Juvenile Delinquents Act, which allowed the state to pursue the child's best interests in a parental manner. As discussed in chapter 6, the family model of juvenile justice has been eclipsed by concerns for both due process and crime control, but is being reconceived through family conferencing, restorative justice, and reintegrative shaming. John Braithwaite (1989: ch.4) criticizes state-based criminal justice systems for taking disputes out of the hands of offenders, victims, families, and communities, and assuming that the interests of offenders and victims are fundamentally opposed.

Both Griffith's and Braithwaite's work owe important debts to Aboriginal justice, which most clearly and eloquently reveals the liberal and adversarial assumptions of Packer's models. Drawing on his study of dispute resolution among the Cheyenne (Llewellyn and Hoebel 1941), Karl Llewellyn (1962: ch. 21) contrasted 'parental' and 'arm's length' models of criminal justice. In the parental model, 'the officials will drum up evidence' for the accused because 'they want to find him innocent; he is part of their team' (ibid: 448). If the accused is factually guilty, the trial is concerned with the restoration of the offender with the victim and the community, not with the isolation and punishment of the offender. 'Its purpose is ... to bring the erring brother, now known to be such, to repentance, to open confession and to reintegration with the community of which he *was and still is regarded as an integral part*' (ibid: 448; see also Sinclair 1994). In contrast, the arm's-length model of criminal justice was more distrustful of officials at the start, but more punitive in the end. The offender was protected by rights, but was not considered as part of the team. The distrust of officials resulted in a formal trial 'before a tribunal artificially sterilized of knowledge of the facts, under a procedure which rigidly eliminates a great deal of relevant evidence ...' (ibid: 444–5). Family models of justice and Aboriginal justice reveal Packer's assumptions of an adversarial criminal process and a liberal reactive state. New models might approach criminal justice with less emphasis on professional and adversarial conflict between the accused and the state and more on reconciling offenders, victims, their families, and their communities.

Packer's Neglect of the Risk of Victimization

Packer wrote before victimization studies had documented widespread underreporting of crime to the police and the pervasive risk of crime. His data set was police-reported crime statistics and he assumed that better clearance rates would control crime. Victimization studies challenged this assumption by demonstrating that the crime-control activities of police and prosecutors affected only a minority of crimes. In many cases, victims were aware that contacting the police about crimes was useless and they feared they would be revictimized by the criminal process. New models of criminal justice should integrate this new knowledge about unreported crime.

The high rate of unreported crime in victimization surveys is subject to different interpretations. It can be constructed as a sign that the criminal justice system has failed and is insensitive to crime victims. As will be seen in chapter 5, this interpretation has inspired reforms which attempt to increase the reporting and prosecutions of sexual and domestic assaults. More generally, victimization studies can provide evidence of a great unsatisfied demand for the criminal sanction and a damning critique of the inadequacy of the current system. When risk is expanded into the fear of crime (which is also increasingly being measured), victimization surveys may be laying the basis for non-diminishing demands for arrests, prosecutions, and criminal justice reform. When the failure of these state-based crime-control activities to affect the incidence rates of most crime is considered,[8] as well as limits to which an adversarial and punitive system can be victim-sensitive, this may be a recipe for unending dissatisfaction.

On the other hand, unreported crime can be seen as a sign of legal pluralism, which can trigger informal and non–state-based reactions to crimes. Victims who do not report crimes to the public police may nevertheless be taking actions themselves to deal with the crime, including the administration of informal sanctions and preventive activities. Crime victims are already more likely to seek compensation from their insurance companies than through state-based compensation or restitution schemes (Hagan 1983). Those with sufficient resources may find private police who are not bound by due-process standards or the need to produce convictions to be more useful in preventing crime and limiting losses than the public police (Brogden and Shearing 1993). The knowledge that the risk of crime is pervasive and unmanageable through traditional crime-control strategies may push victims' rights towards new forms of governance. These include neo-liberal responses such as target-hardening, neighbourhood watch, surveillance, risk-profiling, and insurance (Garland 1996; Ericson and Haggerty 1997). In other contexts, it may lead to regulation of soft targets who can help prevent crime (Braithwaite 1997) or a more fundamental re-examination of the way male identities and sexualities result in sexual violence towards women and children (Braithwaite and Daly 1995). These new forms of governance range the political spectrum, but are united in placing less reliance on the criminal sanction and punishment.

Victimization surveys can be seen as a sign of a 'risk society' (Beck 1992) in which we can calculate, but cannot fully control, risk. The failure to control crime is often seen as a particularly egregious form of government failure and not often assimilated to the greater risks of accidents and disease. The measurement of risk produces a constant, reflexive source of critique. Knowledge about risk can gain 'a new political significance' and constitutes 'the moral statements of a scientized society' (ibid: 23, 176). Victimization studies frequently have this political and moral character. Statistics describing the percentage of women and children who are assaulted and sexually assaulted during their lives have resonance in policy debates in both courts and legislatures. The claims of groups subject to disproportionate imprisonment are also becoming important in policy debates about criminal justice (Roach 1996d). The increased risk that the disadvantaged – women, children, minorities – will suffer crimes and/or imprisonment has been joined with rights discourse to produce a new language of victims' rights. Groups use their disproportionate exposure to documented risks to make new demands on the criminal justice system.

The risk of crime victimization is now measured and known, and should be integrated into any new model of criminal justice. A victims' rights model will be more aligned with the activist state and its desire to manage risk and to recognize group and positive rights. At the same time, old paradigms die hard. One of the dangers of victims' rights is that it will replicate Packer's crime-control assumption that the criminal sanction controls crime and now risk. New knowledge about risk of crime can produce increased demands for the criminal sanction and criminal justice reform. The result may be unending dissatisfaction, as well as conflict with due-process claims. At the same time, however, this new knowledge about the failure of the criminal law to control the pervasive risk of crime could decentre the criminal sanction as a means to prevent and to respond to crime.

New Models of Victims' Rights

Packer's models have remained remarkably durable and still describe important facets of the practice and politics of criminal justice. Nevertheless, they have been persuasively criticized in the three decades since they were first presented. They should now be applied with caution, and there is room for new models of criminal justice.

In order to complement Packer's models, new models of criminal justice will have to have some foundation in present practice, as well as some normative appeal. They should be able to describe the work of legislatures, administrators, and courts (Braithwaite and Pettit 1990), but not be restricted by Packer's assumptions about the limited, liberal nature of governance or the central place of an adversarial system staffed by public-sector professionals. New models should account for the large number of crimes that victims do not report, and incorporate understandings of group rights and risks that have evolved since Packer wrote.

Given the political importance of groups claiming rights on behalf of victims and potential victims, as well as the widespread victimization revealed by victimization studies, any new model of criminal justice must make a place for crime victims and potential crime victims. Having status as a victim can be problematic, and even demeaning. In the context of criminal justice, however, there may be little choice but to recognize victimization. It is not surprising that those representing women, children, various minorities, Aboriginal people, and crime victims stress victimization and potential victimization when they participate in debates *about criminal justice*. When the focus is on other issues – day care, education, employment equity, Aboriginal self-government, safer communities – there should be less stress on victimization. Unfortunately these other issues did not receive as much attention as criminal justice in the 1980s and 1990s. Politics was criminalized, with criminal justice issues going to the top of the public agenda. One of the unfortunate consequences of criminalized politics is that many people will have public identities only as victims, and not as people with other qualities, aspirations, and talents. For the foreseeable future, however, the crime victim or potential victim has an important public identity, and for that reason merits study.

The two models of victims' rights presented here are the punitive model, which relies upon the criminal sanction, and the non-punitive model, which stresses crime prevention and restorative justice. The punitive model can be represented as a roller-coaster. It preserves the linear orientation of the crime-control and due-process models, but the ride is bumpier because of opposition to due-process claims and the well-documented failures of the criminal sanction and public prosecutions to control crime. The non-punitive model can be represented by a circle, which symbolizes successful crime prevention through family and community-building and successful acts of restorative justice, reintegrative shaming, and healing. This model is more holistic and can merge into general issues of health, well-being, and social justice, whereas the punitive model promotes the criminalization and legalization of these issues.

A Punitive Model of Victims' Rights: A Roller-Coaster Model

This model combines the crime-control assembly line and the due-process obstacle course to create a roller-coaster. It is in a state of constant crisis as it responds to the inadequacies of crime control to protect and serve victims, as revealed by victimization studies and accounts of crime victims being revictimized by the adversarial process. It is also in crisis because of the perceived need to defend the criminal sanction from due-process challenges. It features the new political case in which the rights of victims and potential victims are pitted against the accused's due-process claims. The defence of the criminal sanction in the new political case frequently replicates the crime-control assumption that the criminal law can control crimes. Demands by groups of victims and potential victims for the criminal sanction often focus on the equal protection of the criminal law, as opposed to the quality of that actual protection.

Victimization studies revealing high levels of unreported crime play an important role. Each new victimization study confirms the failure of the existing system. Along with reports of victims being treated badly in the existing system, this produces strong demands for criminal justice reform. There may be some recognition of the need for other social, economic, and cultural reforms to reduce crime, but these are less symbolically satisfying and more difficult to achieve. The punitive model places the criminal justice system under constant pressure to improve itself to encourage victims to report their crimes; to prevent revictimization within the criminal process, and to respond to high levels of victimization. Unlike in the crime-control model, for the punitive model good clearance and conviction rates for the minority of crimes reported to police are no longer enough.

There is much less deference to legislators, police, and prosecutors in the punitive model than in the crime-control model. Petitions, advocacy, and private members bills may be used to jump-start the legislative process. Police and prosecutors may find their work subject to critical scrutiny not only from the accused, but from victims and their representatives. Victims demand their rights to protection and solicitude from legislators and criminal justice professionals in strong and sometimes emotional terms. Demands by crime victims and their supporters for standing (see chapter 3) can disrupt the efficiency of a crime-control assembly line designed to encourage the accused and the prosecutor to agree to a guilty plea. Plea bargaining, despite its centrality in the crime-control model, is suspect because it does not include victims or meet their expectations. The assertion of rights, as represented by victims' bills of rights and claims to constitutional security and equality rights, encourages the expression of grievance, in response to both crime and the state's treatment of crime victims.

There are some significant similarities between the crime-control model and punitive forms of victims' rights. They both focus on factual as opposed to legal guilt. It is the commission of the criminal act as reported by victims to researchers or the police, not the state's ability to prove guilt beyond a reasonable doubt or compliance with legal rights, which defines victimization. Support for victims, not faith in the expert judgment of police and prosecutors, produces the operational presumption of guilt that Packer associated with the crime-control model. A punitive victims' rights model tends to divide people into the dichotomous categories of victims and perpetrators while recognizing that in some cases the accused may fall into the former category. There is a tendency to stress the innocence of victims and the guilt of offenders. The punitive mindset, as well as a desire to avoid all appearances of blaming the victim, tends to downplay the overlap in the population and behaviour of some victims and offenders. Crime prevention may be suspect to the extent that it suggests that victims bear any responsibility for the crime. Restorative justice is rejected because of concerns that victims should not have to face offenders and because it places too much emphasis on the offender's rehabilitation.

A punitive victims' rights model resembles the crime-control model in that it assumes that the enactment of a criminal law, prosecution, and punishment controls crime. Some victims' advocates, especially in the United States, demonstrate the same enthusiasm for the criminal sanction that characterizes the crime-control model (United States 1982). This may represent the capture of victims' rights by professionalized interests in crime control (Elias 1986, 1993; Fattah, 1989) or the domination of victims' advocacy groups by those who have experienced the most serious of crimes. The nature of criminal justice politics, which are often mobilized by well-publicized and horrible cases of violence, lead some to conclude that it is 'unrealistic to expect victim advocacy to spearhead the movement toward re-integrative shaming' (Scheingold, Pershing, and Olson 1994: 759). Victim advocacy often focuses on creating new criminal laws in the hope that they will prevent future victimization. Feminist reforms of sexual assault laws and new laws targeting the sexual abuse of children are designed not only to protect the privacy and integrity of victims, but to make convictions easier to obtain. Victim-impact statements and victim involvement at parole hearings are often directed towards greater punishment. Much more directly than due process, victims' rights can enable and legitimate crime control.

Like the crime-control model, punitive forms of victims' rights oppose due-process claims because they divert attention from factual guilt and allow the criminal to go free. The important difference, however, is that victims' rights counter due-process claims by putting forward the argument that victims and groups of potential victims have rights which deserve respect. In California and some other states, victims' bills of rights have included provisions to limit the exclusionary rule (Lungren 1996). In Canada, women's groups and other equality seekers (see chapters 4, 5, and 7) have expressed concern that due-process decisions will frustrate the reporting and prosecution of some crimes. Some feminists have focused on 'making the criminal law work for women' and ensuring that women receive equal and non-discriminatory protection under the criminal law, with less emphasis on how much protection the criminal law can actually provide (Busby 1994; Boyle 1994). Many of the most significant episodes in recent criminal justice politics have involved clashes between those who assert due-process rights and those who assert the security and equality rights of crime victims and potential victims. The new political case does not ignore victims, but it promotes a clash between their rights and those of the accused while reproducing the crime-control assumption that the criminal sanction controls crime.

The punitive model of victims' rights also challenges the idea of victimless crime based on consensual transactions that was so central to Packer's work. Packer's claims about the presence of consent and absence of victims with respect to pornography, prostitution, drugs, and gambling have been vigorously contested since he wrote. His work was done before feminism became a major intellectual and political force or the effects of drugs on disadvantaged communities were recognized. In the absence of any theory about unequal power in society, Packer did not question the genuineness of consent or the effect of crime on disadvantaged groups. Since the time in which he wrote, harm has been expanded to include the risk of future violence, psychological damage produced by anxiety and fear, and contributions to unequal social relations. This expanded understanding of harm demands a greater role for the state. In an age of fiscal restraint and scepticism about social-welfare reforms, however, many demands for state activism are channelled into the criminal process. The punitive model can thus promote a criminalization of politics in which social, economic, cultural, and political problems are primarily addressed through the use of criminal sanction. The criminal sanction is then defended in the new political case against due-process claims on the basis of rights claims by crime victims and groups disproportionately subject to some crimes, with very little attention to how much the criminal law actually promotes the well-being of these groups.

Many of the developments described in this book fall into a punitive victims' rights model because they rely on the criminal sanction and oppose due-process claims by the accused. As will be seen, the politics of criminal justice in the 1990s have been a bumpy roller-coaster ride. A punitive victims' rights model continued to rely on the criminal sanction; found itself in conflict with due-process claims; and failed, despite zero-tolerance strategies, to nullify the risk of crime victimization. Concern about crime victims and disadvantaged groups of potential victims provided a new symbolic and legitimating language for the same old crime-control routine of enacting criminal laws; arresting, convicting, and imprisoning a minority of the people who break those laws; and opposing due- process claims. Victims' rights became the new rights-bearing face of crime control. Because it employs risks and rights, it was much more powerful than crime control.

The major improvement on crime control is that the dissatisfaction of crime victims and disadvantaged groups is no longer ignored. Unlike the crime-control model, which focuses on the organizational interests of police and prosecutors, victims' rights takes victim dissatisfaction with the process and the failure to prevent crime and victimization seriously. This can make the system reflexively critical. By taking victim satisfaction and security as the measure of success, punitive versions of victims' rights may have laid the foundation for eventual recognition of the limits of the criminal law in controlling crime. The corporation and the upper-middle-class homeowner, with their surveillance cameras and private police, have already learned this lesson, but there is a real danger that disadvantaged individuals and groups will be left behind and forced to rely on a crime-control system that fails to control crime and invites due-process challenges.

A Non-Punitive Model of Victims' Rights: A Circle Model

A concern about victims does not produce an inescapable dynamic towards reliance on the criminal sanction and punishment. An alternative direction is away from the roller-coaster of relying on an inadequate criminal sanction and countering due-process claims and towards the prevention of crime and restorative justice once crime has occurred. The processes of both prevention and restoration can be represented by a circle. The least attractive manifestation of the circle may be the gated community with its own private police force. A more inspiring example would be a successful neighbourhood watch or the self-policing of families and communities (Brogden and Shearing 1993). Once a crime has occurred, the circle represents processes of healing, compensation, and restorative justice.

Victimization studies revealing high levels of unreported crime are seen more as a failure of social policy than a failure of the criminal justice system to control crime. Unlike in the punitive version of victims' rights, unreported crime is not automatically viewed with suspicion or alarm. Many crime victims are remarkably non-punitive in their decision not to report crime to the police. To be sure, some non-reporting is related to the inadequacy and inhospitality of the criminal justice system and fears of retaliation from offenders. Some victims, however, do not report crimes because they have found a better way to deal with their victimization that may draw upon strategies such as avoidance, shaming, apologies, and informal restitution. They may also judge the matter to be too minor or inconvenient to justify official intervention or prefer the privacy, time, and control of non-reporting. Unlike in the punitive victims' rights, crime-control, or due-process models, the victim's decision not to invoke the criminal process deserves respect unless it can be shown that it only reflects coercion or the inadequacies of the present system. 'Only a "victim-centred" model would prioritize the interests of victims at the expense of the public interest. No-one has yet managed to develop a victim centred model which is also consistent with due process or crime control' (Sanders and Young 1994: 26). An important step here is to define victims as the best judges of their own interests and not to see their actions as a product of learned helplessness. The prevalence of non-reporting suggests that a non-punitive victims'-rights model shares with the due-process model considerable scepticism about the utility of the criminal sanction.

A non-punitive approach is not deferential to traditional crime-control strategies and agents but, unlike the punitive model, downplays their importance. Families, schools, employers, town planners, insurers, and those who fail to provide social services and economic opportunities are also responsible for crime (Garland 1996; Feeley and Simon 1992). The challenge is to jump traditional jurisdictional lines and not to diffuse responsibility too thinly. Crime prevention can be achieved through social development to identify and provide services for those at risk of crime. Early childhood intervention targeting disruptive and antisocial behaviour and poor parenting skills may help prevent future crime, as well as blur bright line distinctions between victims and offenders. At the same time, more immediate forms of crime prevention, including target-hardening, better lighting, and changing high-risk activities, also play a role. Public health approaches focus much more on the victim than do traditional criminal justice responses which attempt to deter and punish offenders (Moore 1995). Unlike in the punitive model, there is little concern about blaming offenders or not blaming victims. Public health recognizes that offenders and victims often come from similar populations and that those populations are also disproportionately exposed to harms other than crime (Fattah 1993). Crime prevention may evolve into a more comprehensive approach to safety, security, and well-being which does not make hard and fast distinctions between the risk of victimization by crime and other harms and risks.

Once a crime has been committed, the focus is on reducing the harm it causes through healing, compensation, and restorative justice. The circle can be closed without any outside intervention as crime victims take their own actions to heal and attempt to prevent crime in the future. More prosaically, the circle of restoration may simply be a claim on an insurance policy which returns the money the policy-holder invested in insurance premiums (Hagan 1983; Ericson and Haggerty 1997). When the victim does report crime, the circle can be represented by a process of restorative justice which allows the offender to take responsibility for the crime and attempt to repair the harm done to victims. This is often achieved through informal proceedings such as Aboriginal healing circles (Sinclair 1994; Ross 1996), family conferences (Braithwaite and Mugford 1994; Hudson 1996), and victim–offender reconciliation programs (Zehr 1990: 181; Van Ness 1993: 258; Bianchi 1994) in which all of the actors are seated in a circle. All of these interventions will be discussed in subsequent chapters, but they are united by their concern for the welfare of both offenders and victims, informal non-punitive approaches, and community participation. The key players in these circles are the victim, the offender, their families and supporters, not police, prosecutors, defence lawyers, or judges, who may appropriate their dispute (Christie 1977). Victims play the most crucial role, and this gives them some of the power and autonomy that was taken away by the crime. They have the power to decide whether to accept apologies and plans for reparation. In the punitive model, they can only make representations to legislators, judges, and administrators, who retain the ultimate decision-making power.

Restorative justice focuses on factual guilt but explores the reasons why the offender has committed the offence. One reason may be past victimization or deprivation, but this does not produce an 'abuse excuse' (Dershowitz 1994) which, by leading to a verdict of acquittal, denies the suffering of the immediate victim. Restorative justice also marginalizes due-process rights by encouraging the offender to accept responsibility for the offence rather than requiring the state to prove beyond a reasonable doubt that the offender committed the crime and that it complied with the offender's legal rights. Restorative justice entails, however, no permanent opposition to due process (Braithwaite 1989; Braithwaite and Pettit 1990) and it is important that all participants be treated fairly and allowed to speak. Restorative justice works best if offenders voluntarily participate and waive their due-process rights and accept responsibility for the offence. Offenders already do this in many cases when they plead guilty, and they should be more willing to do so in a less punitive system. The greater challenge will be persuading victims to participate, because they may fear or disdain the offender or have unrealistic expectations about the benefits of a formal trial. Some offenders and/or victims will not participate, and trials will be necessary. Especially when offenders do not believe that their activities should be criminal, some of these trials may produce clashes between due process and victims' rights. Although the resulting new political cases are at the core of the punitive model, they are at the periphery of the non-punitive one.

Restorative justice provides a genuine alternative to crime control or due process. The latter two models focus on the state, either as the primary victim of crime or as the perpetrator of rights violations, and largely act upon offenders and victims. The crime-control model imposes punishment on the offender while giving the victim at best indirect recognition and no tangible repair. It embraces a model of justice which is 'preoccupied with the past to the detriment of the future' (Zehr 1990: 72). The due-process model in turn encourages the offender to deny responsibility for the crime and, because of its professional orientation, alienates the offender, the victim, and the larger community. It focuses on rights to the exclusion of duties, including the duty to repair the harm (Bianchi 1994: 38; Morris, 1989: 119).

Some feminists also eschew punitive strategies for both political and practical reasons. Carol Smart (1989: 4) has criticized criminal justice reforms which 'make women embrace their victim status more warmly.' Although violence against women cannot be ignored (Minow 1993), Smart would be sceptical of crime-control strategies which empower police and prosecutors and link women and children as passive victims. Expanded understanding of harm may advance some feminist causes, but also work against others (Cossman et al 1997). Laureen Snider (1994: 76–7) similarly has argued that, 'by focusing feminist energies on villains and victims, political and theoretical attention is directed away from tactics with greater potential to empower and ameliorate.' She advocates a move away from the emphasis on 'injuries and punishment [which] has its origins in anger' (ibid: 76) towards 'non-punitive actions that directly and indirectly alleviate human suffering ... [and] promote healing rather than punishment' (ibid: 103). Feminists who stress the importance of relationships also could support restorative justice because of its emphasis on 'familial relationships and emotional maturity rather than strict notions of guilt' (Heidensohn, 1986: 296). Some feminists support prison abolition on the basis that it is not acceptable 'to try to "get rid of" another person, whether through execution, banishment or caging away with other people about whom we do not care' (Harris 1987: 32; see also Morris 1989). However, this approach is controversial because other feminists are concerned that restorative justice will excuse male violence and reproduce the subordination of women.

Concerns about victims do not necessarily have to be punitive. As demonstrated by their frequent decisions not to report crime, victims can be non-punitive, and their practical interests may not always be in punishment. Protecting the rights of victims through crime prevention and restorative justice could create genuine alternatives to crime control and due process. These changes may not be heralded by an act of Parliament or a judicial decision. They will generally occur at the local level, with increased reliance on public and private forms of crime prevention, victim–offender reconciliation, family conferencing, and Aboriginal justice. These interventions have the potential to take power and control away from the criminal justice professionals who dominate the crime-control and due-process models.

A non-punitive model of victims' rights may also address some concerns about the use of the term 'victim.' A focus on punishment tends to concentrate on what happened in the past and define a person by his or her past victimization. On the other hand, concerns about restoration and prevention look to the future and make room for healing, empowerment, forgiveness, and an identity that is richer for not being circumscribed by victimization. The use of punishment to express solidarity with victims often shatters a social consensus about the need to respect and accommodate groups that have suffered harms and wrongs. Very few can ignore the need to support those who have lost their loved ones to murder, but reasonable people can disagree about whether first-degree murderers should have 'faint hope' hearings after serving fifteen years of their sentence. Few people would disagree with the urgent need to respond to widespread sexual assault of women and children, and domestic violence, but there can be reasonable disagreements about restrictions on the accused's right to call evidence and mandatory charge policies. Less punitive approaches can give those who have been victimized in the past more power and support than crime-control measures which, while increasingly undertaken in the name of victims, often affirm the powers of criminal justice professionals and frequently collide with due-process claims.

Summary

Old models of the criminal process have now been assessed, and new ones based on victims' rights have been articulated. The punitive victims' rights model is new because it employs rights and risk to justify the criminal sanction, but otherwise it is quite similar to the old crime-control model. It replicates Packer's assumption that the criminal law controls crime and his battle between due process and crime control (albeit reconceived as victims' rights). The non-punitive model, however, is a true alternative. It does not rely on punishment to control crime, it treats people fairly and as responsible citizens but not by relying on adversarial adjudication, and it seeks to reconcile the interests of offenders, victims, and their communities through restorative justice and crime prevention. It is tempting to suggest that the crime-control model represents our past; that the due-process and the punitive victims' rights models compete in the present and the future depends on whether punitive or non-punitive forms of victims' rights dominate. True to Packer's original warning, however, any actual system of criminal justice is bound to reflect aspects of all of the models.

There will be a continued need for punishment and incapacitation in the worst cases, and continued conflict between due process and victims' rights. Much will depend on when punitive responses are deemed necessary and if crime prevention and restorative justice are accepted as legitimate responses to crime. In what remains of this chapter, the deep historical roots of the crime-control model and the contingent and fragile development of due process are outlined.

The Dominance of Crime Control before the Charter

Prior to the enactment of the Charter and the 'due-process revolution' of the 1980s, the formal law of the Canadian criminal justice system embraced crime-control values. The few due-process initiatives that occurred were undertaken by Parliament, not the Supreme Court. This runs contrary to Packer's predictions that courts, not legislatures, would be the champions of due process.[9] It also illustrates the dynamic nature of legal and political culture. In the 1980s, the Supreme Court and Parliament switched roles, with the former taking a proactive due-process lead and Parliament being concerned with crime control and victims' rights, frequently in reaction to due-process court decisions (Cohen 1996).

Before the Charter, Canadian courts had limited grounds to intervene in the criminal process. In a 1972 speech in Toronto, Herbert Packer (1973: 1) declined to discuss criminal procedure on the basis that 'the Canadian and US constitutions are quite different, particularly in the feature of judicial review, which in the USA has tended to concern itself almost exclusively with the matter of the processes of the criminal law.' Parliamentary supremacy meant that courts could not directly assess the substantive fairness of criminal laws.[10]

Canadian courts traditionally placed discovering the truth about the factually guilty before the fair treatment of the accused. Justice Ivan Rand rejected the notion that suspects' statements would be inadmissible because the police failed to read the proper warnings. 'It would be a serious error to place the ordinary modes of investigation of crime in a straitjacket of artificial rules ... Rigid formulas can be both meaningless to the weakling and absurd to the sophisticated or hardened criminal; and to introduce a new rite as an inflexible preliminary condition would serve no genuine interest of the accused and but add an unreal formalism to that vital branch of the administration of justice' (*Boudreau* 1949: 9). Thus, *Miranda*-type warnings were dismissed by even the most liberal of Canadian judges before the Charter. Consistent with crime-control concerns about truth and reliability, Canadian courts were concerned only about the propriety of police conduct when doubt was 'cast on the truth of the statement' (ibid: 8). Truth, not fairness, mattered.

Commitment to crime control meant a reluctance to exclude relevant evidence even if unfairly obtained. In *Wray* (1970), the Supreme Court admitted into evidence a gun and an involuntary confession taken from a suspect subjected to a coercive ten-hour interrogation during which the police deliberately kept his lawyer at bay. The gun was admissible as reliable evidence, and the confession was admissible to the extent that its reliability was confirmed when the suspect lead the police to the murder weapon. (*Wray* 1970) The admission of this relevant and truthful evidence was 'unfortunate' for the accused, but not 'unfair' (ibid: 17). There was no 'judicial authority in this country or in England which supports the proposition that a trial judge has a discretion to exclude admissible evidence because, in his opinion, its admission would be calculated to bring the administration of justice into disrepute' (ibid: 13). As will be seen, *Wray* would be decided very differently under section 24(2) of the Charter (*Burlingham* 1995; see chapter 2).

Consistent with their general lack of concern about what happened beyond the courtroom door, the Supreme Court limited the right against self-incrimination to not being compelled to testify in one's own trial. A refusal by an accused to participate in an identification line-up could be used as incriminating evidence (*Marcoux* 1975). The accused's blood and other 'incriminating conditions of the body' could be admitted into evidence even though involuntarily and illegally obtained (*Re s. 92[4] of Vehicles Act [Saskatchewan]* 1958: 331; *Begin* 1955). Under the Charter, the Court would extend the right against self-incrimination from the courthouse to the police station and exclude reliable evidence, including incriminating bodily material, because it was unfairly conscripted from the accused (*Borden* 1994; *Stillman* 1997; see chapter 2).

The crime-control model did not necessarily condone police misconduct, but insisted that it be addressed outside of the accused's trial through civil suits, disciplinary hearings, and criminal prosecutions against the police. During the 1950s, the Supreme Court upheld damage awards stemming from police abuses in Quebec (*Chaput* 1955; *Lamb* 1959), and the right to seek damages was celebrated as the accused's most viable remedy (Martin 1961; Schmeiser 1964: 114). The damage remedy, however, was illusory, except for the most persistent (Tarnopolsky 1975: 254) and ultimately consistent with crime-control values because it required the accused's rights to be vindicated outside of the criminal process. Americans discontent with the Warren Court's reliance on the exclusionary rule looked longingly north of the border. One critic of the Warren Court invoked the Canadian example of crime control by quoting a commissioner of the Royal Canadian Mounted Police (RCMP) who argued that 'when the policeman exceeds his authority, bring him up short, but when he is doing, as most of them are doing, a tough, thankless and frequently dangerous job for you and for all you hold dear, for God's sake get off his back' (Inbau 1966: 270).

Canadian acceptance of broad police powers is best symbolized by writs of assistance which gave members of the RCMP open-ended powers to conduct drug or Customs searches. Consistent with crime-control values, the writs relied on the expertise of police officers to decide when a search was warranted. As late as 1976, there were 935 writs held by RCMP officers which were used to authorize more than 4,000 searches (Griffiths, Klein, and Verdun-Jones 1980: 87–8). As one American commentator noted with some disgust, the writs empowered a police officer 'without prior authorization or subsequent judicial review, to dismantle a house [in a search for narcotics] on their own decision' (Katz 1980: 126). The use of the writs by English Customs officials had been one of the leading grievances in the American Revolution, and such general warrants were specifically prohibited in the American Bill of Rights. In Canada, however, even the reformist Ouimet Commission (Canada 1969: 66–7) refused to recommend their abolition, and the writs were upheld under the Canadian Bill of Rights (CBR) because that statutory bill of rights did not grant Canadians rights against unreasonable searches and seizures, and the writs did not interfere with the accused's right to a fair trial in the courtroom (*Levitz* 1972: 420). Again, judicial concerns about fairness did not extend beyond the courtroom door.

The police also enjoyed broad arrest and detention powers. In 1979, the Supreme Court upheld an obstruction-of-justice conviction for a bicyclist who refused to identify himself to the police after running a red light (*Moore* 1979). Following the crime-control model, the police routinely employed pre-trial detention in order to increase the efficiency of the criminal process (Friedland 1965). Most cases ended with the accused pleading guilty. In 1973, it took on average only seventeen minutes to process each accused along the crime-control assembly line (Baum 1979: 20). Lower court judges, known as magistrates, were not always lawyers (Russell 1987: 204) and shared facilities with the police in 'Public Safety' buildings (Friedland 1968). They did not have the power to reject prosecutions because of police and prosecutorial misconduct (*Osborn* 1970; *Rourke* 1977; *Amato* 1982) and were under no obligation to determine whether guilty pleas were accurate or voluntary (*Adgey* 1973; *Brosseau* 1969). The prosecutor was not required to disclose evidence to the accused (*Duke* 1972; *Caccamo* 1975). Many accused were not represented by defence counsel and this did not violate the right to a fair trial (*Ewing* 1974). As late as 1979, legal aid constituted only 1.6 per cent of total spending on criminal justice (Ericson and Baranek 1982: 222).

Under the 1960 Canadian Bill of Rights (CBR), Canadian courts defined the accused's right in a minimal fashion and refused to grant effective remedies. The right to consult counsel did not include the right to talk to a lawyer in private (*Jumanga* 1976). A drunk-driving suspect required upon pain of criminal conviction to provide a breath sample at the side of the road was not detained and entitled to consult counsel (*Chromiak* 1979). Although a denial of the right to counsel could qualify as a reasonable excuse for not providing a breathalyser (*Brownridge* 1972), the Court would not exclude a breath sample given by a less assertive accused who was also denied counsel. As Laskin J. accurately noted in his dissent, the Court's choice was 'to favour the social interest in the repression of crime despite the unlawful invasion of individual interests ... by public officers ...' (*Hogan* 1974: 80). The guarantee of a fair trial did not ensure the right of appeal so central to the due-process model (*Vallières No.2*, 1973). The prosecutor could appeal acquittals, and Dr Henry Morgentaler's acquittal by a jury was reversed by the Supreme Court without bothering to order a new trial (*Morgentaler* 1975). Parliament recognized the harshness of these approaches and amended the Criminal Code to provide the accused with more appeals and a second jury trial. Similarly, it was Parliament not the Supreme Court that abolished the death penalty. An accused looking for due process before the Charter was better off going to Parliament than to court, at least when the government was not, as in the 1970 October Crisis, prepared to suspend basic liberties such as *habeas corpus* because of fears of an apprehended insurrection. In short, both the law and the practice of criminal justice before the Charter closely resembled Packer's crime-control model. As will be seen in the next section, the values of crime control almost survived the enactment of the Charter.

The Development of Due Process

Although they are the most frequently litigated part of the Charter, the legal rights and remedies of the accused were never at the heart of Pierre Trudeau's patriation project. Support for due process was at the mercy of the intergovernmental bargaining that defined constitutional politics until the late 1980s. The precarious place of due process in the drafting of the Charter, like other messy facts of history, embarrasses claims that due process was an inevitable development necessary to legitimate and distract a criminal justice system that was losing credibility (Habermas 1976: 37, 70; Mandel 1994: 81–7).

As Minister of Justice, Trudeau proposed a Charter that included a guarantee against unreasonable searches and seizures and a strong American-style exclusionary rule (Bayefsky 1989: 58). As Prime Minister, however, he focused on patriation without any mention of due-process rights and remedies (ibid: 78). The 1971 Victoria Charter contained no legal rights or remedies (ibid: 214). If Quebec had agreed, Canada might never have had strong due-process protections. Legitimation crisis or not, provincial consent for a constitutional amendment adding due process would have been unlikely.

In response to the election of the Parti Québécois in 1976, Trudeau introduced Bill C-60 in 1978. This bill included a charter of rights, but again due process was less important than federalism because provinces were allowed to opt into its provisions (ibid: 342). There was only a weak remedial clause that did not empower courts to exclude unconstitutionally obtained evidence or stay proceedings. A 1979 best-efforts draft allowed the provinces to opt both in and out of due-process rights (Romanow, Whyte, and Leeson 1984: 237). Constitutional politics before the final push to patriation suggested that due process was not a priority and would be quickly diluted or abandoned in the face of provincial opposition.

October 1980: When Due Process Really Was for Crime Control

The promise to renew the Constitution during the 1980 Quebec referendum set Trudeau's project of constitutional renewal back on a fast track. Minority language rights were at the heart of the Charter's vision of citizenship rights (Russell 1983), and the federal government again diluted the legal rights and remedies in an attempt to obtain provincial support. By October 1980, the right against unreasonable search and seizure had been watered down to the right 'not to be subjected to search or seizure except on grounds, and in accordance with procedures, established by law' (Bayefsky 1989: 743 s.8). The writs of assistance, however Draconian, were still established by law. Similarly, detainees had rights against detention, imprisonment, and the denial of bail only if the deprivations of liberty were not 'in accordance with procedures established by law' (ibid: ss.9, 11[d]). Those subject to detention or arrest had the right to counsel, but not the right to be informed of that right (ibid: s.10). As under the CBR, only the most knowledgeable and aggressive of accused would benefit from their rights.

The October draft did contain more robust rights such as the presumption of innocence and the right to be tried in a reasonable time, but these rights only ensured fairness in the courtroom. Like all other Charter rights, they were subject to 'reasonable limits as are generally accepted in a free and democratic society with a parliamentary system of government' (ibid: s.1). The reference to a parliamentary system of government would encourage courts to defer to the ability of Parliament to enact criminal laws and procedures and was criticized as a 'Mack Truck' exception to the guaranteed rights. The October draft also inhibited the development of remedies by providing that all Charter rights (except the traditional right against being called as a witness in one's own trial) did not affect existing laws allowing unfairly obtained but relevant evidence to be admitted in criminal trials or the ability of legislatures to provide their own standards of admissibility.

The October draft preserved, behind a thin façade of rights and due process, the unfettered discretion of police, prosecutors, and legislatures fundamental to the crime-control model. It affirmed due process in the abstract while enabling substantial crime-control limitations on these rights (McBarnet 1981: 162). The Court could have tried to impose a due-process revolution, but much of the October 1980 draft of the Charter preserved parliamentary supremacy. The crime-control nature of Canadian law, and in particular the refusal to exclude improperly obtained evidence, would have been preserved while Canadians were sold the idea that their rights were guaranteed. The hollow rights of the October draft were for crime control. They would, however, only have legitimated the criminal sanction to those inclined to be 'mystified by the first man to put on a wig' (Thompson, 1975: 263).

The Joint Committee: Due Process Beats Crime Control

After the collapse of intergovernmental bargaining, the federal government referred the Charter to a special Joint Committee of the House of Commons and Senate. Its televised hearings of presentations from ninety-three groups, six governments, and five individuals had a profound effect in strengthening the Charter and generating public and elite support for the Charter. Alan Cairns has eloquently described the importance of the Joint Committee in the development of the rights consciousness that would flourish under the Charter (Cairns 1991, 1992, 1995). The Cairns thesis is that the Joint Committee gave groups such as women, Aboriginal people, the disabled, and linguistic, ethnic, and racial minorities their own 'stakes in the constitution' (Cairns 1991: 18). Rights became 'an instrument of social recognition' (ibid: 116), and Canadian politicians were introduced to a personal and emotional 'language of shame, pride, dignity, insult, inclusion or exclusion, humiliation or recognition' that they could not soon forget (ibid: 174).

The Cairns thesis can explain much about the politics of victims' rights. Nevertheless, with a few minor exceptions, it does not fit the development of the Charter's legal rights and remedies. Although due-process rights, like equality rights, were weakened by intergovernmental bargaining and strengthened by the Joint Committee process, the public input in the Joint Committee did not come from 'self-conscious minorities' (Cairns 1991: 16), but from more heterogeneous, diffuse, and perhaps weaker interests (Roach 1993a) such as lawyers and civil-liberties groups. Legal rights and remedies were fundamentally strengthened in the Joint Committee process, but they received much less attention than the often 'sexier' topics of discrimination and abortion. Only seven groups addressed the right to counsel, thirteen groups made submissions concerning search and seizure rights, and eight groups spoke to the controversial subject of the exclusion of unconstitutionally obtained evidence (Canada 1980–1, 57: 94–5).[11] The Canadian Civil Liberties Association (CCLA), which claimed a membership of only 5,000 individuals (ibid, 7: 7) was probably the most influential group in beefing up the rights that would be the foundation of Canada's due-process revolution. My suggestion that the legal rights and remedies of the Charter were not nourished by the same politicized sense of identity and grievance as other Charter rights will be more than a historical quibble with Professor Cairns if in subsequent years many groups of Charter Canadians oppose the manner in which the courts interpreted due-process rights. The politicized identities and attachment to equality rights that Cairns eloquently describes create the background for many of the battles between due process and victims' rights recounted throughout this book. The ultimate vindication of the Cairns thesis may be the triumph of legislative policies designed to implement equality rights over judicial interpretations of liberal and individualist due-process rights.

The relative neglect of legal rights and remedies in the development of the Charter is ironic, given that the vast majority of Charter litigation now revolves around them. A document entitled *The Constitution and You* distributed to the public by the federal government in 1982 illustrates how the due-process aspects of the Charter were downplayed. It explained equality rights, with special attention to women's rights and the rights of the disabled, fundamental freedoms, 'native rights,' 'our multicultural mosaic,' the 'right to move around the country,' language rights, and democratic rights. The legal rights were mentioned last, just before the ability of governments to limit rights under section 1 of the Charter, and explained as follows: 'Not that you expect to run afoul of the law, but if it should happen, you'll want to consult a lawyer – right away. Your right to retain a lawyer without delay is written into the Charter' (Canada 1982a: 19). Due process for people accused of crime was not a primary selling point of the Charter, but it has been its most frequent product.

Legal rights and remedies were not ignored by the Joint Committee, and lawyers and civil libertarians obtained some crucial changes. The watered-down search-and-seizure provisions received the most criticism. Alan Borovoy of the CCLA argued that the October prohibition could have upheld an infamous drug raid in Fort Erie where more than 100 patrons of a bar were searched under the expansive legal powers of the Narcotics Control Act and a writ of assistance possessed by one of the officers. The section was a 'verbal illusion in the sense that it may pretend to give us something, but in fact, gives us nothing more than we already have' (Canada 1980–1, 7: 12). The B.C. Civil Liberties Association claimed that the provision was worse than nothing and would justify some of the warrantless searches uncovered by the McDonald Commission into RCMP wrongdoing (ibid, 22: 109). Despite their small membership, the civil-liberties groups effectively invoked well-publicized police abuses. The Canadian Bar Association (CBA) stressed the danger of a standard that could 'be altered by the arbitrary action of a legislature, as well as by the arbitrary action of a public official' (ibid, 15: 8, 24: 43). The lawyers wanted judges, not Parliament, to have the last word. As will be seen in chapter 2, Parliament has frequently had the last word, even though the Charter was amended in the Joint Committee to prohibit unreasonable searches and seizures.

The October draft provided the accused with the right to retain and instruct counsel without delay, but did not require the police to inform detainees of this right. Borovoy successfully proposed that the right be amended so that 'nervous, frightened, bewildered' detainees not be interrogated until informed of the right to counsel (ibid, 7: 13, 22: 109). As noted in chapter 2, this gave the Supreme Court of Canada a textual basis to require the police to provide *Miranda*-style warnings to those they detained or arrested. Civil-liberties groups and the New Democratic Party failed, however, to entrench the right to legal aid, and this omission was later used by the Court as a reason not to require all provinces to provide 1-800 numbers to ensure that detainees could speak to lawyers (*Prosper* 1994; see chapter 2).

Section 26 of the October draft of the Charter would have preserved legislative supremacy for laws governing the admissibility of evidence.[12] It was strongly criticized by civil-liberties groups and defence lawyers, but vigorously defended by police and prosecutors. The CBA argued that it preserved parliamentary supremacy when the Charter would give courts 'an entrenched right to construe every other specified legal right' (Canada 1980–1, 15: 19). In contrast, an association of prosecutors defended section 26 for leaving 'the law of evidence to the type of evolution that we have been used to in this country, that is a combination of parliament and the courts' (ibid, 14: 11). The CBA favoured the judicial supremacy that was fundamental to the due-process model, while the prosecutors wished to conserve legislative supremacy and the crime-control values of the common law.

Civil-liberties groups were careful to distance themselves from the absolute American exclusionary rule. Walter Tarnopolsky of the CCLA argued that deleting section 26 and allowing judges to determine when exclusion of evidence was an appropriate and just remedy 'means exclusion in some cases but not necessarily exclusion in every case if other forms of relief or remedy are available' (ibid, 7: 15). In response to concerns expressed about the American rule, he explained that the courts should 'weigh on the one hand the gravity of the offence, the circumstances, and on the other, the seriousness of infringement ... [and whether] there are other remedies that might be available' (ibid, 7: 27). As will be seen in the next chapter, this approach was much more restrained than that eventually taken by the Supreme Court when enforcing an expanded right against self-incrimination. Even so, the CCLA was criticized by the police chiefs as advocating 'the United States Exclusionary Rule, commonly known as the "Fruit of the Poisoned Tree"' which allowed 'murderers ... [to be] set free because a police officer has made a minor mistake in the procedures he is required to follow' (ibid, 14: 8). Following the crime-control model, the police objected to using the criminal trial as a forum to discipline them and argued that 'society's remedies' for police misconduct 'are found in other disciplinary measures, including the laying of criminal charges against ... [the police officer] – certainly not in having the courts let the murderer go free' (ibid, 14 :9).

The government agreed to delete section 26 in early January 1981 and add a 'general remedies' section allowing courts to order whatever remedy they considered to be appropriate and just in the circumstances (ibid, 36: 18–19). Although not precluding the exclusion of unconstitutionally obtained evidence, this approach would have deferred this controversial question to subsequent judicial development. The Progressive Conservatives subsequently proposed an amendment that evidence shall be excluded if its use would bring the administration of justice into disrepute (ibid, 41: 101–2). Jake Epp, who was otherwise sympathetic to the concerns of the police (ibid, 47: 25), argued that this provision would allow exclusion only in serious cases of police misconduct (ibid, 41: 101). Amid much joking about which party had enjoyed the most success with their amendments, section 24(2) of the Charter was finalized. The only note of caution came from Coline Campbell of the Liberals, who inquired whether the amendment introduced the American 'tainted fruit doctrine' (ibid, 48: 123) and wondered why section 24(2) did not specify the factors to be considered when deciding whether the admission of evidence would bring the administration of justice into disrepute. E.G. Ewaschuk of the Department of Justice reassured her that a judge would consider 'the seriousness of the case, the seriousness of the breach by the police, the manner in which the evidence was obtained' (ibid, 48: 123) before deciding whether to exclude the evidence. Moreover, he argued that the remedy would be triggered only by 'very blameworthy, repugnant and very reprehensive' conduct; in short, when 'the admission of this evidence would make me vomit, it was obtained in such a reprehensible manner' (ibid, 48: 124). As will be discussed in chapter 2, the vomit test did not win judicial favour. In its desire to protect an expanded right against self-incrimination, the Supreme Court developed a quasi-absolutist exclusionary rule which precluded judges from considering the seriousness of the offence charged or the seriousness of the violation.

Following Packer's models, the only opposition to due process in the Joint Committee came from the police and prosecutors, but they had little influence because most of their provincial employers opposed patriation. The Canadian Association of Chiefs of Police were 'strongly opposed to any changes' (ibid, 14: 7) and anticipated that more substantive guarantees of legal rights and remedies would create uncertainty and give the courts more power. Toronto Police chief John Ackroyd argued that the right to a trial in a reasonable time should not be included in the Charter, but more precisely defined in the Criminal Code. He came close to predicting the *Askov* 1990 crisis (discussed in chapter 3) by noting that '"reasonable" is a very vague word' and 'there are cases in the metropolitan Toronto today that are two and a half years and have not come to trial; so, is that a reasonable time? ... could people then be allowed to go free ... because someone ruled that they were not tried within a reasonable time?' (ibid, 14: 14, 17). In the absence of visible public support for crime control,[13] the civil libertarians and lawyers prevailed over the police and prosecutors.

The provinces eventually obtained the ability to enact legislation, notwithstanding the legal rights. This power has never been used in the criminal justice field despite the political appeal of crime control and victims' rights. It has proven unnecessary because Parliament has used ordinary legislation to respond to, and even overturn, unpopular due-process Charter decisions (see chapters 2 and 5). This contrasts with the American experience of courts ignoring legislative attempts to overrule *Miranda*, but it is facilitated by the structure of the Charter, which allows government to justify legislation that violates Charter rights as 'reasonable limits prescribed by law as can be demonstrably justified in a free and democratic society' (Charter, s.1).

Victims' Rights: Absent at the Creation

At this early stage in the development of victims' rights (Rock 1986), there was no testimony before the Joint Committee by victims' groups, and the police, prosecutors, and women's groups did not focus on victims in their submissions. Women's groups were preoccupied with the wide limitations clause, equality rights, and whether the Charter could restrict abortion (Hošek 1983: 286–7). They had relatively little to say about the potential effects of due-process rights on women. The National Association of Women and the Law (NAWL), an association of female lawyers, argued for strengthened due-process protections (Canada 1980–1, 22: 61). They were as dismayed at the hollow rights of the October draft as other lawyers. Other women's groups opposed section 26 because it would allow legislatures to 'say that evidence of a woman or an Indian is not admissible in a court of law, either absolutely or without special safeguards' (ibid, 9: 131, 22: 61). This made the point about the need to entrench strong equality rights. Ironically, however, section 26 might have protected 'rape shield' evidentiary restrictions on the admissibility of the victim's prior sexual conduct from subsequent due-process invalidation (*Seaboyer* 1991; see chapter 5). Women's groups, like most others, were unable to predict how far the courts would take due process.

Groups representing the disabled focused on strengthening equality rights and the right to an interpreter, but a spokesperson for the Coalition of Provincial Organizations for the Handicapped foreshadowed the *Latimer* case when he expressed concerns about 'passive euthanasia' and argued that 'disabled Canadians need to know they are secure from such dangers and that their fellow Canadians ... embrace the right to life and security of the person for everyone, including the disabled (Canada 1980–1, 12: 29). This was an early example of the rights and sense of belonging of disadvantaged groups being associated with the protection offered by the criminal sanction.

The Canadian Jewish Congress (CJC) warned that the accused's right not to be found guilty on the basis of retroactive laws could prevent the prosecution of war criminals for their involvement in the Holocaust. It proposed that the Charter follow article 15(2) of the International Covenant on Civil and Political Rights and allow prosecutions for acts or omissions that were 'criminal according to the general principles of law recognized by the community of nations' even though not contrary to domestic law at the time they were committed. Although recognizing that 'time will eventually destroy the immediacy of the problem of Nazi war criminals,' Maxwell Cohen argued that this change was a 'symbolic gesture to a very dark past' and required because 'no one should be allowed to run free so long as there is a possibility that we have a war criminal who can be identified as such' (ibid, 7: 92). The CJC's recommendation was followed with all-party approval (ibid, 47: 58–9). Parliament later enacted war-crimes legislation, but the Charter amendment only partially insulated it from due-process challenges in another divisive clash between due process and victims' rights (*Finta* 1994; see chapter 7).

With these few exceptions, the debate about due process in the Joint Committee was dominated by civil-liberties groups, lawyers, the police, and prosecutors who faithfully played out the conflict between due process and crime control. Due-process issues generally did not engage women, Aboriginal people, or racial and other minorities. The debates also did not include victims' advocates, who were only beginning to be recognized and cultivated by the government (Rock 1986). The lack of input from these groups set the stage for future confrontations in courts and legislatures between the due-process rights of the accused and the rights of crime victims.

Conclusion

This chapter has outlined four models of the criminal process – crime control, due process, and punitive and non-punitive versions of victims' rights. Packer's crime-control and due-process models should be applied with caution because of empirical and critical research that suggests that due process is irrelevant and counter-productive for most accused, and may enable and perhaps legitimate crime control. These models are also limited by their assumptions about a liberal, adversarial state and their neglect of new knowledges about unreported crime, the risk of victimization, and the revictimization of victims in the adversarial process. New models that recognize victims' rights can build on these new insights and stress crime prevention and restorative justice, or they can attempt to make criminal prosecutions more victim-sensitive and gravitate back to a crime-control assumption that prosecutions and punishment will control crime.

The crime-control model dominated criminal justice discourse before the Charter and might have been preserved had provincial opposition to patriation not forced the federal government to allow lawyers and civil-liberties groups to criticize the weak legal rights and remedies that had been included in early drafts of the Charter. Police and prosecutors opposed attempts to expand due process, but they had little political leverage because their provincial employers opposed patriation. The strengthening of the Charter in the Joint Committee laid the foundation for many of the expansive due-process claims that are examined in the next three chapters. Those who successfully lobbied for due process were small, loosely organized groups of civil libertarians and lawyers. Crime victims were absent at the creation of the Charter, and groups representing women, young people, minorities, and Aboriginal people were preoccupied with other matters, most notably equality rights. These groups developed a stake in other parts of the Charter, but they generally did not anticipate that due process could frustrate the use of the criminal sanction as a means of providing them with equal protection and respect. This set the stage for the conflicts between due process and victims' rights examined in the rest of this book.

2

The Police

At the start of the 1980s, the police enjoyed the benefits of a criminal process oriented towards crime control. Having lost their battle to water down the legal rights and remedies of the Charter, however, they feared an Americanization of the criminal justice system. By the end of the decade, their worst fears were realized. The writs of assistance were a fond memory, and judicial warrants were required to authorize search and seizures. They had to inform even cooperative and drunk suspects about their right to counsel before obtaining confessions or breath samples, and the Supreme Court was prepared to exclude almost all reliable and relevant evidence taken in violation of these *Miranda*-like rules. The image of 'mobile defence counsel' which had been ridiculed at the start of the decade (Ericson and Baranek 1982: 222) was almost required (Jull 1987). The dreams of defence lawyers had come true (Gold and Fuerst 1992).

This chapter examines the due-process revolution as it affected the law concerning police powers. The heart of this revolution was the Supreme Court's willingness to expand the right against self-incrimination from the courthouse to the police station and to enforce this new right with a quasi-absolutist exclusionary rule. Nevertheless, the due-process revolution was moderated by other factors. The Supreme Court made exceptions to facilitate the investigation of drunk driving and refused to require simple technology that would have made mobile defence counsel a reality. The police generally retained robust powers to entrap, arrest, detain, and fingerprint suspects. Many of the Court's decisions balanced due-process rights with concerns about crime control, and occasionally victims' rights. Moreover, Parliament demonstrated a greater concern for crime control and victims' rights, and quickly responded to due-process decisions requiring warrants with legislation that expanded and formalized police search-and-seizure powers. Due process was at times for crime control and victims' rights.

The due-process revolution at first did not attract much criticism. Unlike in the United States during the Warren Court, there was no movement to impeach Chief Justice Dickson or Lamer for being soft on criminals (Baker 1983). The media often failed to realize the implications of the Court's due-process decisions. By the 1990s, however, they began to report the discontent of police and victims' groups with the due-process revolution. The media focused on the Court's activism even though Parliament often had the last word.

The Right to Counsel: *Miranda* and More

The Supreme Court's performance under the Charter confirmed Packer's belief that the right to counsel and protection against self-incrimination were the heart of due process. Nevertheless, it was a surprising development, given the Court's leanings in the past and original expectations about the Charter.

Therens: *The First Shot in the Due-Process Revolution*

A week after the Charter was proclaimed in force, Paul Therens drove his car into a tree. He had been drinking, and single-car accidents are quite common with drunk drivers. The police officer had reasonable and probable grounds to demand that Therens provide a breathalyser sample. Therens cooperated and provided a breath sample, with a blood alcohol level over the legal limit. He did not ask to see a lawyer, and a lawyer would have informed him that it was a serious offence to refuse to provide a breath sample. The police had successfully apprehended an offender and obtained solid evidence of his factual guilt. The prosecutor was prepared to prosecute the offence as a minor summary-conviction offence in the provincial court. Following the crime-control model, the next step would be a guilty plea.

Therens did not plead guilty. Instead, he raised one of the first due-process challenges to police powers that went all the way to the Supreme Court. His lawyer noticed that the police officer had neglected to inform Therens of his right to retain and instruct counsel without delay. As discussed in chapter 1, this right was added to section 10(b) of the Charter by the Joint Committee to ensure that nervous suspects were made aware of their rights. Informing Therens of his rights 'would have occupied only a few moments and could not possibly have delayed or otherwise hindered the investigation' (*Therens* 1982: 473). Although the breathalyser evidence was crucial to the Crown's case, the trial judge excluded it and acquitted Therens because 'the rights of the Crown are not superior to the rights of the individual and the public interest is after all best served when the rights of the individual are defended and protected' (ibid: 474). Due process prevailed over crime control, and a factually guilty person went free because the police constable blundered.

The prosecutor unsuccessfully appealed to the Supreme Court. Rejecting a decision rendered only six years earlier under the Canadian Bill of Rights (CBR; *Chromiak* 1979), the Court refused to limit right-to-counsel warnings to those under arrest. Suspects should be informed and granted the right to counsel whenever they might be in need of legal advice and otherwise unable to contact counsel. Right-to-counsel warnings were also required to respond to 'psychological compulsion, in the form of a reasonable suspension of freedom of choice' (*Therens* 1985: 505). Many people would experience nervousness and psychological compulsion in their involuntary dealings with the police. The police would now have to read them their rights at the point of reasonable apprehension of detention, including in the back of squad cars (*Elshaw* 1991). In contrast, the Warren Court required *Miranda* warnings only when the suspect was detained at the police station (Harvie and Foster 1990, 1996; Roach and Friedland 1996). The Supreme Court was prepared to set the due-process hurdles higher than the most liberal American court.

The Supreme Court also concluded that the admission of the breathalyser sample would bring the administration of justice into disrepute. In an echo of American concerns about deterring police misconduct, the Court reasoned that to admit the evidence 'would be to invite police officers to disregard Charter rights of the citizen and to do so with an assurance of impunity.' If the evidence was admitted, Therens's right to counsel 'would be stripped of any meaning and have no place in the catalogue of "legal rights" found in the Charter' (*Therens* 1985: 662–3). Despite the wording of section 24(2), this deduced exclusion of evidence as necessary to protect at least some Charter rights.

However doctrinally dramatic, *Therens* had limited effects on the police. A police sergeant stated that the ruling 'doesn't bother us' because he was already reading drunk-driving suspects 'a book as thick as a telephone book' (*Globe and Mail*, 25 May 1985). This appeared to give suspects the benefit of every doubt, but in most cases lawyers would only tell suspects that it was a criminal offence not to provide a breath sample. Due process added a veneer of fairness to the mandatory self-incrimination required by the breathalyser law. The police were, however, more concerned about the long-term implications of the Court's liberal and generous approach to Charter rights and remedies.[1] Repeating arguments that had failed in the Joint Committee, the president of the Canadian Association of Chiefs of Police argued that courts were giving Charter rights 'a liberal interpretation ... approaching the same position as American police and American courts ... a continuation of this trend will impinge on the ability of the police to enforce the laws of Parliament and even impinge on the ability of Parliament to govern' (ibid). These dire predictions ignored the low rate of convictions lost because of constitutional violations and increasing prison populations in the United States (Nardulli 1983; Tonry 1995).

Margaret Taylor of Citizens Against Impaired Driving criticized *Therens* as 'one more obstruction' which could lead to the acquittal of drunk drivers and hoped that the police would be 'very scrupulous' in complying with the accused's new rights (*Winnipeg Free Press*, 24 May 1985). Due process forced victims to rely on police compliance. If *Therens* had been better publicized, it would have been unpopular. An 1987 opinion poll found that almost three-quarters of respondents believed the breathalyser evidence should be admitted even if the police had deliberately not informed drunks of their right to counsel (Bryant et al 1990: 22–4). The minority that supported exclusion tended to be less worried about crime and on the left of the political spectrum. There was a considerable gender gap, with 'men more likely than women to exclude the evidence' (Gold et al 1990: 584–5). This was significant, given future clashes between due process and women's rights. In any event, the Court soon balanced its due-process decision in *Therens* with others more solicitous of the interests of the victims and potential victims of drunk driving.

Drunk-Driving Spot-Checks: The Revolution Retreats

A few months after acquitting Therens of drunk driving, the Supreme Court upheld the RIDE spot-check program used in Toronto to deter drunk driving. As in *Therens*, the Court recognized that any stop by the police would result in detention and 'unpleasant psychological effects for the innocent driver' (*Dedman* 1985: 122). Nevertheless, spot-checks were justified in order to deter drunk driving, and because any detention would be short and driving was a licensed activity. Although not a landmark Charter case, *Dedman* received more publicity than *Therens*. Everyone could understand the issue of whether spot-checks should be allowed. The decision was 'welcomed by police and victim support groups' (*Globe and Mail*, 1 Aug. 1985). Defence lawyers, however, warned that Charter challenges might be successful (*Vancouver Sun*, 17 Dec. 1985).

The defence lawyers were wrong, and the Supreme Court upheld spot-checks three years later. They were justified under section 1 of the Charter as reasonable limits on drivers' rights to counsel and against arbitrary detention. The Court listened to the government's evidence that the spot-checks helped deter drunk driving (*Thomsen* 1988; *Hufsky* 1988). Legislation had authorized the violations, and the Court deferred to the legislature. Following the structure of legal doctrine (McBarnet 1981) and the Charter (Ericson 1983), these decisions both recognized expansive rights, but held that their violation was justified. Unlike in *Therens*, the Court saw these as drunk-driving cases and recognized the harms of alcohol-related accidents and the interests of victims and potential victims of drunk driving. The cases also won the Court good press. The lead in the *Toronto Star* on 29 April 1988 was: 'The Supreme Court has sent a message to Canadians: It will not tolerate drinking and driving.' Media and judicial accounts of drunk driving corresponded with the cultural image of the irresponsible killer drunk (Gusfield 1981) and emphasized the importance of using the criminal sanction, as opposed to non-punitive means, to curb drunk driving (Friedland, Trebilcock, and Roach 1990). The actual response to the frequent combination of alcohol and driving was more ambiguous, as represented by the fact that one of the accused had been fined a mere $100 for refusing to provide a breath sample.

The Court upheld spot-checks on the basis that drivers would be detained only briefly. The Court later acquitted a driver who had to wait thirty minutes for the necessary breath-testing equipment to arrive (*Grant* 1991). A fifteen-minute wait was later justified, but only because it was required to ensure that the driver (who had just finished drinking) provided an accurate breath test (*Bernshaw* 1995). The Court was prepared to make exceptions from due process only for reasons of traffic safety. Expressing concerns about police abusing these limited powers, it quickly excluded drugs discovered in a gym bag in a car stopped at a spot-check (*Mellenthin* 1992). The Court made exceptions to due-process doctrine for drunk driving, but was also bound by the limits of the exceptions.

Police Interrogation: The Revolution Continues

Following the path started with *Therens*, the Supreme Court imposed standards on interrogations that were stricter than those imposed by *Miranda* on the American police. A murder suspect's confession was excluded because the police should have waited until she was 'in a sufficiently sober state to properly exercise her right to retain and instruct counsel or to be fully aware of the consequences of waiving this right' (*Clarkson* 1986: 219). The Court criticized the police for interrogating her at the point when an experienced police officer was most likely to obtain a confession. In the crime-control model, the police had acted as diligent professionals getting to the bottom of a case in the most efficient manner possible. In the due-process model, however, they had taken advantage of a suspect who was in no position to exercise her rights.

Clarkson was front-page news. A woman's 'confession about murdering her husband' had been excluded, and she was acquitted because of an absence of other evidence. The Court had made the job of the police in dealing with frequently intoxicated suspects more difficult (*Globe and Mail*, 25 Apr. 1986). The press ignored the possibility that, even without a due-process defence, Clarkson might not have been convicted of murder.[2] Some legal commentators were surprised that the Supreme Court would prohibit police questioning in the absence of a clear waiver and employ an exclusionary rule that was 'for all practical purposes automatic' and did not balance 'the rights of the accused against the interest of society in crime control' (MacCrimmon 1987: 368). Others argued that, as a result of the decision, a 'legal emergency line' was necessary to ensure that all suspects could speak to a lawyer before answering the police's questions (Jull 1987: 385).

The Supreme Court continued to protect suspects from their tendency to incriminate themselves by applying the high waiver standards that had previously governed court proceedings to the more harried atmosphere of interrogations in police cars and police stations (Harvie and Foster 1990, 1996). In one case, a suspect started off well by noting that the right-to-counsel warning 'sounds like an American T.V. programme' and declaring: 'Prove it. I ain't saying anything until I see my lawyer. I want to see my lawyer.' When the detectives confronted him with some evidence, however, he replied: 'When I was in the store I only had the gun. The knife was in the tool box in the car' (*Manninen* 1987: 388). Following the logic of *Miranda* (Paciocco 1987), the Court ruled that the detectives should not have asked the question until the suspect had a reasonable opportunity to contact counsel. As in *Clarkson*, the suspect had not renounced or waived his right by answering questions, and the exclusion of the confession was necessary because it was a serious matter for the police to ignore a suspect's demand for counsel and unfairly goad him into self-incrimination. The media had grown used to such due-process decisions, and the ruling did not make the front page (*Globe and Mail*, 26 Jun. 1987).

This case demonstrated the Supreme Court's commitment to protecting suspects from unfair self-incrimination, but it also illustrated that it was an uphill battle. Even if Manninen had talked to his lawyer, he might still have failed to keep silent as he was processed through the system. The police could have talked to him after he had consulted a lawyer. They would still have had the upper hand, and Manninen might have made another stupid admission. Although the matter is contested, *Miranda* does not appear to have prevented the American police from obtaining confessions. One recent study found that 78 per cent of custodial suspects waived their *Miranda* rights, and 64 per cent of those questioned made incriminating statements (Leo 1996: 280, 286).

Legal Aid, Holding Off, and Technological Fixes

Another aspect of *Miranda* warnings is that suspects must be informed that, if they cannot afford a lawyer, one will be appointed. In American police stations, this warning is frequently meaningless because lawyers are generally appointed by the court to ensure a fair trial, not a fair interrogation (*Gideon* 1963). An American suspect without the resources to find a lawyer who will talk to him at the police station is like a person with chest pains who cannot receive medical treatment until he has a heart attack. As will be seen, the Canadian approach, like our health-care system, is fairer and more egalitarian.

In 1990, a murder suspect who had been informed of his right to counsel asked the detective if there was any 'free legal aid.' The detective replied that he imagined there was legal aid, but, using a typical interrogation tactic, asked the suspect if 'there's a reason for you maybe wanting to talk to one right now' (*Brydges* 1990: 334). The suspect subsequently made incriminating statements before realizing that he needed a lawyer. He got a doctor, but only after the heart attack. The Supreme Court came to the rescue and held that the suspect's right to counsel had been violated because, 'in modern Canadian society,' the right to counsel included both legal aid for those who could not afford it *and* 'the right to have access to immediate, although temporary, advice from duty counsel irrespective of financial status' (ibid: 349). The admission of the incriminating statement would result in an unfair trial. With no other evidence, the accused, like Lana Clarkson, was acquitted of murder. In recognition of the Court's new role in setting standards for police behaviour, and quoting from *Miranda*, the Court declared that the police had thirty days to amend their caution cards to include informing all detainees about legal aid and duty counsel (ibid: 351). This important decision was not big news, and its move beyond *Miranda* was not noted in the press (*Globe and Mail*, 3 Feb. 1990). Without critical attention from the media and interest groups, the Supreme Court could impose due-process standards with very little resistance.

The police complied quickly with the Court's ruling. Most provinces set up toll-free numbers to ensure that all detainees could speak to duty counsel at all hours of the day. The Ontario line served more than 9,000 people in its first year, at a cost of $12 a detainee (Moore 1992: 565). Free duty counsel for everyone was at least cheaper than medicare. A few smaller provinces did not set up toll-free lines and relied upon staff or private lawyers answering phone calls in the middle of the night. In a series of complex judgments, the Supreme Court ruled that, where a province had established a toll-free line, the police had to tell detainees the number (*Bartle* 1994), but that all provinces were not required to establish 1-800 numbers (*Prosper* 1994). It reasoned that the framers of the Charter had specifically refused to entrench a positive obligation to provide legal aid; imposing one would interfere with the spending priorities of government; and that it would be difficult to devise remedies should a province refuse to set up a toll-free number.

In the provinces that did not set up 1-800 numbers, the Court offered a potentially drastic solution. Building on *Clarkson* and *Manninen*, it ruled that the police must not elicit evidence from detainees until they had a reasonable opportunity to contact counsel, even if this meant the loss of the presumption that their breathalyser readings represented their blood alcohol level when driving. In *Prosper* (1994: 360–1), the breathalyser certificate was excluded, even though the police allowed a drunk driver forty minutes and fifteen phone calls in a futile attempt to contact a lawyer on a Saturday. The Court refused to mandate the simple solution of 1-800 numbers and, following the due-process model, it relied on the blunt remedy of excluding evidence.

Justice L'Heureux-Dubé warned in dissent that the Court's holding-off requirement 'effectively rings the death knell of the breathalyser as a device to help take drunk drivers off the road in provinces that do not have 24-hour duty counsel services.' Invoking images of the killer drunk (Gusfield 1981), she predicted that drivers in such provinces were now 'free to drink and drive at leisure, with the inevitable consequences of deaths and serious injuries in the roads' (ibid: 390). This assumed that the presence or absence of due-process doctrine controlled drunk driving. The majority of the public would have sided with the dissent (Bryant et al 1990: 22–4) and been alarmed by headlines such as 'Breath Tests in Jeopardy' (*Globe and Mail*, 30 Sep. 1994). These cases received more critical attention than *Therens* had almost a decade earlier. Combined with other due-process decisions the same year, they indicated 'to some observers – and not just the police – ... that the top court is out of touch, that it deals in lofty principles but is blind to the reality of the street ... The tension is between two issues: crime control versus due process. The court, and especially Chief Justice Antonio Lamer, leans strongly towards due process. Many Canadians, meanwhile, are telling their elected officials that they want the balance in favour of crime control' (*Globe and Mail*, 8 Oct. 1994). The media was finally catching on and reproducing the debates within the Court.

Just as they did not require 1-800 numbers, the courts refused to mandate the video- or audiotaping of interrogations. Although there were successful experiments (Grant 1987), the police did not videotape interrogations of the accused in any systematic fashion and were more likely to record witness statements (Ontario 1993: 154). Recorded witness statements were useful to the police, but the same may not always be true of recorded confessions. When ordering a new trial to hear a suspect's allegations that he had been assaulted during an interrogation, the Ontario Court of Appeal remarked that the issue could have been resolved more accurately and efficiently if the interrogation had only been videotaped (*Barrett* 1993). The Supreme Court restored the accused's robbery conviction on the basis that there was no reason to second-guess the trial judge, who had found the police more credible than the accused (*Barrett* 1995). The Court was again unwilling to require a simple and inexpensive technology that could protect the accused and facilitate more efficient trials (Young 1996: 29). The enforcement of elaborate due-process rules concerning interrogations often hinged on swearing contests between the police and the accused about what had happened in the interrogation room. Judicial reluctance to require technology may have restricted the impact of due-process rules.

The Quasi-Absolutist Exclusionary Rule

In most of the cases in which it found a right-to-counsel violation, the

Supreme Court excluded the evidence. It has been criticized for adopting an American absolute exclusionary rule in defiance of the balancing of interests that, as seen in chapter 1, even civil-liberties groups believed was contemplated under section 24(2) of the Charter (Paciocco 1990). Nevertheless, the Court's approach followed from the logic of expanding the standards of adjudicative fairness and the right against self-incrimination from the courtroom to the police station (Roach 1994: ch. 10). The development of a quasi-absolutist exclusionary rule was also evidence of the autonomous and unpredictable nature of legal reasoning.

In its early cases excluding breath samples and statements, the Court stressed the 'wilful and deliberate' (*Manninen* 1987: 394) nature of the violations. These characterizations were sometimes unfair to police, who were in many cases attempting to comply with their new obligations simply by reading suspects their rights. In the landmark *Collins* (1987) decision, however, the Supreme Court disclaimed any interest in excluding unconstitutionally obtained evidence to discipline the police and articulated a new rationale that related the exclusionary remedy to the accused's right against self-incrimination. Justice Lamer explained that, in right-to-counsel cases, the accused was 'conscripted against himself through a confession or other evidence emanating from him. The use of such evidence would render the trial unfair, for it did not exist prior to the violation and it strikes at one of the fundamental tenets of a fair trial, the right against self-incrimination' (ibid: 19). As Marc Rosenberg (1996: 185) has explained: 'The concept of "fairness of the trial", as explained in *Collins* and its progeny, has very little to do with actual fair trial procedure, and everything to do with the type of evidence obtained and the manner in which it was obtained.' Before the Charter, the idea that improper police conduct could affect the fairness of a subsequent trial or that the accused's right against self-incrimination extended beyond the courtroom would have been quickly rejected.

It was difficult for judges to hold that the administration of justice would not be brought into disrepute by the admission of evidence that made the trial unfair. 'A conviction resulting from an unfair trial is contrary to our concept of justice. To uphold such a conviction would be unthinkable. It would indeed by a travesty of justice' (*Stillman* 1997: 350–1). That the police may not have engaged in flagrant misconduct was not relevant because 'from the accused's perspective (whose trial is *ex hypothesi* proceeding unfairly), it makes little difference that the police officer has a clean conscience in the execution of his duty' (*Hebert* 1990: 20). Finally, the seriousness of the charge could not be relevant because 'the more serious the offence, the more damaging to the system's repute would be an unfair trial' (*Collins* 1987: 21). The Court's commitment to an expanded right against self-incrimination, as well as its rhetorical formulation of the fair-trial test, forced it to ignore the seriousness of both the violation and the charge, even though most had believed that these crime-control factors would be considered in determining whether the admission of unconstitutionally obtained evidence would bring the administration of justice into disrepute.

The Court's quasi-absolutist[3] exclusionary rule was not without its critics. In two cases involving the sexual assault and murder of two young women, Justices L'Heureux-Dubé (*Burlingham* 1995: 410) and McLachlin (*Stillman* 1997: 387) wrote long and thoughtful dissents urging their colleagues to reconsider the rule. Justice L'Heureux-Dubé warned that 'we may be digging ourselves into a hole' with an automatic exclusionary that risks 'frustrating the text of s.24(2), which calls upon courts to evaluate "all of the circumstances" in preserving the reputation of the justice system' (*Burlingham* 1995: 431). Both argued that the quasi-automatic exclusionary rule was contrary to the intent to devise a compromise between the traditional rule of inclusion and the American rule of exclusion. They also both opposed the expansion of the accused's right against self-incrimination, especially when it applied to reliable evidence such as breath or DNA samples. They were joined by one conservative male colleague, but the views of the two female judges on the Supreme Court mirrored the gender gap found in public-opinion research (Gold et al 1990: 584–5).

The Expanded Right against Self-Incrimination

The Supreme Court's commitment to *Miranda* rules and its willingness to exclude evidence taken without full compliance with them was based on its expansion of the right against self-incrimination. In 1975, the Court believed that the right against self-incrimination only protected the accused from being compelled to testify against himself. The fact that an accused refused to participate in an identification line-up was admissible and could be used against her (*Marcoux* 1975). By 1989, however, the Court excluded identification evidence because the accused did not have a reasonable opportunity to contact counsel before participating in an identification line-up. 'Any evidence obtained, after a violation of the Charter, by conscripting the accused against himself through a confession or other evidence emanating from him would tend to render the trial process unfair' (*Ross* 1989: 139). Conscriptive evidence included not only statements, but also reliable evidence such as the breathalyser evidence in *Therens* (1985), and even, as will be seen, DNA matches and murder weapons. The Court extended the standards of fairness that governed the courtroom to the police station.

The Reversal of Wray

The Court's willingness to exclude evidence to enforce this expanded right against self-incrimination was demonstrated by a case that effectively reversed its controversial decision in *Wray* (1970). In that case, the Court admitted a murder weapon obtained as a result of an involuntary confession, as well as the confession, on the basis that both pieces of evidence were true and that courts did not have a discretion to exclude such evidence because it was unfairly obtained. Twenty-five years later, however, it excluded another murder weapon, as well as several incriminating statements made by the accused. The accused's statements were not involuntary, but were obtained in violation of the right to counsel because he was not allowed to speak to his own lawyer, who was away for the weekend. The accused was, however, allowed to speak to another lawyer before he decided to lead the police to the murder weapon in exchange for a promised plea bargain to second-degree murder. The gun was excluded because it was found at the bottom of a frozen river and would not have been obtained without the accused's assistance. This reasoning ensured that the accused was placed in the same position as if his right against self-incrimination had not been violated, but to the public or the victim's family it must have looked like a reward for effectively hiding a murder weapon. The Court defined tainted evidence more broadly than the (in)famous American 'fruit of the poisoned tree' doctrine by excluding the accused's subsequent incriminating statements to his girlfriend even though they were 'but remotely connected to the unconstitutional conduct' (*Burlingham* 1995: 406).

In an oft-quoted passage, Justice Iacobucci affirmed the Court's commitment to due process by arguing that 'even a person accused of the most heinous crimes, and no matter the likelihood that he actually committed those crimes, is entitled to the full protection of the Charter' (ibid: 408). The Court did not even bother to overrule *Wray*, and Justice L'Heureux-Dubé, who argued in her dissent that a reasonable person would not exclude the evidence, 'took great exception' (ibid: 431) at the suggestion that she was advocating a return to it.[4] Although the accused was not acquitted and was already serving time for another similar murder, the case was reported as another victory for the 'ardent advocate[s] of ensuring due process for accused people.' Justice L'Heureux-Dubé was described as a 'lone voice on the country's top court' because of her 'tough stand on crime' (*Globe and Mail*, 31 May 1995). The media reproduced the struggle between crime control and due process on the Court for wider public consumption.

Summary

The Supreme Court went well beyond *Miranda* by requiring the police to inform suspects of their right to counsel whenever they were detained and by requiring information about state-funded duty counsel who can provide legal advice regardless of financial status. This included informing suspects of the 1-800 numbers established in most provinces which ensured that suspects could talk to a lawyer at all hours of the day. Contrary to crime-control values, police were required to hold off eliciting evidence until there was a reasonable opportunity to contact a lawyer. A violation of any of these requirements generally resulted in the exclusion of evidence, to ensure that the accused received a fair trial. The Court did not hesitate to exclude reliable and important evidence unfairly conscripted from the accused. The right to counsel and the expanded right against self-incrimination had their own autonomous dynamic. Not even civil-libertarians expected in 1982 that a quasi-absolutist exclusionary rule would develop or that reliable real evidence such as the gun in *Burlingham* would be excluded to protect the accused from self-incrimination.

Herbert Packer would not have been surprised that the Supreme Court adopted the right to counsel as the focal point of its due-process revolution. For Packer, the right to counsel, both in the police station (*Miranda* 1966) and in the courtroom (*Gideon* 1963), was the engine of due process. Without defence lawyers, the state would not be forced to prove its case, and the legal rights of the accused would not be vindicated. Packer's critics have taken a less romantic view of defence lawyers and stressed their role as a cog in the crime-control assembly line (Ericson and Baranek 1982). There are limits to the utility of the legal advice that even the most diligent defence lawyer can provide. For example, the defence lawyer or duty counsel called by a drunk-driving suspect in the early hours of the morning can only explain that refusing to provide the breath sample is a criminal offence. Suspects continue to talk detectives after being informed of their rights (Leo 1996). Even if a confession or other self-emanating evidence is excluded, there may still be enough evidence to convict the accused of at least some offence. Although right-to-counsel decisions such as *Prosper* (1994) and *Burlingham* (1995) were the focus of critical media attention in the mid-1990s, they may not be fundamentally inconsistent with crime control. In any event, in other contexts, the courts were less committed to due process.

Investigation, Arrest, and Detention: Crime Control Affirmed

The investigative process prior to the invocation of the right to counsel was stacked against the accused and designed to facilitate the police discretion that is a fundamental part of the crime-control model. This was the case both before (Ericson 1981, 1982) and after the Charter, with even the formal law enabling the police.

Investigative Stops

The most common encounter with police power is being pulled over when driving or stopped as a pedestrian. As discussed above, the Supreme Court was careful not to frustrate organized spot-checks designed to detect and deter drunk driving (*Dedman* 1985; *Hufsky* 1988; *Thomsen* 1988). The Court went further and held that the random stopping of motorists was justified for reasons of highway safety (*Ladouceur* 1990). Although random stops violated the driver's right against arbitrary detention, they were justified as an attempt to catch unlicensed drivers who were at greater risk of being involved in traffic accidents. Risk was constructed for crime-control ends, and the Court assumed that random stops would reduce traffic accidents. Unlike the right-to-counsel cases, the majority did not go as far as even more conservative American courts which had held that reasonable suspicion was required to justify traffic stops (*Prouse* 1979).

Four of the judges most committed to due process vehemently dissented in *Ladouceur* (1990: 29) on the basis that 'the roving random stop would permit any individual officer to stop any vehicle, at any time, at any place. The decision may be based on a whim. Individual officers will have different reasons.' They were concerned that for every unlicensed driver apprehended, many more would be stopped by a police car, 'siren blaring, lights flashing,' and be forced 'to prove his or her legitimacy on the road.' As will be discussed in chapter 7, the dissenters were also concerned that police might use their unfettered discretion to harass minorities.

The dissenters in *Ladouceur* made dire predictions about the effects of the decision on innocent drivers, but the media seemed surprisingly unconcerned. The *Globe and Mail* (1 Jun. 1990) buried the case in a short story on page 14, and the *Montreal Gazette* (1 Jun. 1990) similarly ran a short story with the comforting headline 'Spot Checks Needed to Stop "Highway Carnage": Top Court.' The media were not interested in this pre-packaged conflict between due process and crime control, perhaps because there were no representatives of police or victims to speak out against the decision.

When There Is No Exclusionary Rule

When the police were not acting for traffic-safety reasons, the courts were more concerned about police relying on hunches when making investigative stops or conducting searches (*Duguay* 1989; *Mellenthin* 1992). The courts, however, could provide only the remedy of excluding evidence when the police hunch was correct. The exclusionary remedy was strong in that it allowed the factually guilty to go free, but it was weak because it did not protect the innocent. Canadians remained more reluctant than Americans to sue the police civilly, in part because of the low level of damages ($500 was a typical award for a violation of Charter rights) and because, if they lost, they would have to pay not only their own legal costs, but those of the police (Roach 1994: ch.11; Roach and Friedland 1996). Complaints against the police were another a possibility, but often a hassle, with even less rewards for the complainants (Landau 1994). Given this dearth of remedies, it was not surprising that the Charter's guarantee against arbitrary detention and imprisonment was one of the least litigated of due-process rights (Young 1991; Quigley 1997: ch.7).

Entrapment

At first glance, the development of an entrapment defence affirmed the movement towards due process. The Supreme Court left behind its pre-Charter reluctance to recognize the defence (*Amato* 1982) and made clear that it would stay proceedings regardless of the factual guilt of the accused (*Mack* 1988: 540). On closer examination, however, entrapment doctrine accommodated police discretion and displayed none of the scepticism towards the criminalization of consensual offences that Packer (1968: 290) associated with the defence. Police could still offer an accused an opportunity to commit a crime, provided they had a reasonable suspicion that the person was already engaged in criminal activity or the police were pursuing 'the genuine purpose of investigating and repressing criminal activity' in an area 'where the particular criminal activity is likely occurring' (*Barnes* 1991: 9–11). This latter category justified a random request for 'some weed' to a pedestrian on Vancouver's busy Granville Mall (ibid) and the increasing use of undercover police officers who posed as prostitutes or johns. The police were enabled by statute to use reverse stings in which they sold drugs, and were allowed by courts to make several phone calls to set up a drug buy (*Showman* 1988). The entrapment defence applied only if the police engaged in extreme forms of abuse that would make the average person commit the crime (*Mack* 1988). Entrapment affirmed due-process values, but at the same time accommodated much crime-control discretion. It did not, as Packer had hoped, inhibit the enforcement of drug and prostitution offences based on consensual transactions (see chapter 4).

Arrest

The police retained robust powers to arrest and search people. Warrantless arrests were allowed so long as the police had reasonable and probable grounds to believe that the person was guilty. Hunches were not enough, but perfection was not required (*Storrey* 1990: 327). Once an arrest was made, the police could search the person and the immediate surroundings even without reasonable and probable grounds to believe they would find evidence or weapons. In *Cloutier* (1990), the police literally won a victory over the lawyers when the Supreme Court acquitted two police officers of assault after they had frisked a lawyer arrested for unpaid parking tickets. The same year, however, a closely divided Court drew the line at the rectal search of a person arrested for unpaid parking tickets (*Greffe* 1990). In dissent, Chief Justice Dickson argued that 'the reasonable person would be shocked and appalled to learn that an accused, unquestionably guilty of importing a sizable amount of heroin, was acquitted of all charges ...' (ibid: 173). The Chief Justice's dissent was the lead for most reports of the case, but even with headlines like ' "Obviously Guilty" Drug Dealer Free' (*Toronto Star*, 14 Apr. 1990), the story did not make the front page or generate critical commentary.

Fingerprinting

The police also retained the discretion to fingerprint a person arrested for a serious offence. One of the earliest controversies over police powers arose when the Saskatchewan Court of Appeal struck down this power because it allowed the police to fingerprint people when doing so was not necessary to solve the crime (*Beare* 1987). The police viewed this decision with alarm and hired J.J. Robinette, a top lawyer, to intervene in support of the Crown's appeal. They need not have bothered, as the Supreme Court reversed the decision on the day of the hearing because of the importance of fingerprinting to the administration of justice. Even without supporting reasons, this oral judgment won praise. The *Montreal Gazette* (19 Dec. 1987) editorialized that 'to hold that the state should not fingerprint accused persons until they have been convicted ... would be to deprive the state of essential policing and judicial tools. Justice, including the victim's right to see justice done, would be denied more often than it is now.' This was an early example of the media invoking concerns about crime control and victims' rights in response to due-process decisions.

When the reasons in *Beare* were released a year later, they argued that fingerprinting had traditionally 'been permitted because of the felt need in the community to arm the police with adequate and reasonable powers for the investigation of crime' (*Beare* 1988: 71). The Court concluded that the discretionary nature of the power was not defective. Stricter legal requirements 'could seriously impede criminal investigations ... Discretion is an essential feature of the criminal justice system ... Police necessarily exercise discretion in deciding when to lay charges, to arrest and to conduct incidental searches ...' (ibid: 75–6). The Court deferred to and celebrated the police discretion which was the hallmark of the crime-control model.

Bail and Pre-Trial Detention

After arrest, the police retained the power to decide whether to release a person. Despite recognizing the difficulty of predicting future danger, the Supreme Court upheld preventive detention on the basis that 'the bail system ... does not function properly if individuals commit crimes while on bail' (*Morales* 1992: 107). The Court also upheld a reverse onus which required those charged with drug trafficking to establish why they should not be detained (*Pearson* 1992). The Court portrayed pre-trial detention as exceptional despite the fact that half of the admissions to Ontario's jails were those awaiting trial, and one in five accused acquitted at trial had been imprisoned before trial (Ontario 1995: 113, 123). The Court's decision was probably warmly received by the public, who read headlines such as 'Accused Drug Dealers Face Tougher Bail Rules' (*Montreal Gazette*, 20 Nov. 1992).

While upholding pre-trial detention to prevent flight and future crime, the Supreme Court struck down detention in the public interest as excessively vague. Disregarding that the provincial jails were full of those awaiting trial, Chief Justice Lamer reasoned that, 'since pre-trial detention is extraordinary in our system of criminal justice, vagueness in defining the terms of pre-trial detention may be even more invidious than is vagueness in defining an offence' (*Morales* 1992: 103). As is consistent with due-process values, he was sceptical about discretion and concluded that 'a standardless sweep does not become acceptable simply because it results from the whims of judges and justices of the peace rather than the whims of law enforcement officials. Cloaking whims in judicial robes is not sufficient to satisfy the principles of fundamental justice' (ibid: 101). In dissent, Justices Gonthier and L'Heureux-Dubé argued that detention in the public interest was necessary for 'the good governance of society and the rule of law' and that the Court should place greater trust in judicial discretion. Their views lost in Court, but eventually prevailed in Parliament.

In 1997, Parliament responded by authorizing the denial of bail for 'any other just cause ... and, without limiting the generality of the foregoing, where detention is necessary in order to maintain confidence in the administration of justice, having regard to all the circumstances, including the apparent strength of the prosecution's case, the gravity of the nature of the offence, the circumstances surrounding its commission and the potential for a lengthy term of imprisonment' (*Criminal Code* s.515[10] as am. S.C. 1997 c.18 s.59). The reference to any other just cause tracked the words of section 11(e) of the Charter, which guaranteed the accused the right not to be denied reasonable bail without just cause. The vagueness of the due-process guarantee was used to authorize pre-trial detention on grounds other than risk of flight and future crime. The other words of the new section redefined public interest to ensure that accused would be denied bail in notorious and shocking cases. Parliament's reply to the Court's decision received no debate in the House of Commons and little media attention. Despite the constitutional nature of its due-process rulings, the Supreme Court did not always have the last word on police powers.

In its bail decisions, the Court accommodated crime-control concerns about the risk of flight and future crime. It may also have helped to legitimate high rates of pre-trial detention and disproportionate detention of black and Aboriginal accused by creating the illusion that pre-trial detention was exceptional and determined in a fair manner (see chapter 7). On the other hand, the need to create an illusion of fairness was not that strong. Legitimation crisis or not, Parliament could reverse the Court's only due-process decision on bail with little opposition and in the name of crime control.

Summary

The Supreme Court affirmed robust police powers to stop, entrap, arrest, fingerprint, and detain suspects. Once the police had some grounds to believe a crime had been committed, the presumption of factual guilt, typical of the crime-control model, applied. The courts responded to the worst abuses of police power, but even then Parliament sometimes had the last word.

Search and Seizure: Due Process, Crime Control, and Victims' Rights

While due process dominated the right-to-counsel cases, and crime control dominated the arrest and detention cases, search-and-seizure law was the most contested. Due process and crime control competed within judicial doctrine (McConville, Sanders, and Leng 1991: 179) often through separate approaches to rights and remedies. In the name of crime control and, increasingly, victims' rights, Parliament frequently replied to the Court's due-process decisions striking down warrantless searches.

The Writs of Assistance Go Down

The writs of assistance as the embodiment of crime-control deference to the police might have been doomed once the Charter was amended to guarantee a right against unreasonable search and seizure. Such a conclusion, however, discounts the contingent nature of legal culture. The B.C. Court of Appeal upheld the writs in one early case on the basis that police officers still had to have a reasonable belief that drugs were present and that, unlike the Fourth Amendment, the Charter had no explicit warrant requirement (*Hamill* 1984). The Supreme Court eventually ruled that the writs were unconstitutional because they authorized searches without prior judicial approval, but admitted the marijuana seized in this case because the police relied in good faith on the old writs (*Hamill* 1987). In its first search-and-seizure case, the Court liberally borrowed from Warren Court decisions (*Katz* 1967) which attempted to prevent unreasonable searches by creating a presumption that all warrantless searches were unreasonable (*Hunter* 1984). Judges would generally have to decide whether there was probable cause for the search, and they would not defer to the expertise of the police even when the search revealed reliable and irrefutable evidence of a crime.

Parliament Responds with Telewarrants

In response to civil-liberties concerns, the government imposed a moratorium on the issue of new writs of assistance in the mid-1970s. In 1981, however, Solicitor General Robert Kaplan proposed issuing new writs to fight 'an invasion of hard drugs' on the West Coast (*Globe and Mail*, 20 Nov. 1981). Without any mention of the Charter, this proposal was widely criticized on civil-liberties grounds, and Kaplan eventually decided in 1983 that, even if the writs were held to be constitutional, they could not 'be rehabilitated in public opinion' (*Globe and Mail*, 12 Jul. 1983). That same year, the Law Reform Commission of Canada (1983b: 30) concluded that the writs should be abolished, but that the Criminal Code should be amended to allow warrants to be secured quickly over the telephone. Telewarrants were enacted with all party approval in 1985, with Minister of Justice John Crosbie arguing that they were needed to respond to the danger that the police, without writs of assistance, would be unable to seize evidence before it was destroyed. He also noted that the use of telewarrants had survived constitutional challenge in the United States (Hansard, 20 Dec. 1984: 1390). Charter challenges had given the writs the final push, but pre-Charter media and civil-libertarian criticism played an important role. In any event, the repeal of the writs provoked Parliament to authorize more efficient telewarrants.

Regulatory Searches: The Due-Process Revolution Retreats

The Supreme Court's first search-and-seizure decision arose not in a typical criminal case, but in one involving the investigation of a newspaper conglomerate, Southam News, for anti-competitive offences. The Court held the search was unreasonable because it was authorized by the chief enforcement officer and not based on probable cause (*Hunter* 1984). The government did not even attempt to justify the legislation under section 1 as a reasonable limit on the corporation's right. The director of Combines Investigation who had authorized the search and lost the case was not worried because, 'in operational terms,' it was not 'really that significant a decision for us' (*Globe and Mail*, 18 Sep. 1984). Search warrants could still be obtained under the Criminal Code, and combines investigators still had ample powers to demand that corporations produce relevant business documents. Nevertheless, many commentators (Petter 1986: 490; Manfredi 1993: 112; Mandel 1994: 230–4; Bakan 1997: 91) argued that the case demonstrated how the nineteenth-century liberal values of due process would be used to restrain the modern state and how wealthy corporations would be able to make the most effective use of the Charter at the expense of the victims of corporate crime.

These critics were more concerned about the symbolic and ideological message of the Court's decision than about its actual effects. Even at the level of doctrine, the Court soon retreated. In the same way as it made allowances for the deterrence of drunk driving, the Court began to make exceptions to allow regulatory searches of corporations. In *Thomson Newspapers Ltd.* (1990), it decided that probable cause was not needed before a corporation's documents were subpoenaed. Justice La Forest concluded that due-process requirements would 'immunize perpetrators of anti-competitive offenses from discovery and prosecution' and 'defeat the purposes of the Act' (ibid: 486, 545). Justice Wilson, one of the Court's strongest voices for due process, dissented on the grounds that the law unfairly forced targets to incriminate themselves, but even she subsequently held that income tax officials did not have to satisfy *Hunter* standards before demanding documents (*McKinlay Transport Ltd.* 1990). The Court also upheld the powers of provincial regulators to demand employment records and inspect workplaces without warrants or probable cause (*Potash* 1994). It did find minor flaws in the Income Tax Act's search-warrant provisions, but fixed them by giving judges a discretion whether to grant the warrant (*Baron* 1993). Even in the self-incrimination context, the Court was not soft on corporate crime and held that individuals could be compelled to testify against their corporations (*Amway Corp*, 1989) and could be convicted of regulatory offences on the basis of business records that they were compelled by statute to make (*Fitzpatrick* 1995).

All in all, the argument that due process hindered the successful prosecution of corporate crime is not persuasive. It ignores the ability of the courts to make contextual distinctions (McBarnet 1981) and the sympathy the Court displayed for the concerns of regulators and the victims of corporate crime. Attempts to pit due process against the rights of victims of corporate crime may be another form of symbolic and criminalized politics that obscured more fundamental reasons why traditional forms of crime control did not effectively reduce corporate crime.

Blood and Drunk Driving

In two early cases, the Supreme Court excluded blood samples because they had been taken without a warrant from drunk drivers (*Pohoretsky* 1987; *Dyment* 1988). The Court emphasized the seriousness of taking blood and conscripting the accused against himself. The Court went much further than the leading Warren Court precedent (*Schmerber* 1966) which held that taking a blood sample did not result in unfair self-incrimination or an unreasonable search (Harvie and Foster 1990: 760–3). Surprisingly, these decisions were not front-page news (*Winnipeg Free Press*, 5 Jun. 1987; *Calgary Herald*, 9 Dec. 1988). The media, the potential watchdog of crime-control and victims' rights interests, seemed to be asleep at the switch.

Parliament Responds with Blood Warrants and 'Killer Drunk' Offences

Parliament was not asleep and, before the decisions discussed above were even rendered, gave police new powers to obtain warrants, by telephone if necessary, to obtain blood samples from unconscious drunk drivers involved in accidents causing harm or death. These new police powers were enacted in 1985 along with new offences of impaired driving causing death and bodily harm. The demands of due process provoked a new legislative focus on the 'killer drunk' (Gusfield 1981). Minister of Justice John Crosbie defended the new laws as a response to the demands of 'organizations of people who are concerned about the rights of victims ... people whose relatives had suffered terrible injuries in auto accidents caused by an impaired driver and from organizations whose families have had someone die as a result of impaired driving' (Hansard, 20 Dec. 1984: 1385). Two representatives of Mothers Against Drunk Driving testified in committee that they were 'shocked' and 'appalled' when the drunk drivers who killed their sons were charged with drunk-driving offences that did not recognize that deaths had occurred (Canada, JLAC, 12 Feb. 1985, 12: 5–7). Crosbie matched the due-process 'right not to have one's person's interfered with' with the competing 'right of the public to be secure and people to be protected from injuries when on public highways, the rights of society as a whole' (Hansard, 20 Dec. 1984: 1388). Rights rhetoric did not privilege due process, but rather produced a countervailing concern with the rights of victims and potential victims, and the elevation of the societal interest in crime control to the status of a right.

The new blood warrants and 'killer drunk' offences were extremely

popular. The opposition Liberals took credit for introducing similar legislation before their defeat and, even though the legislation was given second reading five days before Christmas, offered to speed its drunk-
driving provisions through to support other holiday initiatives against
drunk driving (Hansard, 20 Dec. 1984: 1391). Due process was only a
temporary obstacle[5] as Parliament enacted new measures in the name of
crime control and victims' rights.

Privacy, Risk, and Warrantless Searches

The Supreme Court invalidated a number of warrantless investigative
techniques, including the use of a wire to record conversations (*Duarte*
1990); the use of hidden video cameras to record illegal gambling in a
hotel room (*Wong* 1990); and the use of electronic beepers to track cars
(*Wise* 1992). The first decision was the most controversial because it made
illegal consent intercepts which allowed informers and police officers to
wear a wire without judicial authorization. The Law Reform Commission
of Canada (1986: 28), the Warren Court (*Lopez* 1963), and most Canadian courts approved of these intercepts on the basis that the people
whose conversations were surreptitiously recorded risked that they were
talking to an informer who could testify against them and thus had no
reasonable expectation of privacy. The Supreme Court saw the issue differently. It was concerned about the 'total absence of prior judicial supervision of this practice' (*Duarte* 1990: 13). Justice La Forest dramatically
placed privacy before crime control by arguing that a 'society which
exposed us, at the whim of the state, to the risk of having a permanent
electronic recording of our words every time we opened our mouths
might be superbly equipped to fight crime, but would be one in which
privacy no longer had any meaning' (ibid: 11).

The *Duarte* decision did not draw much public attention immediately
after its release (*Globe and Mail*, 26 Jan.1990), but within a year became a
cause célèbre as police blamed it for sending 'the undercover officer out
without a life line ... We've had officers robbed, stabbed, shot at, and it's
not getting better.' To the police, the Court's due-process decision meant
that 'the best evidence is not admissible' (*Globe and Mail*, 26 Jul. 1991).

Parliament Responds with Lifelines and General Warrants

In 1993, Minister of Justice Perrin Beatty introduced legislation in reply
to the Supreme Court decisions discussed above. He explained that the

Court's judgments in *Duarte* (1990), *Wong* (1990), and *Wise* (1992) 'significantly affect the way police and other agents of the state can do their jobs.' He promised that the new legislation would 'increase the effectiveness of both the police and Crown prosecutors, in accordance with the recommendations of the Supreme Court. We are talking about the resources police officers need to perform their duties satisfactorily' (Hansard, 25 Feb. 1993: 16491–2). As they had over a decade ago in the Joint Committee, the police argued that due process made their jobs difficult.[6] In the face of Court decisions that made explicit the crime-control costs of due process, this time they won.

The most important amendments for the police were those to respond to *Duarte* and to provide what the Justice minister dramatically described as 'an electronic lifeline to permit police and others in potentially dangerous situations to have their conversations surreptitiously intercepted by backup teams' (Hansard, 25 Feb. 1993: 16491). The NDP Justice critic echoed these concerns by saying that he wanted 'the policeman who is going under cover to be protected, to have a lifeline back to his colleagues, the other policemen' (ibid: 16564). Another member wanted 'everyone to know that we in the Liberal Party support the police in this area,' especially if 'the Charter is being respected' (ibid: 16558). The amendments allowed a judge to issue a sixty-day warrant for a consent intercept on reasonable grounds that an offence had been committed and the intercept would discover information concerning the offence. Unlike regular wiretap warrants, it was not necessary to demonstrate that other investigative methods had been tried or to notify the target after an unsuccessful intercept. Even though the Supreme Court had strongly criticized the use of wires without warrants, the new amendments allowed the police to avoid having to obtain a warrant if there was either 'a risk of bodily harm to the person who consented to the interception; and the purpose of the interception is to prevent bodily harm' or an urgent situation where a warrant could not be obtained 'with reasonable diligence' (*Criminal Code* s.184.1,184.4 as am. S.C. 1993 c.40). A judicial decision decrying the dangers of warrantless wires produced legislation authorizing them. Due process provoked a crime-control response.

The only opposition to these 'lifeline' provisions came from lawyers. Unlike in the Joint Committee on the Constitution (see chapter 1), no civil-liberties group appeared. The Canadian Bar Association (CBA) stressed that the Supreme Court had indicated that all warrantless searches were 'prima facie unreasonable' and even compared the new authorization of warrantless wires to the infamous writs of assistance because they allowed the police unfettered and undocumented discretion (Canada 1993c: 4:5, 4:14). The lawyers did not win this battle because due process now had to be defended on the basis of a Supreme Court decision that had overruled settled legislative policy and had been widely criticized for threatening police safety.

Parliament responded to *Wong* (1990) with a new general warrant provision that allowed a judge to authorize 'any device or investigative technique or procedure or do any thing described in the warrant that would, if not authorized, constitute an unreasonable search or seizure in respect of a person or a person's property' (*Criminal Code* s.487.01 as am. 1993 c.40 s.15). The only restrictions on the general warrant was that it should respect the privacy of people 'as much as possible' (ibid s.487.01[4]) and not interfere with bodily integrity. This amendment employed the Court's present and future due-process doctrine for crime-control ends. The scope of searches that could be authorized would henceforth expand in lock step with the Court's definition of an unreasonable search and seizure. As due process expanded, so, too, would the legislative authorization for crime control. Due process defined crime control.

The Justice minister justified the general warrant as a response to the Court's decisions and as means to ensure that 'the police and other enforcement officials can use video and other surveillance technology such as electronic tracking devices' (Hansard, 25 Feb. 1993: 16492). Ian Waddell, the NDP Justice critic, defended the legislation on the basis that it allowed judges to issues warrants only 'where it is clearly indicated the request meets the test of the Charter' (ibid: 16563). The procedural standards of prior authorization and probable cause required by the Charter had become the benchmark of legislative wisdom. No one in Parliament spoke about the dangers of authorizing in advance unknown technologies or the wisdom of employing these means to investigate crimes based on consensual transactions. No one questioned whether it was worthwhile to employ videotaping to convict men who consented to sex in public washrooms (*Le Beau* 1988) or who gambled in hotel rooms (*Wong* 1990). Due-process doctrine made the law more complex and technocratic, but it did not provide a vehicle for challenging the use of the criminal sanction in relation to crimes based on consensual transactions.

The Wiretap Business

Warrants authorizing the use of wiretaps were frequently challenged under the Charter. The cases generally involved long and complex drug conspiracy charges and they provided a cottage industry for some defence lawyers. Before the Charter, the Supreme Court had restricted the accused's ability to challenge a wiretap warrant by presuming the authorizing judge had not erred (*Wilson* 1983). Under the Charter, however, the Court ruled that the accused's right to make full answer and defence required access to the sealed packet containing the information on which the warrant was granted (*Dersch* 1993; *Durette* 1994). The door was opened to due-process challenges of wiretaps. Previous studies had indicated that many warrants were issued even though probable cause and other legal requirements had not been adequately established (Law Reform Commission of Canada 1983a; Hill 1996). Now that the packet was opened, defence lawyers discovered similar inadequacies in wiretap warrants (*Garofoli* 1990). In part because of these challenges,the use of wiretaps declined dramatically during the Charter era.[7] Due process, along with fiscal concerns, restrained some police activity.

In 1993, Parliament codified the new procedures devised by the courts for challenging wiretaps and repealed the automatic statutory exclusionary rule that applied to unlawfully intercepted communications (*Criminal Code* s. 189[1]–[4] repealed S.C. 1993 c.40 s.10). Henceforth such evidence would be excluded only if the Court concluded under section 24(2) of the Charter that its admission would bring the administration of justice into disrepute. As will be seen in the next section, the Court was often reluctant to exclude evidence obtained through an unreasonable search, especially if the police had made some efforts to obtain even a defective warrant. The Minister of Justice euphemistically presented this retreat to the minimum standards of the Charter as 'simplifying the rules of admissibility of evidence' (Hansard, 25 Feb. 1993: 16492). Constitutional minimums replaced more rigorous statutory standards designed to deter illegal wiretaps. When defence lawyers objected, they were met with a customary reply: what could possibly be wrong with Charter standards? In this case, the due-process protections of section 24(2) of the Charter were for crime control because they replaced a stricter rule designed by an earlier Parliament to deter illegal electronic surveillance. The Court, not Parliament, was now the guardian of due process, and the minimum guarantees of the Charter were effectively maximum standards.

The Not-So-Absolute Exclusionary Rule

In stark contrast to the quasi-absolute exclusionary rule used to enforce the expanded right against self-incrimination, the Supreme Court was

quite reluctant to exclude evidence obtained from simple search-and-seizure violations. In *Collins* (1987), the Court suggested that the admission
of real evidence which existed prior to the violation would generally not
affect the fairness of the trial or trigger a presumption of exclusion. The
distinction between pre-existing real evidence, such as drugs or guns, and
self-incriminating evidence, such as a statement or breath sample, served
as an automatic rule for a number of years. It was criticized for devaluing
section 8 of the Charter relative to other Charter rights (Delisle 1987;
Elman 1987), but it implicitly deferred to crime-control interests by making it more difficult to exclude evidence that was often crucial to the
prosecution (Roach 1994). In contrast to its enforcement of the right
against self-incrimination, in the search-and-seizure context, the Court
struck 'a balance between the tory value of community and the liberal values of individual rights and liberty' (Brock 1992: 301).

The Court refused to classify the results of illegal electronic surveillance as evidence which affected the fairness of the trial, despite a strong
argument by Justice Wilson that there was no principled distinction
between such evidence and confessions which triggered the expanded
right against self-incrimination. (*Wong* 1990: 469). This meant that
lengthy challenges to wiretap warrants often produced no tangible remedy for the accused. In response to an abuse of a traffic stop, the Court
opened the door to the exclusion of drugs and other pre-existing real evidence under the fair-trial test (*Mellenthin* 1992), but later restricted this to
cases where the accused's participation was required to find the evidence
(*Stillman* 1997). Even then, the Court recognized crime-control values by
allowing the prosecutor to demonstrate that the evidence would have
been legally discovered in any event (Roach 1996a).

In most cases, evidence obtained through a search-and-seizure violation would be excluded only if the seriousness of the violation outweighed the seriousness of the charge. In the writs-of-assistance and
wiretap cases, there was no question of excluding the evidence, because
the police relied in good faith on their statutory powers (*Hamill* 1987;
Duarte 1990; *Garofoli* 1990). As in the United States (*Leon* 1984), evidence
seized under defective warrants was also admitted. The idea that evidence
could be excluded because of a typographical error in a warrant was good
drama, but it was fiction. The police had to do something pretty flagrant
to have evidence excluded because of a search-and-seizure violation. It
was not the vomit test promised by Justice officials when section 24(2) was
drafted (see chapter 1), but it was pretty close.[8] The Court did not ignore
crime-control considerations and classified even property offences and

the cultivation of marijuana as serious offences (*Wise* 1992; *Grant* 1993). The Court's reluctance to exclude most unconstitutionally obtained drugs betrayed none of the scepticism about drug law enforcement that Packer suggested accompanied due process. The Court interpreted the right against unreasonable search and seizure in a generous due-process manner, but did not pay the crime-control price of frequently excluding illegally seized evidence.

DNA Evidence

Testing bodily samples for DNA first occurred in England in the *Pitchfork* case, when the entire male population of a village volunteered samples to help find an offender who had raped and murdered two females (Gelowitz 1988). Like blood testing for drunk driving, DNA testing has strong victims' rights implications and is especially useful in crimes involving rape. It also has some due-process attractions because, as occurred in the Guy Paul Morin and David Milgaard cases, it can exonerate the wrongfully convicted. Nevertheless, DNA testing sits uneasily with other due-process values because of its focus on factual guilt and the idea that the innocent have nothing to hide.

The courts did not take a uniform position on DNA testing. An early Ontario Court of Appeal judgment suggested that the police could seize hair samples for DNA testing as part of their common-law powers of search incident to arrest (*Alderton* 1985). In a series of cases, including two involving serial killer Alan Legere, the New Brunswick Court of Appeal took a more restrictive approach and held that the police violated section 8 of the Charter when they took hair and bodily samples without a warrant or the accused's consent (*Legere* 1988, 1994; *Stillman* 1995). In all of these cases, however, the Court of Appeal accommodated crime control and victims' rights by admitting the DNA samples under section 24(2) of the Charter. Seizures of hair or saliva were not a serious affront to human dignity, and community reactions to brutal and horrifying murders were considered. Due process was recognized, but did not trump crime control and victims' rights.

The Supreme Court was more committed to due process and willing to exclude bodily samples used for DNA testing. In *Borden* (1994), the Court excluded evidence of a DNA match given by an accused. The accused had consented to the sample in relation to an investigation of a sexual assault that had not involved semen (he was convicted and served four years), but was not told by the police that the samples would be used in their investigation of the rape of a sixty-nine-year-old woman at a nursing home. The Court held that, without this information, the accused had not validly waived his rights or consented to the sample. Without valid consent, there was no statutory authorization at the time for warrants to obtain bodily substances for DNA testing. The case received unfavourable media attention as part of a string of decisions that raised the question of whether 'the highest court [has] lost touch with reality' (*Globe and Mail,* 8 Oct. 1994). The lead in the Canadian Press report was: 'A man accused of raping a 69-year-old Nova Scotia woman will never serve a day in jail for that crime – despite DNA evidence linking him to it ... the freeing of a man who was proven "beyond a scintilla of doubt" to have raped a 69-year-old woman at a senior citizens' home is a good thing, his lawyer says' (*Winnipeg Free Press,* 3 Oct. 1994). The media again echoed the legal debates between due process and crime control,[9] but it was sympathy for victims that eventually forced Parliament to act.

Parliament Responds with DNA and Body-Impression Warrants

In 1995, legislation authorizing the seizure of bodily samples for DNA testing was introduced and fast-tracked through Parliament with all party approval. A few weeks after a private member's bill had been introduced calling for DNA warrants to 'fill a gaping hole in the criminal justice system' (Hansard, 7 Jun. 1995: 13374), Minister of Justice Allan Rock introduced the amendments for second reading, thanking 'all members of all parties in the House whose collaboration and agreement will make it possible for us today to consider and approve this bill, allowing quick and effective action on an important measure to improve Canada's system of justice and ... another step forward in the government's safe homes and safe streets agenda' (Hansard, 22 Jun. 1995: 14489). He noted that DNA evidence had been widely used, but that 'several courts, including the Supreme Court of Canada in the recently issued Borden decision, have pointed out that no law in Canada specifically permits us to take blood samples in order to carry out genetic analyses for medical and legal purposes' (ibid). He stressed that the legislation complied with the procedural protections of the Charter by requiring a judge to issue a warrant upon a showing of probable cause (ibid: 14490). The possibility of DNA exonerating an accused had been highlighted in the news because Guy Paul Morin had recently been acquitted of the murder of Christine Jessop on the basis of DNA evidence. Some defence lawyers, perhaps anticipating the challenge to the DNA evidence in the O.J. Simpson case, criticized the bill for not regulating laboratory procedures or independent tests by the accused (*Globe and Mail*, 23 Jun. 1995). The allure of science, combined with a sense that only the factually guilty had something to lose, explained some of the popularity of the bill.

The crucial factor, however, was sympathy for victims' rights and the attendance of the family of Tara Manning, a fifteen-year-old who had been raped and killed in her own bed the previous year in Montreal. Her father and brother had initially been suspected, but were exonerated when they voluntarily provided DNA samples. Her killer was eventually convicted on the basis of a DNA match (*Globe and Mail*, 5 May 1997), but at the time there was great concern that his DNA samples would be excluded from his trial. Allan Rock studiously avoided reference to the Mannings in his short speech,[10] but Lucien Bouchard, then leader of the opposition, made it clear that the House was considering the bill 'with exceptional speed ... and with unanimity rarely seen ... [because of] the seriousness of what happened to Mr. Manning's family' (Hansard, 22 Jun. 1995: 14490). He noted that the victim's family had toured 'Canada far and wide with petitions in order to convince the justice system to come up with the means to arrest criminals in the future. While Tara Manning paid for this flaw in the Criminal Code, others will be spared, because we will now be able to equip police investigators and the justice system with the means to provide the vital evidence' (ibid: 14491). Bouchard seemed to assume that Criminal Code authorization of DNA testing would somehow have prevented this awful murder. The Manning family had previously called for the override of Charter rights under section 33 to be invoked so that legislation could be enacted, notwithstanding due-process rights. The victim's father argued, 'The most important right that we have is the right to life. When the right to life is taken away, I don't see the problem of taking a swab from the inside of somebody's mouth to see if that DNA is the DNA that is, in this case, inside my daughter' (*Globe and Mail*, 25 May 1995). The Bloc's critic on the Status of Women praised the bill, noting that DNA testing was most often used in sex crimes and that 'women welcome any measure aimed at protecting them against physical and sexual violence' (Hansard, 22 Jun. 1995: 14495). The Deputy Speaker of the House concluded the short and unanimous debate on the bill by thanking 'the Manning family for being with us tonight for this very special occasion' (ibid: 14497). Victims' rights emerged as a powerful force that justified the new legislation.

The emotion of victims' rights allowed Parliament to enact popular[11] legislation before it left for its summer recess. Families of murdered children played the dominant role in campaigning on behalf of crime victims. In an alliance of victims' rights and crime control, the police supported the bill, but also wanted a DNA data bank, which they promised would allow them to solve unresolved sexual-assault and homicide cases. Some grass-roots organizations were not as impressed. Julia Kubanek of the Vancouver Rape Relief and Women's Shelter was concerned that the legislation would detract attention 'from the thousands of sexual assaults that occur every year and place public resources and attention on a small number of sensational crimes,' as well as make it more difficult to obtain convictions in cases where the certainty of DNA testing was not available (*Globe and Mail*, 23 Jun. 1995). Victims' rights initiatives that focused on high-profile cases shared the symbolism of due-process discourse, even while they engaged and countered it.

Following *Borden* (1994), the Supreme Court excluded DNA samples taken from an unwilling accused in another case that was investigated before DNA warrants were available. Justice Cory warned that the police must 'respect the dignity and bodily integrity of all who are arrested. The treatment meted out by agents of the state will often indicate the treatment that all citizens of the state may ultimately expect' (*Stillman* 1997: 344).[12] In dissent, Justice L'Heureux-Dubé argued that the police should be able to take DNA samples at least 'in the case of highly reprehensible crimes, such as murder or sexual abuse, where the identity of the person may be difficult to establish otherwise, considering the fact that such crimes may typically occur in private' (ibid: 368, 375–6). For her the issue was complicated by concerns about equality and victims' rights. Reading her opinion, one could not help but compare the horrendous violence inflicted on the victim with the minimal intrusion of the police taking hair samples for DNA testing.

Consistent with its growing interest in clashes on the Court between due process and crime control, *Stillman* was reported on the front page as 'DNA Evidence Gathering Curbed' (*Globe and Mail*, 21 Mar. 1997). The majority of the Court, however, went out of its way to suggest that the new legislation authorizing warrants satisfied constitutional standards (*Stillman* 1997: 343). Even in Stillman's own case, there was still admissible DNA evidence, because the Court found that the police had legally seized mucous found in a tissue discarded by the suspect in the police station after he had cried during an interrogation in violation of his rights under the Young Offenders Act. The media treatment of the case presented an image of the courts restricting the ability of the police to control crime and being insensitive to victims. The doctrinal landscape was more complex and ambiguous because the Court had accommodated crime-control values and allowed Parliament to authorize and regulate police powers.

The Supreme Court found the taking of the accused's teeth impressions in *Stillman* to be a particularly unreasonable seizure. The impressions were needed to see if they matched a bite on the victim's stomach. Justice Cory stressed that the two-hour procedure was 'a lengthy and intrusive process ... very different' from the taking of fingerprints. Justice L'Heureux-Dubé found the procedure to be less troubling, noting that the impressions were taken 'by a dentist according to professional standards' (ibid: 382), which apparently did not include consent to treatment. Parliament quickly responded to the ruling by providing for warrants to obtain body impressions if there were reasonable grounds to believe an offence has been committed; that the impression would provide information concerning the offence and it was in the best interests of the administration of justice to issue the warrant (*Criminal Code* s.487.091 am. S.C. 1997 c. 18). There was little public debate and no effective opposition from civil-libertarians or defence lawyers. The most intrusive form of police investigation that resulted in the exclusion of evidence in *Stillman* was reauthorized and legitimated by legislation and warrants. Once again, a due-process decision had provoked Parliament to act in the name of crime control and victims' rights.

Feeney

In *Feeney* (1997), the Supreme Court delivered yet another controversial decision restricting police search powers. The Court reversed its own rule that the police could enter homes without a warrant to make an arrest because under the Charter 'the privacy interest outweighs the interest of the police' (*Feeney* 1997: 154). The evidence, including a shirt stained with the blood of the eighty-six-year-old murder victim, was excluded because the police admitted that, even under the old rule, they did not have adequate grounds to arrest the accused and conduct the search. Justice Sopinka appealed to due process by arguing that the fact the police were correct in their 'hunch' about the accused's involvement did not 'legitimize' their actions and that the price of a lost conviction was 'fully justified in a free and democratic society' because of the importance of respecting the accused's rights (ibid: 159, 170). In her dissent, Justice L'Heureux-Dubé appealed to crime control. She was appalled that the majority had presented the police 'as lawless vigilantes, flagrantly and deliberately violating the Charter at every turn' whereas any more restraint would have left them open to criticism 'for allowing a murderer to remain at large in the community' (ibid: 204). She combined support for the police with sympathy for the 'helpless victim' who had been subject to a 'random' and 'savage beating' (ibid: 205).

Like the DNA cases discussed above, *Feeney* was heavily criticized by the police and victims' groups and was met with a quick legislative reply. A page one story in the *Globe and Mail* (9 Aug. 1997) portrayed the case as 'the latest sign of the top court's determination to set tough new rules for police and prosecutors' and featured criticism by the victim's family that the Supreme Court was more concerned about the rights of a brutal murderer than about those of the victim. The more mundane facts that the accused was subject to a new trial and that the Court quickly responded to the public and police outcry by allowing a transition period were buried in the fiftieth and fifty-fifth paragraphs of the story. Jeffrey Simpson argued that the decision was another indication that the Court's Charter rulings 'are now more important in determining a range of criminal law matters than anything Parliament decides' (*Globe and Mail*, 6 Feb. 1997).

Parliament Responds with Entry and Arrest Warrants and Exceptions

Simpson's fears about Court domination were unwarranted because Parliament quickly enacted new legislation which provided for warrants and telewarrants to enter a dwelling to make an arrest. Like Parliament's response to *Duarte* (1990), the legislation also authorized warrantless searches if 'exigent circumstances' existed. The Court in *Feeney* had been reluctant to recognize this exception to the warrant requirement, but Parliament defined it to include circumstances in which the need to prevent the imminent loss or destruction of evidence made it 'impracticable to obtain a warrant.' The police were also allowed to obtain judicial authorization to dispense with their traditional warnings that the police were entering a dwelling if the warnings would expose them or others to harm or result in the loss of evidence. A due-process decision stressing the importance of warrants resulted in legislative authorization of warrantless searches and entries without announcement.

The government defended the new law as giving 'the police as much flexibility as possible given the limitations imposed by the Charter' (Hansard, 31 Oct. 1997). Reform Party members used its introduction as an opportunity to criticize the Supreme Court. Chuck Cadman, a victims' rights advocate, argued that 'a convicted killer found covered in the blood of your loved one may walk away unpunished because the police were unable to wake him from a drunken stupor before entering the premises to make an arrest. It is another classic example of how our justice system continues to revictimize' (Hansard, 31 Oct. 1997). Following the trend in the DNA cases, resistance to due process became a victims' rights issue, and victims' groups joined the police in opposing the Court's decision and supporting the legislation. Defence lawyers argued that the bill was unconstitutional and defied the Court's judgment, but, unlike in the Joint Committee on the Constitution, their views were unpopular, given the facts of the case, and did not prevail. Parliament emphasized the importance of its reply to the Court with a preamble which declared that 'circumstances may nonetheless exist that justify entry into a dwelling house' without a warrant. Although the case did not involve domestic violence, and women's groups did not testify in committee, Parliament also relied on the 'societal importance of providing peace officers with the ability to effectively respond to urgent calls for assistance, particularly in the context of domestic violence,' to justify exceptions to the warrant requirement. As will be seen in chapter 5, similar statements figured in the preambles to Parliamentary replies to due-process decisions that affected the rights of women as victims and potential victims of sexual and domestic assault. The *Feeney* episode underlined again the important alliance between victims' groups and the police and Parliament's willingness to respond quickly to due-process decisions restricting police search powers.

Was Due Process for Crime Control?

The search-and-seizure cases fall into a distinct pattern. Due-process decisions holding that various warrantless investigative techniques were unreasonable searches were all greeted in short order with new legislation authorizing the impugned searches, usually, but not always, with a warrant. In this sense, due process was ultimately for crime control, and the decisions of the Supreme Court provoked legislation from Parliament that gave the police more investigative powers. These new powers would be legitimated either by a judicial warrant based on probable cause or by Parliament's statement that warrants were not necessary. Judicial decisions concerning the right against unreasonable search and seizure were particularly amenable to such responses because of the emphasis that the Court placed on prior legislative and judicial authorization of searches.

The courts were reluctant to extend the common law to authorize searches, and this forced Parliament to do this crime-control work. The pattern was perfected in the general warrants where the scope of legal and judicial authorization automatically expanded with due-process protections.

The search-and-seizure cases offer the strongest support in this chapter for the critical thesis that due process was for crime control. Although the Supreme Court embraced due-process values more strongly than even the Warren Court, the end result often accommodated crime control and victims' rights. As McBarnet (1981) has suggested, the Court's own jurisprudence simultaneously affirmed due-process values in the abstract while making ample accommodations for crime control. Contrary to the fears of progressive critics, the Court made exceptions from probable-cause standards to allow regulatory searches. Due-process decisions allowing the accused new opportunities to challenge wiretap warrants were balanced by a judicial reluctance to exclude such evidence under section 24(2) of the Charter and Parliament's repeal of a stricter statutory exclusionary rule. Most unconstitutionally seized evidence was admitted under section 24(2), with courts stressing crime-control factors such as the good faith of the police, the seriousness of the charges, and the importance of the evidence. Many search-and-seizure cases were drug cases, but the Court displayed no scepticism about the criminal sanction and concluded that all drug offences, including those involving marijuana, were serious. Due process was not, however, a charade. The Court excluded DNA matches and murder weapons because it was bound by the logic of its expanded right against self-incrimination. Nevertheless, the overall trend in the search-and-seizure cases was to qualify due-process decisions impugning warrantless searches with decisions to admit evidence and invitations to Parliament to expand and legitimate police search powers in the name of crime control and victims' rights.

It could be argued that my conclusion is unduly cynical. After all crime control is a legitimate value (McConville, Sanders, and Leng 1991; Brock 1992) and the Court's decisions at least encouraged Parliament to enact warrant procedures. Decisions such as *Hunter* (1984), *Duarte* (1990), *Stillman* (1997), and *Feeney* (1997), however, romanticized the new constitutional requirement of prior judicial authorization of searches on the basis of probable cause established under oath. A person unaware of the practice of criminal justice could conclude that warrants were issued only after a full-dress adversarial hearing in open court before a judge. Nothing could be further from the truth. Most warrants were issued by justices of the peace who, while judicial officials, were often not lawyers, and even wiretap warrants obtained from judges were almost always granted. The police typed up their 'story' of the investigation (Roach and Friedland 1996: 334) and there was no one representing the suspect. Both before (Law Reform Commission 1983a: 83–92) and after the Charter (Hill 1996), warrants were frequently granted without adequate attention to whether probable cause was established or the place to be searched and the items to be seized adequately defined. The warrant procedure may have legitimated crime control by promoting the illusion of compliance with due-process standards.

Conclusion

Starting with the Joint Committee's decision in 1981 to strengthen the legal rights of the Charter, the police faced many due-process challenges to their powers. The Supreme Court embraced due process more strongly than many had anticipated and imposed stricter *Miranda* rules than even the Warren Court. To the surprise of many, the Court expanded the right against self-incrimination from the courtroom to the police station and enforced it with a quasi-absolute exclusionary rule. Even here, however, due process was not the only value, and the Court made exceptions for drunk driving spot-checks. The Court's surprising and rigorous commitment to an expanded right against self-incrimination demonstrated the dynamic and autonomous nature of legal culture. Captured by its own logic of due process, the Court excluded important evidence in cases with very sympathetic victims.

On the other hand, the Court's treatment of other police powers demonstrated that crime control still played an important role in legal doctrine. It upheld proactive and random virtue testing, warrantless arrests and searches, fingerprinting, and preventive detention. Even when the police went over the line, the courts were reluctant to use their blunt and strong remedies. The search-and-seizure cases displayed both a willingness to take the logic of due process to great lengths and a more traditional reluctance to exclude illegally seized evidence from a criminal trial. The Court affirmed due process when interpreting Charter rights and recognized crime control when deciding whether to exclude evidence. The search-and-seizure cases also provoked frequent legislative replies as Parliament responded to the Court's decisions with new legislation providing warrants for any investigative technique that might otherwise be an unreasonable search or seizure. Judicial due process invited legislative intervention in the name of crime control, and increasingly victims' rights. The next chapter explores whether due-process innovations in criminal trials were for crime control and examines the emerging role of crime victims and other third parties in the criminal trial.

3

The Criminal Trial

Like *Miranda* rules and warrant requirements, the criminal trial in which the accused was represented by a lawyer and forced the prosecutor to prove guilt beyond a reasonable doubt was an important symbol of the due-process model of criminal justice. The irony, however, was that most cases ended in guilty pleas or prosecutorial withdrawals with minimal judicial involvement. Packer recognized that the guilty plea was the most efficient disposition of a case, and thus a goal for police and prosecutors, who dominated the crime-control model. He did not, however, anticipate that guilty pleas might also serve the organizational interests of defence lawyers and judges (Ericson and Baranek 1982) and that some accused with valid due-process claims might plead guilty to avoid the hassle of a trial (Feeley 1979). He also did not anticipate how guilty pleas might be vulnerable to criticism for not meeting the expectations of crime victims or how criminal trials and plea bargains alike might prevent the victim, the accused, and the community from achieving restorative justice.

This chapter examines changes to the criminal trial process during the Charter era. There were signs of a due-process revolution as accused exercised new rights to demand speedy trials and full disclosure. They also successfully challenged criminal laws for failing to respect the presumption of innocence and imposing punishment without fault. In response to due-process violations, courts stayed prosecutions and struck down offences. Nevertheless, the due-process revolution was partial and there was significant support for the critical thesis that due process was for crime control. In particular, disclosure and speedy trial decisions led to administrative reforms designed to increase the efficiency and legitimacy of the guilty-plea process. The courts retreated from some of their due-process decisions and did not ignore concerns about efficient crime control and victims' rights.

As it did in chapter 2, victims' rights will make an appearance. Victims staked out a modest role in the criminal trial process by claiming that their Charter rights were violated. In addition, they were given a minor role in plea bargaining and, as will be examined in chapter 9, a greater role in sentencing. These were significant changes, but the criminal trial process remained dominated by professionals. Defence lawyers and judges made their due-process mark, and victims were consulted and claimed rights, but prosecutors still called the shots in most cases.

Speedy Trials: Fairness or Efficiency?

Before the Charter, the courts refused to use their common-law powers to combat trial delay (*Rourke* 1977), and police and prosecutors objected to the inclusion of the right to a trial in a reasonable time in the Charter. They were not opposed to speedy trials per se, because 'the speedy conviction of the guilty advances crime control interests to the same extent that the speedy acquittal of the innocent protects the accused's liberty and security interest' (Code 1992: 5). They were, however, concerned about the vagueness of the guarantee and the possibility that courts might stop prosecutions because of delay. Many of their fears would have been addressed by speedy-trial legislation introduced in 1984 (ibid: 79) This legislation, however, died on the order paper, and the courts filled the vacuum left by the legislature and did so in a manner more concerned with due process than with crime control.

The courts struggled with defining a reasonable time for a trial. Unlike many who refused to believe that accused really wanted speedy trials or were harmed by delay, Justice Lamer took a bold approach which went further than American law in assuming that the accused suffered prejudice from delay. He also refused to consider the state's crime-control interests in conducting a prosecution after substantial delay. Justice Lamer wanted objective standards based on how quickly efficient districts disposed of cases independent of 'the difficulties which a particular police force, Crown office or court may face in preparing or trying a case that result from institutional inadequacies such as lack of personnel, facilities etc.' (*Mills* 1986: 548). He also convinced the Court that a stay of proceedings was the minimal remedy for a violation of the right. Like the quasi-absolute exclusionary rule used to enforce the expanded right against self-incrimination, this remedy was deduced from the nature of the right even though it would result in 'automatically allowing persons guilty of serious criminal acts to go free simply because someone has caused delay that can be regarded as unreasonable' (ibid: 571). The comparative empirical approach combined with the automatic remedy of a stay set the stage for one of the most controversial cases of the era.

Askov

Elijah Askov was charged with threatening and extorting Peter Belmont to pay a 50 per cent commission on any exotic dancers that Belmont booked in Toronto. Askov was also charged with weapons offences for brandishing a sawed-off shotgun and a knife while making this business offer to Belmont. Askov was denied bail for almost six months after his arrest in November 1983. He was committed for trial after a preliminary inquiry in September 1984. The next available trial date was October 1985. Because of overbooking in the Peel court, the case could not be heard until September 1986. With the court finally ready to hear the case, Askov's lawyers instead successfully argued that the proceedings should be stayed because his right to a trial in a reasonable time had been violated by the twenty-three month delay between committal and trial. In ordering the stay, the trial judge cryptically observed that 'those responsible for the proper administration have known about this systematic [sic] delay for at least five years; yet nothing has been done about it' (Askov 1990: 463).

There was indeed a larger story behind the case. The judges in Peel and throughout Ontario were in the middle of a political struggle with the government to have more judges appointed and more courtrooms built. Despite their guaranteed independence, judges relied on governments to construct, maintain, and staff their courthouses and to appoint more judges. Like others in government, they lobbied for increased resources. The Charter, however, gave them special powers. In 1988, the Chief Justice of Ontario warned the government that 'if the needs of the justice system are not given priority, then the Government will have to be prepared to tell a person who has been robbed, or whose home has been broken into, or whose child has been knocked down by a drunken driver that the accused person has been released because there are not sufficient funds to prosecute him within a reasonable time' (Howland 1988: 8). Despite these strong words, Ontario's attorney general Ian Scott remained reluctant to put more resources in the system. He believed that judges and prosecutors, like others in government, would have to learn to use their existing resources more efficiently.

Despite its Chief Justice's pleas about the seriousness of the delay problem in Peel, the Ontario Court of Appeal reversed the trial judge's stay of proceedings. Following the crime-control model, the Court of Appeal assumed that Askov was factually guilty and only complained about the delay when he thought he could obtain a stay of proceedings rather than an expedited trial (*Askov* 1987: 299–300). The Supreme Court restored the stay of proceedings and stressed that 'all accused persons, each one of whom is presumed to be innocent, should be give the opportunity to defend themselves against the charges they face and to have their name cleared and reputation re-established at the earliest possible time' (*Askov* 1990: 474). Justice Cory invoked the 'exquisite agony' of an innocent accused awaiting trial, whereas the Court of Appeal had imagined a guilty person laying in wait for a loophole. The Supreme Court found the twenty-three month delay to be unreasonable. Despite the 'unfortunate and regrettable' effects of a stay on crime control, due process must prevail. In reasoning similar to that used to justify the quasi-absolutist exclusionary rule discussed in chapter 2, Cory J. concluded that 'to conclude otherwise would render meaningless a right enshrined in the Charter as the supreme law of the land' (ibid: 490).

Askov could have been a due-process case of importance only to those who faced a two-year trial delay. Nevertheless, the Court gathered, on its own initiative, data which indicated that the 'average time' it took for a trial to commence in Montreal was about three months (*Askov* 1990: 489; Code 1992; Baar 1993). 'Making a very rough comparison and more than doubling the longest waiting period to make every allowance for the special circumstances in Peel,' the Court then held that trials should commence in between six and eight months (*Askov* 1990: 490). By following Justice Lamer's comparative empirical approach, the Court articulated the type of objective guidelines that Parliament had failed to enact. Unfortunately, it also made a basic social-science mistake by focusing on the average and not the slowest cases which were in greatest danger of being stayed (Baar 1993: 316).

In addition to its (mis)use of social-science evidence, the Supreme Court also concluded that the cause of delay in Peel was a lack of resources, not inefficient case processing by prosecutors and courts. The Court criticized Ontario's delay-reduction initiative, which included case management, disclosure of the prosecutor's evidence to the defence, and early plea discussions, as 'obviously insufficient' because it 'stressed more efficient use of the region's available facilities rather than the provision of additional resources' (ibid: 487). Cory J. added that 'more resources must be supplied to this district perhaps by way of additional Crown Attorneys and courtrooms' (ibid: 488). The Court endorsed Chief Justice Howland's understanding of insufficient resources as the cause of delay over Attorney General Scott's belief that inefficient practices were to blame (Code 1992: 129).

As Ontario's Chief Justice had previously done (Howland 1988), Justice Cory predicted that an outraged and frightened public would blame the government, not the courts, for the stays (*Askov* 1990: 475). The government, however, provided the media with statistics that created the impression that the courts had declared an amnesty for criminals. Contrary to the Court's intentions, the *Askov* crisis was constructed as one which pitted the courts' insistence on due process against the government's interests in crime control and victims' rights (Bogart 1994: 208).

Après Askov: *The Deluge of Stays*

In a display of the power that a single Supreme Court decision can have in the due-process model, courts and prosecutors followed the six-to-eight-month guidelines quite literally. In the first five months after *Askov*, 30,000 criminal charges were either stayed by courts or withdrawn by prosecutors (Code 1992: 113). By November 1991, this charge count would top out at 51,791. In addition, close to 64,000 more minor provincial and municipal offences were also stayed (Baar 1993: 314, 319–20). The criminal-charge count was periodically released by the attorney general to the press and resulted in screaming headlines that left the impression that a wholesale amnesty for criminals, if not actual anarchy, was occurring. Nevertheless, the *Askov* charge count and its threat to crime control were inflated. The statistics reported charges, not cases. Most accused faced multiple charges. Askov faced five, and drunk-driving cases, which accounted for more than a quarter of all the charges withdrawn or stayed (Baar 1993: 320), resulted in the dual charge of 'over 80' and 'impaired' even though the accused could legally be convicted of only one. In a banner front-page headline, the *Toronto Star* (19 Dec. 1991) reported that '2,400 drunk driving cases [had been] dropped' although the actual case count was half this charge-based figure. The *Askov* charge-count figures also collapsed charges that were stayed by courts and withdrawn by prosecutors. Some of these charges would have been dropped in any event because of pre-*Askov* standards of delay, lack of evidence, and plea bargains. The media also did not report that 90 per cent of criminal charges in Ontario were not 'Askoved' and proceeded to their normal disposition (Baar 1993: 320).[1]

The Court attracted more criticism when Justice Cory commented at an academic conference that 'the rigidity of the interpretation [of *Askov*] given by some people came as a shock ... We were not aware of the extent of that impact' (*Globe and Mail*, 17 Jul. 1991). Representatives of drunk-driving victims complained that the dismissal of charges was 'irresponsible beyond belief ... We've worked 10 years to get drunk drivers off the road and they're putting them back on faster than we can get them off' (*Toronto Sun*, 20 Dec. 1990). Ontario's attorney general Howard Hampton was not about to be blamed for the delay and sent letters of condolence to victims of crime whose charges were stayed (*Toronto Sun*, 11 Nov. 1990). Both Chief Justice Lamer and the Ontario government appointed task forces to examine ways of clearing up and preventing future delays. Defence lawyers begin to see that the due-process victory of *Askov* had provoked forces that would lead to more efficient crime control and sympathy for crime victims. Brian Greenspan, for example, rejected the increasingly popular idea that the criminal process should be 'working as efficiently as a General Motors production line' (*Globe and Mail*, 22 Aug. 1991). In response to the quality-control crisis of *Askov*, however, the crime-control assembly line was refurbished and speeded up.

In response to *Askov*, the Ontario government spent $39 million and appointed twenty-seven new provincial court judges and sixty-one new Crown attorneys. (Code 1992: 114; *Globe and Mail*, 11 Jul. 1991). It also committed $314 million to building new court facilities in Peel and other centres (*Toronto Star*, 9 Oct. 1991). This influx of resources helps explain how the number of charges disposed in Ontario courts actually increased during the *Askov* crisis. In 1988–9, trial courts had disposed of 503,432 charges across Ontario, but in 1990–1, during the height of the *Askov* crisis, 608,702 charges were disposed (Ontario 1993: 16). Despite fears of guilty people roaming the streets, there was only a slight decline in Ontario's prison population in the year after *Askov*, and thereafter the prison population continued to expand. Michael Mandel (1994: 228) has concluded that *Askov* only resulted in 'a constitutional diversion of public sector funds from the service sector to the repressive sector, with the overall result of more people in jail.' Like the search-and-seizure cases examined in chapter 2, the Court's due-process decisions provoked a crime-control response from the other arms of the state. The due-process *Askov* crisis actually resulted in more efficient crime control.

The Court Retreats in Morin

The administrative response to *Askov* was practically important, but not part of the public drama of due process being pitted against crime control and victims' rights. The Supreme Court was not able to revisit *Askov* until

March 1992, when it heard of an appeal of a typical drunk-driving case that had been stayed because of a thirteen-month delay. The Court charitably acknowledged that the public reaction to *Askov* had been 'mixed.' Borrowing Packer's argument that due process could cleanse the system of trivial cases, Justice Sopinka asserted that 'many applaud the result which has in their view unclogged the system of much dead wood in the form of charges that should not have been laid or, having been laid, ought to have been dropped.' He went on, however, to acknowledge the vastly more popular opinion that *Askov* was perceived as 'an amnesty for criminals, some of whom were charged with very serious crimes ... accused persons are discharged when they have suffered no prejudice to the complete dismay of victims who have suffered, in some cases, tragic losses' (*Morin* 1992: 7). This followed the media in overestimating the practical effects of *Askov* and reproducing fears about an amnesty for criminals and the consequent reactions of victims. Justice McLachlin similarly argued that, when cases were stayed, 'victims conclude that justice has not been done and the public feels apprehension that the law may not be adequately discharging the most fundamental of its tasks' (ibid: 29). The Court recognized crime control and victims' rights as legitimate concerns that should temper the accused's rights to a speedy trial.

The Court did not explicitly overrule the *Askov* guidelines, but stressed that they were not 'to be applied in a purely mechanical fashion' like a limitation period (ibid: 20). It provided longer guidelines of eight to ten months for the majority of often simpler cases which are heard in provincial court. It underlined the flexibility of its new guideline by holding that the thirteen-month delay was reasonable. The Court also recognized a social interest, not in the speedy trials that Justice Cory has praised in *Askov*, but in trials after substantial periods of delay. The accused's behaviour, including the bringing of due-process challenges, would be relevant in determining the reasonableness of the delay (ibid: 17), and the accused's failure to object to delay would support an inference of no prejudice from the delay (ibid: 28). Chief Justice Lamer dissented on the basis that the Court was departing from *Askov* by requiring the accused to prove prejudice (ibid: 6). As Packer suggested, due process was vulnerable not only to public hostility, but also to subtle changes in judicial attitudes.

Summary

Askov was best known as a due-process decision that resulted in the stay of more than 51,000 charges in Ontario. Of all the due-process cases examined here and in chapter 2, it received the most public criticism and left lingering suspicions about the judiciary's respect for crime control and victims' rights. A closer analysis, however, reveals much more ambiguity. The Court was not immune from public criticism and significantly retreated in *Morin*. As pointed out by McBarnet (1981), its own jurisprudence was flexible enough to embrace both the accused's due-process interests and the interests of the public and victims, at first in speedy trials (*Askov* 1990), and subsequently in trials after considerable delay (*Morin* 1992). The Court was not prepared to remain committed to due process when the crime-control and victims' rights prices became high and well publicized. Moreover, it suggested that governments respond to its speedy-trial decisions by adding judges, prosecutors, and courtrooms. Although mired in fiscal troubles, the Ontario government obliged. One of the most controversial due-process cases of the era actually resulted in more resources for crime control.

Disclosure: Fairness or Efficiency?

It was not a coincidence that Peel, the slowest district 'anywhere north of the Rio Grande' (*Askov* 1990: 489), was also known as 'No Deal Peel.' The *Askov* problem of delay was closely linked with charge screening, disclosure, and plea bargaining.[2] If prosecutors were unable because of resource constraints or hard-line policies to plea-bargain, the backlog of cases would increase. Disclosure of the prosecutor's case to the defence facilitated plea bargaining by forcing prosecutors to assemble their case and by placing defence lawyers in a position where they can intelligently make a deal for their clients. Without early disclosure and plea bargaining, the system was very inefficient and risky. If too many cases were settled in the few harried minutes before court started, judges would be, as they sometimes were in Peel, idle for a good part of the working day. If not enough cases were settled, then accused like Askov would be sent home because the judges were too busy. Askov's due-process remedy was a stay of proceedings, but society's remedy for systemic delay was more guilty pleas. Disclosure and plea bargaining were the oil that kept the crime-control assembly line operating smoothly.

Disclosure was, however, best known as a due-process protection for the accused. The Warren Court, in one of its landmark due-process decisions, declared that the prosecutor must, at the accused's request, disclose all exculpatory evidence (*Brady* 1963). Reflecting their lack of concern about due process, Canadian courts held that disclosure was not required under the Canadian Bill of Rights (*Duke* 1972: 479) and refused to ensure that the accused received full disclosure of the prosecutor's case in preliminary inquiries (*Caccamo* 1975). The issue came to a head when a public inquiry blamed the wrongful conviction of Donald Marshall Jr on the failure to disclose inconsistent statements made by witnesses (Nova Scotia 1989: 72). It echoed earlier recommendations by the Law Reform Commission of Canada (LRCC 1974a, 1984) that the Criminal Code be amended to require disclosure. Parliament did not act and, as in *Askov,* the Supreme Court again filled the space left by the legislature.

Stinchcombe

William Stinchcombe, a Calgary lawyer, was convicted of embezzling $1.9 million from clients and sentenced to nine years' imprisonment. His secretary gave testimony that suggested that Stinchcombe may have been acting as a business partner, not a lawyer, for the clients who lost the money. She had spoken twice to the police before giving this testimony, but refused to be interviewed by her former boss's lawyers. Stinchcombe wanted the police recordings of those conversations. The trial judge denied the request, and the Alberta Court of Appeal dismissed an appeal without bothering to write reasons. Like Askov, Stinchcombe received a warmer reception in the Supreme Court.

The Supreme Court used the case to announce a general principle that the prosecutor was required, at the accused's request, to disclose all relevant non-privileged information in his or her possession at an early stage of the case. The Court invoked Donald Marshall's wrongful conviction as a justification for requiring full disclosure. It deduced the right to disclosure from the accused's 'right to make full answer and defence,' which was described as 'one of the pillars of criminal justice on which we heavily depend to ensure that the innocent are not convicted' (*Stinchcombe* 1991: 9). It also stressed the ideal that prosecutors were impartial ministers of justice more interested in the truth than in winning. The Court ordered that the conversations between the police and Stinchcombe's former secretary be disclosed to Stinchcombe and a new trial held. A person who had lost $1.6 million was bitter, commenting: 'we're going to go through this ... again.' Another victim, however, accepted the decision because 'the legal rights of people is sacrosanct' and the prosecutor 'will have another kick at the cat.' Stinchcombe, who had been out on bail during his appeal, praised the decision as a 'good thing for the law itself' (*Calgary Herald,* 8 Nov. 1991).

Although the Court based its decision on the accused's rights, it also cheerfully noted that full and early disclosure 'will foster the resolution of many charges without trial, through increased numbers of withdrawals and pleas of guilty' (*Stinchcombe* 1991: 14). The Court cited a study showing a quarter of cases were settled at disclosure conferences and that disclosure had doubled guilty pleas and tripled Crown withdrawals (LRCC 1984: 8). The fact that due process might facilitate more efficient crime control was no conspiratorial secret and was warmly acknowledged by the Court during the height of the *Askov* crisis.

Après Stinchcombe*: Increasing and Legitimating Plea Bargaining*

The Court's decision in *Stinchcombe* left many unanswered questions and created much work for police, prosecutors, defence counsel, and the courts. As will be seen in chapter 5, the ability of defence lawyers to obtain access to the records of sexual-assault victims became a controversial issue that was not anticipated at the time *Stinchcombe* was released. The actual case had to return to the Supreme Court a second time after the judge at Stinchcombe's new trial stayed proceedings because the police were unable to produce the originals of their interviews with Stinchcombe's secretary. The Court of Appeal overturned the drastic remedy of a stay of proceedings, quoting with approval Justice McLachlin's statements in *Morin* (1992: 29) that, as a result of stays, 'victims conclude that justice has not been done and the public feels apprehension that the law may not be adequately discharging the most fundamental of its tasks' (*Stinchcombe* 1994: 565). Having learnt its lessons from the wholesale stays that followed *Askov*, the Supreme Court affirmed that a stay was not an appropriate remedy because the Crown had not engaged in any misconduct and could disclose only information in its possession (*Stinchcombe* 1995). It was later drawn back to using a stay in a controversial case in which a rape crisis centre shredded its counselling records (*Carosella* 1997; see chapter 5).

Despite the ability of an occasional accused to obtain a stay, there were strong arguments that *Stinchcombe*, like *Askov*, ultimately served the interests of more efficient crime control. The police produced more paper work to ensure that the prosecutor could disclose full files. In one police force alone, it required two new clerks, a photocopying machine, and an annual expenditure of $90,000 for paper (Ericson and Haggerty 1997: 314). Unlike in the United States, the prosecutor was not required to hand over only information that could help the accused, but all relevant material. Most of the *Stinchcombe* file was composed of police reports and witness statements that would usually make the case for the prosecution and an early guilty plea.

Administrative responses to *Askov* and *Stinchcombe* were largely designed to increase and legitimate plea bargaining. Before the Charter, plea bargaining was 'a dirty little secret' (Parker 1972: 310) and 'something for which a decent criminal justice system has no place. There has to be a trial' (LRCC 1974–5: 14). These attitudes mirrored Packer's (1968: 157) assumption that, without a trial, the accused could not be treated fairly. By 1989, however, the LRCC had changed its tune (p. 8) and concluded that plea bargaining (now sanitized as 'plea discussions') was not 'an inherently shameful practice' and should be recognized and regulated. Similarly, the widely respected Martin Task Force appointed in the wake of *Askov* concluded that the advent of the Charter and legal aid went 'a long way toward alleviating any concern about the propriety of a broad discretion to conduct resolution discussions.' The 'Charter-enhanced quality' of the police investigation meant that most accused should be expected to plead guilty (Ontario 1993: 286).

The Martin Task Force called for prosecutors to screen charges at an early stage. 'Fifteen minutes of the time of one Crown counsel, during which one case is screened early on, and weeded out because it is fatally weak, may save many hours of judicial, administrative, police, witness, prosecutorial and publicly funded defence time' (ibid: 140). 'No Deal Peel' with its reputation for overcharging was not the model.[3] Early and full disclosure would not only ensure compliance with *Stinchcombe*, but place prosecutors and defence lawyers in a position in which they could reach an appropriate disposition 'without the expense, inconvenience and trauma of a full trial' (ibid: 288). Despite noting that as many as two-thirds of defence lawyers did not even bother to ask for disclosure, the Martin Task Force rejected the Marshall Commission's recommendations that disclosure be automatic because of concerns about increased costs and delay in cases in which the accused did not bother to put up a fight (ibid: 210–11). Accused were encouraged to plead guilty by sentencing discounts that penalized them for going to trial and losing. Prosecutors were advised that they could not 'expect an accused person to waive the constitutional right to a trial' (ibid: 312) for nothing. Judges were advised to go along with sentence deals unless they brought the administration of justice into disrepute (ibid: 327). Judges were also encouraged to facilitate plea bargaining at pre-trial conferences by expressing views about the appropriate sentence and being available to take the guilty plea and sentence the accused (ibid: 368). The task force hoped that this judicial involvement would 'enhance the public perception of the practice of resolution discussions' (ibid: 350). Plea bargaining was no longer a 'dirty secret' hidden in the corridors of the courtroom, but was now openly facilitated in the judge's office.

Plea bargaining was also legitimized on the basis that it spared victims the trauma of the criminal trial (LRCC 1989: 10; Ontario 1993). This benefit might come with the price of a sentence reduction and/or charge reduction that might leave the victim believing that his or her suffering had not been adequately acknowledged by the professionals who ran the crime-control assembly line. The Martin Task Force recognized this danger and suggested that victims be consulted about plea bargains 'where appropriate and feasible' (ibid: 305). Nevertheless, victims would not have a veto because 'the mere fact of having been victimized' did not give them 'any insight into how criminal law, or the criminal trial process, works' (ibid: 307). The monopoly of crime-control professionals remained, and victims' rights were used to support crime control without really empowering crime victims.[4]

In summary, the dramatic due-process decisions of *Askov* and *Stinchcombe* facilitated a greater emphasis on plea bargaining. In this functional sense, due process was for crime control. The Martin Task Force's recommendations for charge screening, disclosure, and judicial involvement may have made plea bargaining a fairer process, but they were also designed to speed up and legitimate the crime-control assembly line in which the vast majority of cases were resolved without a trial.

Third Parties Use the Charter to Join the Criminal Trial

Although left on the periphery of a renewed plea-bargaining process, crime victims fought their way into the criminal trial by claiming their Charter rights were violated. Cases recognizing the standing of victims and other third parties seemed monumental because they challenged the view, prevalent in both the crime-control and the due-process models, that the criminal trial was a bipolar affair between the state and the accused (Martin 1996; Cameron 1996). Nevertheless, the extent of the third-party revolution can be overstated. Victims and other third parties gained entry primarily to fight defensive battles by challenging subpoenas and requesting publication bans. The focus was on minimizing their revictimization in the criminal process. Their rights claims were often rejected and, even when recognized, were balanced against the rights of the accused and the media. In the most serious cases, victims and other third parties were not guaranteed a right to appeal.

The media was the first third party to gain entry into the criminal trial. This was ironic because the media's interest in freedom of expression and crime victims' interests in privacy were frequently at odds. In *Dagenais* (1994), the Canadian Broadcasting Corporation (CBC) challenged a publication ban restraining it from broadcasting the fictionalized 'Boys of St Vincent' series until the trial of four priests in Ontario for sexual abuse of boys in training schools was completed. The Ontario Court of Appeal took the traditional approach and held that the CBC as a third party had no right to appeal the sweeping publication ban (*Dagenais* 1992). As it would in refusing to hear claims by rape crisis centres that sexual-assault victims' equality and privacy rights were violated by disclosure of their records (*Beharriell* 1995), the Ontario Court of Appeal clung to the idea that the prosecutor and the accused were the only parties in a criminal trial. It also took a traditional hierarchical approach to the rights at stake by indicating that if there was 'a conflict between freedom of expression and fair trial, then the right to a fair trial is held to be paramount' (*Dagenais* 1992: 332). Third parties would not be heard in a criminal trial and, even if they were, their rights would be trumped by those of the accused.

The CBC appealed the publication ban to the Supreme Court, which, as in the due-process context, was more receptive to innovative claims. The Court found it had jurisdiction under an obscure provision which allowed the CBC to leap-frog from the trial court to the Supreme Court without an appeal being heard by the Court of Appeal. The Court recognized that this discretionary procedure failed to 'provide optimal protection for important rights (eg. freedom of expression)' (*Dagenais* 1994: 305), but it was better than nothing.[5] The Court also declared that trial judges had a discretion to grant standing to the media to make submissions and even call evidence that a proposed publication ban violated freedom of expression.

Dagenais not only gave third parties a procedural stake in the criminal trial, but outlined a new framework for balancing competing rights claims. The Court rejected a clash-of-rights approach which presumed that the accused's right to a fair trial was in irreconcilable conflict and should trump freedom of expression. Henceforth, judges should attempt to maximize both the accused's fair-trial rights and the public's right to freedom of expression by reasonable alternatives that would protect a fair trial, but less severely limit expression. This framework created doctrinal space for reconciling the accused's rights with the rights of third parties, and hence cooled out winner-take-all conflicts between due process and victims' rights. It also attempted to shift debate from the symbolic and confrontational level of what right in the abstract should prevail towards more practical and contextual issues. The problem, however, was that third parties would be heard only to the extent that they claimed their rights had been violated. Having drunk from the intoxicating waters of rights, it was unlikely that third parties would be satisfied by compromises. The *Dagenais* approach was an admirable attempt at pragmatism, but also a recipe for disappointment and frustration. The rights of third parties were no longer ignored and rejected, but even if accepted would be balanced with other rights.

The new procedural and substantive stakes of third parties in criminal trials were played out the next summer as the media, a victim of sexual assault, and the families of murdered girls intervened in Paul Bernardo's trial. The result was the sort of pragmatic compromise that *Dagenais* promised, but little satisfaction. The families of Leslie Mahaffy and Kristen French were granted intervenor status on the basis that they had an unique perspective on whether videotapes showing their daughters being sexually assaulted and tortured should be shown in open court. Jane Doe was granted standing because of her interests in videotapes that showed Bernardo sexually assaulting her (*Bernardo* 1995a). The trial judge accepted the increasing role of victims in criminal trials as a 'healthy evolution,' but one that should 'never interfere with or be seen to interfere with the accused's right to a fair trial, the orderly process of the court's business and the Crown's overriding historical obligation to represent the whole of society' (*Bernardo* 1995b). Following *Dagenais*, he had less trouble granting numerous media outlets, including an author with a book contract, standing to argue that the tapes should be shown. The family of crime victims and a victim had been allowed in the trial, but so, too, had the media. The trial was an example of a new political case in which the accused's and the media's rights were pitted against the rights of victims.

Dagenais was intended to avoid a clash of rights, but it promoted one by allowing the media and the victims to make their best case in an adversarial format. The media stressed the importance of freedom of expression, especially given the previous publication ban of Karla Homolka's plea bargain. Bernardo argued that restrictions on the public display of the videotapes would also harm his right to full answer and defence, but offered to give up this argument if the victims and the prosecutor agreed to a plea bargain to second-degree murder. The victims' families were offended by the media's arguments and the prospect of yet another plea bargain. They asserted a broad range of rights, including their right to freedom of religion; freedom of conscience; security of the person; the right not to be subjected to cruel or unusual punishment; and the equality rights of children, women, and the families of victims of violence. They argued that the public display of the videotapes would inflict 'harm, embarrassment, guilt, helplessness, despair and other physical and psychologically trying emotions upon the families' (*Bernardo* 1995b). Jane Doe wanted not only no showing or playing of the tapes in open court, but also no discussion of their contents. With both the media and the victims being encouraged to rely on claims of Charter rights, the stakes and the accompanying rhetoric were raised very high.

The trial judge issued a Solomonic judgment that the public in the courtroom would be allowed to hear, but not see, the tapes. This was the sort of pragmatic compromise encouraged by *Dagenais*, but it pleased few. The trial judge did not recognize the many rights the victims had claimed, but he acknowledged that the public display of the tapes would cause them 'tremendous, psychological, emotional and mental injury.' He also recognized the media's concerns about freedom of expression, but concluded that '"open justice" is a concept, a principle, that can be more than adequately achieved without pictorially displaying the indignity suffered by these young victims' (ibid). One newspaper publisher argued that the trial judge's compromise made no one happy, and 'a clear-cut decision one way or another would have been more appropriate' (*Globe and Mail*, 31 May 1995). The victims' families were also not satisfied and appealed to the Supreme Court, which simply denied leave to appeal without reasons. The victims' families subsequently initiated separate civil proceedings to argue that various Charter rights required courtrooms to be closed when the tapes or other forms of child pornography were shown as evidence (*French Estate* 1996; see chapter 9).

In the end, the *Bernardo* videotape decision highlighted the tensions of giving third parties a stake in criminal trials. Third parties, including the media and victims, gained a new procedural role in the criminal trial, but one that was premised on the assertion of Charter rights. This led to polarized and extreme demands that pitted against one another the accused's due-process rights; the media's interest in freedom of expression; and the interests of crime victims and their families in privacy, security, and equality. The contextual balancing approach outlined in *Dagenais* encouraged judges not to declare ultimate victors in the clash of rights and to devise pragmatic compromises. Such decisions did not please parties who, in order to enter the fray, had been required to assert their rights. The rights of crime victims and other third parties could be asserted in the criminal trial, but they frequently would not be satisfied.

The Presumption of Innocence: Honoured in Its Breach

The crime-control model relied on a 'presumption of guilt' based on the experience of police and prosecutors in identifying the factually guilty, while the due-process model relied on a presumption of innocence based on the beliefs of defence lawyers and judges. The presumption of innocence could become a 'self-fulfilling prophecy' (Packer 1968: 160, 167) by demanding proof beyond a reasonable doubt and giving the accused the benefit of many defences not related to factual guilt. The invention of the presumption of innocence as the 'one golden thread' running 'throughout the web of the English Criminal Law' (*Woolmington* 1935: 480) smacks of exaggeration and legitimation (Mandel 1994: 196). Both before and after the Charter, the presumption of innocence was frequently honoured in its breach. The legitimation thesis must, however, explain why the courts so openly and eagerly embraced exceptions to this revered principle. The answer may be found in their ability to accept contradictory logics and their growing acceptance of victims' rights.

The Supreme Court's first Charter case dealing with the presumption of innocence became a due-process landmark. Chief Justice Dickson matched the 'golden thread' rhetoric by declaring the presumption of innocence 'a hallowed principle lying at the very heart of criminal law' which ensured 'that until the State proves an accused's guilt beyond all reasonable doubt ... it reflects our belief that individuals are decent and law members of the community until proven otherwise' (*Oakes* 1986: 333–4). Stirring words to be sure, but ones that would not ring true to accused who, before they entered the courtroom, were exposed to the presumption of guilt shared by police, prosecutors, and the public.

Oakes had been charged with possession of narcotics for the purpose of trafficking after he was found with eight vials of hash oil. The Court held that the Narcotics Control Act (NCA) violated the presumption of innocence because it required only proof beyond a reasonable doubt of possession of any amount of narcotics before requiring the accused to prove that he or she did not have the intent to traffic in the drugs. The Crown's proof that Oakes had drugs did not prove beyond a reasonable doubt that he was a drug dealer, and Oakes could be convicted even though there was a reasonable doubt about his intent to sell the drugs.

The fact that it was more probable than not that Oakes would sell some of his eight vials was enough for a police officer or a prosecutor, but not for the court. The reasonable-doubt standard reflected due-process values which gave high priority to avoiding even minor risks of convicting the innocent. It informed the Court's subsequent expansive interpretation of the presumption of innocence, but not its willingness to accept limitations on this right under section 1 of the Charter.

The conclusion that the reverse onus violated the presumption of innocence did not end the matter. The state could still prove that such a violation was a reasonable limit under section 1 of the Charter, and here the Court was somewhat more attracted to the logic of crime control. It readily accepted that curbing drug trafficking was a pressing and substantial objective that could justify limiting a Charter right. This particular reverse onus, however, did not rationally advance the war against drugs because it applied to 'a small or negligible quantity of narcotics' (ibid: 350) where there was not even a probability of trafficking. As drafted, the law offended the common-sense expertise of police and prosecutors by presuming that someone found with one joint was going to sell it. Parliament might have saved the reverse onus by redrafting it to apply only to those, like Oakes, who were found with significant quantities of drugs. This was, of course, not necessary because judges and juries almost always convicted such accused of possession for the purpose of trafficking. *Oakes* demonstrated the Court's ability to advance and qualify due-process rights (McBarnet 1981; Ericson 1983) and to reject and accept crime-control logics of probability.

Because it was one of the Court's first decisions under the Charter, *Oakes* was front-page news. Defence lawyers wrongly predicted that 'a lot of other sections ... will be struck down' (*Globe and Mail*, 1 Mar. 1986). The victory for Oakes was somewhat less exciting. The decision did not overturn his conviction for possession of the hash oil, and his lawyer suggested that it just meant that his client will 'have to pay his fine' (*Winnipeg Free Press*, 1 Mar. 1986) The Court's mediation of due-process and crime-control values was an elite professional discourse that made a minimal difference in the lives of those it was intended to protect.

The grand rhetoric of the *Oakes* case could be seen as technique to legitimate the imposition of the criminal sanction, but the legitimation thesis must explain the large number of cases in which the Court subsequently upheld violations of the presumption of innocence. Two years after *Oakes*, Chief Justice Dickson found himself dissenting from a decision to require those in possession of guns to prove they had a valid licence. The majority stressed the importance of gun control and argued that the accused was in the best position to prove whether he had a licence (*Schwartz* 1988: 88). Requiring an intoxicated person found in the driver's seat of a car to prove that he or she had no intent to drive violated the presumption of innocence but, as in the right-to-counsel context, the violation was justified to combat the 'the threat to public safety posed by drinking and driving' (*Whyte* 1988: 98). Chief Justice Dickson, like the police, prosecutors, and public, was shocked at the prospect that a drunk 'found slumped over the steering wheel in a vehicle with the lights on, keys in the ignition and engine warm' (ibid: 115–16) could be acquitted. The Court openly placed the efficient control of guns and drunk driving before the celebrated reasonable-doubt standard.

The Court offered concerns about victims as a reason for accepting violations of the presumption of innocence. In *Keegstra* (1990: 71), it accepted the requirement that the accused prove the defence of truth because 'the relatively small possibility of truthfulness' did not outweigh 'the harm caused through the wilful promotion of hatred.' A court less concerned about the harms of hate propaganda to racial and religious groups might have insisted, as the minority did, that the state with its superior resources should have to prove that hate propaganda was untruthful. In *Downey* (1992: 20), the Court decided that presuming that everyone who lived with a prostitute was guilty of pimping violated the presumption of innocence, but was required in order to protect prostitutes from having to testify against their pimps. Justice Cory argued that 'prostitutes are a particularly vulnerable segment of society. The cruel abuse they suffer inflicted by their parasitic pimps has been well documented ... It would be unfortunate if the Charter was used to deprive a vulnerable segment of society of a measure of protection' (ibid: 20).[6] In *Audet* (1996), a majority of the Court upheld a judge's presumption that a teacher remained in a position of trust and authority when he had sexual contact with his fourteen-year-old former student during the summer vacation. Although criticized by some legal commentators for ignoring the presumption of innocence (Stuart 1996a: 340; Boisvert 1996), the case was interpreted by the media as issuing 'a blunt warning to teachers: Sexually abuse a student and you are going to jail, even if the young person consents' (*Toronto Star*, 31 May 1996).

In summary, the presumption-of-innocence cases demonstrated how the Charter allowed the Court both to recognize and to qualify the most celebrated due-process right. The judges could reject the crime-control logic that the accused was probably guilty when interpreting the right, but then accept it when determining whether the limit on the right was reasonable. The ease with which the Court accepted violations of the presumption of innocence suggested that respect for due process was not all that important in legitimating the criminal sanction. Victims' rights emerged as an alternative source of justification and legitimation of the criminal sanction.

Substantive Criminal Law

Herbert Packer argued that a due-process model of criminal justice would reduce reliance on the criminal sanction by making it more difficult to investigate and prosecute crimes based on consensual transactions. The fate of Packer's predictions and Charter challenges to such 'victimless' crimes is examined in the next chapter. The somewhat surprising effects of the Charter on homicide laws is discussed here.

Striking Down Felony Murder

Due process can be triggered by sympathetic cases, and the Supreme Court's first Charter foray into homicide came in a case involving a cautious and unlucky robber. Vaillancourt did not carry a gun and insisted on being given three bullets from his accomplice's gun. While he was acting as a lookout in a robbery, his accomplice became involved in a struggle and fatally shot one of the pool hall's patrons. The accomplice got away, but Vaillancourt, the cautious but unlucky robber, was caught. He was convicted of murder because the Criminal Code provided that robbers were responsible not only for that crime, but for any other crimes that they ought to have known would occur during the robbery, and that they were guilty of murder if death resulted from the possession or use of a gun. It did not matter that Vaillancourt had not intended to kill or even harm a person, or that the victim's death was unforeseeable.

This felony-murder rule had been criticized by academics for its harshness, but had been upheld because of the supremacy of Parliament in defining criminal laws. The Supreme Court struck it down in *Vaillancourt* because it imposed a murder conviction even when death was not objectively foreseeable (*Vaillancourt* 1987: 138). Lamer J. articulated a much broader principle that 'it may well be that, as a general rule, the principles of fundamental justice require proof of a subjective *mens rea* with respect to the prohibited act' (ibid: 133). Although supported by some criminal-law theory, this proposition would have entailed a judicial rewriting of many offences which did not require proof of subjective fault related to a prohibited act. After having articulated this principle, Justice Lamer demonstrated the flexibility of legal reasoning by restricting it to a 'very few' crimes which, because of their special stigma and penalty, required proof of subjective awareness of the prohibited act (ibid: 134). Even as it charted new paths in striking down felony murder, the Supreme Court staked the path for a retreat based on the notion that only a few offences had a stigma which required proof of subjective fault.

Unlike with the presumption of innocence, the Court was loathe to justify violations of fundamental justice under section 1 of the Charter and quickly concluded that the legitimate objective of deterring crimes with weapons could be achieved more proportionately by 'very stiff sentences when weapons are involved in the commission of the crime of manslaughter' (ibid: 139). In the end, Vaillancourt did not receive the stiff sentence contemplated by Justice Lamer. He pleaded guilty to robbery and, in consideration of his time already served awaiting his successful appeal, received a suspended sentence (Barnett 1989: 16). Justice McIntrye dissented from the whole enterprise on the basis that the courts should not invalidate Parliament's law simply to reclassify Vaillancourt as a person guilty of manslaughter as opposed to murder (ibid: 122–5). Justice L'Heureux-Dubé also argued in dissent that the Court should not forget that victims were killed and not engage in 'an egregious example of misplaced compassion' for offenders who were 'already proven to be a "hijacker", a "kidnapper", a "rapist", or an "arsonist" ... willing to cause bodily harm to commit the offence' (*Martineau* 1990: 386–7). She also pointed out that the American courts had upheld felony-murder laws, at least when capital punishment was not imposed (ibid: 379)

Vaillancourt, like most other early due-process decisions, received little media attention or public criticism. On 4 December 1987, the *Vancouver Sun* ran a Canadian Press story on page 10 with the heading 'Top Court's Ruling on Murder Provision Gives Pair New Trials.' The story noted that the death had been caused by Vaillancourt's accomplice and that the accused would be subject to a new trial. An op-ed piece in the *Toronto Star* on 13 December 1987 praised the decision for preventing 'future injustices in circumstances where a killing is accidental or otherwise unintended' and concluded that 'Vaillancourt is a lucky man because the Supreme Court was able to use the Charter of Rights and Freedoms.' Unlucky in life, Vaillancourt was lucky in law.

In another case, involving the well-publicized shooting of Barbara Turnbull during a Mac's Milk robbery in suburban Toronto, the Court held that the accomplices could be guilty of attempted murder only if they knew that such a crime was likely to occur (*Logan* 1990). Attempted murder, like murder, was one of the 'very few offences' (ibid: 398) that required a minimal subjective-fault element under section 7 of the Charter. Even this decision did not draw much attention from the media. The shooting and trial had been front-page news, but the Court's decision was reported on page 15 of the *Toronto Star* on 14 September 1990, with an emphasis on the fact that even though the accomplices had been acquitted of attempted murder, they were serving sentences for armed robbery ranging from thirteen to twenty years. Turnbull, paralysed because of the shooting but attending university, commented that she had no strong feelings about the Court's decision. Without the spectre of the criminal going free or aggrieved victims or interest groups, the media was not captivated by, and perhaps did even not understand, the Court's bold rewriting of the murder laws.

Upholding Felony First-Degree Murder

The same day as it released its decision in *Logan* and *Martineau*, the Supreme Court balanced the scales by upholding felony first-degree murder and its penalty of twenty-five years' imprisonment without eligibility for parole. A charge of first-degree murder was generally reserved for planned and deliberate murder, but also included the killing of police officers and prison guards, and any murder committed during a hijacking, sexual assault, kidnapping, or hostage taking. This latter provision mirrored the logic of the felony-murder provisions struck down in *Vaillancourt* and *Martineau* because it based a first-degree murder conviction not on subjective fault, such as planning and deliberation in the killing, but on the commission of another serious offence. On the same day, the Court embraced the conflicting logics of murder based on subjective fault and first-degree murder based on the commission of another serious crime.

Chief Justice Lamer upheld felony first-degree murder because it was no longer possible 'to classify unintentional killings as first degree murder' since *Martineau* required 'proof beyond a reasonable doubt of subjective foresight of death' (*Luxton* 1990: 71). Due-process decisions requiring subjective fault for murder justified a broad crime-control definition of felony first-degree murder. Increased punishment was also justified because the underlying crimes all involved 'the illegal domination of the victim' (ibid: 72). The Court had first articulated this rationale in a case in which a child had been sexually assaulted and killed (*Paré* 1987) and applied it in a companion case in which the accused ran over the victim after attempting to sexually assault her (*Arkell* 1990). Due process and victims' right combined to justify felony first-degree murder.

The Court also upheld the severe punishment in part because first-degree murderers could apply to a jury to become eligible for parole after they had served fifteen years in prison. As examined in chapter 9, victim-advocacy groups and the police were opposed to these 'faint hope' hearings and were subsequently able to restrict them. Felony first-degree murder remained politically attractive, and Parliament added stalking and the use of explosives by a criminal organization to the list of offences in 1997. These amendments followed high-profile cases in which women were stalked and murdered by their ex-partners and a child was killed by an explosion in a biker-gang war. Felony first-degree murder was a vehicle to recognize the suffering and domination of victims even though the Court struck down felony murder by focusing on the accused's subjective fault.

Expanding Manslaughter

After striking down felony murder, the Court retreated and refused to use the Charter to invalidate most other crimes.[7] This retreat reflected a changing Court's diminishing enthusiasm for rewriting the Criminal Code; a desire to acknowledge the harm caused to the victim; and a concern about the risk of unlawful acts. In 1992, the Court concluded that accused could be convicted of unlawfully causing bodily harm even if they did not intend or foresee the bodily harm. There was 'no principle of fundamental justice preventing Parliament from treating crimes with certain consequences as more serious than crimes which lack those consequences' (*DeSousa* 1992: 125). As Justice L'Heureux-Dubé had suggested in her *Martineau* dissent, once some threshold of fault was crossed, the harm that the accused had actually caused to the victim should determine society's response.

This idea also motivated the Court to hold a person who had injected cocaine into the victim with her consent responsible for manslaughter even if there was no objective foreseeability that the victim would die. A wide definition of manslaughter was required 'to deter dangerous conduct which may injure others and in fact may kill the peculiarly vulnerable' (ibid: 380). Following Justice L'Heureux-Dubé's dissent in *Martineau*, Justice McLachlin argued that 'the criminal law must reflect not only the concerns of the accused, but the concerns of the victim, and where the victim is killed, the concerns of society for the victim's fate. Both go into the equation of justice' (ibid: 381). Justice Lamer's arguments that it was unfair to punish a person for causing death if not even a reasonable person could have seen the risk of death were rejected as blaming the victim for her 'peculiar vulnerability' or 'thin skull' (ibid: 376). Concern about victims and the risks of unlawful acts, not the individual fault of the accused, was used to legitimate the imposition of punishment.

Although the Court was concerned about protecting the peculiarly vulnerable victim, that concern did not extend to the odd accused. It insisted on a 'single, uniform legal standard of care' (ibid: 384) that was the same whether the accused was a police officer experienced with guns who claimed he accidentally shot a detainee (*Gosset* 1993) or a teenaged mother with little education charged with killing her baby by denying the necessities of life (*Naglik* 1993). Solicitude for victims who may have unexpectedly died was combined with crime-control and punitive victims' rights approaches towards accused who engaged in unlawful acts which resulted in even unforeseeable deaths.

Summary

The Court balanced its abolition of felony murder with an acceptance of felony first-degree murder and an expansion of manslaughter. As in the presumption-of-innocence cases, the Court was able to accept contradictory logics at the same time. In the felony-murder cases, it focused on the accused's subjective intent regardless of the harm to the victim or the illegality or risk of the offender's conduct. In the felony-first-degree-murder and manslaughter cases, however, it focused on the suffering of dominated and vulnerable victims and the fact that the accused was engaged in unlawful and risky activity. Due-process restrictions on murder convictions were used to justify a broad definition of felony first-degree murder and its severe punishment.

Regulatory and Corporate Crime

In one of its first Charter cases, the Supreme Court struck down a provincial law that prohibited driving without a licence regardless of whether drivers knew or should have known that their licences had been suspended because of their poor driving records. The offence had been enacted by the B.C. legislature after the Supreme Court had acquitted an accused of driving without a licence because it had a reasonable doubt about whether he knew that his licence was suspended (*Prue* 1979). The legislature reacted to this decision with legislation that ensured not only that other poor drivers would not be given a reasonable doubt about their subjective fault, but that they would be convicted even if a reasonable person in their position would not have known that the licence was suspended. The Supreme Court concluded that the new law imposed absolute liability that could punish the morally innocent who had done nothing wrong. It was clear that the accused's liberty was a stake because there was a minimum penalty of seven days' imprisonment. Justice Lamer recognized the importance of keeping bad drivers off the road, but concluded that the government had not justified 'the risk of imprisonment of a few innocent' drivers, given the less drastic alternative of a strict liability offence 'open to a defence of due diligence, the success of which does nothing more than let those few who did nothing wrong remain free' (*Re: Section 94(2) of the B.C. Motor Vehicle Act* 1985: 316).

Like the Court's decision the previous year striking down warrantless searches by combines investigators (*Hunter* 1984), this one provoked concerns that the Court and the Charter were placing barriers on the successful prosecution of regulatory and corporate crime (Monahan and Petter 1987; Tollefson 1991; Mandel 1994). These critics assumed that tough criminal laws and prosecutions would deter corporate crime despite evidence that softer strategies employing publicity and shaming might be more effective (Braithwaite 1997). Even if prosecutions worked, the critics ignored the Court's strong hint, eventually realized in *Irwin Toy Ltd.* (1989), that absolute liability could still be used against corporations because they did not enjoy life, liberty, or security of the person protected under section 7 of the Charter. All a legislature had to do was to pay the political price of enacting offences that applied only to corporations. The fact that this did not occur suggested that the reluctance to prosecute corporate crime could not simply be blamed on the courts and the Charter.

Professors Monahan and Petter (1987: 96) argued that the *B.C. Motor Vehicle Reference* was based on 'a narrow and anachronistic view of the function of penal law and of the relationship between individuals and the state' which prohibited the criminal law from allocating to bad drivers the responsibility of determining whether their licence had been suspended. They failed to recognize that the less restrictive alternative of a strict liability offence still imposed responsibilities on bad drivers to demonstrate that they had acted reasonably in determining whether their licence had been suspended. To be fair, however, the less restrictive alternative of strict liability came under attack, and corporations enjoyed some success in lower courts in arguing that it violated the presumption of innocence by requiring them to establish a defence of due diligence (*Ellis-Don Ltd.* 1990).

In *Wholesale Travel* (1991), however, the Supreme Court upheld a strict liability offence that required a corporation to demonstrate that it exercised due diligence to avoid misleading advertising. The responsibility of taking reasonable precautions could be allocated to corporations and others who entered a regulated or licensed field. In stark contrast to the critics' vision of the courts as the champion of a nightwatchman state, the majority celebrated the positive state that protected people 'from cradle to grave ... from waking to sleeping' (ibid: 239) even as the welfare state eroded. As in the manslaughter cases, victims were not ignored. Invoking images of children labouring in dirty and dangerous workplaces, Justice Cory argued that regulatory legislation played 'a legitimate and vital role in protecting those who are most vulnerable and least able to protect themselves' (ibid: 249–50). As in the manslaughter cases, the Court was concerned about victims and potential victims of risky activities. With three others, Chief Justice Lamer dissented and in most cases would have given the accused the benefit of a reasonable doubt about its negligence. This position could have hindered much regulation, but it did not win the day.

The media failed to recognize that the contour of the vast majority of offences in Canada were on the line. The case merited a short and confused Canadian Press story on page 4 of the *Globe and Mail*'s 25 October 1991 'Report on Business.' The lead suggested that those charged with false advertising were required to 'prove they did everything they could to avoid making an incorrect claim,' while the penultimate paragraph more accurately described the due-diligence defence as requiring the accused to show 'they took all reasonable precautions.' No mention was made of the broader implications of the ruling or of the impassioned differences of opinion among the judges. If the minority had won one more vote, corporate executives might not have been informed of the good news over breakfast. As noted in chapter 2, the media's relative indifference towards or ignorance of the intricacies of due process created room for radical versions of it. The majority of the Court, however, was more cautious and concerned about crime control and potential victims.

The *B.C. Motor Vehicle Reference* was not the final word on how British Columbia would regulate bad drivers who drove with suspended licences.

A year after the Court's decision, the legislature deleted the reference to the offence being one of absolute-liability, but retained the minimum sentence of seven days' imprisonment. The Supreme Court upheld this mandatory penalty on the basis that, while it could constitute cruel and unusual punishment in the odd case, they would consider only reasonable hypotheticals (*Goltz* 1991). This was a retreat from an early decision that struck down a seven-year mandatory sentence for importing drugs on the far-fetched chance that it would be used against a teenager coming home from Florida with a joint of marijuana (*Smith* 1987). The Court had taken away absolute liability, but allowed mandatory imprisonment. A subsequent decision, however, took away imprisonment by holding that the offence remained one of absolute liability because a driver could be convicted without having received notice of his licence suspension (*Pontes* 1995). This last case supported critics who argued that the Court interfered with British Columbia's efforts to keep bad drivers off the roads. At the same time, however, the Court preserved strict liability offences which placed significant obligations on those who engage in regulated activities, and allowed absolute liability offences so long as individuals were not imprisoned.

Failure to prosecute corporate and regulatory crime cannot be blamed on the Court and the Charter. As was the case with respect to regulatory searches, discussed in chapter 2, critical concerns that the Charter would roll back state regulation were overstated and ignored other social, economic, and political forces that were much greater threats to state regulation. The critics also ignored the ability of courts to retreat from their due-process decisions, make contextual distinctions and embrace contradictory logics.

Conclusion

At first glance, due process revolutionized the criminal trial by giving accused new rights to demand speedy trials and disclosure and to challenge the fairness of criminal laws. On closer examination, however, the revolution was partial, with some evidence to support the critical conclusion that due process was for crime control. Despite concerns about an amnesty for criminals following *Askov* (1990) and concerns about the prevention of wrongful convictions in *Stinchcombe* (1991), the long-term effect of those decisions was to increase the efficiency and the legitimacy of the guilty-plea process typical of the crime-control model.

In other contexts, the relation between due process and crime control was less clear. The courts interpreted the presumption of innocence broadly, but upheld violations of this celebrated right because of concerns about the victims of drunk driving, hate propaganda, prostitution, sexual abuse, and corporate and regulatory crime. The courts restricted the offence of murder to ensure the subjective fault of the accused, but expanded the offence of manslaughter and upheld felony first-degree murder to recognize harms to victims and the risks of unlawful conduct. The murder cases were concerned with protecting the odd accused who did not realize the consequences of his or her actions while the manslaughter and felony-first-degree-murder cases were concerned with recognizing the suffering of vulnerable and dominated victims.

Third parties fought their way into the criminal trial by claiming their Charter rights were violated. Crime victims, as well as the media, won a procedural stake in criminal trials and appeals, but no guarantee that their rights would be recognized. Crime victims were encouraged to assert rights, only to have them rejected by the courts or balanced with the rights of the accused and the media. As will be seen in the next chapter, however, the assertion of Charter rights on behalf of victims and potential victims of crimes played an important role in legitimating the criminal sanction with respect to what Packer believed were victimless crimes particularly vulnerable to due-process challenges.

4

Victimless Crimes?

According to Herbert Packer (1968: 151–2), the rise of due process should have resulted in a corresponding decline in the use of the criminal sanction with respect to 'victimless' crimes based on 'consensual' transactions. The proactive police behaviour necessary to enforce laws against prostitution, drugs, gambling, vagrancy,[1] abortion, euthanasia, and obscenity and other forms of speech, and the laws themselves, would be challenged by accused claiming their rights in court. Due process would slow down and disrupt the 'assembly-line justice' (ibid: 292) that surrounded many of these crimes and provide an outlet for social ambivalence about their criminalization.

Packer's claims about the presence of consent and absence of victims have subsequently been challenged. He wrote before feminism became a major intellectual and political force. Although most feminists supported Packer's belief that abortion should be decriminalized, they did so for different reasons. Their concern was not so much difficulty of enforcement, or even liberty, but equality for women. Some feminists vigorously contested Packer's claims that prostitution and pornography were consensual and victimless. In the absence of any theory about unequal power in society, Packer did not question the genuineness of consent or the effect of crime on disadvantaged groups. Since the time he wrote, harm has been expanded to include the risk of future violence, psychological damage produced by anxiety and fear, and contributions to unequal social relations. Expanded understandings of harm also implicated the role of the state. Packer's individualistic, liberal assumptions about the limited, adversarial role of the state were challenged. Canada followed the international lead and was much more receptive than the United States to attempts to criminalize the content of speech in order to protect disadvantaged groups.

This chapter serves as a transition from previous chapters, which were rooted in conflicts between crime control and due process, to the new law and politics of criminal justice based on conflicts between victims' rights and due process. Each controversial case examined here merits a book of its own (Brodie, Gavigan, and Jenson 1992; Morton 1992b; Lacombe 1994; Cossman et al 1997). My purpose, however, is to examine changing approaches to the criminal sanction and the dynamics of the new political case. The political case of Packer's generation involved the conflict between an accused claiming due-process rights and the state claiming to represent community values and morality (Wolfenden 1957; Devlin 1959). The political case of my generation was more complex and evenly matched because it involved a conflict between an accused claiming due-process rights and representatives of groups of victims and potential victims claiming rights to security and equal protection of the criminal law.

My point is not to resolve these complex conflicts, but to illustrate how they evolved since Packer's time. The political cases discussed here should not be confused with what George Fletcher (1995) has referred to as the 'new political trial' in the United States. Both involve politicized groups aligning themselves with crime victims and the criminal sanction, but the new Canadian political cases were more likely to include direct discussion of the equality and other rights of crime victims and potential victims. In a typically Canadian fashion, they were also more likely to produce judicial decisions upholding the criminal sanction or new criminal laws enacted by Parliament, as opposed to the riots which sometimes accompanied jury acquittals after new American political trials.[2]

This chapter also introduces the pluralistic politics of victims' rights. The claims examined in this chapter range from pro-life arguments that the aborted foetus was an innocent victim that required protection by the criminal sanction, to anti-pornography feminist arguments for the criminalization of violent and degrading pornography as a means to protect the equality rights of women. Within each group, there were controversial and divisive debates about the use of the criminal sanction. For example, some groups representing the disabled supported Sue Rodriguez's attempt to legalize assisted suicide, while others opposed it. Similarly, feminists were divided in their approach to prostitution and pornography. Nevertheless, decisions to defend the criminal sanction precisely where it had been most controversial were significant. The focus on the equal protection of the criminal law sometimes replicated the dubious crime-control assumption that the criminal law controlled crime. This assumption was still employed in other less contentious contexts, but increasingly the advantaged began to recognize that the criminal law did not control crimes like break and enters and robberies. They invested in security systems and private police. The disadvantaged groups examined in this chapter, however, often had to rely on the criminal sanction's false promise of security and equality and had to defend the new political case. They had their agendas and politics criminalized by the perceived need to defend the criminal sanction from due-process challenges.

This chapter will also engage some of the diverse and vibrant literature that had developed around the Charter. Christine Boyle (1994) has argued that the equality rights of women and other disadvantaged groups should not be ignored in the criminal justice field. As will be seen, equality rights were used to uphold some of the criminal laws examined in this chapter. The equality-rights perspective is an important addition to criminal justice discourse; it explains how claims in support of the criminal sanction can be grounded in rights. It also sheds light on the new political case which pitted due-process claims by the accused against equality and security claims by disadvantaged groups of potential victims. Sociologically, politically, and legally, it was more realistic than Packer's bipolar approach, which ignored all those affected by crime except the accused and the state. However, it tended to focus on preserving and extending the criminal sanction in a non-discriminatory fashion and may, in judicial and legislative discourse, have fallen into the trap of assuming that the criminal law controlled crime. More emphasis was placed on the equality rather than the quality of the criminal law's protection. Professor Boyle and many other feminists were well aware of the limitations of the criminal law and the need for broader social, economic, cultural, and political reforms to improve the position of disadvantaged groups vulnerable to crime. The defence of the criminal sanction in the new political case, however, forced many equality-seekers to stress the importance of the criminal law and downplay the value of alternative strategies. This contributed to the criminalization of politics in which equality claims focused on the limited and often symbolic benefits of the criminal law.

Rainer Knopff and Ted Morton (1992, 1996) have argued that the Charter has given equality-seekers, whom they identify as post-materialistic elites who identify in terms of gender, race, disability, and sexual orientation, a new ability to use the courts for strategic ends. Like the equality-rights perspective, this work sheds some light on the new political case. Nevertheless, it discounts the deep divisions among feminists and groups representing the disabled about the appropriate role of law. In the criminal justice arena, the 'Court Party' most often fought defensive battles in which they invoked equality rights, not as a sword, but as a shield, to arguments made by defence lawyers on behalf of hate-mongers and pornographers. In criminal cases, the Women's Legal Education and Action Fund (LEAF, 1996) most often lined up on the side of the state and, with respect to pornography, on the same side of the case as social conservatives. In the next chapter, it will be seen that feminist groups fought similar defensive battles in the context of sexual-assault laws. They lost in Court only to be vindicated in Parliament. In the criminal justice field, the Court Party was neither a unified party nor one that depended on the Court.

Prostitution

Packer (1968: 328) criticized prostitution laws as 'an attempt to secularize an essentially moralistic judgment.' He was scandalized by police officers attempting to enforce prostitution laws by posing as customers and argued that the police were the most visible, intrusive, and unsavoury when they did the least important work (ibid: 284). His scepticism about the utility of criminalizing prostitution was confirmed by the fact that prostitution offences were processed through the assembly line with trivial penalties (ibid: 329).[3]

Pressing and Persistent

Ironically, the most successful due-process challenge to prostitution laws came before the Charter. In *Hutt* (1978), the Supreme Court quashed the conviction of a woman who had explained to an undercover officer that she was a 'working girl, a prostitute' and had negotiated a price for sexual activities. Justice Spence ruled that only 'pressing or persistent conduct' created a nuisance and that this solicitation did not qualify. He expressed somewhat exaggerated fears that 'hundreds of pedestrians every day who request free rides in automobiles' would be guilty of a more expansive offence and that a person's home could also be deemed a public place (ibid: 422). He was also concerned about the assembly-line process of trivial punishment and held that the $1 fine imposed on Hutt was unfair because she had not been present in court to make representations (ibid: 425). Following Packer's prediction, this due-process decision helped decrease the use of the criminal sanction. A year after the decision, there were only 674 soliciting charges, as compared with 1,684 charges the previous year (Canada 1985: 421). In 1981, the Court acquitted another prostitute who, while plying her 'trade energetically,' did not pressingly and persistently solicit an undercover police officer (*Whitter* 1981: 5). The year after that ruling, only 220 soliciting charges were laid (Canada 1985: 421). Municipalities then enacted their own by-laws prohibiting soliciting, but these, too, were struck down by the Court as infringing Parliament's exclusive jurisdiction over criminal law (*Westendorp* 1983: 337). The Supreme Court derailed the crime-control assembly line without any appeal to the Charter.

The New Soliciting Law: Crime Control Affirmed

Following the recommendations of police and municipalities and rejecting law-reform proposals for a nuisance-based approach (Canada 1985), the Conservative government enacted a new criminal sanction prohibiting any public solicitation for the purpose of prostitution. Minister of Justice John Crosbie defended the new law in crime-control terms by arguing it was required to help the police and citizens 'regain ... control of the streets and neighbourhoods in certain urban areas of this country' (Hansard, 9 Sep. 1985: 6373).[4] The judiciary was criticized for having 'emasculated' the previous law 'as an effective piece of enforcement machinery' (ibid: 6375), and potential Charter challenges to the new crime were ridiculed on the basis that 'no one has an inalienable right to offer or to sell or purchase sex on the streets.' Freedom of speech and of association did not give participants in street prostitution 'the right to violate the rights of others' (ibid: 6377). The possibility of a due-process challenge upped the rhetorical ante so that the public had a right not to see or suffer public solicitation.

The new soliciting law was vigorously opposed as a punitive and piecemeal approach whose burden fell on the most disadvantaged female prostitutes. Svend Robinson of the New Democratic Party (NDP) argued that the legislation failed 'to come to grips with the fact that prostitution is a fundamental social and economic problem, a problem which reflects the broader sense of exploitation and degradation of women in our society' (Hansard, 9 Sep. 1985: 6383). Criminalization would promote a 'vicious cycle of arrest, fine, back to prostitution, more violence and ultimately, in many cases, death' (ibid: 6382). He expressed concern that communities victimized by street prostitution had been 'manipulated ... as guinea pigs in the fight by police forces for this repressive legislation' (ibid). The rights and concerns of communities victimized by street prostitution were being used for crime control.

Many feminist groups joined with civil-liberties and gay and lesbian organizations in opposing the new law (Shaver 1994). The National Action Committee on the Status of Women (NAC) advocated a repeal of soliciting and bawdy-house offences because 'the true causes of prostitution are social and economic.' They urged a comprehensive approach that targeted child abuse and pornography and provided alternative housing and employment to the women and children employed in prostitution (Canada 1985: 351, 363). Other feminists, however, took a more punitive approach (ibid: 362, 520). The Ontario Advisory Council on the Status of Women (1984: 31–2) proposed that males who solicited a female person to have 'illicit sexual intercourse' be subject to an indictable offence. They also argued that 'there is a real victim in prostitution – the prostitute herself. All women, children and adolescents are harmed from prostitution, more than any other feature of our society ... Prostitution functions as a form of violence against women and young persons. It is certainly a blatant form of exploitation and abuse of power' (ibid: 33). A common concern about the victimization of women by prostitution could lead feminists both towards and away from the criminal sanction.

The new law dramatically increased crime-control activities such as arrests and prosecutions, but failed to control street prostitution. By 1987, there were 9,243 police reported soliciting incidents. In 1987 alone, the Toronto police spent $1.8 million in laying 3,835 soliciting charges (Canada 1989: 29, 37). The new law was enforced by policemen posing as customers and policewomen posing as prostitutes. Although the Supreme Court recognized an entrapment defence (*Mack* 1988), it did not apply to random virtue testing in strolls (*Barnes* 1991; see chapter 2). For embarrassed customers, an entrapment defence would only prolong the process as punishment (Feeley 1979). For prostitutes, a conviction, fine, and even imprisonment was a cost of business. All this crime-control activity, however, did not control the crime. The Department of Justice's own evaluation, heavily influenced by police reports, concluded that in Vancouver and Toronto 'the legislation had virtually no success in moving prostitutes off the street' (Canada 1989: 76).

Charter Challenges: Crime Control and Victims' Rights

The number of soliciting charges might have been even higher if some lower courts had not ruled that the new law infringed freedom of expression and association. Given its previous track record on the issue and its new activism under the Charter, it was quite possible that the Supreme Court would strike the new soliciting law down. In 1990, however, it upheld it, as well as laws prohibiting bawdy houses. Seven governments intervened in support of the legislation, and only the Canadian Organization for the Rights of Prostitutes intervened to oppose it. The absence of feminist groups such as LEAF that had already started to intervene in other Charter cases (LEAF 1996; Razack 1991) was significant. It meant that a potentially strong feminist voice against the legislation was not heard and that most of LEAF's interventions in criminal matters were in favour of the criminal sanction.[5]

Both Chief Justice Dickson for the majority and Justice Wilson for the minority agreed that the objective of the new soliciting law was eliminating 'the social nuisance arising from the public display of the sale of sex' (*Re: ss.193 and 195.1(1)(c) of the Criminal Code (Man.)* 1990: 132,73). The minister of justice had made the same claim even though the legislation departed from the Court's prior decisions that only pressing and persistent solicitation constituted a nuisance (*Hutt* 1978). In upholding the new restrictions on freedom of expression, Dickson C.J. stressed the fact 'that other attempts at legislation in this area have failed for various reasons' and that legislation did not have to be 'perfect' to survive under the Charter (*Re: ss.193 and 195.1(1)(c) of the Criminal Code (Man.)* 1990, 76, 75). The majority of a Court quickly becoming famous for due process was concerned about the efficiency of crime control and prepared to defer to Parliament.

It was ironic that the Court was more deferential to prostitution legislation after the enactment of the Charter than before. This deference, however, was part and parcel of the Court's new responsibilities under the Charter (Roach 1996c). Although the law was criminal, the Court's deferential approach was associated with non-criminal Charter cases distributing resources among competing groups (*Irwin Toy Ltd.* 1989) and the fear that, like the U.S. Supreme Court before the New Deal, it could be dragged into protecting 'economic rights' and ruling on matters of 'pure public policy' (*Re: ss.193 and 195.1(1)(c) of the Criminal Code (Man.)* 1990: 100, 104; *Skinner* 1990: 6). As Packer suggested, due process was fragile because courts as unelected institutions were constantly under pressure not to interfere with the democratic will, especially recent laws such as the soliciting law.

Lamer J. also upheld the new soliciting law, but he attempted to justify it as a response to victimization caused by prostitution, including the problems of juvenile prostitution, drugs, and pimping. He quoted with approval a brief prepared by the Ontario Advisory Council on the Status of Women which argued that 'prostitution functions as a form of violence against women and young persons' and was 'a symptom of the victimization and subordination of women and of their economic disadvantage' (*Re: ss. 193 and 195.1(1)(c) of the Criminal Code (Man.)* 1990: 118). Picking up on this theme, he argued that prostitution was 'degrading to the individual dignity of the prostitute' and 'a vehicle for pimps and customers to exploit the disadvantaged position of women in our society' (ibid: 118). He foreshadowed developments in obscenity law by approving of the law's attempts 'at minimizing public exposure to this degradation.' The concerns of one women's group[6] were used to support the law despite the fact that most feminist organizations had opposed it as punitive and piecemeal. Victims' rights were used to legitimate crime control.

Justice Wilson dissented on the basis that the law was overly broad and applied even when there was no possibility of a social nuisance or adverse effects on others. She noted that Parliament had not yet criminalized prostitution itself, and speculated that it may have believed that the prostitute was 'the real "victim" of prostitution' or that it 'may have realized that they could not send the female prostitute to prison while letting the male customer go' (ibid: 136). Justice Wilson sided with the women's groups who had advocated decriminalization. Unlike Justice Lamer, she was cautious about making claims about victimization and degradation, and recognized the limitations of the criminal law in responding to the social problem of prostitution.

The soliciting law continued to be enforced in the 1990s, but the debate evolved. The risk that prostitutes would be murdered or would kill was calculated and emphasized both by the Canadian Centre for Criminal Justice Statistics (1997) and by the media. (*Toronto Star,* 14 Feb. 1997). Even in cases where there might be doubt about criminalizing consensual transactions between adults, the risk of other harms such as violence and AIDS was used to support the criminal sanction and police intervention. The criminal sanction was offered as a response to measured risk (Beck 1992), but with little evidence that it could reduce it.

Another development was community and police attempts to shame johns, by publicizing their names and sending them to 'john schools' designed to educate men arrested for soliciting about the health and criminal justice risks entailed in public prostitution and to reinforce the message that street prostitution was not a victimless crime. Victims were defined broadly to include the communities affected by street prostitution, women wrongfully identified and propositioned as prostitutes, prostitutes and their families, and customers (sometimes described as sex addicts) and their families. Almost everyone was a victim. Because they

attempted to shame and persuade offenders, john schools shared some of
the characteristics of reintegrative shaming (Braithwaite 1989) while also
relying on risk and surveillance concepts (Ericson and Haggerty 1997).
Their supporters argued they were a more effective and integrative form
of social control, and their detractors saw them as a neo-Victorian attempt
to enforce morality on wayward men. In any event, they were often more
intrusive for offenders than processing through the crime-control assembly line and they justified intervention in the name of victims' rights.

   Juvenile prostitution also received special attention and bolstered the
case for the criminalization of prostitution. In 1985, Parliament created
the separate, more serious offence of soliciting a person under eighteen
for the purposes of prostitution. It was not enforced, because police
could not use those under eighteen years of age in enforcement stings.
The offence was expanded in 1997 so that it applied when an undercover
officer represented him- or herself as under eighteen and the accused
could point to no evidence that he had any other belief (S.C.1997 c.16
s.2). As in *Downey* (1992; see chapter 3), this incursion on the presumption of innocence will likely be upheld as necessary to protect juvenile
prostitutes as vulnerable victims.

   A new aggravated offence of living off the avails of a prostitute under
eighteen was also created in 1997, with a mandatory minimum five-year
penalty. This increased the threat of punishment without responding to
the causes of juvenile prostitution. As in child-sexual-abuse cases, witnesses under eighteen were allowed to use videotaped evidence and
screens so they would not have to face the accused when they testified.
These provisions were efforts to increase reporting and minimize the secondary victimization of the adversarial trial process. In response to international concerns and laws, Canadian law was also extended to allow
child-sex tourism and child abuse outside of Canada to be prosecuted
within Canada. As will be seen, support for the criminal sanction with
respect to many of the crimes examined in this chapter came from international law, and the new demand for the criminal sanction did not stop
at Canada's borders. Victims' rights were nourished by international
sources (Cairns 1995; see chapter 9).

   The symbolic nature of the 1997 legislation was underlined by its preamble, affirming international commitments to respect the rights of children and to protect them 'from all forms of sexual exploitation and
sexual abuse, and to take measures to prevent the exploitative use of children in prostitution.' At a time of record levels of youth homelessness
and unemployment, the government argued that these new and difficult-

to-enforce criminal offences meant 'our Canadian youth matter a great
deal ... It is important to send a strong message of social disapproval with
respect to the abuse, exploitation and prostitution of young people.
Young people deserve our respect. Young people need our protection'
(Hansard, 10 Jun. 1996: 3547). In committee, however, those who worked
with juvenile prostitutes and who had been juvenile prostitutes stressed
the need for social and health services rather than tougher criminal sanctions (Canada, JLAC, 26 Nov. 1996). A representative of the Canadian
Organization for the Rights of Prostitutes also argued that increased
criminalization 'will actually endanger the well-being of youth working in
the sex trade ... If young people are choosing prostitution over their families or social services, perhaps those latter institutions are the ones where
the genuine problems lie' (ibid, 27 Nov. 1996). This was an argument
that resisted the criminalization of the social, economic, educational, and
family problems that lead teenagers into prostitution.

The use of the criminal sanction increased dramatically in the Charter
era with no apparent reduction in street prostitution. The type of due-
process challenges that Packer advocated had much greater success
before the Charter was enacted, but only inspired Parliament to enact a
new law making any public solicitation illegal. The Supreme Court
upheld the new soliciting law from Charter challenges on the crime-control basis that it targeted public nuisances and the punitive victims' rights
basis that it protected prostitutes from exploitation and degradation. The
Court was also concerned about deferring to Parliament's criminal-law
solution to this complex problem. Many feminists opposed the new law,
but they did not intervene to support the Charter challenge. Support for
the criminal sanction continued in the 1990s, with greater emphasis on
juvenile prostitution at home and abroad, well-documented risks associated with prostitution, and community activism that attempted to shame
and educate johns about the many victims of street prostitution.

Drugs

Packer (1968: 332) was concerned that due-process violations 'have
become habitual because of the great difficulty that attends the detection
of narcotics offenses.' Decriminalization could prevent due-process violations and assist minorities and the urban poor who bore the brunt of
drug enforcement. Reflecting on students who were busted for drugs
during the 1960s, he also argued that 'nothing but gratuitous misery will
result from the occasional imposition of criminal conviction on a person

who possesses for his own use drugs' (ibid: 341). Some of Packer's liberal views were reflected in the LeDain Commission's advocacy of decriminalization of marijuana possession (Canada 1972), but were generally not implemented in either the United States or Canada. In response to due-process decisions, the police armed themselves with warrants and other enabling laws. Courts in both the United States and Canada found ways not to exclude illegally seized drugs (*Leon* 1984; *Silveira* 1995). Due process did not slow the war against drugs.

Prohibitions on the cultivation and possession of marijuana were unsuccessfully challenged under the Charter. The Quebec Court of Appeal held that Parliament had not acted in an arbitrary or irrational manner in criminalizing marijuana and distinguished the legal use of alcohol on the basis of different 'cultural traditions' towards the two drugs. The Supreme Court did not even bother to hear the case (*Hamon* 1993). There was more success in persuading trial courts to allow the medicinal use of marijuana, but the courts ordered only limited exemptions from the law. Even though the police and lawyers among others argued that the possession of marijuana should be decriminalized (Fischer 1997), the new Controlled Drugs and Substance Act (CDSA) continued to criminalize it, albeit only as an assembly-line summary-conviction offence. 'In terms of cannabis possession, the CDSA ... does not reform, but just confirms what the criminal justice system has been practising for a long time. The punishment provisions still entail full "criminal" sanctions and have a labelling effect. Over 500,000 other Canadians carry such a criminal label already' (Fischer et al 1996: 176). As occurred in relation to child prostitution, hate propaganda, and obscenity, the use of the criminal law was defended as necessary to meet Canada's international obligations.

Gambling

Packer (1968: 347) believed that gambling, like drugs, should be decriminalized. It was consensual and widespread, and required intrusive and proactive police enforcement. There was some liberalization of gambling laws after the Charter was enacted, but not because of the Charter. Parliament reduced some restrictions in order to support the horse-racing industry. It allowed the provinces to license lotteries and casinos in order to increase their revenues. The criminal sanction still played an important role in regulating gambling. Criminal convictions for violating the terms of provincial lottery licences were upheld from due- process challenges (*Furtney* 1991), and Aboriginal people failed to convince the courts they had Aboriginal rights to run lotteries (*Jones* 1991) or high-stakes gambling (*Pamejewon* 1996) without provincial licences. Some presumptions relating to gaming houses violated the presumption of innocence, but most special investigative powers were upheld. Parliament responded to a case that prohibited video surveillance of illegal gambling with new legislation authorizing warrants for such surveillance (*Wong* 1990; see chapter 2). Neither the Court or Parliament expressed concern about using intrusive technology or the criminal sanction to criminalize a consensual transaction. Some argued that criminal prohibitions were required to protect the victims of gambling such as gambling addicts and their families, but these arguments did not prevail over more immediate concerns about increasing governmental revenues.

Abortion

Early in his career, Packer identified abortion as an area where the criminal sanction was inefficacious (Packer and Gampell 1959). Criminal restrictions on abortions created a 'crime tariff' that made them more expensive and dangerous (Packer 1968: 344). He also was sceptical about whether the most disadvantaged women would benefit from 'moderate reforms' (ibid) such as Canada's 1969 abortion law which legalized abortions if a hospital committee believed that the continuation of a pregnancy would be a risk to a woman's health. Packer championed decriminalization of abortion, but without referring to the equality rights or even the liberty of women.

The Supreme Court's 1988 decision to invalidate the criminal sanction against performing or receiving an abortion without the approval of a hospital committee seems to be a spectacular affirmation of the ability of due process to restrict the use of the criminal sanction (*Morgentaler* 1988). Even as hardened a Charter critic as Michael Mandel (1994: 420) concluded that 'the repeal of the abortion law was the only unqualified good result to come from the Supreme Court of Canada to date.' Abortion was the one 'victimless crime' in which Packer's predictions seem to have been realized.

Nevertheless, the claim that abortion was victimless was contested, and the criminal sanction did not completely wither away. Attempts to reintroduce the criminal sanction in 1989 were narrowly defeated. The criminal sanction was subsequently used to regulate pro-life protests at abortion clinics. More generally, the Court's understanding of how the abortion law affected women and infringed their rights laid some of the foundation for acceptance of the criminal sanction with respect to hate propaganda and pornography.

Morgentaler

A few weeks after the enactment of the Charter, Dr Henry Morgentaler announced plans to open abortion clinics in Toronto and Winnipeg. He was charged with conspiracy to breach the abortion law by performing abortions without the approval of a hospital committee. He challenged the constitutionality of the abortion law without success before both the trial judge and the Ontario Court of Appeal. They concluded that the Charter did not allow courts to review the substantive fairness of laws and was intended to be neutral on the abortion issue (*Morgentaler* 1984, 1985).[7] Judicial culture was dynamic and soon changed, with Supreme Court decisions proclaiming the courts' power to review the substantive fairness of criminal laws (see chapter 3).

Although the abortion law was upheld and Dr Morgentaler acted in clear violation of it, he was acquitted by a Toronto jury. Jury acquittals of Dr Morgentaler were nothing new, but this time he employed American jury-selection experts and asked prospective jurors whether they had any religious, moral, or other beliefs relating to abortion that would cause them to convict or acquit regardless of the law or the evidence (Morton 1992b: 184). The Crown did not raise jury selection as a ground of appeal, but in an early example of third parties joining the criminal trial, four pro-life groups attempted to intervene in the Ontario Court of Appeal to argue that their members had been unfairly excluded from the jury. They were denied access on the traditional basis that 'in a criminal proceeding, the Crown represents the public interest and it alone is given the right to appeal from an acquittal' (ibid: 207). As seen in chapter 3, the Ontario Court of Appeal resisted the claims of third parties to intervene in the criminal trial, but such interventions were subsequently made possible under the Supreme Court's more innovative jurisprudence. Courts continued to grapple with the fairness of jury selection in a heterogeneous society in which some groups identified with the accused and others identified with the victim (see chapters 7 and 8).

Security from Stress and Anxiety

The most influential judgment striking down the abortion law was written by Chief Justice Dickson with the concurrence of Justice Lamer. Drawing on concerns previously expressed in right-to-counsel (*Therens* 1985: 505) and speedy-trial (*Mills* 1986: 538–9) cases, he argued that the delay and uncertainty of committee approval resulted in 'state-imposed psychological trauma' for women (*Morgentaler* 1988: 465). Although she based her decision on a woman's right to choose an abortion, Justice Wilson also agreed that the Charter could protect people against 'psychological trauma' (ibid: 566). As will be seen, the idea that the Charter should protect individuals from state-imposed stress and anxiety was soon translated into the idea that the Criminal Code should serve the same purpose in order to protect crime victims and potential victims (*Keegstra* 1990).

This enlarged understanding of security of the person did not go unchallenged. Justice Beetz defined security of the person more narrowly as access to medical treatment to protect life and health without fear of the imposition of the criminal sanction (ibid: 492). In his dissent, Justice McIntyre ridiculed the idea that the Charter should be concerned with the psychological effects of the law: 'it is hard to imagine a governmental policy or initiative which will not create significant stress or anxiety for some and, frequently, for many members of the community'(ibid: 535). He feared anti-smoking policies could be challenged because they 'produce much stress and anxiety among smokers and growers of tobacco' (ibid: 536). He also argued that the expanded understanding of security from stress and anxiety offered women false peace of mind because 'the mere fact of pregnancy, let alone an unwanted pregnancy, gives rise to stress ... there is really no psychologically painless way to cope with an unwanted pregnancy' (ibid: 536–7). This argument ignored the real delay and uncertainty created by the abortion law, but underlined the difficulty of using either the Charter or the criminal law to protect victims from an expanded understanding of harm.

The Rejection of the Foetus as Victim

The Court relied upon the prosecutor's concession that it did not have to decide whether the foetus had Charter rights (*Morgentaler* 1988: 479, 564). Pro-life groups, like pro-choice groups, were not represented in the appeal and they would have made no such concession. The next year, the Court again ducked the issue, in civil litigation commenced by Joe Borowski, who argued that the Criminal Code's legalization of committee-approved abortions violated the Charter rights of the foetus (*Borowski* 1989). Civil litigation was an outlet for the strong claims made on behalf of victims and potential victims who believed they were not adequately protected by the criminal law (see chapter 9). The issue could no longer be avoided as the Court returned from its 1989 summer holidays to overturn an injunction secured in civil litigation by Jean-Guy Tremblay which prohibited his ex-girlfriend, Chantal Daigle, from obtaining an abortion. Like *Borowski*, this case was also moot because Chantal Daigle had gone to the United States to obtain an abortion in the twentieth week of her pregnancy. The Court nevertheless rejected the notion of foetal or father's rights in order 'to try to ensure that another woman is not put through an ordeal such as that experienced by Ms. Daigle' (*Tremblay* 1989: 648). Pro-lifers had failed to convince the courts that the foetus was a victim that required the protection of the criminal sanction.

The government introduced a bill recriminalizing abortion unless a doctor concluded that the physical, mental, or psychological health or the life of the woman was threatened by the continued pregnancy. Pro-choicers opposed the bill because it recriminalized abortion at all stages of pregnancy and left doctors open to the threat of private prosecutions. Private prosecutions, like civil litigation, were a feature of victims' rights because many of those claiming rights on behalf of victims were unwilling to rely on public prosecutions. Pro-choicers relied upon *Morgentaler*, and in particular Justice Wilson's argument that abortion was a matter for a woman's conscience. At times, they went beyond individualistic, due-process concerns and argued that abortions should not be 'dictated by economic necessities' and that there was a need for attention to 'such crucial matters as birth control, counselling, social services, violence, battering, child care, housing or conditions of remorseless poverty' (Brodie, Gavigan, and Jenson 1992: 75). The focus on Charter arguments against recriminalization meant, however, less emphasis on these broader issues (Bogart 1994). Politics were criminalized and legalized even if, as in the abortion context, the criminal sanction was ultimately defeated.

Pro-lifers criticized the bill because of its requirement that only one doctor agree and its wide definition of health to include psychological health. The later reflected both Chief Justice Dickson's and Justice Wilson's broad definitions of security of the person. In a demonstration of the flexibility of victims' rights claims, they portrayed the aborted foetus as the ultimate victim. 'We are told that "the unborn is innocent"; that it is "the weakest stage of all of us"; that it "has done no wrong"; and that it is "without defence"' (Brodie, Gavigan, and Jenson 1992: 81). Pro-lifers employed the language of murder, violence, and child abuse to depict abortions in the most unfavourable light (ibid: 83). The foetus was 'presented as helpless and vulnerable, the most innocent of innocent victims' (ibid: 123). Punitive forms of victims' rights often stress the innocence of victims and the need to punish the perpetrator, and pro-life discourse was no exception. In the end, the bill was passed by the House of Commons, but defeated by a tied vote in the Senate. A parliamentary reply to a due process decision was derailed, and the decriminalization achieved by *Morgentaler* narrowly prevailed.

The Criminal Sanction Again

In response to escalating pro-life protests, the Ontario government applied for injunctions against picketing at abortion clinics and doctors' homes. The judge saw the case as 'a clash of constitutional values' (*Dieleman* 1994: 281), pitting the protestors' freedom of expression against 'the psychological well-being of women patients and their related interests in privacy and equality' (ibid: 311). In ordering the injunction, he stressed the concern in *Morgentaler* about stress and anxiety, as well as concerns about 'emotional damage,' 'psychological harm,' and 'freedom from humiliation and embarrassment' found in subsequent Court decisions upholding hate propaganda, obscenity, and soliciting offences, and publication bans of the complainant's identity in sexual-assault trials (ibid: 301–13). He also noted that murders of doctors in the United States 'generate a sense of fear and insecurity on the part of abortion providers everywhere' (ibid: 317). The idea in *Morgentaler* that women should be free from emotional damage and anxiety caused by the abortion law developed into a concern about protecting women and doctors from anxiety, fear, and the risk of violence by, if necessary, imprisoning protestors for contempt of court.

Similar injunctions were also obtained against Operation Rescue protests in British Columbia, but were ineffective. (Campbell and Pal 1991: 34) In November 1994, a Vancouver doctor who performed abortions was shot and almost killed. In response, the B.C. legislature enacted a law making it an offence to interfere or protest within access zones around abortion clinics. Like the Ontario injunction, this law was intended to ensure that women could receive abortions in 'an atmosphere of security, respect and privacy' (*Lewis* 1996: 498). It was soon challenged by a pro-life protestor who was charged for carrying a sign ('Our Lady of Guadalupe Patron of the Unborn Please Help Us Stop Abortion') within fifty metres of a clinic. The courts eventually ruled that the restriction on freedom of expression was justified to ensure that women had access to the clinic without experiencing anxiety and distress (ibid).

While rejecting the criminal sanction, the decisions of Chief Justice Dickson and Justice Wilson in *Morgentaler* articulated an understanding of harm that was used to justify the criminal sanction both in the abortion and in other contexts, including the Court's decision to uphold obscenity and hate-propaganda offences. A concern about protecting women from state-imposed stress and anxiety was translated to a concern about protecting them from the same harms and risk of violence imposed by pro-life demonstrators. Abortion was decriminalized, but Packer's scepticism about the criminal sanction was rejected by those on all sides of the abortion issue.

Assisted Suicide

Voluntary euthanasia and assisted suicide did not receive much attention from Packer, but he would likely have opposed criminalization of these consensual crimes. He would have assumed that consent was freely given and been critical of the use of the criminal law to enforce morality. His judgment that these activities should be decriminalized would have been bolstered by the fact that they were difficult to enforce.

Sue Rodriguez's attempts to use the Charter to decriminalize assisted suicide captured the public imagination. Her argument was personal and compelling. As a victim of ALS, she would eventually be unable to move, speak, swallow, or breathe. She asked for an exemption from the offence of assisting suicide so that she could legally wait until she required assistance in ending her life. Under the law, she would be required to end her life while she was physically able to do so without assistance or suffer a slow and painful death. In the end, she did neither and received illegal assistance in ending her life.

The *Rodriguez* case raised conflicting claims of rights, victimization, and the public interest. In a 5-4 decision, the Supreme Court upheld the prohibition on assisted suicide. Drawing on Chief Justice Dickson's expanded definition of security of the person in *Morgentaler,* the majority readily conceded that the offence caused Rodriguez 'physical pain and psychological stress in a manner which impinges on the security of her person' (*Rodriguez* 1993: 64). Nevertheless, the Court concluded that this denial of security of the person was in accordance with the principles of fundamental justice. These principles were informed by consideration of the public interest and morality typical of the older crime-control model, as well as concerns about potential victims typical of a newer punitive victims' rights model.

Justice Sopinka stressed for the Court that the law reflected 'the policy of the state that human life should not be depreciated by allowing life to be taken' (ibid: 69). This policy was supported by community values because, 'to the extent that there is consensus, it is that human life must be respected and we must be careful not to undermine the institutions that protect it' (ibid: 78). He adopted a conservative approach to the criminal sanction (Devlin 1959) by arguing that the state served 'as a role model for individuals in society' and that 'allowing the state to kill will cheapen the value of human life ... To permit a physician to lawfully participate in taking life would send a signal that there are circumstances in which the state approves of suicide' (*Rodriguez* 1993: 78–9). The idea of the state as role model was rehabilitated from its Victorian overtones by the fact that the right to life was itself protected under section 7 of the Charter. As will be seen in the hate-propaganda and pornography context, the Court was not embarrassed about proclaiming and defending moral values, as long as they could be called Charter values (*Keegstra* 1990; *Butler* 1992).

Justice Sopinka also justified the Court's decision to uphold the criminal sanction by an appeal to victims' rights and the risk that a person's consent to suicide might not be genuine. He made repeated references to the need to protect 'the vulnerable' without ever specifying who they were (Weinrib, 1994: 630). He may have been referring to the submissions of an intervenor, People in Equal Participation (PEP; 1993: 1), who represented 'persons with severe disabilities and is dedicated to enhancing the quality of life for the disabled.'[8] This advocacy group argued that 'the legal vacuum that would be created by declaring section 241(b) of the Criminal Code invalid would only add to the discrimination already facing disabled persons in Canada' (ibid: 3). In their view, there was 'a direct relationship between the lack of services afforded to disabled persons and their desire to commit suicide' (ibid: 13) and 'a just and compassionate community would ... affirm their value as human beings and supply them with essential financial, rehabilitative, emotional and social assistance' (ibid: 11). These remedies were, of course, not available in the new political case, which could only decide whether the criminal sanction should be applied. The demands of the disabled for various services were criminalized in a debate over whether or not the criminal sanction should be applied.

Like Justice Lamer in the *Prostitution Reference*, Justice Sopinka stressed 'the state's interest in protecting the vulnerable' through the criminal sanction (ibid: 69). He supported a punitive form of victims' rights which channelled support for the disabled into the criminal sanction, as opposed to more expensive services that might prevent some suicides. He also ignored the divisions within the disabled community about Rodriguez's case. Although PEP, joined by pro-life groups, supported the law, two other groups representing the disabled supported Rodriguez. They were concerned that courts not ignore the discriminatory effects of facially neutral laws, like the assisted-suicide law, on the disabled. The Coalition of Provincial Organizations of the Handicapped (COPOH; 1993: 13–14, 19) argued that it was 'grossly stereotypical to assume that a disabled person who wants to die is motivated by the disability itself' and that 'freedom of choice ... self-determination and autonomy are ... essential components of true equality' for the disabled. Groups representing the disabled did not act as a monolithic Court Party. A recurring difficulty was who could speak for the victims or potential victims. Approaches, like that taken by the majority of the Court, which did not acknowledge this difficulty ran the greatest risk of using victims for other causes such as crime control.

The majority's belief that the criminal sanction protected the vulnerable was also based on risk analysis. It quickly moved from uncalculated risks that the 'vulnerable' would be coerced into suicide to the prospect of that risk being realized. Risk could be presented in the actuarial language of the social sciences or, as in this case, through a more emotive parade of horribles. In any event, it was constructed to support the criminal sanction even in the absence of evidence that the criminal law could control the risk. The alternative interpretation that the criminal law would not deter those caregivers prepared to end the lives of the vulnerable was ignored.

In her dissent, Justice McLachlin stressed how the assisted-suicide law restrained Rodriguez's liberty (ibid: 87), not softer concerns about security of the person from stress and anxiety. She criticized the majority for overestimating the risk that allowing Rodriguez to obtain an assisted suicide would 'open the doors, if not the floodgates, to the killing of disabled people who may not truly consent to death.' It was unfair to require Rodriguez 'to bear the burden of the chance that other people in other situations may act criminally to kill others or improperly sway them to suicide' (ibid: 90). She made a classically liberal argument that the individual should not be sacrificed for social or utilitarian ends.[9] As will be seen in the next section, Justice McLachlin found herself in the minority when she made similar arguments in *Keegstra* (1990), and her conclusion in *Seaboyer* (1991) that the accused should not be sacrificed to the social interest in the 'rape shield' law resulted in a strong dissent and a parliamentary reply designed to advance the social goal of encouraging reporting of sexual assaults.

The reaction to the Court's decision to uphold the law was mixed. Close to three-quarters of Canadians supported doctor-assisted suicide in an opinion poll taken shortly after Rodriguez's death (*Victoria Times Colonist*, 4 Mar. 1994). At the same time, both the Canadian Medical Association and a Senate committee concluded that euthanasia should not be legalized. The majority of the Senate committee (Senate of Canada 1995: 71), like the majority of the Supreme Court, stressed the need to maintain 'the fundamental social value of respect for life' and to prevent abuses 'with respect to the most vulnerable members of society.' Ignoring the fact that suicide itself was legal, they feared repealing the law would send a message to young people, especially Aboriginal youth, that suicide was acceptable (ibid: 72). This assumed that the criminal law could respond to the social, economic, political, and cultural conditions that contributed to high suicide rates among Aboriginal people. The minority of the committee stressed the unfairness of the law towards those who, because of physical disability, required assistance in suicide. The Court Party, including Rodriguez's lawyer and the intervenors in the case, simply moved down Wellington Street only to achieve the same result.

In summary, the *Rodriguez* case and subsequent debate demonstrated considerable support for the criminalization of what Packer would have believed was a victimless crime. The Court's judgment in *Rodriguez* combined a conservative crime-control deference to Parliament's ability to define public morality with a punitive victims' rights argument that the criminal law was required to protect the vulnerable and to respond to the risk of coercion. These latter concerns were supported by some groups representing disabled people, but other groups argued that the sanction discriminated against those who could not take their own lives because of a disability. Justice McLachlin took a more individualistic due-process approach which rejected curtailing Rodriguez's liberty because of possible abuses in other cases. Her approach would fail in *Keegstra*, and would result in controversy when it prevailed in sexual-assault cases.

Hate Propaganda

In 1970, Canada ratified the International Convention on the Elimination of All Forms of Racial Discrimination, which called for state parties to make the dissemination of ideas based on racial superiority and hatred an offence punishable by law. That year an offence prohibiting the wilful promotion of hatred was added to the Criminal Code. Packer and other American liberals would have supported only hate-propaganda laws targeting clear and present dangers of violence and would have been suspicious of the new law because it targeted the content of speech.

In any event, there were few prosecutions because of requirements that the attorney general approve prosecutions and prove a wilful intention to promote hatred (*Buzzanga* 1979). In 1984, a parliamentary committee argued that the above safeguards were no longer necessary 'now that we have an entrenched Charter of Rights, [which] can be used to shield any Canadian who feels he is being improperly prosecuted under the hate propaganda provisions' (Canada 1984c: 70). Due process was used to justify reforms that would facilitate prosecutions. A year later, the Fraser Committee recommended that private prosecutions be allowed and that the law also apply to the promotion of hatred on the basis of sex, age, or disability. The minister of justice announced his intention to repeal the requirements of wilful promotion and the attorney's general consent (Canada 1985: 318). This never occurred, and the focus soon shifted to the defence of what had been criticized as a law that inadequately prohibited hate propaganda.

Keegstra

James Keegstra was charged in 1984 with wilfully promoting hatred against Jews. Keegstra, who had also been the mayor of Eckville, Alberta, had taught his high-school students for more than a decade that Jews were responsible for depressions, anarchy, wars, and revolutions, and were 'subversive,' 'sadistic,' 'money-loving,' 'power hungry,' and 'child killers' (*Keegstra* 1990: 12). By the time of his hate-propaganda trial, he had been fired from his teaching position and been denied re-election as mayor. He might have been left in 'richly deserved obscurity' (Borovoy 1988: 53) had a criminal prosecution not been commenced. The prosecution lasted over a decade and resulted in an influential precedent linking equality rights with support for the criminal sanction.

Denying Keegstra's argument that the hate-propaganda law infringed his freedom of expression, the trial judge concluded that Keegstra's expression violated the equality and speech rights of its targets (*Keegstra* 1984). After a seventy-day trial, Keegstra was convicted and fined $5,000. He successfully appealed to the Alberta Court of Appeal, which held that the law was an unjustified violation of freedom of expression because it applied even when there was no danger of anyone acting on the hate message. This was the clear-and-present-danger approach that could be expected from Packer. Kerans J.A. argued that the anxiety caused by hate messages was only 'a psychological pin-prick' because they did not enjoy acceptance. 'Nobody enjoys being the target of name-calling, but the sense of outrage and frustration may be bearable if that abuse is rejected by the community as a whole' (*Keegstra* 1988: 169). As will be seen, all the members of the Supreme Court would take the psychological harms of hate speech more seriously.

The prosecutor's appeal to the Supreme Court was well publicized and attracted a number of intervenors. Six governments argued in support of the law, as well as the Canadian Jewish Congress, the Human Rights League of the B'nai B'rith, Interamicus, and the Women's Legal and Education Action Fund (LEAF). The Canadian Civil Liberties Association (CCLA) argued that the legislation was an unjustified restriction on freedom of expression. In a 4-3 decision, the Court upheld the law. Chief Justice Dickson wrote the majority decision, joined by Justices Wilson, L'Heureux-Dubé, and Gonthier. This alliance combined the two judges most receptive to due-process claims (Dickson and Wilson) with the two judges least receptive (L'Heureux-Dubé and Gonthier) (Morton, Russell, and Withey 1995: 45). It could, however, perhaps be explained by a common receptiveness to the claims of 'the Court Party' of politicized groups who had developed a stake in the equality rights of the Charter (ibid). In this context, however, these groups intervened on the side of the state and the criminal sanction. The dissenting judgment was written by Justice McLachlin with the agreement of Justices Sopinka and La Forest, all judges with good due-process credentials. *Keegstra* was typical of the new political case because it pitted the equality rights of disadvantaged groups against the due-process rights of the accused.

All the judges on the Supreme Court recognized the psychological harms caused by hate speech. Justice McLachlin rejected the Court of Appeal's clear-and-present-danger approach by arguing that 'to view hate propaganda as "victimless" in the absence of any proof that it moved its listeners to hatred is to discount the wrenching impact that it may have on members of the target group themselves. For Jews ... statements such as Keegstra's may raise very real fears of history repeating itself' (*Keegstra* 1990: 118–19). Chief Justice Dickson also concluded that hate propaganda caused 'very real harm' to target groups, including 'emotional damage ... of grave psychological and social consequence ... The derision, hostility and abuse encouraged by hate propaganda therefore have a severely negative impact on the individual's sense of self-worth and acceptance' (ibid: 36). The references to 'psychological' and 'emotional damage' harkened back to his concerns in *Morgentaler* about the effects of the criminal law on women seeking abortions. An understanding of harm first developed to recognize the due-process rights of women as potential accused was used on behalf of victims of hate propaganda to support the criminal sanction. The Chief Justice also related hate propaganda to words which 'can in themselves constitute harassment ... a response of humiliation and degradation from an individual targeted by hate propaganda is to be expected. A person's sense of human dignity and belonging to the community at large is closely linked to the concern and respect accorded the groups to which he or she belongs ...' These references to 'humiliation' and 'degradation' foreshadowed the Court's decision to uphold the obscenity provisions of the Criminal Code from Charter challenge (*Butler* 1992).

Risk played an important role in both judgments. Chief Justice Dickson justified the criminal sanction as a response to 'the possibility that prejudiced messages will gain some credence, with the attendant result of discrimination, and perhaps even violence, against minority groups in Canadian society' (ibid: 37). Risk discourse was merged with rights discourse (Ericson and Haggerty 1997), and risk included that of both violence and discrimination. The Chief Justice argued that it was 'well accepted that Parliament can use the criminal law to prevent the risk of serious harm, a leading example being the drinking and driving provisions of the *Criminal Code*' (*Keegstra* 1990: 59). This comparison invoked the aura of both scientific and moral certainty surrounding the risk of drunk driving (Gusfield 1981), as well as the Court's willingness to make exceptions from due process to facilitate the investigation of that crime (see chapter 2). By employing risk in this way, he turned civil-libertarian arguments about the risk of deterring legitimate expression on their head. Every example that Justice McLachlin provided of 'a chilling effect on defensible expression by law-abiding citizens' (ibid: 115, 120–1) was met with a counter-example of discrimination or violence that might flow from hate propaganda. Both sides operated without empirical evidence as to the magnitude of the risk, and both constructed risk for their own purposes.

Chief Justice Dickson and Justice McLachlin debated not only the relevant risks, but also the relevance of equality rights. Chief Justice Dickson adopted a submission by LEAF that moved from the uncontroversial position that government-sponsored hate would violate equality rights to one that 'government action against group hate,' here the criminal sanction, 'promotes social equality' and 'deserves special constitutional consideration' (ibid: 44). This argument mirrored the development of the *Morgentaler* idea that the state should not impose stress and anxiety to the broader proposition that it should use the criminal law to prevent stress and anxiety. It also assumed that the criminal sanction effectively promoted social equality and protected potential victims of hate propaganda. The Court downplayed the importance of education and non-punitive means to reject Keegstra's hateful ideas and assumed that the criminal law was necessary and capable of controlling the harms and risks of hate speech. In her dissent, Justice McLachlin refused to make this jump and argued that equality rights were not relevant because the case involved the discriminatory teachings of a private citizen, not governmental action (ibid: 100–1).

The two judges also disagreed about the appropriate role of the state. Chief Justice Dickson contemplated an activist state that was benevolent (Moran 1994) and 'uniquely Canadian' (*Keegstra* 1990: 34). He preferred the dissenting theories of American critical race theorists to 'the view, reasonably prevalent in America at present, that the suppression of hate propaganda is incompatible with the guarantee of free expression' (ibid: 34; *R.A.V.* 1992). Reflecting the support that 'Charter Canadians' or the 'Court Party' received from international sources (Cairns 1992), he argued that Canada's 'international commitment to eradicate hate propaganda and, most importantly, the special role given equality and multiculturalism in the Canadian Constitution' required the criminalization of hate propaganda. Justice McLachlin assumed an adversarial state that threatened rather than protected its citizens (Moran 1994). She relied on American cases and notions of vagueness, overbreadth, and chill which found their origin in the American distrust of the state. Her views were similar to Packer's assumptions about a limited adversarial state, while Dickson's views were compatible with the more activist state required to protect victims and manage risk.

In the end, the law was upheld with the majority stressing the symbolic value of the criminal law as 'a form of expression' which sent the message 'that hate propaganda is harmful to target groups and threatening to a harmonious society.' The Court assumed that the 'many, many Canadians who belong to identifiable groups surely gain a great deal of comfort from the knowledge that the hate-monger is criminally prosecuted and his or her ideas rejected' (ibid: 53–4). The 'strong message' sent by the criminal law and the comfort conferred on identifiable groups was diluted by Keegstra's almost successful due-process challenge and the $3,000 fine that he received after six more years of due-process challenges and appeals (*Keegstra* 1996). His community's actions in firing him as a teacher and not re-electing him as mayor were in many ways more severe than the fine he received (Borovoy 1988: 53). The fact that he was prosecuted may have made him more defiant and impervious to shame. His endless appeals resulted in publicity and symbolic politics.

Zundel

Following the attorney general's refusal to prosecute Ernst Zundel's denial of the Holocaust as hate propaganda, Sabina Citron, a Holocaust survivor, commenced a private prosecution under a then obscure Criminal Code provision which made it a crime to wilfully publish news that the accused knew was false and that would cause injury or mischief to a public interest. Although the case was eventually taken over by the attorney general's office, which had the resources needed to conduct long trials and appeals, private prosecutions were an important expression of victims' rights. They were, however, suspect in both crime-control and due-process models of criminal justice because they circumvented the expert-judgment and fairness obligations of public prosecutors (Ontario 1993).

Zundel's first trial lasted seven and a half months and ended in a conviction and a sentence of fifteen months' imprisonment. In addition, Zundel could not publish anything about the Holocaust for three years as a condition of probation. This offered the victims of his hate something more tangible than the fines in *Keegstra*, but the conviction came at the price of Holocaust survivors and historical experts being subject to abusive cross-examination by Zundel's (and Keegstra's) lawyer, Douglas Christie. The exposure of victims to the adversarial trial process invited a second victimization. Alternatives to prosecutions such as public denunciations and shaming might give victims more dignity and control of the process.

In any event, Zundel's conviction was overturned on appeal because the trial judge had not made clear to the jury that the prosecutor had to prove that Zundel knew that his Holocaust denial was false (*Zundel* 1987). As in the hate-propaganda law (*Buzzanga* 1978), the courts made it difficult to obtain convictions by raising the standard of subjective fault that the prosecutor must establish beyond a reasonable doubt. The Court of Appeal also held that the trial judge had overreacted by disallowing all questions when Christie improperly attempted to ask prospective jurors questions about their views about Jews. A court subsequently allowed

Christie to ask jurors in Imre Finta's trial whether they belonged to organizations that supported the new war-crimes laws. As discussed in chapter 7, this raised concerns that Christie had succeeded in keeping Jews off the jury. Jury selection was a controversial issue in the new political case because it implicated the rights of both the accused and the victim.

Zundel's new trial lasted four months and ended with a conviction and a nine-month jail sentence. The Ontario Court of Appeal upheld the conviction, but the Supreme Court decided 4-3 that the law was an unjustified violation of freedom of expression. Justice McLachlin wrote the majority judgment and revisited many of the themes of her dissenting judgment in *Keegstra*. In turn, the dissenting judgment reflected many of the themes found in the majority's judgment in *Keegstra*. Victories in judicial doctrine, whether they be for due process or victims' rights, were fragile. As Packer predicted, the personnel and attitudes of courts could change and they had a great capacity to qualify and distinguish their precedents.

The Supreme Court in *Zundel* (1992) went well beyond the Warren Court (*Garrison* 1964) in holding that even deliberate and conscious lies were protected expression. As in *Keegstra*, both the majority and minority acknowledged the pain that Zundel's Holocaust denial must have caused among its victims, particularly survivors (*Zundel* 1992: 475, 510). After this, however, they parted company, with the majority stressing the risk that the law would chill legitimate expression, and the minority stressing the risk that it would result in discrimination against disadvantaged groups. Justice McLachlin attempted to infuse freedom of expression with equality values by arguing that 'much of the speech potentially smothered, or at least "chilled", by state prosecution of the proscribed expression is likely to be the speech of minority or traditionally disadvantaged groups' (ibid: 517). The attempt to defend the decision in terms of its outcome for minorities was a testament to the impact of *Keegstra* in entrenching equality analysis of speech offences.

In their dissent, Justices Cory and Iacobucci defined the harm of false hate speech broadly to include 'humiliation and degradation' and 'discrimination and the exclusion of a group subjected to historical disadvantage' (ibid: 474–5, 479). They contemplated an active role for the state by suggesting that the targets of hate propaganda would feel disowned if the state did not prosecute Zundel. Quoting an article by a critical race theorist urging courts to consider 'the victim's story' (Matsuda 1989: 2379), they warned that while 'one can dismiss the hate groups as an organization of marginal people ... the state is the official embodiment of the society we live in' (ibid: 474). This revived the conservative idea of the state as a role model, but one which acted in the name of Charter values as opposed to conventional morality. The minority blended concerns about the reactions of victims, equality rights, and an active role for the state to justify the use of the criminal sanction. Educational and preventive measures to ensure that Zundel's lies were denounced and did not gain a following were dismissed as second-best strategies that did not carry the strong symbolic weight of the criminal law.

The gains of recognizing equality rights and the harms and risks of hate speech in *Keegstra* were quickly countered by the decision in *Zundel*. Judicial doctrine recognizing due process or victims' rights was unstable and subject to qualification. Whatever side won the new political case was bound to receive a qualified, and perhaps only temporary, victory. Keegstra's conviction was upheld after a decade of appeals, but resulted in a fine that was denounced by target groups as 'getting away with murder' (*Vancouver Sun*, 13 Jul. 1992). The fine and the due- process challenges undercut the strong message of the criminal law. These two cases also contributed to a criminalization of politics by focusing on the symbolic value of the criminal law and the struggles of the new political case, as opposed to other more expensive and less contentious means to address the social problems revealed by hatred of minorities.

Pornography

Herbert Packer (1968: 324) believed that 'the only valid purpose' of obscenity laws was to prevent a public nuisance. Any other justification would be a disguise for the enforcement of morals which should be left to the 'church, the school, and the home' (ibid: 320). As late as 1975, the Law Reform Commission of Canada (p. 4) similarly argued that pornography was a 'victimless' crime. Less than twenty years later, two members of that commission, Antonio Lamer and Gerald La Forest, would sign on to a landmark Supreme Court ruling that justified the prohibition of violent, degrading, dehumanizing, and child pornography regardless of its nuisance value (*Butler* 1992). Another crime once challenged as victimless became reinvigorated as one that responded to the risks of victimization and inequality.

Scientific Claims of Harm

Many successful victims' rights initiatives relied on the prior production and politicization of knowledge about the extent of victimization. Victimization studies documenting widespread sexual violence against women and children played an important role in building a foundation for the legal reforms examined in the next two chapters. The same was true for pornography. In 1968, Packer argued that, unlike in the case of drinking and driving, there was no evidence linking pornography to harm.[10] This claim became contested in the next two decades so that 'all actors involved in the pornography debate ... [could mobilize] the scientific discourse to justify their respective positions on the criminalization of pornography' (Lacombe 1994: 139). For civil libertarians, the risk of violence was not clear enough to overcome their concerns about the risk of legitimate speech being chilled. For conservatives, the social-science data suggested that Parliament had a reasonable basis for legislating and that the courts should not interfere. For the Fraser Committee and some feminists, a concern for the equality rights of women justified some obscenity laws even if the research did not yet establish that pornography was 'a significant causal factor in the commission of some forms of violent crime, in the sexual abuse of children, or the disintegration of communities and society' (Canada 1985: 99). Risk was measured by social science, but plugged into broader normative and legal theories.

Failed Legislation

Several failed attempts in the 1980s to amend obscenity laws created the background for the Supreme Court's reinterpretation of obscenity law in *Butler* (1992). In 1984, the Liberal government introduced a bill that would have redefined obscenity to include material with the dominant characteristic of 'sex, violence, crime, horror or cruelty through degrading representations of a male or female person or in any other manner' (ibid: 132). The centrality of degradation to the proposed definition of obscenity was inspired by a 1978 parliamentary committee report that had adopted new feminist understandings of pornography,[11] as well as some judicial decisions holding that degrading and dehumanizing depictions of sex and violence exceeded community standards (*Douglas Rankine Co.* 1983: 70). This bill died on the order paper before the election of the Conservatives in 1985.

In 1986, the new government introduced a new bill that defined obscenity very broadly as 'any visual matter showing vaginal, anal or oral intercourse, ejaculation, sexually violent behaviour, bestiality, incest, necrophilia or other sexual activity' and prohibited child pornography with anyone who was or appeared to be under eighteen years of age.

Whereas the Liberal bill had been influenced by some feminist under-standings of obscenity, this one was inspired by social conservatives (Lacombe 1994: 104–9). It was opposed by feminist groups who 'wanted laws that outlaw the degradation of women ... [not] laws that were going to be Victorian and outlaw healthy human sexuality' (Campbell and Pal 1989: 139). Despite Gallup polls suggesting that it was supported by two of three Canadians (ibid: 142), the bill was also allowed to die. In 1987, it was replaced by another bill, which dropped the reference to 'other sexual activity' in its definition of pornography and took a nuisance-based approach to 'erotica.' Civil libertarians and librarians campaigned against the bill, while social conservatives, although initially supportive, came to fear that it would liberalize the existing law. As with the 1989 abortion bill, the fact that this bill did not please the opposing extremes contributed to its demise. Because the courts had not struck down the existing law under the Charter, however, the burden of inertia favoured criminalization.

The National Action Committee on the Status of Women (NAC) opposed the two Conservative bills and argued that a new criminal law alone was inadequate. What was required was better funding for battered women, incest survivors, and rape victims; better jobs for women; and education efforts to combat gender stereotypes in the media (Lacombe 1994: 121–2). This approach prioritized pornography in the context of a comprehensive strategy to reduce violence against women. As will be seen, however, this sense of perspective was lost when women's groups were faced with due-process challenges to the existing obscenity law. As in the hate-propaganda context, the focus soon shifted to the defence of what many had criticized as an outdated and ineffective law.

Butler

The failure of the legislature to act meant that the future of obscenity law depended on the judiciary. The landmark case involved 240 counts of obscenity against a video-store owner. The case would have been easy for Packer because the store owner had posted a notice that 'if sex oriented material offends you, please do not enter' (*Butler* 1992: 134). Much more, however, was at stake than the regulation of nuisance. The trial judge acquitted Butler of most charges on the basis that, under the Charter, Parliament could no longer outlaw explicit sex, but only violent or dehu-manizing sexual material that 'effectively reduces the human or equality rights or other Charter rights of individuals' (*Butler* 1987: 121). The Charter would allow the criminal sanction only in the name of the rights of victims. This ruling reflected a growing emphasis in judicial decisions on violent, degrading, or dehumanizing depictions and equality rights that was best captured by the Liberal's 1984 pornography bill. This approach was not uniform, and the Manitoba Court of Appeal convicted Butler on all counts because the videos contained 'prurient materials devoid of a redeeming meaning' and not even worthy of protection as free expression (*Butler* 1990: 231). This approach mirrored the Conservative's proposed definitions of obscenity as virtually all explicit sex.

In the Supreme Court, six governments intervened to support the obscenity law, as did the conservative Group against Pornography, and LEAF. The governments' arguments combined older 'moral concerns about decency, immorality, abnormal sex and family decline ... with newer concerns about sexual violence, the degradation of women, and gender harm' (Gotell 1997: 97–8). The Canadian Civil Liberties Association and the British Columbia Civil Liberties Association argued that the legislation could not be justified under section 1 of the Charter, with the former making traditional civil-libertarian arguments about the importance of free expression and the dangers of overbreadth, and the latter arguing for 'sexual plurality and diversity' (ibid: 78). Like Justice McLachlin in her *Zundel* judgment, some civil libertarians recognized that equality concerns should be integrated into their more traditional concerns about liberty.

As in *Keegstra*, LEAF lined up on the side of the criminal sanction. Building on *Keegstra*, it argued that 'pornography is a form of hate propaganda against women' (LEAF 1996: 215; Mahoney 1992). Like the majority in *Keegstra* and the minority in *Zundel*, LEAF defined harms to include not only the risk of violence, but 'systemic discrimination against women through systemic bias and subordination' which 'deter women's equal access to participation in community life ... Sex toys do not generally run for prime minister' (LEAF 1996: 215–16). LEAF also built on lower court decisions that had focused on harm to women and equality rather than sexual morality. 'Whereas the traditional approach is concerned with materials deemed scurrilous, disgusting, indecent and immoral, this line of cases identifies as obscene material that is dehumanizing, degrading, subordinating and dangerous for women' (ibid: 207). Consistent with the conservatism of legal doctrine, LEAF built its case on precedents.

Although *Butler* has been depicted as a LEAF victory, the bulk of its factum addressed a losing argument – namely, that pornography based on violence and threats of violence did not deserve protection as expression because it conflicted with gender equality. Much of this argument was devoted to what was described as 'a growing body of legal and social scholarship, evidence, expert and victim testimony, and official acknowledgement that pornography is a systematic practice of exploitation and subordination based on sex that differentially harms women' (ibid: 208). As suggested above, however, the social science was heavily supplemented by legal and normative arguments.

LEAF's intervention in *Butler* has been controversial. Lise Gotell (1997: 93–4) argued that 'the LEAF factum presents women as powerless victims of male sexual violence' and that taking the perspective of female victims of male violence was 'a rhetorical tactic that serves to insulate LEAF's arguments from critique and contestation.' Appeals to personal experience were a common characteristic of the otherwise very different groups that sought to change the law to reflect their experience as victims or potential victims, and this helped explain the divisive and emotive nature of new political cases. Following *Keegstra*, the LEAF factum also stressed the use of the criminal law and did not advert to alternative strategies to counter violent and degrading images of women and gender inequality. This was curious because LEAF's understanding of pornography drew on Catharine MacKinnon's work in connection with a Minneapolis ordinance which relied more heavily on civil litigation. Acknowledgment of alternatives to the criminal sanction would have created a real danger that the law would be struck down as a disproportionate means of protecting women. Whatever their views on the place of the criminal sanction in reform, LEAF's lawyers were forced as a matter of legal strategy to emphasize the importance and necessity of the criminal sanction.

LEAF's approach has been defended as 'simply attempting to force the State to extend its protection in order to fulfil its promise of security of the person for all women. In other words, we want criminal law to work for women. This is an equality argument' (Busby 1994: 175). The criminal law was taken as a given and it was assumed that, if it could only be made 'to work for women.' it would fulfil its promise of security. This replicated the crime-control' assumption that the criminal law controlled crime. The rights of women, as victims and potential victims of male violence, were constructed for crime control.

The Supreme Court upheld the obscenity law in *Butler* by holding that, when interpreted in light of the new line of cases stressing violence and degradation, it was a justified limit on freedom of expression. In an example of the type of legislative classification that defied parliamentary agreement, Justice Sopinka quickly divided pornography into three categories:

1 / explicit sex with violence which would almost always be obscene; 2 / explicit sex which subjects people to degrading or dehumanizing treatment which will be obscene 'if the risk of harm is substantial'; and 3 / explicit sex which will generally not be obscene unless it involves children (*Butler* 1992: 150–1).[12] The Court accepted the category of degrading and dehumanizing pornography even though the Fraser Committee believed the term was 'too imprecise and too broad' and could include 'much of which appears as mainstream pornography' (Canada 1985: 269–70). Unlike Packer, the Court was sceptical about consent and concluded that 'consent cannot save materials that otherwise contain degrading or dehumanizing scenes. Sometimes the very appearance of consent makes the depicted acts even more degrading or dehumanizing' (*Butler* 1992: 146–7). Unlike Packer, the Court did not accept consent as an argument for decriminalization.

The Court placed little emphasis on the social-science evidence that examined the links between pornography and violence. The linkage was 'not susceptible of exact proof,' but Parliament 'was entitled to have 'a reasoned apprehension of harm' resulting from the desensitization of individuals exposed to materials which depict violence, cruelty and dehumanization in sexual relations' (ibid: 164). The Court did not expect much from the social-science evidence and resolved any dispute about the evidence in favour of the government. This could be explained by the Court's increasing reluctance to re-evaluate the evidence on which governments acted (*Irwin Toy Ltd.* 1989) and its willingness, since the prostitution cases and *Keegstra*, to apply this more deferential standard in the criminal context of the new political case.[13]

As in *Keegstra*, the harm and risk created by the expression was emphasized. The social science demonstrated that pornography could 'potentially victimize women' (ibid: 164). The harm of pornography was anything that 'predisposes persons to act in an antisocial manner as, for example, the physical or mental mistreatment of women by men, or what is perhaps debatable, the reverse' (ibid: 150). Harm included psychological damage. 'Materials portraying women as a class as objects for sexual exploitation and abuse have a negative impact on the individual's sense of self-worth and acceptance' (ibid: 159) and can 'wreak social damage in that a significant portion of the population is humiliated by its gross misrepresentation' (ibid: 162). The harms of pornography were located in the subjective perceptions of its targets – namely, the 'degradation which many women feel as "victims" of the message of obscenity' (ibid: 166). This built on the Court's recognition of subjective harms in *Mor-*

gentaler and Justice Lamer's reference to degradation in the *Prostitution Reference*. Consistent with the emotionalism of victims' rights, individual feelings of 'self-worth' and 'humiliation' became a justification for the criminal sanction.

The Court rejected the conservative idea that Parliament could legislate any particular vision of morality, but suggested that legislating morality on the basis of Charter values was perfectly acceptable (ibid: 156; Dyzenhaus 1991: 376). The Court stressed the important symbolic role of the criminal sanction in demonstrating 'our community's disapproval of the dissemination of materials which potentially victimize women' (ibid: 164). Parliament was justified in criminalizing ideas that were contrary to values of equality. As in *Keegstra*, it rejected the American approach which would have struck down a *Butler*-type statute as an attempt to regulate the content of speech and to require adherence to an 'approved' viewpoint on matters of social controversy (*American Booksellers Assn. Inc.* 1985: 328; *R.A.V.* 1992). Perhaps because Canadians were more comfortable with a conservative tradition that openly allowed the state to take sides on moral issues, the Supreme Court upheld hate propaganda and obscenity laws precisely because they were content-based, and denounced ideas contrary to the new Charter value of equality.

Butler promoted a legalized and truncated politics to the extent that it marginalized the social and economic alternatives to the criminal sanction that NAC had emphasized in its opposition to the Conservative's pornography bills (Lacombe 1994: 121–2). The adversarial challenge of litigation also led to a loss of perspective, with Catharine Mackinnon quoted as saying that the Court's decision was 'a stunning legal victory for women, this is of world historic importance' (*Globe and Mail*, 29 Feb. 1992). Such a conclusion emphasized the symbolic importance of including equality concerns in judicial doctrine more than any realistic judgment about the impact that the decision would have in reducing violence against women and children. Sheila Noonan (1992: 16) was more sanguine about the effects of *Butler* and raised an important question: 'in spite of juridic pronouncements sympathetic to the victimization of women and children, how much has actually been accomplished?' *Butler* fitted into a pattern of victims' rights being for crime control. An old obscenity law was upheld, not on the basis of crime-control deference to Parliament's expression of public morality, but on the new rationales of risk and equality rights. The equality rights of victims and potential victims and the risk of sexual violence and psychological harm were used to relegitimate a law previously challenged as moralistic and victimless.

The Aftermath of Butler

The day after the *Butler* judgment, Minister of Justice Kim Campbell announced her government's decision to enact new legislation against child pornography. Just before Parliament dissolved for the 1993 election, Parliament enacted legislation which prohibited the depiction of people under eighteen years of age engaged in explicit sexual activity. Possession of such material was made an offence in order 'to curb the flow of child pornography' (Hansard, 3 Jun. 1993: 20329). The bill received all party approval despite arguments by media and arts groups that the breadth of the prohibition could seriously inhibit legitimate expression. The government argued that, by enacting the new offences, they were 'taking important steps to protect children from sexual abuse and exploitation' and providing 'the satisfaction of going home this summer knowing that this country is a better place to live' (Hansard, 3 Jun. 1993: 20328, 20330). This suggested that the complex social and cultural problems presented by the sexualization and sexual abuse of children could be alleviated by the enactment of a new criminal sanction. Several members cited *Butler* as legitimating the legislation,[14] and the Liberal Justice critic suggested that 'we have the invitation from the Supreme Court of Canada to do something about child pornography' (ibid: 20870). *Butler* legitimated the expansion of the criminal sanction to cover child pornography.

Due-process challenges to obscenity laws, like those to hate-propaganda laws, allowed defenders of the laws to lose sight of the limitations of the criminal sanction and the need for broader and more expensive strategies to achieve equality and prevent the victimization of disadvantaged groups. In so doing, they contributed to the criminalization and legalization of broader issues of gender and sexuality. The defence of the criminal sanction in the name of victims' rights and the focus on the equal protection of the criminal law came dangerously close to replicating the crime-control assumption that the criminal law controlled crime.

Conclusion

With the exception of abortion and revenue-related gambling-law reforms, the Charter failed to facilitate the decriminalization of what Packer believed were victimless crimes. The same concern with protecting woman from psychological harm that led to the invalidation of the abortion law in *Morgentaler* also justified the criminalization of some pro-life protests, hate propaganda, and degrading pornography. Harm was redefined to include psychological harm from stress and anxiety; the risk of violence or coercion; and discriminatory practices which contributed to the social inequality of women, children, the disabled, and racial and religious minorities. The very idea of victimless crime was effectively contested by new knowledges about the risk of victimization, emotional testimonies of the experience of victimization, and claims that rights could be protected only by the criminal sanction.

The new ambitions for the criminal sanction were great, but were often not realized. The use of the criminal sanction frequently resulted in long and divisive struggles in appeal courts between due process and victims' rights. In some cases, Parliament introduced new criminal sanctions such as the soliciting and child-pornography laws. The defence and creation of the criminal sanction reinforced the willingness of legislators and litigators to criminalize politics by focusing on the strong symbolic message of the criminal sanction as opposed to more expensive strategies to achieve equality and prevent victimization. The defence of the criminal sanction in the name of victims' rights at times replicated the crime-control assumption that the criminal law controlled crime. There was more concern about equalizing the benefits of the criminal law than assessing the quality of its protections.

The groups that defended the criminal sanction and asserted the rights of victims and potential victims did not march under a single banner. Some disabled people supported Sue Rodriguez's challenge to the assisted-suicide law and some did not. Many feminists opposed the 1985 sanction against soliciting for prostitution; some did not. There were likewise various feminist positions on the criminalization of pornography. Although equality seekers won some victories, the Court Party was far from united. Even the victories were contingent because judicial doctrine was just as unstable and symbolic when it recognized victims' and equality rights as when it recognized due process. The victory of *Keegstra* was qualified by the loss of *Zundel*, and a parliamentary reply to *Morgentaler* was only derailed by a tie vote in the Senate. The heady optimism of some feminists about *Butler* was eroded by the way it was subsequently applied by legislators, administrators, and courts. Although the Court claimed to be protecting the vulnerable from undefined risks in *Rodriguez*, the case was a loss for most equality-seekers. As will be seen in the next chapter, feminist groups failed in their defence of sexual-assault laws from due-process challenges only to achieve success in Parliament. As was observed in this chapter, these new political cases set the accused's due-process rights against the equality and security rights of victims and potential victims and relied on the old crime-control assumption that the criminal law could control crime.

5

Women

As suggested in chapter 4, feminists played an important role in defending the rights of crime victims and potential crime victims with respect to some crimes that Packer believed to be victimless. Feminists were, however, not united on whether the criminal sanction should be used to respond to the harms of prostitution and pornography. Nevertheless, there was more consensus about the need for new laws and strategies to respond to the prevalence of sexual and domestic violence against women. Efforts in the 1970s focused on raising awareness and reducing harm through rape crisis centres and shelters for battered women. In the 1980s, there was more emphasis on achieving legal reforms to make the crimes easier to report and to prosecute. These legislative reforms were subject to due-process challenges throughout the 1990s. Ironically, feminists enjoyed less success in defending reformed sexual-assault laws in Court than in those cases discussed in chapter 4. The feminist wing of the 'Court Party' (Knopff and Morton 1992, 1996) lost its defensive battles in court only to win in Parliament. In both battles, however, they argued that the equality rights of women as victims and potential victims of male violence should be considered and supported the criminal sanction.

Although women have been the most influential group of crime victims and potential crime victims in achieving criminal-law reforms (Elias 1986, 1993; Rock 1986), feminists have not seen themselves as part of a larger victims' rights movement. They have been concerned that focusing on victims could allow women to be blamed for male violence and contribute to their disempowerment (Clark and Lewis 1977; Snider 1994: 100). They have resisted attempts to assimilate their challenge to criminal justice with other victims' rights initiatives because violence against women 'has to do with a sexist, patriarchal society. It has to do with a lack of economic power. It's different from break and entry victims, victims of assault in bars, and what not' (Rock 1986: 222). In this and subsequent chapters, I hope to respect the specificity of various groups' experiences, but also to place them in the larger context of the changing law and politics of criminal justice. In chapter 4, linkages were drawn between the use of the criminal sanction to respond to hate propaganda and pornography, and the understanding of harm in abortion and other cases. In chapter 6, the influence that strategies to reduce violence against women had on attempts to reduce the sexual abuse of children will be examined.

The success enjoyed in reforming sexual-assault laws was not matched with respect to child care, equal pay, and poverty among women and their children. Governments in the 1980s and 1990s gave women criminal justice victories, but social welfare defeats (Gotell 1997: 69). As former minister of justice John Crosbie candidly explained, 'one of the reasons ... for giving justice issues a major push was the fact that the government did not have much money. The government did not feel it could introduce big spending programs, it had to try to get the deficit under control' (quoted in Lacombe 1994: 105). Gender politics were criminalized to the extent that the criminal sanction was used as the most visible and least expensive policy instrument to respond to the concerns of women's groups. To be sure, other issues such as tax- and family-law reform surfaced, but not with the sustained nature of reforms concerning wife assault and sexual assault.

It was not clear whether women's groups challenged the very nature of due process and crime control or whether they attempted to equalize the protection of the existing system so that the criminal law worked for women (Busby 1994: 175). These issues will be addressed in this chapter in the context of changing approaches to the law of self-defence and the prosecution of wife assault. The *Lavallee* (1990) defence and domestic-assault charge policies recognized the prevalence of violence against women, but may not have fundamentally changed the nature of due process or crime control, including its limited ability to increase liberty or security. A nascent alternative to crime control and due process might, however, be found in feminist corrections which broke down the dichotomy of offenders and victims.

The criminalization of gender politics through sexual-assault law reform set the stage for its legalization in a series of political cases that pitted due-process claims by the accused against the equality and security claims of women as victims and potential victims. The mega political cases of *Seaboyer* (1991), *Daviault* (1994), *O'Connor* (1995), and *Carosella* (1997) will be examined in this chapter. In the media, and even in Court, these political cases were portrayed as divisive battles between feminists and defence lawyers. The adversarial dynamic of the cases encouraged each side to seek total victory. As occurred in relation to pornography and hate propaganda, the battle to preserve inadequate criminal laws from due-process challenges facilitated a loss of perspective and a replication of the crime-control assumption that the criminal law controlled crime.

This chapter also examines the parliamentary replies to these political cases. They differed from the ones discussed in chapter 2 because they pitted the equality and security rights of women, not the crime-control interests of police and prosecutors, against due-process claims by the accused. Moreover, they increasingly tracked the dissenting opinions of Supreme Court judges and were much more legalistic and abstract than the sexual- and wife-assault reforms of the 1980s, which themselves have been criticized for decontexualizing violence against women. These replies also featured symbolic and non-enforceable preambles proclaiming the ability of the criminal law to protect the equality and security rights of women and children, as well as the due-process rights of the accused. Despite their own desires for more comprehensive reforms, many feminists felt compelled to play defence against due process and devoted much energy in the 1990s to the defence and resurrection of the criminal sanction.

Female Criminality: Due Process or Victims' Rights?

In 1970, the Royal Commission on the Status of Women applied Packer's vision of due process to women and argued for decriminalization so that about 3,000 women a year, including a disproportionate number of Aboriginal women, would not be sent 'to jail for offences relating to vagrancy, attempted suicide, public intoxication and drug addiction' (Canada 1970: 378–9). As examined in chapter 4, much of this decriminalization did not occur, and in 1985 commentators still noted that there was 'nothing "criminal" about the majority of offences committed by women' (Boyle et al 1985: xvii). Due-process reforms, such as ensuring that people were not imprisoned because they were too poor to pay their fines (*Hebb* 1989), would benefit the vast majority of female offenders who were still imprisoned for non-violent offences (Johnson and Rodgers 1993: 107). As will be suggested in subsequent chapters, however, due process may be necessary to reduce the imprisonment of disadvantaged groups, but it was not sufficient.

Battered Women and Self-Defence

In 1996, there were ninety-eight women serving time for murder or manslaughter (Canada 1996a: 208). The vast majority of them had killed people they knew and reported having been abused in the past (Canada 1990: 52; Shaw, Rodgers, and Blanchette 1992: 16). One response to female criminality was to argue that a woman's past victimization by battering should be considered in determining whether she acted in self-defence. This was an attempt to make due process work for women. Like other due-process reforms, however, it did not reduce imprisonment. Most women who killed their male partners did not qualify for the reformed defence (Ratushny 1997) and still pled guilty to some offence (Shaffer 1997).

Walker's Cycle of Violence and Learned Helplessness

Increased knowledge about how women were victimized by crime played a role in many of the initiatives examined in this chapter. Research into battered woman's syndrome (BWS) was both influential and controversial (Shaffer 1990; Grant 1991). In 1979, psychologist Lenore Walker published her first major study on battered women. In it she emphasized the prevalence of wife assault: 'If you are a woman, there is a 50% chance it could be you!' (Walker 1979: 19), as well as the fact that the violence affected middle- and upper-class women. (ibid: 21). Walker presented accounts of 120 women 'as victims in order to understand what the toll of such domestic violence is like for them' (ibid: xvi). She then articulated a theory of learned helplessness and a three-stage cycle of violence to explain why women stayed in abusive relationships. Her work and the subsequent use of BWS illustrated why some feminists were uneasy with a focus on victims.

Walker suggested that women stayed in abusive relationships not because of financial dependency or fear, but because of a psychological pathology of learned helplessness that was similar to that experienced by dogs and rats who did not take opportunities to escape after receiving random electric shocks (ibid: 46–8). Battered women, like abused dogs, might have to be 'dragged' (ibid: 46, 53, 239) by others out of the abusive situation. As will be seen, this controversial theory could support mandatory arrest and prosecution for domestic violence against the wishes of victims (ibid: 209–10). Walker also outlined a three-stage cycle of violence which 'helps explain how battered women become victimized, how they fall into learned helplessness behaviour, and why they do not attempt to escape' (ibid: 55). The first phase was a tension-building stage where the woman attempted to placate the man's growing anger. The second phase was acute and often unpredictable battering involving a 'lack of control' and 'destructiveness' (ibid: 59) not seen in the incidents of battering that may have occurred in the first phase. The immediate aftermath for the victim was 'helplessness' (ibid: 63) similar to that experienced by disaster victims. The third phase was characterized by kindness and loving behaviour from the batterer, which, along with learned helplessness, explained why women remained in abusive relationships.

Lavallee

During her three- to four-year relationship with Kevin Rust, Angelique Lyn Lavallee had been the victim of physical abuse requiring numerous trips to hospital emergency rooms. On the night that she killed Rust, Lavallee was assaulted by him and hid in a closet to avoid him. Rust loaded and handed a gun to her (*Lavallee* 1990: 101). As he was leaving the room, Lavallee fatally shot him in the back of the head. In the police car on the way to the police station, Lavallee stated that 'he told me he was gonna kill me when everyone left' and 'I hope he lives. I really love him' (ibid: 102).

At trial, the defence called a psychiatrist, Dr Fred Shane, who concluded that Lavallee was a battered woman and had been subject to numerous cycles of violence. Dr Shane presented Lavallee as a victim of 'learned helplessness, if you will, the fact that she felt paralysed, she felt tyrannized ... there were steel fences in her mind which created for her an incredible barrier psychologically that prevented her from moving out.' Shooting at Rust was a product of her 'underlying rage ... [and] the feeling that she had to do something to him in order to survive, in order to defend herself' (ibid: 124). At the same time, however, Lavallee had a 'victim mentality, this concentration camp mentality, if you will, where she could not see herself be in any other situation except being tyrannized, punished and crucified physically and psychologically' (ibid: 124). Lavallee was at one moment a helpless victim with no way to imagine any escape and at another a person whose understandable rage at being beaten motivated her to self-help.

The trial judge allowed Dr Shane's testimony, but warned the jury that it was of limited weight because it was based on interviews with Lavallee and her mother that were not subject to cross-examination. The jury acquitted and the Manitoba Court of Appeal decided that Dr Shane's evidence was not admissible and, without it, no reasonable jury would have acquitted Lavallee (*Lavallee* 1988). For the Court of Appeal, the abuse suffered by Lavallee was a matter that might have supported a charge of manslaughter, but otherwise was not relevant. *Lavallee* was argued in the Supreme Court without any intervention from interest groups[1] and the parties in their factums were concerned about whether Dr Shane's expert evidence was admissible. The Supreme Court restored the acquittal and held that the expert testimony was admissible because without it the accused 'faces the prospect of being condemned by popular mythology about domestic violence' (*Lavallee*, 1990: 125). The expert testimony was seen in a benevolent light: 'we need help...and help is available from trained professionals' (ibid).

The Court relied on BWS to reject the idea (*Whynot* 1983) that a battered woman could not have a reasonable apprehension of death unless she faced imminent harm. Despite Walker's (1979: 61) own conclusion that the onset of acute battering was unpredictable, Justice Wilson cited another psychologist (Blackman 1986) who concluded that 'it may in fact be possible for a battered spouse to accurately predict the onset of violence before the first blow is struck, even if an outsider to the relationship cannot' (*Lavallee* 1990: 119). BWS was one reason why the jury must consider 'the history, circumstances and perceptions' (ibid: 125) of the accused in determining whether she had a reasonable belief that there was no other way to save herself. Justice Wilson also noted that 'women are typically no match for men in hand-to-hand combat' and that requiring a woman to wait until an assault was under way would 'be tantamount to sentencing her to "murder by instalment"' (ibid: 121).

Although she quoted Dr Shane's testimony that Lavallee had a 'victim' and a 'concentration camp mentality' that made her come back to her abusive partner 'in a magnetic sort of way' (ibid: 124),[2] Justice Wilson attempted to qualify the potentially negative image of Lavallee as helpless in a number of ways. One was to note that 'environmental factors' such as 'lack of job skills, the presence of children to care for, fear of retaliation by the man' (ibid: 123) may contribute to a woman's reluctance to leave an abusive relationship. The latter factor was particularly important, given studies which suggested that women were more likely to be killed after they separated from abusive partners (Crawford and Gartner 1992: 44). Justice Wilson also adapted the principle of no duty to retreat from one's home to the context by arguing that 'a man's home may be his castle but it is also the woman's home even if it seems to her more like a prison in the circumstances' (*Lavallee*, 1990: 124). Effectively avoiding criticisms that Walker's theory did not account for battered women who nevertheless do not act in self-defence (Downs 1966: 148, 154), Justice Wilson warned that 'the fact that the appellant was a battered woman does not entitle her to an acquittal. Battered women may well kill their partners other than in self-defence' (*Lavallee* 1990: 126). The decision did not recognize an 'abuse excuse' (Dershowitz 1994) that acquitted women simply because they had been battered.[3]

Lavallee was front-page news, and most reactions were favourable. A past director of the Women's Legal Education and Action Fund (LEAF) described it as 'a victory for women' (*Calgary Herald*, 4 May 1990), and another spokesperson said the judgment was 'exceptional and wonderful' because 'it recognizes the cycle of violence women endure and the effect of ongoing abuse' (*Globe and Mail*, 4 May 1990). Pat Marshall, who later chaired the Panel on Violence against Women, commented that 'we can be very proud of our Supreme Court ... Its recognition of this case as self-defence is a very important step along that road to equality' (*Toronto Star*, 4 May 1990). A manager of a support centre for battered women was less optimistic because 'we'll now have a "battered wife syndrome" and I don't think every woman who is battered has a psychological syndrome' (*Calgary Herald*, 4 May 1990).

The immediate praise for *Lavallee*, like that for *Butler* (1992), was premature. The Court did not back away from the case, but different judges placed less emphasis on equality and the experience of women. Four years after *Lavallee*, the Court affirmed that imminent threats were not required and prior threats were relevant, but on the due-process basis that 'it is the accused's state of mind that must be examined, and it is the accused (and not the victim) who must be given the benefit of a reasonable doubt' (*Petel* 1994: 104). Martha Shaffer (1997: 17) found only three cases in which women were acquitted of the murder or manslaughter of their abusive partner on the basis of *Lavallee*. Following the Manitoba Court of Appeal's suggestion in *Lavallee*, BWS was most frequently considered as a mitigating factor when a woman pled guilty to manslaughter in order to avoid the risk of a murder conviction and mandatory life imprisonment (ibid: 18–19). A judge appointed to examine the applicability of *Lavallee* to past cases found valid self-defence claims among only three of ninety-eight women who applied (Ratushny 1997). A representative of the Elizabeth Fry Society commented that 'no woman will leave prison as a result of the decision' (*Toronto Star*, 27 Sep.1997). Like disclosure and speedy-trial standards examined in chapter 3, *Lavallee* enabled and legitimated guilty pleas while it held out the promise of acquittals. Whether seen as a case about due process, equality, or victims' rights, *Lavallee* did not disrupt the crime-control assembly line for women who killed their abusers.

Alternative Approaches

Given the limits of *Lavallee*, are there other more promising strategies? One alternative was articulated by the Task Force on Federally Sentenced Women, which took a more holistic approach to women who committed crimes. Although not ignoring the abuse the women suffered, the task force did not rely on BWS or images of passive and helpless victims.[4] It emphasized the need for prevention of 'violence which breeds violence' and called for 'community-based restorative justice options, and an alternative Aboriginal justice system' (Canada 1990: 1–2, 52). It listened to the federally sentenced women when they 'expressed needs for respect, for support and for the chance to take responsibility for their lives …' (ibid: 63). The women ultimately had responsibility for their own rehabilitation and should be given the opportunity to make their own choices. These opportunities included counselling, education, skill development, and alcohol and drug addiction programs. Gender issues were not decontextualized or criminalized into issues about whether or not the criminal sanction should be applied. Consistent with Braithwaite's (1989) theories, the task force also stressed the need for offenders to be reintegrated with their families and communities. As will be discussed in chapter 8, the healing approach that the task force advocated was influenced by Aboriginal justice. Given the limitations of *Lavallee*, a feminist and culturally sensitive approach to corrections is also needed.

Wife Assault: Crime Control or Victims' Rights?

Packer wrote before the risk and distribution of crime were measured through victimization studies. Ignoring the incidence of crime not reported to the police, he assumed that greater efficiency in processing reported crimes would control crime. Hence, the inaccurate but rhetorically powerful name of the crime-control model. By establishing that the police were dealing only with the tip of the iceberg, victimization studies could have challenged the logic of crime control and indicated the limited relevance of the criminal justice system. As will be seen, however, this did not occur, and the high incidence of unreported crime was most often constructed as a reason for criminal justice reform.

The most influential victimization study in the wife-assault context was a 1980 report that concluded that one in ten Canadian women who were married or in a relationship with a live-in lover were battered by their partners (MacLeod 1980: 21).[5] Despite the author's own warning that 'no definitive statement about the incidence of wife abuse can be made' (ibid: 16), one in ten became 'a magical figure' (Rock 1986: 275; Hilton 1989: 327) which inspired criminal justice reform. The statistic that one in ten Canadian women had been assaulted by their partners did not require any particular policy response. It could be evidence of the deep patriarchal roots of male violence in Canadian society, the limited relevance of the criminal law, and the immediate need for more shelters and educational and economic reforms. Nevertheless, it was interpreted as justifying a new response by police and prosecutors that was based on 'a clear, publicly advertised policy applying the same standards of non/arrest to family violence as to assault outside the family' (MacLeod 1980: 64).[6]

In 1982, a parliamentary committee on family violence stressed the need to focus on the act of violence, with 'no exception for people who are married or intimately related' (Canada 1982c: 13). It argued that 'cases of wife beating should regularly be processed through the criminal justice system' without the victim's consent, even while recognizing that such processing would not ensure the accused's rehabilitation or 'make up for the pain that the victim has suffered' (ibid: 16). Like the 1985 prostitution law, the committee's report was originally greeted with laughter in the House of Commons (Hansard, 12 May 1982: 17334), but Parliament eventually got serious and unanimously approved a resolution encouraging 'all Canadian police forces to establish a practice of having the police regularly lay charges in instances of wife beating, as they are inclined to do with any other case of common assault' (Hansard, 8 Jul. 1982: 19119–20). Parliament looked to police forces to implement its strategies to reduce wife assault, and the next year amended the Criminal Code to allow the police to make arrests when they did not witness the assault. As mandatory[7] arrest policies sought to protect victims, they also controlled them. In this sense, victims' rights were for crime control.

The crime-control orientation of mandatory arrest policies was reflected in the first major and still oft-quoted study on their implementation by the London, Ontario, police. The primary measurement of success was that sixty-eight assault charges were laid by the police in the first four months of the policy, compared with six in the six months before the policy, that the new charges were more likely to result in jail or a fine and that the number of victim initiated charges had declined (Burris and

Jaffe 1983: 311–13). The next year, an American study suggested that
arrest was more effective than separation and counselling in preventing
future assaults over a six-month period (Sherman and Berk 1984). It
quickly became a policy classic even though its findings were not replicated in many subsequent studies. The lead researcher tried to dissociate
himself from the mandatory-arrest policies, but his original findings had
a life of their own and were constructed for crime-control ends (Sherman
et al 1992; Lerman 1992).

Mandatory arrest and charge policies relied on victimization studies
documenting the risk of male violence. A B.C. policy was prefaced with
the statement that 'an average of two women every week were killed by
their partners. Researchers and professionals working with assaulted
women estimate that each year one in eight women, living in a relationship with a man, will be assaulted. In addition, research indicates that as
many as 35 violent episodes may have occurred before a woman seeks
police intervention' (Valverde, MacLeod, and Johnston 1995: 324). An
Ontario policy deployed slightly different statistics to similar effect (ibid:
351). Crime control in a risk society (Beck 1992) became a matter of
attempting to respond to risks that were easier to calculate than to control. Although figures like 'one in ten' could suggest the limits of crime
control, they were employed to justify more crime-control activities. Zoe
Hilton (1989: 327) has argued that '"one in ten women" became the focal
point of the wife abuse issue when the Canadian Government took own-
ership of it. Attention was directed to official facts and figures, not the
underlying system which supports abuse: patriarchy.' Victimization studies invited 'zero tolerance' criminal justice policies because theoretically
the risk could be reduced to zero. This set the stage for continued criminal justice reforms every time a new victimization study revealed that risk
had not been reduced.

Mandatory-arrest policies stressed formal equality and the understanding of wife assault as violence. 'Hence the descriptive assertion – wife
assault is like other assaults – and the normative demand – charge and
prosecute men who assault their wives' (Martin and Mosher 1995: 15). As
will be seen, a similar focus on the violence of sexual assault motivated
the 1983 sexual-assault reforms. Gillian Walker (1990: 107) has suggested
that this approach dissolved 'the gender and relational aspects' of the
assault and allowed 'the most seemingly radical aspects of feminist mobili-
zation [to be tied] into a conservative law and order framework of social
control.' It facilitated the criminalization of gender politics. For example,
the minister responsible for the status of women refused to promise any

money to implement the Panel on Violence against Women's expensive and comprehensive recommendations for workplace, education, and health care reforms, but quickly endorsed the crime-control aspects of the report by saying that her government would adopt zero tolerance of violence against women (*Globe and Mail*, 30 Jul. 1993).

There were also echoes in mandatory arrest and charge policies of the controversial idea that battered women were subject to learned helplessness (Walker 1979; *Lavallee* 1990). British Columbia's policy balanced 'the demands of the criminal justice system with the best interests of the victim' (Valverde, MacLeod, and Johnston 1995: 324). The reference to the best interests, as opposed to the wishes, needs, or even rights of the victim equates battered women with children. Although sometimes unavoidable, the frequent grouping of women and children in official discourse promoted images of passive and helpless victims. Even when the best interests of the woman (whoever defined them) were ascertained, the B.C. policy required them to be balanced against the demands of the criminal justice system. This was the language of bureaucratic power and crime control; not the empowerment of victims. The Ontario policy also called for prosecution regardless of the victim's wishes. Prosecutors were advised to discuss 'the public wrong aspect of domestic violence' with victims (ibid: 354) and to give victims 'statistical information' that 'the majority of battered women who have gone to court report a reduction or termination of violence after court' and that 'sons of batterers are one thousand percent more likely to beat their wives' (ibid: 353). Victimization studies were used to inform battered women about what was in their best interests and the best interests of their children. The intended result was a victim who cooperated in the prosecution.

The policies as written had ideological significance, but did not represent actual practice. The Winnipeg Family Violence Court relied on probation, with prosecutors still dismissing more than 30 per cent of the cases (Canadian Centre for Criminal Justice Statistics 1994c: 7). An award-winning survey of 128 wife-assault cases in 1995–6 by the *Toronto Star* (3 Nov. 1996) concluded that, while a significant percentage of convicted wife-assaulters received a jail sentence, more received 'a slap on the wrist' in the form of a suspended sentence, or a conditional or absolute discharge. The real scandal, however, was that 37 per cent of the cases ended when the victim either recanted or did not appear for trial. The victims' decisions were not given presumptive respect, but were seen as a sign of their intimidation and the need for police and prosecutors to follow the practice of other jurisdictions 'winning the fight against this crime' by relying on independent evidence. In the wake of the stories, new family-violence courts, one which relied on evidence independent of the victim, were established. Crime control could be perfected by removing the victim from the process.

The power of victims under mandatory-arrest policies was largely the power of defiance of official authority and pleading at sentencing (McGillivray 1987). Even this limited power was reduced. The Alberta Court of Appeal resisted women's pleas that their partners not be imprisoned by relating them, not to forgiveness or a pragmatic concern for financial survival, but to BWS resulting in the 'loss of self-esteem' and 'a sense of powerlessness and inability to control events' (*Brown* 1992: 353). The Court cited *Lavallee* as justification for the 'imprisonment of the man as not only an instrument of the deterrence of other men, but also as an instrument of breaking the cycle of violence in that man's family even at the risk of the relationship coming to an end during the enforced separation' (ibid: 355). The assault victim was marginalized and pathologized by initiatives taken in her name. Victims' rights were for crime control.

Alternative Approaches

A less punitive approach to wife assault would challenge the crime-control 'idea that charging, prosecuting and sentencing comprise the entire realm of significant or meaningful actions' (Martin and Mosher 1995: 43). 'Approaches to stopping the violence may include help with child care, education or training, financial or housing assistance, getting in touch with spiritual or cultural roots, rekindling or creating support networks' (MacLeod 1995: 202). Police intervention would play a role, but victims would be given options other than criminal prosecutions. For example, Saskatchewan provided for civil remedies such as emergency-intervention orders to remove the abuser, and victim-assistance orders, including monetary compensation (The Victims of Domestic Violence Act: SS.1994 c.V-6.02). Civil remedies to facilitate separation and ending the relationship may also be appropriate. Family conferences bringing together the victim, the offender, and their families might also play a role in some cases. They could be 'victim-centred' and allow the victim to 'confront the offender in her own words in her own way with all the hurt she has suffered' (Braithwaite and Daly 1995: 222). Unlike in mandatory-arrest policies, the victim would have a veto over any plan of action (ibid: 223). Family relations and abuse of trust and authority would not be a factor to increase punishment,[8] but a resource to shame offenders and to assist in their rehabilitation and reintegration.

Many women's groups opposed the use of family conferences or restorative justice in cases of domestic violence. They were concerned that victims could be blamed for the violence and be coerced into agreements because of imbalances of power (Stubbs 1995: 280–3). Reintegration may frequently not be an appropriate goal. Nevertheless, there was a danger that family conferences were dismissed simply because they were not punitive. Both civil remedies and family conferences departed from mandatory arrest and prosecution policies by taking power away from police, prosecutors, and judges, and by attempting to give battered women some choices. They will not work in all cases, but they did not squeeze pressing concerns about the prevalence of violence against women into the old boxes of due process and crime control.

Victims' Rights: The 1983 Sexual-Assault Law

As was the case with wife assault, victimization studies and studies documenting the sexist treatment of female victims laid the foundation for the 1983 reforms. A victimization study based on interviews with 551 women in Winnipeg in the late 1970s found that 6 per cent had been raped and 27.2 per cent had been sexually assaulted, with only 12 per cent of the former and 7 per cent of the latter reporting the crime to the police (Gunn and Minch 1988: 13). This research was used by the Canadian Advisory Council of Women in a 1981 pamphlet which concluded that '1 in every 17 Canadian women is raped at some point in her life; 1 in every 5 women is sexually assaulted ... a woman is raped every 29 minutes in Canada – a woman is sexually assaulted every 6 minutes' (quoted in Canada 1984b: 143). Like MacLeod's 'one in ten' figure for wife assault, these statistics effectively combined research and advocacy and were constructed to create a demand for criminal justice reform.

Another influential study documented low rates of police founding and convictions in rape cases. Clark and Lewis (1977) explained their findings as a product of sexism in which women were protected by rape laws only because of male interest in their sexuality. A man owned the sexuality of his wife, but not that of the chaste wives or daughters of other men. This explained why a man could not legally rape his wife (ibid: 161) and why an accused could ask questions about whether the victim had sex with other men (ibid: 156). These two aspects of rape law figured prominently in the 1983 reforms, as did recommendations that rape be reconceived as an assault which invaded any person's physical integrity and autonomy (ibid: 166). Like wife assault, sexual assault was deliberately defined as a product of violence, not coercive sexuality (Smart 1989: 45, 33). Clark and Lewis (1977: 198) were not unaware of the need for interventions other than criminal-law reform and stressed the importance of rape crisis centres and 'a complete re-education of all members of society.' Their greatest impact, however, was in charting the course for rape-law reform.

Rape as Assault

The 1983 reforms replaced the offences of rape and indecent assault with three categories of sexual assault patterned on the assault provisions of the Criminal Code. Following Clark and Lewis, the analogy with assault was designed to 'recognize the element of violence' and invasion of 'the integrity of the person' in sexual offences (Hansard, 7 Jul. 1981: 11300; 4 Aug. 1981: 20041). Aggravated sexual assault and sexual assault causing bodily harm would apply to the more serious forms of sexual assault such as rape.[9] Women's groups concluded that including psychological damage as an aggravated form of sexual assault would 'be more of a problem than a benefit' (quoted in Los 1994: 34). As discussed in chapter 4, psychological harm was recognized and given constitutional status first in *Morgentaler* as a rationale for not using the criminal sanction, and later in *Keegstra* as a reason for the criminal sanction.

Although the new offences expanded the range of prohibited conduct, they did not make the criminal sanction more punitive. The new sexual-assault offence could be prosecuted as a summary-conviction offence with a maximum of six months' imprisonment.[10] Law-and-order Conservatives thundered that the new law was 'a fraud perpetrated upon the female population of the country ... We have equated what we knew to be rape with a serious speeding ticket' (Hansard, 4 Aug. 1982: 20042). Prosecutors unsuccessfully lobbied to retain special penalties for rape (Snider 1985: 343), and some feminists argued that 'lowered penalties speak loud and clear to society that the crime is no longer as serious as it once was'(Cohen and Backhouse 1980: 103). The government, supported by women's groups such as the National Action Committee (NAC) and the National Association of Women and Law (NAWL), persisted in the hope that a less punitive approach would result in better protection of the physical integrity of victims. The number of cases prosecuted under the new law increased dramatically, but they were punished much more leniently than under the old rape law.[11] In their attempts to obtain better protection of the physical integrity of women, most feminist groups were prepared to move to an assault model, even though it reduced punishment. This was an important example of a victims'-rights initiative that was more concerned with increasing protection for victims than with increasing punishment for offenders.

In keeping with the spirit of much early feminist law reform, including the wife-assault policies, the 1983 reforms emphasized gender neutrality. Women could be prosecuted for sexual assault, and the crime no longer required penetration. Even though the equality rights of the Charter would not be proclaimed in force for another three years, Minister of Justice Jean Chrétien emphasized that 'an effort has been made throughout the bill to de-gender the Criminal Code provisions relating to sexual offences in keeping with the equality rights guaranteed by the Charter of Rights' (Hansard, 4 Aug. 1982: 20039). Flora MacDonald hoped that repealing rape laws would diminish the stigma of rape and encourage women 'to report sexual assaults against them without the additional fear of being branded as immoral by society' (ibid: 20042). This echoed Lorenne Clark's argument that 'the whole idea of rape is historically associated with a woman being damaged goods or a commodity no longer ... valued' (Canada, JLAC 6 Jan. 1982, 91: 12–13). The vision of equality expressed by these women engaged substantive values as opposed to the minister's understanding of equality as the same treatment of men and women.

The 1983 reforms also featured important changes in the law of evidence. Judges were prohibited from warning juries about the dangers of uncorroborated testimony. Some defence lawyers criticized this reform as based on 'the feminist belief that just because a woman complains of rape, she should be believed,' but others recognized that corroboration was not required for most other crimes (*Vancouver Sun*, 13 Jan. 1983). The new legislation also repealed the doctrine that the victim's failure to raise a 'hue and cry' would be held against her because 'her silence may naturally be taken as a virtual self-contradiction of her story' (*Kribs* 1960: 405). As will be seen in the next chapter, courts would became more sensitive about the reasons for delays in reporting and would allow sexual-assault prosecutions concerning events decades ago. Both the corroboration and recent-complaint doctrines were based on distrust of women, and the evidentiary changes challenged the sexism of what had once been seen as neutral and natural.

The new law also contained so-called rape-shield provisions which restricted the ability of the accused to introduce evidence of the victim's past sexual conduct. Evidence of the victim's sexual reputation became inadmissible. The victim's sexual history with people other than the accused was also inadmissible unless required to rebut the prosecution's evidence concerning past sexual conduct, to prove the identity of the perpetrator, or to establish sexual activity with others on the same occasion. This was a strong 'rape shield' law (Spohn and Horney 1992) and a response to a Supreme Court decision which had interpreted an earlier reform designed to protect the victim from being asked questions about her sexual history at trial as actually making her a compellable witness at a closed preliminary hearing (*Forsythe* 1980). This decision had been criticized by Justice Wilson for exposing victims to more 'embarrassment' than even the old common law (*Konkin* 1982: 295; Boyle 1981; Shilton and Derrick 1991). It was reversed by a provision that the victim would not be compellable at a preliminary closed hearing to determine if her sexual history fell into the categories that were admissible under the new law. This reply to *Forsythe* foreshadowed the dialogues between the Supreme Court and Parliament that would become louder under the Charter.

The 'rape shield' in the 1983 law was much less than feminists wanted. NAC unsuccessfully argued in committee that 'the accused's knowledge of the past sexual history of the complainant is irrelevant ... Any person who can be sexually assaulted must be able to rely on the protection of the law regardless of their past sexual history' (Canada, JLAC, 6 Jan. 1982, 91A:9). This argument was taken up without success by the New Democrats.[12] Feminists would later vigorously defend the 'rape shield' provision against Charter challenges and lobby for its legislative reinstatement, but at the time it seemed to be more of a defeat than a victory (*Winnipeg Free Press*, 5 Jan. 1983).

The relevance of the victim's sexual history was connected with the controversial *Pappajohn* (1980) defence which allowed a man to be acquitted of rape on the basis that he honestly, but unreasonably and mistakenly, believed the woman had consented. The 1983 reforms required judges to instruct juries to consider the reasonableness of the man's mistaken belief. Svend Robinson of the NDP would have gone farther and proposed that there must be reasonable grounds for a mistaken belief. He argued that it is 'not good enough for him to rely upon perverse or irrational grounds; for him to say, for example, that because her husband told him that she was really enjoying it, even though she was crying and saying no, that he should be acquitted.' Although supported 'by every national women's organization, the chiefs of police and over 22,000 men and women who signed petitions urging that we accept the principle that no means no,' his amendment was easily defeated (Hansard, 4 Aug. 1982: 20046). A decade later, Parliament required the accused to take reasonable steps to discover if the victim consented, and expanded the rape-shield provision to apply to prior sexual conduct with the accused, but only after the Supreme Court struck down the 1983 'rape shield' as a violation of the accused's Charter rights (*Seaboyer* 1991).

Due Process versus Victims' Rights: The New Political Cases

The rest of this chapter will examine a series of political cases pitting the accused's due-process claims against the security and equality rights of women as victims and potential victims of sexual assault. In the media and sometimes the Court, the cases were presented as divisive clashes between defence lawyers and feminists. Women's groups had less success in defending sexual-assault laws and prosecutions from due-process challenges than more controversial crimes such as pornography examined in chapter 4. These due-process victories meant that women's groups, not just the police, became strong critics of the Supreme Court. The parliamentary replies embraced the logic of dissents in the Supreme Court and increasingly reflected gender politics that were criminalized and legalized.

Seaboyer

Although fundamental to attempts to increase reporting and counter the sexist image of the 'unrapeable' sexually active woman (Clark and Lewis 1977), the 'rape shield' was vulnerable to Charter challenge because it categorically excluded evidence that the accused might want to introduce, especially in relation to the controversial defence that he honestly, but unreasonably, had a mistaken belief that the victim consented. An early article entitled 'Sparing the Complainant "Spoils" the Trial' (Doherty 1984) foreshadowed the confrontation between due process and victims' rights.

In 1991, the Supreme Court decided 7–2 that the evidentiary restrictions were an unjustified restriction on the accused's right to full answer and defence. Justice McLachlin started from the due-process 'precept that the innocent must not be convicted ... One has only to think of the public revulsion at the improper conviction of Donald Marshall in this country or the Birmingham Six in the United Kingdom to appreciate how deeply held is this tenet of justice' (*Seaboyer* 1991: 387). Unlike in *Canadian Newspapers Co. Ltd.* (1989), where an unanimous Court had followed LEAF's (1996:

39–41) arguments that a publication ban on victims' names was necessary to increase the reporting of sexual assaults, the Court in *Seaboyer* was not prepared to restrict the accused's defence (ibid: 396). It was one thing to restrict media claims of freedom of expression in order to increase reporting, but quite another to restrict the accused's right to call evidence. A possibly innocent accused should not be sacrificed for the social goal of increased reporting and deterrence of sexual violence.

Alluding to LEAF's (1996: 182) arguments, Justice McLachlin noted 'it has been suggested that s.7 should be viewed as concerned with the interest of complainants as a class to security of the person and to equal benefit of the law as guaranteed by ss.15 and 28 of the Charter' (*Seaboyer* 1991: 385). Even if this were so, it would not matter because a violation of the accused's 'right to present a full and fair defence would violate s.7 in any event' (ibid: 385). In a clash of rights, the accused's prevailed over the victim's.[13] As in her dissents in *Rodriguez* and *Keegstra* (see chapter 4), Justice McLachlin gravitated towards the classically liberal due-process position that an accused's liberty should not be sacrificed for social interests. In her two-page analysis concluding the legislation could not be justified under section 1 of the Charter, she argued that Parliament had struck 'the wrong balance between the rights of complainants and the rights of the accused' because it had transgressed the traditional rule of excluding defence evidence 'whose value is not clearly outweighed by the danger it presents' (ibid: 403). The judgment recognized the rights of women as victims and potential victims of sexual assault, but quickly reverted to the traditional primacy of the rights of the accused.

Although the Court struck out Parliament's evidentiary restrictions, it devised new common-law guidelines in an attempt to find 'a middle way that offers the maximum protection to the complainant compatible with the maintenance of the accused's fundamental right to a fair trial' (ibid: 381). As discussed in chapter 3, such pragmatic compromises were often unappreciated after each side in the new political case had been encouraged to demand their rights. These guidelines attempted to regulate sexist forms of reasoning about the victim's past sexual conduct but were quickly rejected in the media and in Parliament. Parliament did, however, follow the Court's guidelines by extending its new restrictions to the victim's prior sexual conduct with the accused. As in the wife-assault reforms discussed above, courts were encouraged to determine whether an assault had occurred without reference to the accused's and the victim's relationship.

In her dissent, Justice L'Heureux-Dubé did not start from individualistic, liberal premises about the primacy of the accused's due-process rights. Rather, she combined a feminist concern about women as victims of sexual assault and rape myths with more traditional crime-control concerns about discovering the truth about crime and encouraging the reporting of crime to the police. Citing the expanded understanding of security of the person that had played a role in *Morgentaler* and *Keegstra* (see chapter 4), she noted 'that many, if not most women live in fear of victimization' (ibid: 340). She refused to focus on 'the narrow interests of the accused' (ibid: 370) and following the recognition of a social interest in speedy trials in *Askov* (1990), argued that the legal rights of the Charter included the interest of the 'complainant, and indeed the community at large ... in the reporting and prosecution of sexual offences' (ibid: 370). Unless the 'accused has the right to a biased verdict' (ibid: 372), his rights were not at stake. She confidently declared that 'the conclusions reached in these reasons are absolutely un-contentious' (ibid: 379). Everyone should accept that any evidence excluded under the law was 'prejudicial and irrelevant' (ibid: 368). Justice L'Heureux-Dubé hoped that the issue would not become 'a battle between feminists and defence lawyers' (ibid: 368, quoting Boyle 1981: 265), but it became just that because both opinions trivialized or ignored the arguments of the other side.

The two judges displayed different approaches to legal analysis and rhetorical styles. Justice McLachlin was the traditionalist who argued that the legislation infringed a rule of evidence 'familiar to all those who practise in our criminal courts' (ibid: 391). Like the former law professor she was, McLachlin J. tested the law in a Socratic fashion, with hypotheticals of evidence that could be excluded under its provisions. She assumed that juries would follow instructions not to infer that a woman was less believable or more likely to consent because of her past sexual conduct. In contrast, Justice L'Heureux-Dubé was the critical upstart who argued that Parliament had a ' marked, and justifiably so, distrust of the ability of the courts to promote and achieve a non-discriminatory application of the law in this area' (ibid: 376). She fought the hypotheticals (Gilligan 1982) by complaining that many of them were 'pure fantasy and have absolutely no grounding in life or experience' (*Seaboyer* 1991: 359). They were a sexist exercise of the 'pornographic imagination' (Sheehy 1989: 755–7; Acorn 1991) because they depended 'to some degree, upon the acceptance of stereotypes about women and sexual assault and the will to propagate them' (*Seaboyer* 1991: 359). L'Heureux-Dubé J. debunked the traditional faith that juries followed instructions by citing social-science surveys indicating that mock jurors were less likely to convict when they knew about the victim's sexual history (ibid: 342–4). *Seaboyer* captured the energies and imaginations of legal elites in part because it played out struggles and tensions within the legal academy about the nature of scholarship and the limits of legitimate inquiry.

Risk played a role in both judgments. Justice McLachlin invoked the 'real risk that an innocent person may be convicted. The price is too great in relation to the benefit secured, and cannot be tolerated in a society that does not countenance in any form the conviction of the innocent' (ibid: 402). In contrast, Justice L'Heureux-Dubé examined victimization studies which suggested that 'at least one woman in five will be sexually assaulted during her lifetime' (ibid: 334) and that 'many, if not most women live in fear of victimization' (ibid: 340). The majority's risk was due process's traditional concern about convicting the innocent; the minority's risk was the well-documented risk of sexual assault.

The two opinions also differed in their approaches to the *Pappajohn* (1980) defence. Justice McLachlin concluded that the law prevented valid *Pappajohn* defences because 'the basis of the accused's honest belief in the complainant's consent may be sexual acts performed by the complainant at some other time or place' (ibid: 393). Such evidence, for Justice L'Heureux-Dubé, could not be relevant if the judge and jury were 'operating in an intellectual environment that is free of rape myth and stereotype about women' (ibid: 363). For feminists, it was 'the confluence of *Pappajohn* and *Seaboyer* that was so dangerous' (Shaffer 1992: 210). The parliamentary reply would allow the controversial defence to be revisited and, following the tradition of the 1983 reforms, would address both evidentiary rules and the offence of sexual assault.

Media Reaction

Unlike many early due-process decisions that restricted police powers, *Seaboyer* was front-page news. The vice-president of NAC warned that 'now the rights of the woman will be violated and courtrooms can again be used to put the victim on trial' (*Montreal Gazette*, 23 Aug. 1991). A spokesperson for NAWL called the decision 'a devastating blow to women and children who are victims' (*Halifax Chronicle Herald*, 23 Aug. 1991). Lee Lakeman of the Canadian Association of Sexual Assault Centres stated that the decision 'is a slap in the face to those women who defy the odds' by going to court (*Globe and Mail*, 24 Aug. 1991). These comments, which relied on images of violation and violence, as well as headlines that the 'rape shield' had been struck down, made it seem as though the

Supreme Court was literally assaulting women. This assumed that the presence of the technical evidentiary restrictions protected women. Judy Rebick predicted that the decision 'will have a chilling effect on women charging men with rape' (*Toronto Star*, 24 Aug. 1991) and there were several stories written by women who explained that they would no longer report being sexual assaulted because they did not want to be condemned for their past sexual history (*Halifax Chronicle Herald*, 26 Aug. 1991; *Vancouver Sun*, 26 Aug. 1991). One rape victim wrote that her 'hollow feeling, that sense of irretrievable loss, returned' when she heard about the decision. She stressed the dangers of secondary victimization by the court process: 'Having one man brutalize me in such an intimate, personal way killed a part of me. Having the same thing done again in public by the very system that is supposed to bring me justice could have very well destroyed me' (*Montreal Gazette*, 10 Sept. 1991).

Others focused on the symbolic significance of the decision. Pat Marshall, who a year before had lauded the Court for *Lavallee* (1990), declared it 'a sad day for women in Canada' (*Montreal Gazette*, 23 Aug. 1991). As was the case with the *Zundel* decision that followed *Keegstra*, the Court was not proving to be a reliable ally for the 'Court Party.' Judy Rebick argued that the 'symbolic meaning is that the rights of a rapist are more important than the rights of a rape victim' (*Toronto Star*, 24 Aug.1991). A legislative reply was necessary not only to assure sexual-assault victims that it was safe to report the crimes, but also to obtain symbolic recognition of the rights of women that had been slighted by the Court. The new political case pitted feminists against defence lawyers in a symbolic confrontation over whether the rights of women or the accused were more important.

Legislative Reaction

The result in *Seaboyer* had been anticipated by a parliamentary subcommittee on the status of women. In order to protect women from 'brutal interrogation about their sexual history and reputation,' it recommended that Parliament re-enact the 'rape shield' law, using its controversial power to pass new legislation notwithstanding the legal rights of the Charter (Canada 1991: 43–4). The chair of the committee repeated the call for the section 33 override shortly after the Court's decision (*Winnipeg Free Press*, 30 Aug. 1991). An override to restore the old law might seem drastic, but it would have been more partial than the eventual result.

Minister of Justice Kim Campbell was prepared to respond quickly to

Seaboyer, but was counselled by a coalition of women's groups and sexual assault centres to consult widely. The result was an innovative grass-roots consultation that was praised as a model for future law reform (McIntyre 1994) and denounced as a 'victory for interest group politics' (Martin 1993). The consultation helped expand the legislative reply from a reintroduction of a modified 'rape shield' to include a preamble, 'no-means-no' provisions defining consent, and the modification of the *Pappajohn* defence. It can be contrasted with the criminalization of stalking a year later when Minister of Justice Pierre Blais acted without consultation with women's groups and ignored their demands for a preamble and a more comprehensive approach (Cairns-Way 1994). The dominant image in the stalking debate was of passive, fearful female victims and their children (Hansard, 6 May 1993: 19015) as opposed to the more assertive 'No Means No' campaign that accompanied the *Seaboyer* legislation. Victims' rights legislation without input from victims and their supporters tended to produce top-down crime-control measures that could exploit the suffering and fear of victims. Grass-roots involvement provided partial resistance to the legalization and criminalization of politics.

Bill C-49 was presented by Campbell as legislation 'that will restore the confidence of victims of sexual assault in the criminal justice system and … articulate for all Canadians the delicate balance between the rights of victims and the rights of accused persons' (Hansard, 8 Apr. 1992: 9504–5). The rights of victims[14] and the accused were front and centre as the new political case moved to Parliament, whereas they were rarely mentioned in debates about the 1983 reforms. Campbell argued that the new 'rape shield' provisions were 'essential in order to protect victims from embarrassment, to preserve their privacy and dignity and to encourage their co-operation in prosecutions' (ibid: 9507). Even as the new provision protected victims, it sought their 'cooperation' in efficient crime control. In a manner similar to the proclamation and qualification of due-process rights (McBarnet 1981), the preamble declared that sexual history would be 'rarely relevant,' while the enabling legislation contained a far more complex and open-ended formula. Mirroring media accounts that portrayed the striking down of the 'rape shield' as violence, Campbell suggested that the new law protected victims' safety and security, at least from the secondary victimization of the trial process. 'I could not put victims of sexual assault at risk of an uncertain application of the law. As I have often said, individual women and men who have suffered victimization must never be put in a situation where they are victimized again' (Hansard, 8 Apr. 1992: 9508).

The bill received all-party approval. The Liberal critic equated it with 'fundamental justice for women who are placed in a very vulnerable position in our society' and the recently decided *Butler* (1992) decision which had related pornography 'to violence against women and violence against children' (Hansard, 8 Apr. 1992: 9509–10). Ian Waddell of the NDP praised the 'strong law' for its contribution to equality for women, and as part of a 'movement toward having some of the old Canadian values back when Canada was a peaceful country' (ibid: 9527). Statistics that a sexual assault occurred every seventeen minutes, with only 1 in 100 perpetrators being charged, were frequently cited in the debates (ibid: 9513, 9524, 9534, 9536). Fear also played a role, with Dawn Black of the NDP hoping that more men would become 'afraid for their daughters, their sisters, their partners, their mothers and their friends' (ibid: 9514). Marlene Catterall hoped that the bill would 'overcome the automatic powerlessness that women feel' (ibid: 9531), and Mary Collins argued that the bill 'will empower women to take control, in many ways of their lives. It will have a very beneficial effect on men too' (ibid: 9519). Lynn Hunter of the NDP spoke of educational efforts to get across the message of 'No Means No' (ibid: 9532–5). They did not speak in one voice, but women dominated the debates in the Court, the media, and Parliament about the 'rape shield.'

In committee and the media, there was the battle between feminists and defence lawyers that Justice L'Heureux-Dubé had hoped to avoid. Brian Greenspan, of the Criminal Lawyers Association of Ontario, stated that he hoped that the bill 'never gets out of committee,' while Judy Rebick of NAC warned: 'we are going to have a fight ... because women always have to fight for anything' (*Globe and Mail*, 13 Dec. 1991). Marlys Edwardh, of the Criminal Lawyers Association, warned of the 'the risk of putting people in jail to educate them ... we need ... other areas of education – judicial education, education of male children' (Canada, JLAC, 14 May 1992, 1: 42–3). Sheila McIntyre of LEAF 'fundamentally disagreed' and invoked 'the successful campaign against drinking and driving as our model' (ibid, 2: 8; see also 2: 23, 26, and 1A: 4). The politicians supported the educational effects of the law, with Mary Clancy arguing that 'all of us who support this bill say not only can you legislate attitudes, but you must' (Hansard, 15 Jun. 1992: 12039). The preamble was defended for its educative role, but the minister of justice refused to include it in the actual text of the law. She wrongly predicted that it would be included in commercial criminal codes used by judges, lawyers, and the public (ibid, 6 Jun. 1992, 6: 62). All participants in the debates assumed that not only criminal justice officials, but the public would become aware of the new law.

The preamble stated that Parliament enacted the law 'to promote and help to ensure the full protection of the rights guaranteed under sections 7 and 15 of the *Canadian Charter of Rights and Freedoms*.' In one breath, Parliament invoked the security and equality rights of women and children, and the due-process rights of the accused. By recognizing 'the prevalence of sexual assault against women and children,' Parliament departed from the gender neutrality of earlier reforms and followed the feminist approach of Justice L'Heureux-Dubé's dissent. LEAF's proposals to recognize the specific position of 'Aboriginal women, Black women and women of colour, elderly women, immigrant women, Jewish women, lesbians, poor women, refugee women, sex trade workers, women without full citizenship, women who have a disability' (Canada, JLAC, 14 May 1992, 2A :21–2) were rejected. Kim Campbell argued that 'the power of this legislation is that it speaks to all women' and was concerned about leaving a group out of the list (ibid, 6 Jun. 1992, 6: 44). The NDP and the Liberals, however, supported the listing of 'doubly disadvantaged' women and complained that the bill 'is still a bill for white, middle-class – this time – women' (Hansard, 15 Jun. 1992: 12035, 12041). The preamble, like section 15 of the Charter, had become a site for the politics of recognition (Cairns 1985; Taylor 1992), but some politicians feared the dangers of underinclusion.

The bill modified the *Pappajohn* defence by requiring the accused to take reasonable steps in the circumstances known to him to find out if the victim consented. Defence lawyers did not object because 'judges and juries impose their own inherent objective standards when making such considerations' (Canada, JLAC, 21 Jun. 1992, 5: 12–13).[15] Despite its being a symbol of everything that was wrong and male about the criminal law, defence lawyers let the *Pappajohn* defence go without a fight. This suggested that it was more of a symbol than a practical reality. The least abstract part of the bill was its definition of when consent could not be legally obtained. 'No Means no' was clearly defined so that a woman could express, by words or conduct, a lack of agreement to engage or continue to engage in the activity. She would also not consent if incapable of consenting or if induced by an abuse of a position of trust, power, or authority. This provision was evidence that legislatures could at times 'provide a respite from the abstraction and detachment of the courts' (Fudge 1989: 458; Hughes 1993). The rest of the legislation depended on specific adjudicative facts and the case-by-case balancing of the accused's and the victim's competing rights. The new definitions of consent stood out because they provided definitive and educative statements which recognized the physical and moral autonomy of women as potential victims of sexual assault.

Summary

The prompt legislative response to *Seaboyer* belied Professor Judy Fudge's (1989: 455) fears that 'feminists may no longer be able to call upon the legislature to constrain the courts, whilst the legislature may be able to rely upon the courts to absolve itself of political responsibility' (see also Sheehy 1991; Dauvergne 1994). Even though Parliament responded to *Seaboyer* in a more comprehensive fashion than it would subsequent due-process victories, the result reflected the criminalization and legalization of gender politics. The politicians responded to *Seaboyer* by focusing on the most punitive and least expensive of the subcommittee on the status of women's proposals to reduce violence against women.[16] At the same time, the 'No Means No' provisions demonstrated a modest ability to escape the defensive and legalistic nature of subsequent legislative replies to due-process decisions.

Many of the fears and hopes that accompanied *Seaboyer* and Bill C-49 were exaggerated. Despite predictions that *Seaboyer* would chill the reporting of sexual assault, 'time series analysis of the number of reports of sexual assault following the Supreme Court decision reveals that the incidence of reports was unaffected' (Roberts 1994: 419). Despite its widespread publicity, the passage of Bill C-49 also did not increase reporting (ibid: 420). It is, however, premature to dismiss the educative potential of the 'No Means No' provisions (Dauvergne 1994: 298; Spohn and Horney 1992). *Seaboyer* and Bill C-49 were turning points in the changing law and politics of criminal justice. Although *Keegstra* (1990) and *Butler* (1992) recognized that the accused's rights would have to be balanced with the equality and security rights of victims and potential victims, Bill C-49 was the first recognition of this phenomena at the legislative level. It indicated that parliamentary replies to due-process decisions affecting women would be more high-profile and controversial than those affecting the police.

Daviault

Henri Daviault was a seventy-two-year-old chronic alcoholic who testified that he had consumed seven or eight bottles of beer before arriving at the home of his wife's friend, a sixty-five-year-old woman confined to a wheel-chair because of partial paralysis. They each had some brandy, after which the victim fell asleep in her wheelchair. Daviault then apparently consumed the entire bottle of brandy, producing an estimated blood alcohol level between 400 and 600 milligrams per 100 millilitres. Such a level, at least five times the prohibited level for drunk driving, would have produced a coma or death in a non-alcoholic. It did not have that result on Daviault. When the victim awoke in the early hours of the morning, he blocked her attempts to go to the bathroom, threw her from her wheel-chair, attempted to rape her, struck her in the face when she tried to call 911, demanded that she perform fellatio, and showed no reaction when she squeezed his testicles to the point that they later turned black. After these assaults and sexual assaults, Daviault made his way home, unlocked the door, and took off his clothes, something that his wife testified he had trouble doing when he was really drunk (Healy 1995a).

Daviault was acquitted of sexual assault on the basis of extreme intoxication producing a state of automatism. The trial judge accepted the victim's story about what happened and Daviault's factual guilt, but acquitted because the prosecutor could not prove the accused's intent beyond a reasonable doubt. As in the murder cases discussed in chapter 3, proof of subjective fault 'before imposing on the accused the socio-moral stigma that follows a guilty verdict' was more important than the 'protection of society' (*Montreal Gazette*, 1 May 1991). The Quebec Court of Appeal overturned the acquittal on the traditional basis that, while intoxication could be a defence to mentally complex crimes such as murder and robbery, it could not be a defence to more basic crimes such as assault and sexual assault (*Daviault* 1993). If Daviault was too drunk to be aware of what he was doing, it was sufficient that he was to blame for becoming so intoxicated. In influential dissents, Chief Justice Dickson had criticized this approach as unfair because it denied the accused the right to call relevant evidence just because he was charged with assault or sexual assault and assumed that he had a guilty mind just because he had been drinking (*Leary* 1977; *Bernard* 1988). As he had in *Pappajohn* (1980), the Chief Justice trusted the good sense of the jury to dismiss outrageous defences. Although it was presented as just such an outrage, the Supreme Court's decision in *Daviault*, like the majority's formulation of new common-law guidelines in *Seaboyer*, was intended to be a moderate compromise between convicting people because they were drunk and allowing the intoxication defence in all cases.

Daviault successfully appealed to the Supreme Court, which ordered a new trial in which he would have an opportunity to establish a new defence of extreme intoxication. Justice Cory concluded that it offended both fundamental justice and the presumption of innocence to substitute the fault of becoming drunk for Daviault's intent or voluntariness at the time of the sexual assault. He concluded that 'to deny that even a very minimal mental element is required for sexual assault offends the Charter in a manner that is so drastic and so contrary to the principles of fundamental justice that it cannot be justified under s.1 of the Charter' (*Daviault* 1994: 62). This did not, however, embrace the Dickson position, which would allow the accused to benefit from any alcohol-related reasonable doubt about the accused's intent. The new defence would apply only in rare cases in which intoxication deprived the accused of the basic awareness of what he was doing (*Bernard* 1988). In another example of judicial acceptance of limits on the presumption of innocence (see chapter 3), the accused would have to establish this limited defence on a balance of probabilities (*Daviault* 1994: 68). Although the public would soon see the Court's position as extreme and lacking in 'pragmatism' (*Toronto Star*, 11 Oct. 1994), it was, within legal discourse, a compromise that many believed to be unprincipled. Chief Justice Lamer and Justice LaForest signed on, but only because the majority's position was the most consistent with the Dickson approach, 'which goes much further' (*Daviault* 1994: 25–6).

In dissent, Justice Sopinka defended the traditional rule that intoxication should not be a defence to assault or sexual assault. It would not offend the Charter to convict Daviault of sexual assault because he was morally blameworthy for 'voluntarily becoming so intoxicated as to be incapable of knowing what he was doing.' He distinguished sexual assault from murder because neither 'the stigma or the available penalties demand as a constitutional requirement the subjective intent to commit' the prohibited act (ibid: 38). Sexual assault was more like manslaughter, and the accused's risky conduct in becoming so intoxicated was blameworthy.

Unlike *Seaboyer*, *Daviault* was not argued as a new political case that pitted the accused's due-process rights against the security and equality rights of a group vulnerable to crime. As Isabel Grant (1996a: 257–8) noted, 'the majority judgment in *Daviault* reads as if there is only one party with anything at stake in the decision: the accused. His disabled female victim is largely invisible and there is no mention of the gendered nature of sexual assault in our society nor of the implications of excusing violence against women on the basis that the accused was very intoxicated.' No attorneys general or interest groups such as LEAF intervened, and the Court did not consider victimization studies documenting the increased risk of assaults from men who drank regularly and to excess. *Daviault* was not argued as a new political case or an issue of risk, but it soon became one.

Media Reaction

Public reaction to *Daviault* was fierce. The *Toronto Star*'s 1 October 1994 headline was: 'Drinking Ruled a Rape Defence – Feminists Outraged at Supreme Court Decision.' The paper later editorialized that the Court's 'appalling' ruling 'completely neglects the impact on the victim' and 'declared open season on women' (*Toronto Star*, 11 Oct. 1994). A NAC spokesperson described the decision as 'totally, totally unacceptable ... This will set a precedent for men to claim they were under the influence of alcohol or whatever and that they were not responsible for their reactions' (*Halifax Chronicle Herald*, 1 Oct. 1994). Of the ninety Supreme Court decisions that year, 'as far as most Canadians are concerned there was only one ... For weeks the ruling was fodder for radio hotline shows and newspaper letter-to-the-editor writers.' Opposition to *Daviault* united both 'feminists and law-and-order-advocates' (*Montreal Gazette*, 31 Dec. 1994).

One reason why the decision enraged so many was the manifest vulnerability of the victim. 'The facts of the case, that the victim was elderly and disabled, and that she was literally dragged from her wheelchair and sexually assaulted, brought the issue into stark focus for the public' (Grant 1996b: 383). The media seized on these facts and the outrage of critics, whereas an earlier decision that had acquitted a man of murder because he was sleepwalking (*Parks* 1992) was not so reviled. The story was kept alive by five subsequent acquittals in the nine months following the decision. The six unsuccessful uses of the defence and the reversal on appeal of two of the five acquittals received less attention (Drassinower and Stuart 1995). As it had with *Seaboyer*, the media reaction created the climate for a quick legislative reply.

Legislative Reaction

Soon after the decision, a Liberal senator introduced a private member's bill that would make it an offence punishable by up to fourteen years' imprisonment to commit assaults and sexual assaults while intoxicated.

This followed the majority's suggestion in *Daviault* (1994: 68, 46) that, if Parliament was concerned about the implications of the new defence of extreme intoxication, it could 'fashion a remedy which would make it a crime to commit a prohibited act while drunk.' Justice Dickson had proposed a similar solution and it was favoured by most law reformers. The new crime would have actually increased Daviault's exposure to imprisonment, because sexual assault had a maximum penalty of ten years' imprisonment. Nevertheless, Minister of Justice Allan Rock criticized the bill as raising 'the spectre of having a drunkenness discount which would give people who intoxicate themselves an option to have a lesser penalty for the same crime' (Hansard, 27 Mar. 1995: 11037).

Given that the offence of aggravated sexual assault was infrequently charged, women's groups reasonably feared a wholesale migration of cases down to any new intoxication-based offence. The Metro Action Committee on Public Violence against Women and Children (METRAC) was also concerned that such an offence would hide violence against women 'socially and statistically by calling it "criminal intoxication"' (Canada, JLAC, 20 Jun. 1995, 112A: 59). They noted that an intoxication-based crime might have a disproportionate effect on 'certain groups vulnerable to biases in law enforcement, such as Aboriginal men' (ibid, 112A: 58). Sheila McIntyre advised against a new intoxication-based offence because of 'the danger ... that, in the name of women' Parliament will enact 'Draconian measures, punitive, reactionary measures' (*Globe and Mail*, 2 Nov. 1994). As with the 1983 reforms, concerns about victims did not lead to the most punitive response.

A few days before a National Day of Action to protest the decision, the minister of justice introduced Bill C-72. The bill took away the *Daviault* defence for violent offences. Following Justice Sopinka's dissent, it provided that it was not a defence if 'the accused, by reason of self-induced intoxication, lacked the general intent or the voluntariness required to commit the offence.' Getting drunk and involuntarily interfering with the bodily integrity of another person was deemed to be a marked departure 'from the standard of reasonable care recognized in Canadian society' sufficient to convict an accused of assault or sexual assault. The bill included a preamble recognizing concerns that 'self-induced intoxication may be used socially and legally to excuse violence, particularly violence against women and children' and affect their rights under sections 7, 15, and 28 of the Charter (*Criminal Code* as am. S.C. 1995 c.32). A preamble again engaged the symbolic stakes of the dispute and served as a vehicle for the politics of recognition.

Bill C-72 became another battle between feminists and defence lawyers. Susan Bazilli of METRAC praised it as 'a major victory for women' (*Vancouver Sun*, 25 Feb. 1995), while defence lawyer Clayton Ruby criticized it for 'punishing someone who does not have a guilty mind in the same way as someone who does have the guilty mind' (*Globe and Mail*, 31 May 1995). In committee, the Quebec bar unsuccessfully argued that the bill should be referred to the Supreme Court to determine its constitutionality.

At second reading, Minister of Justice Allan Rock stressed the 'close association between violence and intoxication, the disproportionate effect of such violence on women and children, and the extent to which that violence deprives women and children of the equality rights to which they are entitled under the charter' (Hansard, 24 Feb. 1995: 11039). In committee, Rock stressed risk as documented by victimization studies which indicated that 'the rate of assault for women living with men who drank heavily – five or more drinks at one time – was six times higher then for those whose partners didn't drink at all' (Canada, JLAC, 4 Jun. 1995, 98: 16; Sheehy 1995: 7–8). Like prostitution, intoxication was legal, but criminal justice interventions were justified in both cases because of data[17] which indicated that it was associated with risks of other crimes. Risk could be more easily measured than controlled (Beck 1992), but this fact could be obscured by relying on the old crime-control assumption that the criminal law controlled crime and now risk.

At third reading, Rock portrayed the bill as a crime-control measure and part of the government's 'safe homes, safe streets agenda,' which included toughening the Young Offenders Act, gun control, DNA testing, and 'broadening the rights of victims in the criminal justice process' (Hansard, 22 Jun. 1995: 14470–1). He argued that the bill was fair to victims of crime and ensured 'accountability for the aggressor.' The bill was politically useful because it could be presented both as a response to the risk of violence against women and children and as part of a campaign to be tough on crime and respect victims.

The bill received all-party approval. The Bloc Québécois supported it as a measure directed at violence towards women[18] while the Reform Party supported it as a crime-control and victims' rights measure without stressing women or children. Ian McClelland of Reform sounded like a Nixon Republican attacking the Warren Court when he argued that Canadians were 'upset and disgusted' with Supreme Court decisions that lacked 'common sense' and were 'better suited for a faculty club.'[19] Victims' rights were invoked for crime control and against due process.

Summary

The *Daviault* saga reflected the criminalization and legalization of politics. Almost everyone accepted an individualistic discourse that portrayed the most severe intoxication associated with alcoholism as a matter of individual choice and criminal responsibility.[20] The idea that alcoholism was a disease needing treatment (Packer 1968: 345–7) was passé (Grant 1996b: 399).[21] Within the dominant paradigm of criminalization, there was some flexibility, and women's groups helped educate politicians about the disproportionate effects that an intoxication-based offence could have on the disadvantaged. This insight did not, however, produce scepticism about the criminal sanction, and women's groups also opposed an intoxication-based offence because of victims'-rights concerns about plea bargaining and inappropriate labelling of those who committed drunken assaults and sexual assaults.

The legislation endorsed the dissenting opinion of Justice Sopinka and did not expand the scope of the debate, as Bill C-49 had. Although the public may have believed that Parliament was abolishing the defence of intoxication, the legislation only affected a handful of cases and did not stop the Supreme Court from using the Charter to expand the intoxication defence for more mentally complex crimes such as murder (*Robinson* 1996). As in some police-powers cases (see chapter 2) and murder cases (see chapter 3), the Supreme Court went to great lengths to protect the accused from any unfairness. *Daviault* was not argued as a new political case, but it soon became one. The Court's due-process decision could not survive in the face of public criticism and concerns expressed by both equality-seekers and law-and-order advocates about the victims of intoxicated assaults and sexual assaults. Although men were also victims of intoxicated assaults, the political legitimation for the new law was the rights of women and children as victims of male violence. The new legislation was based on the assumption that the criminal law could control crime and the risk of crime associated with intoxication.

O'Connor

Bishop Hubert O'Connor was accused of raping and indecently assaulting four Aboriginal students between 1964 and 1967, when they attended a residential school in northern British Columbia. The case received extensive media coverage because it involved the highest Roman Catholic official to be charged with sexual crimes and symbolized both the recent recognition of the sexual abuse of children (see chapter 6) and the victimization of Aboriginal people in residential schools (see chapter 8). It was part of a 'bulge of recently reported but historical charges, often dating back twenty of more years,' concerning sexual offences (Holmes 1997: 85). For many victims and accused, an unjust past was on trial. Defence lawyers responded to historical cases by attempting to undermine the victim's credibility by seeking their school, social welfare, medical, and counselling records in order to discover 'drug and alcohol abuse, psychological problems, criminal records or susceptibility to influence,' including the controversial false memory syndrome (FMS) (Paciocco 1996b; Oleskiw and Tellier 1997). Their efforts were defended as necessary to counter stale allegations, but criticized for putting the victim on trial and attempting to introduce irrelevant and prejudicial material.

Without hearing from them, a judge ordered the victims to authorize their employers and therapists to give copies of their complete files to the prosecutor, who would then give them to the accused. The prosecutor was reluctant to follow this sweeping order because of concerns that disclosure would 'revictimize the victims' and result in 'gender bias'(*O'Connor* 1995: 28). Many of the records were eventually disclosed to the defence, and the trial judge denied repeated applications by the accused for a stay of proceedings. The trial judge, however, stayed proceedings early in the trial because the prosecutors had failed to disclose drawings that one of the victims had made to describe her sexual abuse. The abrupt end of the trial was reported on the front page as traumatic 'not only to the complainants but also to our leadership. As native people we've come through a system where in our view it appears there is no justice' (*Globe and Mail*, 8 Dec. 1992).

The stay of proceedings was reversed by the Supreme Court. As discussed in chapter 3, the Court was concerned not to repeat the *Askov* (1990) experience by enforcing the broad disclosure requirements of *Stinchcombe* (1991) through the use of the most drastic remedy. L'Heureux-Dubé J. concluded that the accused's rights would not be irreparably harmed by late disclosure, especially because there was only 'a possibility' that the drawings might have helped the defence lawyers in their cross-examination of the victims (*O'Connor* 1995: 46). Although the prosecutors' failure to make full disclosure was 'shoddy and inappropriate,' it was related to their genuine 'desire to protect the privacy interest of the complainants' (ibid: 43).

In the due-process model, the result of individual cases can be secondary to how the Court resolves the doctrinal issues.[22] *O'Connor* was a loss for sexual-assault victims because a 5–4 majority indicated that, once the victims' records came into the prosecutor's possession, they would have to be disclosed to the defence under *Stinchcombe* (1991). Any concerns about the victim's privacy 'disappear where the documents in question have fallen into the possession of the Crown' (*O'Connor* 1995: 14). At most, the victim, like the accused, should be warned about the dangers of incriminating themselves by giving their files to the prosecutor. The majority approached the disclosure of files in the prosecutor's possession from a bipolar due-process perspective that was concerned only with ensuring fairness between the state and the accused.

When the records remained in the possession of third parties, the majority was prepared to balance the accused's rights against the privacy interests of victims. Like the *Seaboyer* majority, however, they trusted trial judges to strike the right balance. The accused had to demonstrate only that records were possibly relevant in order to justify requiring the third party to give them to the judge. The accused should not be placed in the 'Catch 22' position of having to prove the relevance of documents he had never seen, and the courts should not 'lose sight of the possibility of occasioning a miscarriage of justice by establishing a procedure which unduly restricts an accused's ability to access information which may be necessary for meaningful full answer and defence' (ibid: 17–18). After the judge received the records from the third parties, he or she would balance their importance to the accused's defence against the damage to the victim's privacy, dignity, and security of the person, including her 'psychological integrity' (ibid: 53). There was, however, no mention of equality rights or the crime-control interest in encouraging reporting.

In her dissent, Justice L'Heureux-Dubé returned to the themes of her *Seaboyer* dissent. Because 'sexual assault is a crime which overwhelmingly affects women, children and the disabled,' their equality rights and the danger of 'systemic re-victimization' by disclosure of their records must be considered (ibid: 57, 59). In addition, the 'interest in encouraging the reporting of sexual offences and the acquisition of treatment by victims' (*O'Connor* 1995: 69) should not be ignored. The majority was encouraging defence lawyers to seek access to irrelevant and prejudicial material by authorizing a 'fishing expedition' on the basis of 'bare, unsupported' assertions (ibid: 64). 'The vast majority of information' in therapeutic records was not relevant because therapy was an exploration of 'feelings of doubt and insecurity ... not a fact-finding exercise' (ibid: 65). Unlike the majority, she was not impressed by 'the sheer number' of cases in which defence lawyers had obtained therapeutic records to determine, for example, whether 'therapy ... influenced the memory of the alleged events' (ibid: 23).

A companion case affirmed that rape crisis centres and other third parties would have standing to argue before the trial judge and on appeal that the production and disclosure of their documents would violate the Charter (*Beharriell* 1995). Victims and their supporters had interests distinct from those of prosecutors (Chapman and McInnes 1996: 214). Like the media (*Dagenais* 1994; see chapter 3), they should have a procedural stake when criminal proceedings threatened their Charter rights. The Court's ruling redressed the unfairness of victims being ordered to produce their documents without even being heard, and reaffirmed the procedural foundation of the new political case pitting the accused's rights against the rights of victims and their supporters. Being allowed to play, however, did not guarantee a win. This procedural victory was accompanied by a substantive loss as the majority refused to consider equality rights and the social interest in encouraging reporting. Once the documents fell into the prosecutor's possession, even the victim's privacy rights would not be considered. Victims and their supporters were allowed to play the rights game in court, but they would frequently lose.

Carosella

The victim in *Carosella* consulted the Windsor Sexual Assault Centre in 1992 about how to lay charges against a former teacher who she alleged had sexually assaulted her when she was a teenager in 1966. She meet with a counsellor for under two hours, and it was not clear whether they discussed only the procedure for laying charges or the incidents in question (Holmes 1997). What was clear was that the counsellor's notes were shredded in 1994 pursuant to the centre's new policy of destroying records of cases with police involvement if they were not subject to a court order. The centre argued that this policy was 'forced upon them by present Court practices' and was necessary 'to reduce further victimization to the clients it serves' (*Carosella* 1997: 297). The victim was not informed about the centre's decision to shred her records and had agreed to allow the records to be given to the trial judge (ibid: 295). In this sense, the case was more about the institutional interests of the sexual assault centre than the wishes of the particular victim.

The trial judge held that the accused's right to a fair trial and full answer and defence had been violated because he was deprived of material that might provide a basis for questioning the victim's credibility. As in *O'Connor*, the trial judge stayed proceedings (*Carosella* 1994: 308). This time, the Supreme Court upheld the stay in a 5-4 decision. For the majority, Justice Sopinka returned to the heady due-process days of *Askov* (1990) by holding that the accused need not establish any prejudice to prove that his Charter rights were violated. He stressed the 'possibility' that the counsellor's notes could have revealed inconsistencies in the victim's story (ibid: 308). The majority did not seriously consider the minority's arguments that the notes were not likely to have been helpful to the accused. On the other hand, Justice L'Heureux-Dubé, in her dissent, impatiently dismissed the accused's argument as the 'popular refrain' of defence lawyers (ibid: 327) and a request for 'a fishing expedition' (ibid: 331, 341). The two judgments were also miles apart on their evaluation of the Rape Crisis Centre's destruction of the notes. The majority denounced the centre's conduct as a shocking attempt to subvert the rule of law (ibid: 311),[23] while the minority depicted it as an understandable, almost praiseworthy, attempt to protect victims (ibid: 341-2). The judgments had degenerated into a battle between defence lawyers and feminists that did not treat the other side respectfully or take it seriously.

Media Reaction

O'Connor was reported in the *Globe and Mail* (15 Dec. 1995) as a ruling 'against rape victims,' with the Court's reversal of the trial judge's stay buried in the twenty-sixth paragraph of the story. The media were now aware that the direction of the doctrine was more important than the outcome of the case. As in *Seaboyer* and *Daviault*, the public drama pitted outraged feminists against self-righteous defence lawyers. Diane Oleskiw, a lawyer for one of the rape crisis centres subpoenaed in *Beharriell*, argued that 'for the accused to gain access to all that emotion-based information is another rape in itself,' while Alan Gold, who had intervened on behalf of the Ontario Criminal Lawyers' Association, argued that counselling records were crucial in revealing 'a kind of indoctrination where a therapist encourages a belief in a victim, hardening the memories or filling in the blanks ... These people have no concern about the presumption of innocence and the possibility of convicting innocent people. I'm delighted the Supreme Court didn't buy into that' (ibid). The lawyers took their cue from the bitterly divided Court and played out the battle of defence lawyers against feminists in the media.

Carosella produced predictions from prosecutors that the decision was, like *Askov* (1990), 'a big "get out of jail" free card.' There was no mention that under proposed legislation accused would probably not be able to obtain access to counsellors' notes (*Globe and Mail*, 7 Feb. 1997). The issue of document destruction by rape crisis centres had already been featured in the media. A law professor was quoted as saying: 'If I worked in a women's shelter, I'd be burning records right now ... If it goes to court, it will be used against the people you've worked with' (*Winnipeg Free Press*, 14 Oct. 1994b), while defence lawyers argued that shredding policies were 'almost vigilantism' (*Globe and Mail*, 8 Dec. 1994) that could backfire on the victim. Media and court discourses converged and both depicted battles between feminists and defence lawyers.

Legislative Reaction

As it had with Bill C-72, the government introduced legislation to respond to the *O'Connor* ruling shortly before a meeting with a coalition of women's groups. This caused the *Globe and Mail* (3 Jun. 1996) to editorialize that the minister of justice was 'changing the law of the land every time an interest group makes a fuss' The government argued that the bill was not a reversal of *O'Connor*, but an attempt to ensure that 'the rights guaranteed by our charter are guaranteed to all people, be they accused of criminal offences or complainants or witnesses in criminal proceedings' (Hansard, 4 Feb. 1997: 7664). Nevertheless, the bill was 'a direct, almost point by point repudiation of the majority judgement ... vindicating the approach taken by the minority' (Feldthusen 1996: 562). Although they eventually supported it, the Reform Party found debates on the bill agonizing. They approved of its consideration for victims, but were concerned that the restrictions placed on access to records might protect a woman who was not a 'true' victim, but rather subject to FMS. Reluctant to invoke due-process fears about wrongful convictions, they portrayed the wrongfully accused man as the 'true victim' and were concerned about families being split by false allegations. The Liberals took some glee in pointing out that, when they proposed a bill to protect victims, the Reform Party was concerned about the accused's rights.

Like the previous two bills, Bill C-46 featured a preamble that recognized the prevalence of sexual violence against women and children and its effects on their rights under sections 7, 8, 15, and 28 of the Charter. Unlike the majority's opinion in *O'Connor*, the preamble expressed concern that 'the compelled production of personal information may deter complainants of sexual offences from reporting the offence to the police and may deter complainants from seeking necessary treatment, counselling or advice.' The legislation followed the dissent in *O'Connor* by setting out ten allegations that alone or together were not sufficient to establish that the record was relevant. The allegations included the fact that the record related to past or present treatment or counselling; to the subject matter of the proceedings; or to the victim's credibility; or that it might disclose a prior inconsistent statement. This followed the tradition of Bill C-49's definition of consent by spelling out what was not adequate and based on sexist assumptions. It did, however, beg the question of what records were relevant, especially if the accused did not yet have access to them. In an attempt to meet these stringent requirements, defence lawyers would insist on preliminary inquiries in which they could cross-examine victims in an attempt to establish grounds for production (Holmes 1997). This could make things worse for individual victims. The actual effects of court reforms were difficult to predict because of adaptive behaviour in the adversarial system (Feeley 1984).

Bill C-46 reversed the more extreme due-process requirements of *O'Connor*. Judges were required to consider the victim's privacy and equality rights and society's interests in encouraging the reporting of sexual offences before ordering the production or disclosure of documents in the prosecutor's possession. This reduced the prosecutor's *Stinchcombe* disclosure requirements in the context of sexual offences, but did not go as far as LEAF's attempts to privilege the records. Judges were also required to balance the factors noted above before ordering the production of records for their own examination. This followed the dissent's concern about the effects on the victim of production to the judge and a distrust of the ability of trial judges to make non-discriminatory decisions if left to their own devices.[24]

In committee, groups representing sexual assault centres, women, and prosecutors supported the legislation while expressing a preference for the 'no means no position ... that is no records would ever be relevant at any time' (Canada, JLAC, 11 Mar. 1997). The legislation was defended by the Ontario Coalition of Rape Crisis Centres as 'a message to the women and children in this country that you will provide some protection for their rights' (ibid). The legislation was also defended as 'necessary to protect even the existence' of sexual assault centres by offering women who sought assistance privacy. The Criminal Code amendment, however, did not secure funding for centres even though they would incur costs when arguing in court that their records should not be produced or disclosed. Sheila McIntyre of LEAF defended the complex legislation as 'a fine piece of legal analysis. It's not politics ... the justice department and the women lawyers who actually read the whole Constitution outlawyered the defence.' The legislation was important because it told the five-judge majority that they were 'wrong in constitutional law' (ibid, 6 Mar. 1997). These comments revealed how far the politics of violence against women had become legalized (Fudge 1989; Mandel 1994; Bakan 1997). Feminist groups successfully responded to, but had their agendas defined by, due-process decisions.

The issue became another battle between defence lawyers and feminists. Defence lawyers argued that the legislation was unconstitutional and that it could result in wrongful convictions based on FMS. They invoked the Martensville case and even strained to suggest that the wrongful conviction of Guy Paul Morin might not have been overturned if the defence could not have used records to attack the credibility of the informants (Canada, JLAC, 13 Mar. 1997). In turn, a representative of the Ontario Coalition of Rape Crisis Centres argued that she was not aware of any false memory cases and that, given the treatment of victims within the criminal justice system, 'I think we're going to weed out anybody who would be crazy enough to lie about being sexually assaulted and attempt to go through this system' (ibid, 11 Mar. 1997). This reproduced the presumption of guilt that Packer associated with the crime-control model, albeit based on sympathy for victims who were brave enough to face the adversarial criminal process.

Summary

Bill C-46 continued the trend to legalized politics by adopting the procedures, rhetoric, and balancing contemplated by Justice L'Heureux-Dubé in her *O'Connor* dissent. Like Bill C-72, it did not go beyond the parameters of the Court's due-process decision. Its effectiveness remains an open question. It may prevent defence lawyers from obtaining records of the type that were shredded in *Carosella* or disclosed in *O'Connor*, but it will not prevent them from trying both at preliminary inquiries and through Charter challenges to the legislation. Bill C-46 remained a defensive victory for feminists and one that stopped short of LEAF's (1996: 443) argument that all counselling records should be privileged and inadmissible. The new law has already been declared unconstitutional by several trial judges and seems destined to return to the Supreme Court. The debate between Parliament and courts continues, and Parliament may not have the last word. These debates in both courts and legislatures will continue to pit defence lawyers against feminists in symbolic and legalistic battles about whether rights claims on behalf of the accused or women and children should prevail.

Conclusion

The length of this chapter reflects the central place of attempts to respond to violence against women in the development of victims' rights. As will be seen in the next chapter, attempts to respond to sexual abuse of children have followed similar patterns. The preambles to the parliamentary replies made explicit the linkage between attempts to protect women and children.

Strategies to combat violence against women gravitated in crime-control directions which stressed the interests of police and prosecutors and relied on the dubious assumption that criminal laws, arrests, and prosecutions controlled crime. Mandatory arrest and prosecution policies for domestic assault empowered police and prosecutors even when victims objected. They assumed that the wishes of victims were a product of coercion or pathology. Like the 'battered woman syndrome,' they portrayed victims as passive and helpless. Victims' rights initiatives ran the greatest risk of reproducing crime control when they did not listen to victims and dismissed their wishes.

The tendency to decontextualize both the sexual and the relational aspects of violence against women also supported a crime-control approach. Because the focus was on whether a legally defined assault had occurred, the knowledge of criminal justice professionals was privileged, and any desire by victims to situate violence in the context of ongoing relationships was rejected. The assault paradigm improved on sexist assumptions, but it was inadequate to explain the reasons for violence or what, besides incapacitation, was necessary to prevent it in the future. An alternative approach could be found in correctional policies towards female criminality and family conferences. Crime could be situated in the past treatment and present opportunities of both offenders and victims. Offenders must accept responsibility, but there was a possibility of their reintegration in healthy social structures that could minimize the risk of future violence. These alternatives to crime control and due process would not be appropriate or work in all cases, but they should not become a taboo subject simply because they do not rely on punishment.

The new political cases examined in this chapter became increasingly legalistic and defensive. Bill C-49 enacted in response to *Seaboyer*, like the 1983 sexual-assault reforms, addressed both substantive and evidentiary law reform. In contrast, Bills C-72 and C-46 defensively engaged Supreme Court decisions by codifying the logic of the dissenters in *Daviault* and *O'Connor* while adding symbolic preambles. Feminists outlawyered defence lawyers with complex doctrinal manoeuvres, but even their victories were truncated, and perhaps temporary. Like the legal doctrine that they mirrored, the legislative replies simultaneously proclaimed and qualified the rights of women. Complex legislative victories may be eroded by subsequent interpretations and due-process challenges.

As they were contested in Court, the media, and Parliament, the new political cases degenerated into divisive, symbolic and legalistic battles between defence lawyers and feminists. The justices of the Supreme Court seemed increasingly unwilling to fully appreciate the other side's argument. In any event, judicial attempts to make pragmatic compromises were quickly dismissed, first in the media and then in Parliament. In such a polarized climate, the desire to understand the other side waned. The new political case also increased the emphasis placed on the criminal sanction. Energy and good will were diverted from other projects, and the educational and symbolic value of criminal laws, particularly preambles, was overestimated. An even greater danger was the reproduction of the old crime-control assumption that the criminal law controlled crime, and the new assumption that the proclamation of the rights of victims ensured their realization. These assumptions thrived because the ideological stakes in the law were precarious and threatened. In the heat of the battle for the equal protection of women in the criminal law, the actual protection that the law offered was assumed.

6

Young People

Criminal justice policies towards young people reflect many of the themes discussed throughout this book. Children were recognized in the 1980s as victims and potential victims of sexual violence. In turn, criminal laws were reformed in attempts to facilitate reporting, prosecutions, and convictions. New concerns for the rights of victims were used to justify the crime-control activities of police, prosecutors, and other professionals. Some attempts to facilitate prosecutions of child sexual abuse have been subject to due-process challenges and resulted in new political cases similar to those examined in chapters 4 and 5. Statutory rape and vagrancy offences for convicted sex offenders were struck down, but Parliament quickly responded with new legislation. At the same time, courts upheld Parliament's modest attempts to make it easier for children to testify. In contrast to post-charge delay (see chapter 3), they allowed sexual-abuse cases to proceed despite decades of pre-charge delay. In contrast to their exclusion of unconstitutionally obtained evidence (see chapter 2), they admitted much evidence from young children in criminal trials. These cases were all new political cases which set the accused's due-process claims against those of victims and groups of potential victims.

Attitudes towards young people charged with crime also changed dramatically. They were no longer seen as children in need of parental-type guidance, but as individuals with at least the same rights and many of the same responsibilities as adults. The 1984 Young Offenders Act (YOA), like the Charter, moved the system towards due process. As in the adult system, however, due process did not increase liberty or reduce reliance on the criminal sanction. Many more young people were imprisoned or placed under state supervision than under the parental Juvenile Delinquents Act (JDA). This raised the familiar issue of whether due process enabled and legitimated increased crime control or whether it was only consistent with increased prison and probation populations.

This chapter concludes with an exploration of alternatives to crime control and due process for young people. These include non-punitive strategies which stress the prevention of youth crime through early social-welfare interventions and the use of restorative justice such as family conferences. These approaches could link childhood victimization with teenage offending. In so doing, they could break down the present dichotomy of perceptions of young people as either vulnerable, innocent, and helpless victims in need of crime-control protection or irresponsible, predatory criminals prepared to exploit their due-process rights.

Sexual Abuse: Victims' Rights and Crime Control

Packer's (1968: 309, 315–16) arguments that incest and statutory rape were 'imaginary' crimes that should be repealed because they enforced morality reflected the times in which he wrote. Counselling for both the victim and his or her family, not criminal prosecutions, was seen as the appropriate response in the 1960s (McGillivray 1990). One Canadian commentator concluded in 1972 that, because of the time, trauma, and difficulty of obtaining criminal convictions, 'people working in this field believe that there are only rare occasions when the criminal law should be used. Parents should not be punished but should be helped ...' (Van Stolk 1972: 76). Before the late 1970s, there were few references to the abuse of children in the reports of provincial child-protection services, and the focus was more often on battered children. The reporting of sexual abuse to child-welfare authorities increased dramatically in the 1980s, and with it demands for the use of the criminal sanction (Canada 1984b: 127; Rogers 1990: 19). There was also a growing recognition that many children placed in training and residential schools had been sexually abused (Bala 1997).

The Badgley Report

As was the case for violence against women, victimization studies played a significant role in the recognition of sexual abuse of children. In 1984, the Badgley Committee made headlines by reporting that 'sometime during their lives one, about one in two females and one in three males have been victims of unwanted sexual acts. About four in five of these incidents happened to these persons when they were children or youths' (Canada

1984b: 175). These 'magic figures' (Rock 1986; Sullivan 1992) were based on interviews with more than 2,000 adults and included acts of exposure, threatened sexual assault, unwanted touching, attempted sexual assault, and sexual assaults (Canada 1984b: 179–81). Most sexual abuse of children was not reported to the police, and for 'three in four female victims and about nine in ten male victims, these incidents had been kept as closely guarded personal secrets' (ibid: 187). The Badgley Committee argued that these victimization studies revealed 'an evident and urgent need to afford victims greater protection than that now being provided.' Moreover, 'children and youths have the absolute right to be protected from these offenses' (ibid: 193). Risk had been measured and should be reduced to zero.

High rates of victimization could have been constructed as a sign of the limited relevance of the criminal sanction, but this was not done. Instead, the Badgley Committee stressed the need for a more victim-sensitive criminal sanction. Like the Clark and Lewis (1977) and MacLeod (1980) studies discussed in chapter 5, it charted the course for criminal-law reforms. The media joined in the demands for criminal justice reforms by arguing that, in light of Badgley's data, 'no decent society can fail to do all in its power to prevent it, to punish the perpetrators and to protect the innocent victims' (*Toronto Star,* 4 Aug. 1984). The result has been described by Anne McGillivray (1990: 553) as 'a shift away from the immediate value of criminal prosecutions to the victim (a value often outweighed by the harm done to the victim by the process) towards the value of the prosecution to the community.'

Although it incorporated the insights of doctors, psychologists, and social workers, the Badgley Report focused on the inadequacy of the criminal law. It demonstrated enthusiasm for the criminal sanction by recommending broad and tough criminal offences for child sexual abuse, juvenile prostitution, and child pornography. Unlike Packer, and the Law Reform Commission of Canada (1978: 25–9), it did not recommend that the crime of incest be repealed. The Badgley Committee's focus on the criminal sanction was in part dictated by the constitutional division of powers which required the federal government to enter the field of child welfare through the use of the criminal law or, more expensively and less visibly, through its spending powers. The federal government's reluctance to expand or maintain its spending powers contributed to the criminalization of politics. Like women's groups, children's advocates enjoyed more success in obtaining new criminal sanctions than more costly and less dramatic interventions.

Although the committee criticized the 1983 sexual-assault reforms for not recognizing 'the peculiar vulnerabilities of children,' its proposals were quite similar. Morals-based offences such as seduction under the promise of marriage and gross indecency should be repealed, and most new offences should be gender-neutral. Gender-neutrality was not, however, related to sexual equality, but the data which revealed that boys, as well as girls, were subject to sexual abuse. Statutory rape should be retained and expanded to cover fourteen- and fifteen-year-old girls because of the particular harms of early pregnancy. New offences such as sexual touching and invitation to sexual touching should be worded broadly to focus on the invasion of bodily integrity. Older teenagers were to be protected by new offences based on the 'abuse of trust' (Canada, 1984b: 59)

Following the changes made in 1983, fundamental reforms of evidentiary laws were necessary to eliminate traditional distrust of the testimony of the victim. Every child should be competent to testify, and requirements for the corroboration of the testimony of children who did not understand the oath should be abolished. The remaining rules relating to recent complaint should be abolished, and spouses should be compellable to testify against each other in sexual-abuse cases. Courts should be more inclined to allow witnesses to give hearsay evidence about out-of-court statements they heard children make even if the child did not testify at the proceeding (ibid: 71). The committee also recommended restrictions on publishing the names or identifying information of child witnesses and that 'rape shield' restrictions on the admissibility of prior sexual conduct be extended to children.

Like many in the early 1980s, the Badgley Committee underestimated the impact of the Charter. In a cursory five-page chapter, it concluded that the Charter did 'not imply the paralysis of law enforcement' and that every one of its recommendations were justified as 'an appropriate and tailored response to the special needs and substantial vulnerabilities of Canadian children and youths' (ibid: 460–1). The issue of whether new criminal laws were 'Charter proof' and the new political case pitting due-process rights against the rights of victims had not yet emerged. Six years later, however, another report on child sexual abuse would urge the government to monitor due-process challenges and fight the new political case by defending the criminal sanction as a necessary protection for children (Rogers 1990: 62). As will be seen, Badgley's enthusiasm for absolute liability (*Hess* 1990) and vagrancy offences (*Heywood* 1994) ran into Charter trouble.

The Badgley Committee advocated criminalization without much attention to what victims wanted. The written submissions from victims of child abuse suggested that 'few victims or persons who had known victims (13.3 per cent) adopted a punitive approach towards child sexual offenders. About one in three (35.7 per cent) called for counselling for victims, family members and offenders. There was little concern among this group about the need to amend legislation ...' (Canada 1984b: 25). The committee did not give these representations much weight. As was the case with mandatory arrest policies for wife assault, approaches which marginalized victim input were more likely to result in crime-control strategies.

Badgley's findings that most sexual abuse of children was committed by men confirmed feminist insights, but was not stressed in the report. Lorenne Clark (1985: 100) argued that, despite increased punishment and services for victims, 'things will go on just as they have so long as men are socialized to regard women and children as property, and to link male sexuality with power, authority, and violence.' Clark's argument supported a comprehensive approach to sexual abuse similar to the one she advocated a decade earlier with regards to sexual assault (Clark and Lewis 1977). As with the 1983 sexual-assault reforms, new criminal laws were easier to achieve.

The Legislative Response

In 1986, Bill C-15 was introduced, with Minister of Justice Ray Hnatyshyn arguing that the high incidence of sexual abuse as documented by Badgley demonstrated that the criminal law had failed and must be reformed (Hansard, 4 Nov. 1986: 1037). The bill honoured 'a responsibility to protect children from sexual abuse and exploitation and to deter those who would seek to victimize them' (ibid: 1036). New knowledge about the risks of victimization was quickly translated into deterrence-based crime-control measures. The existing law not only failed to protect against risk, but also failed to provide 'young girls and boys ... the equal degree of protection of the law required by our Charter of Rights' (ibid: 1037). Like the 1983 sexual-assault reforms, new criminal laws could respond to the risks of victimization and protect the rights of victims.

Equality was defined as gender-neutrality, with statutory rape being replaced with new offences that protected both girls and boys. The present law did 'not adequately cover the full range of sexual behaviour that children may be induced to engage in' (ibid: 1037). A new sexual-interference offence prohibited direct or indirect touching in order to provide 'an almost absolute protection to children under 14 years of age from being touched for a sexual purpose' (ibid: 1037). Following Badgley, a separate offence of inviting sexual touching was also created. This offence responded to the risk created by those who had tried but not succeeded in sexually touching a child. The third new offence was sexual exploitation by an accused 'in a position of trust or authority' towards a young person between fourteen and seventeen years of age. For all three offences, the accused would not have a defence that he believed the young person to be older unless he took all reasonable steps to ascertain the victim's age. This was, however, more of a defence than recommended by Badgley or available under the old statutory-rape offence. Young offenders under sixteen years of age could use the victim's consent as a defence provided they were less than two years older than the victim and were not in a position of trust, authority, or dependency. This was also more liberal than Badgley's proposals, which had led to fears about criminalizing much teenage sexual activity (Sullivan 1992). The new law also abolished the 'victim-blaming' (Boyle et al 1985: 63–4) provision that protected only chaste girls who were not more to blame than the accused for the sexual activity. Like the 1983 sexual-assault reforms, these offences defined criminal conduct more broadly in an attempt to better protect the physical and sexual integrity of victims, but also allowed more lenient treatment. All three offences could be prosecuted as summary-conviction offences subject to six months' imprisonment. In the hope of increasing successful prosecutions, more lenient punishment was contemplated. Again a concern for victims did not always produce the most punitive response.

Bill C-15 also tried to make it easier for children to testify. Following the 1983 reforms, the legislation abolished corroboration and recent complaint requirements. It 'stopped well short' (McGillivray 1990: 562–3) of Badgley's recommendation that children's hearsay statements be admissible without requiring them to testify, but allowed videotaped evidence to be introduced and then adopted by children when they testified. As originally introduced, the bill provided that the accused could be removed from the courtroom when a child testified. In response to Charter-based concerns, the accused was allowed to remain, but a screen between the accused and the victim could be used. As will be seen, these last two provisions attracted due-process challenges.[1]

Like many victims' rights initiatives, the bill was greeted with all-party approval. The Liberal Justice critic, however, warned that more attention should have been paid to 'the requirements of the Charter for fair trials, free speech and free access' (Hansard, 4 Nov. 1986: 1041). Svend Robinson of the NDP noted that, while some argued that Badgley's estimates of the incidence of sexual abuse were 'excessive and unreasonable. Whatever the extent, it is now clear that this Parliament must take firm and effective action now to deal with that crisis' (ibid: 1042). He warned of the dangers of not focusing on 'all forms of abuse, including poverty, neglect, hunger, homelessness as well as … physical and sexual abuse' (Hansard, 23 Jun. 1987: 7509). In one of the few references to interventions outside the criminal justice system, Robinson suggested 'that education at home, school, church and elsewhere is the best way for children to develop in a sexually healthy and mature fashion' (Hansard, 4 Nov. 1986: 1047). The criminalization of politics, however, meant that issues such as child sexual abuse, juvenile prostitution, and child pornography received more attention than child poverty and other forms of neglect that could not be addressed by the criminal sanction.

Some defence lawyers criticized the bill, particularly provisions enabling young children to give evidence and repealing corroboration requirements. Bob Wakefield was concerned that 'victims' groups generally were not interested in the judicial process,' but only in obtaining convictions and harsh sentences, and that the government, in an attempt to 'smooth the road to conviction,' had similarly ignored 'judicial values' (Canada, JLAC, 16 Dec. 1986, 4:4–4:5). Defence lawyers were beginning to recognize that victims were the new face of crime control. In contrast, prosecutor Wendy Harvey defended the legislation by arguing that 'children suffer at the hands of defence lawyers, at the hands of prosecutors, and at the hands of the judges themselves' (ibid, 4: 7). She foreshadowed her own concerns as one of the prosecutors in *O'Connor* (1995) by arguing that the accused and defence lawyers should not have access to videotapes because 'it is a war out there' (ibid, 4: 14). This was a victims' rights approach which agreed with many of the aims of crime control, but departed from its deference to the expertise of the professionals in the system. At least one member of the committee rejected the well-publicized concerns of defence lawyers on the basis that the Badgley Report made it clear 'that Canadians are fed up with sexual abuse of children and they want the federal government to do something about it' (Vallance 1988: 187).

As Anne McGillivray (1990: 556) has suggested, Bill C-15 was 'an effect of criminalization rather than the cause' because reporting of child sexual abuse had already increased under the 1983 sexual-assault reforms, and most charges continued to be laid under that law (Roberts 1996).

There was an extensive publicity campaign about the new law, with more than 4 million pamphlets distributed (Schmolka 1992: 4). After the law was proclaimed in force in 1988, some increase in reported child sexual abuse was documented in some cities. Most victims were girls, many under five years of age, and most accused were men known, but not related, to the victim. Conviction rates were generally high, with most cases resulting in short periods of incarceration. However, not enough attention was paid to treating offenders to prevent recidivism or to early intervention by child-welfare authorities (Rogers 1990).

The Evidence Counter-Revolution

As seen in chapter 2, the Supreme Court developed a quasi-automatic exclusionary rule under section 24(2) of the Charter in order to enforce an expanded right against self-incrimination. This section examines a less well-known, but more important, evidence counter-revolution. It was not motivated by judicial concerns about the accused's rights, but rather by judicial attempts to facilitate the prosecution of child-sexual-abuse cases (Healy 1995b; Paciocco 1996b).

Reform of the hearsay rule was a crucial part of the evidence counter-revolution.[2] The hearsay rule generally prohibited witnesses from telling the court about statements heard from third parties on the basis that it was unfair to accept these statements for their truth when the person who made them was not before the court and subject to cross-examination. As in *Seaboyer* (1991), *O'Connor* (1995), and *Carosella* (1997) (see chapter 5), cross-examination of witnesses by defence lawyers was thought necessary to ensure fairness and respect the accused's right to make full answer and defence. At the same time, the hearsay rule was always riddled with exceptions. The Badgley Committee recognized that the hearsay statements of children about sexual abuse would be valuable and recommended a new exception.(Canada 1984b: 393). Parliament did not provide such an exception in Bill C-15, but the courts soon addressed the issue.

The impetus for hearsay reform came in a case in which a doctor was acquitted of sexually assaulting his three-and-a-half-year-old patient. Shortly after her private examination, the young girl told her mother that the doctor had 'put his birdie in my mouth, shook it and peed in my mouth' (*Khan* 1990: 95). Forensic evidence found a mixture of semen and saliva on the child's clothes. The trial judge ruled that the little girl was too young to testify and that her statement to her mother was inadmissible hearsay. He acquitted Dr Khan, commenting that 'however suspicious I remain to this moment, the Crown has fallen just short of proof of the accused's guilt beyond a reasonable doubt' (ibid: 96). The Supreme Court reversed this shocking acquittal and reformed the hearsay rule to facilitate the prosecution of child-sexual-abuse cases that before had been 'automatically dropped' (McGillivray 1990: 579).

The Supreme Court approached the evidentiary issues raised by the case 'in view of the increasing number of prosecutions for sexual offenses against children and the hardships that often attend requiring children to re-tell and re-live the frequently traumatic events ...' (*Khan* 1990: 100). The trial judge had erred in 'letting himself be swayed by the young age of the child. Were that a determinative consideration, there would be danger that offenses against very young children could never be prosecuted' (ibid: 99). Building on precedents from child-protection hearings, McLachlin J. concluded that the hearsay statement to the mother was admissible because it was necessary, the child having not been allowed to testify at trial,[3] and reliable, the child having no motive to falsify a story that emerged without prompting and was supported by real evidence. This generally accorded with Badgley's recommendations that reliable and necessary hearsay statements about child sexual abuse be admitted.

When children did testify, the Supreme Court abandoned their traditional distrust of their statements (*Kendall* 1962). Justice Wilson warned that 'the standard of the "reasonable adult" is not necessarily appropriate in assessing the credibility of young children' (*B.(G)*. 1990: 220). As in *Lavallee* (1990), objective standards would have to be individualized to accommodate victims and groups of potential victims. Two years later, the Court commented that 'since children may experience the world differently from adults, it is hardly surprising that details important to adults, like time and place, may be missing from their recollection' (*W.(R)* 1992: 143). A new willingness to accept children's testimony was required if they were to 'receive the full benefit of the protection that the law seeks to afford them' (Canada 1984b: 374) and the accused was not to benefit 'from the youthful age of his victim' (*B.(G.)* 1990: 180–1). Justice Wilson, who had played an important role in the development of the section 24(2) quasi-automatic exclusionary rule, expressed concerns that 'imposing too restrictive a standard on ... [children's] testimony may permit serious offenses to go unpunished and perhaps to continue' (ibid).

Part of the evidence counter-revolution involved judicial deference to Parliament's attempt to make it easier for child witnesses to testify. These were new political cases pitting due process against victims' rights, but they received little publicity and no legislative replies because they recognized the rights of child witnesses. In *L.(D.O)*. (1993), the Supreme Court upheld 1988 amendments allowing videotaped statements by children to be introduced as evidence. In a terse judgment for the Court, Chief Justice Lamer concluded that the provision was a legitimate 'response to the dominance and power which adults, by virtue of their age, have over children' and an attempt to accommodate 'the needs ... and interests of young victims of various forms of sexual abuse, irrespective of their age' (ibid: 294). The reform was relatively minimal because it required that the child adopt the statements and be available for cross-examination in court. At times, videotaped statements benefited defence lawyers by revealing inconsistencies between the child's testimony and his or her earlier statement (Bala and McCormack 1994: 346). Unlike the 'rape shield' or the post-*O'Connor* legislation, it did not challenge the accused's ability to engage in cross-examination.

Justice L'Heureux-Dubé also wrote a long concurring judgment which brought together many different strands of victims' rights. She criticized the majority and Badgley for failing to 'recognize that the occurrence of child sexual abuse is one intertwined with the sexual abuse of all women, regardless of age' (*L.(D.0)*: 303). She stressed the need to consider 'the innate power imbalance between the numerous young women and girls who are victims of sexual abuse at the hands of almost exclusively male perpetrators' when '"truth" is being sought before a male-defined criminal justice system' (ibid: 302–3). Not even the preambles of Bills C-49, C-72, and C-46 had singled out girls as opposed to boys for protection from sexual abuse. Justice L'Heureux-Dubé combined her feminist focus on male violence against females with a concern about victims. The legislation was needed because 'we live in a society which continues to blame even the most innocent of victims' (ibid: 304). Child victims of sexual abuse were 'generally scared, helpless and in emotional turmoil' and the use of videotapes would reduce 'stress and trauma' and the second victimization of the trial process (ibid: 321). The law was also justified by reference to Canada's international commitments to protect vulnerable groups, in this case those under the age of eighteen (ibid: 321). She was not persuaded with the Manitoba Court of Appeal's argument that the section did not effectively serve its purpose because children still had to be cross-examined. Consistent with the crime-control model, she argued that the admissibility of videotaped statements encouraged guilty pleas. Her arguments reflected many of the themes in victims' rights, but overestimated the value of videotapes in reducing the trauma of the trial process and the sexual abuse of children.

The Supreme Court also upheld the use of screens between the accused and the victim. Writing for the Court this time, Justice L'Heureux-Dubé rejected the bipolar due-process focus on the accused and the state, and stressed the need for 'multifaceted considerations, such as the rights of witnesses, in this case children, the rights of accused and the courts' duties to ascertain the truth' (*Levogiannis* 1993: 333). In this case, she seemed more realistic about the limits of the legal reforms by noting that 'young complainants, shielded by the screen, remain predominantly subject to the rigours of the court-room and cross-examination' (ibid: 339). She also adverted to the risk that juries would view victims as less credible when they did not face the accused.(ibid: 341). In any event, screens were expensive and not available in all courtrooms.

The evidence counter-revolution was practically more important than the development of an automatic exclusionary rule under section 24(2) of the Charter because it affected the evidentiary rulings made every day in routine cases across the country. As suggested above, it was influenced by an increase of child-sexual-abuse cases and was motivated by concern about the position of child witnesses.

The Pre-Charge Delay Counter-Revolution

At the same time that they refused to hear cases because of less than a year of post-charge delay, courts allowed cases to proceed based on decades-old allegations of sexual abuse. Like the evidence counter-revolution, this one was less well known than *Askov* (1990; see chapter 3), but practically more important because it allowed numerous historical sexual-abuses cases to proceed (Holmes 1997), including the *O'Connor* and *Carosella* cases discussed in chapter 5. My point is not to engage the merits of either these developments, but to illustrate the flexibility of legal discourse and the way the courts focused on due process in some contexts, and concerns about victims in others.

In 1991, an unanimous Supreme Court reversed a stay of proceedings entered when a trial judge had concluded that delay by the accused's daughters in reporting sexual assaults alleged to have commenced in 1957 was 'ludicrous.' The Court recognized the 'courage and emotional strength' required to report sexual abuse by family members[4] and expressed concern that 'if proceedings were to be stayed based solely on the passage of time between the abuse and the charge, victims would be required to report incidents before they were psychologically prepared for the consequence of that reporting' (*L.(W.K.)* 1991: 328). Perhaps reflecting concerns about the way *Askov* (1990) was being applied in Ontario at the time, the Court added that 'establishing a judicial statute of limitations would mean that sexual abusers would be able to take advantage of the failure to report which they themselves, in many cases, caused. This is not a result which we should encourage. There is no place for an arbitrary rule' (ibid: 329). This argument demonstrated not only awareness of the dilemmas faced by those sexually abused by a family member, but also a crime-control assumption that most accused were factually guilty and responsible for the delay.

Statutory Rape

Until 1988, it was an indictable offence punishable by life imprisonment for a man to have sexual intercourse with a girl under fourteen years of age, regardless of the girl's consent or his belief about her age. The Badgley Committee recommended that this absolute-liability offence be retained on the crime-control basis that 'there will seemingly always be men, young and old, who do not accept that it is wrong to have sexual intercourse with young girls. For these men, detection and prosecution may act as a deterrent' (Canada, 1984b: 50–1). In a preference for the criminal sanction over condoms, it also recommended that the sanction be extended to protect girls under sixteen years of age from the risks and harms of early pregnancy and sexually transmitted diseases.

As discussed above, the committee underestimated the extent to which its proposals were vulnerable under the Charter. In an early example of the new political case, the Supreme Court declared the statutory-rape offence unconstitutional, but split on whether the rights of the accused or the victim should prevail. The majority of the Court approached the constitutionality of the law in an abstract fashion typical of the due-process model and ignored that one accused had already pled guilty and that sexual-assault charges had been withdrawn against another only because the twelve-year-old victim 'did not indicate her lack of consent to the appellant because she was too scared' (*Hess* 1990: 185–6). Justice Wilson stressed the maximum penalty of life imprisonment and concluded that 'to imprison a "mentally innocent" person is to inflict a grave injury on that person's dignity and sense of worth' (ibid: 171). Focusing on the criminal act as opposed to the accused's fault would treat the accused as 'little more than a means to an end. That person is in essence told that because of an overriding social or moral objective, he must lose his freedom even though he took all reasonable precautions to ensure that no

offence was committed' (ibid). This argument was similar to the individualistic and anti-utilitarian reasoning used in the political cases examined
in chapter 5. As with the felony-murder cases (see chapter 3), the Court
went beyond the U.S. Supreme Court, which had upheld a similar statutory-rape offence (*Michael M.* 1981).

Justice McLachlin dissented on the basis that the violation of the
accused's rights was necessary to protect young girls from pregnancies,
'grave physical and emotional harm,' and 'exploitation,' including juvenile prostitution (*Hess* 1990: 193–4). Like the Badgley Committee, she
argued that the law was not 'unduly draconian' because of sentencing discretion and the fact that all a man needed to do to avoid liability was 'to
refrain from having sex with girls of less than adult age unless he knows
for certain that they are over 14' (ibid: 198). She maintained that the law
was an effective deterrent, 'as exemplified by terms such as "jail bait"'
(ibid: 195). This crime-control approach focused on the criminal act and
was more consistent with the Court's willingness in the manslaughter
cases to uphold a broad use of the criminal sanction in an attempt to
deter people from risking serious harm (*Creighton* 1993; see chapter 3).

Even though it was a new political case like those examined in the last
chapter, the Court's decision was not front-page news. A Canadian Press
story reported that 'the old statutory rape law has been invalidated by the
Supreme Court as fundamentally unjust,' but noted that Parliament had
already replaced the offence with a new offence (*Winnipeg Free Press*,
15 Sep. 1990). The new offence prohibited any sexual touching of a child
under fourteen years of age and allowed the accused a defence that he or
she thought the child was older only if 'all reasonable steps' were taken to
ascertain the child's age.[5] The type of crisis observed in chapter 5 was
averted because a new criminal sanction to protect victims was already in
place.

Vagrancy

Packer (1968: 78) predicted that status-based offences like vagrancy were
'very much on their way out' because they gave the police and courts
unfettered discretion to convict someone for doing nothing. As examined in chapter 4, Parliament repealed a law in 1972 that made it an
offence to be a prostitute who could not give a good account of herself. It
left on the books, however, a vagrancy offence which made it a crime for a
convicted sex offender to loiter in or near a school ground, playground,
public park, or bathing area. The offence was rarely used and had been

rendered useless when Parliament forgot to amend it when the section numbers of sexual offences were changed. Following Badgley's recommendation, however, this error was corrected and the law soon gained more prominence (Canada 1984b: 60, 329).

Robert Heywood, a retired schoolteacher, was convicted of two counts of sexual assault in 1987 against young girls. Two years later, he was arrested and convicted for loitering in a playground. He was photographing young girls' crotches while they played. The trial judge found that Heywood had an evil or malevolent intent and sentenced him to three months' imprisonment and three years' probation. In late 1992, however, the British Columbia Court of Appeal reversed Heywood's conviction because the legislation as written did not require either a malevolent intent or notice to sex offenders that they could be convicted for loitering. The Court of Appeal was also concerned that the offence applied automatically for the entire lives of all sex offenders. Southin J.A. expressed 'the fervent hope that Parliament will not be discouraged from forthwith enacting a better measure to enable the police to keep convicted sexual offenders away from places where children congregate and that the police will have the capacity and the will to enforce it' (*Heywood* 1992: 528). She enforced due process, but invited a legislative reply in the name of crime control and victims' rights.

Parliament responded before the 1993 general election with new provisions which gave courts the discretion to ban those convicted of sexual crimes against children from attending public parks, public swimming areas, school grounds, playgrounds, or community centres,[6] and from having a position of trust and authority over children. Minister of Justice Pierre Blais presented the new law as 'bad news for child molesters. Those individuals who are convicted of child molestation can now find themselves subject to a prohibition order that can last for life' (Hansard, 10 Jun. 1993: 20671). Two Liberal members were not convinced. Beryl Gaffney criticized the bill because 'it leaves the individual judge with far too much discretion' (Hansard, 10 Jun. 1993: 20703), and Albina Guarnieri suggested that 'the millions of victims and potential victims of violent crime in this country' would 'ask why a convicted sex offender who is considered sufficiently dangerous to be barred from being around children is allowed on the street at all' (Hansard, 6 May 1993: 19065). Demands for crime control and protection of potential victims were not easy to satisfy.

The Supreme Court still had Heywood's fate in their hands, but, as in *Hess*, the policy issue had been pre-empted by Parliament's early intervention. For the majority, Justice Cory found the law unconstitutional because 'it applies without prior notice to the accused, to too many places, to too many people, for an indefinite period with no possibility of review. It restricts liberty more than is necessary to accomplish its goal ... to protect children from becoming victims of sexual offenses' (*Heywood* 1994: 514, 517). The new legislation was praised as an example of a less intrusive means to advance the important objectives of the old law (ibid: 523). Like his *Daviault* decision the same year, this decision was criticized for not considering the interests and rights of victims and potential victims (Grant 1996a: 230–1). Four judges dissented and stressed the prevalence of child sexual abuse. Justice Gonthier constructed risk for crime-control ends by interpreting 'the difficulty of predicting who will cross-offend or repeat offend' as a reason to justify the absolute ban on all convicted sexual offenders even though, on due-process grounds, it would be a reason for not using the criminal sanction. In rejecting claims that the law infringed the presumption of innocence, he assumed the perspective of a helping professional by arguing that the law 'does not assume recidivism, but rather, provides the means to prevent it ...' The law was also defended on more traditional crime-control grounds for providing 'useful means for law enforcement officers to take immediate preventive steps' (ibid: 499).

Unlike the *Hess* statutory-rape decision four years earlier, the Court's decision in *Heywood* made the front page. The media were increasingly aware of the new political case, and reporters, like judges, had their own inclinations towards due process and victims' rights. Sean Fine's lead in the *Globe and Mail* on 25 November 1994 was that 'sex offenders will no longer be banned for life from hanging around parks, schoolyards and playgrounds.' He quoted Priscilla de Villiers of CAVEAT as stating that the decision indicates 'how far our courts, and particularly the Supreme Court, has gone from reflecting a need for public safety.' This was followed with another story featuring critics of the decision (*Globe and Mail*, 30 Nov. 1994). In contrast, David Vienneau's lead in the *Toronto Star* on 25 November 1994 was the Court's 'tacit' approval of the 1993 law. He quoted lawyers who predicted the new law would be used against convicted paedophiles. The symbolic battles of the new political case were played out in courts, legislatures, and the media.

Summary

Changing approaches to the sexual abuse of children followed many of the same patterns observed in chapter 5 with respect to wife assault and sexual assault. Victimization studies helped raise awareness and concerns about the prevalence of child sexual abuse. The criminal sanction was reformed to increase reporting and prosecutions even though the extent of victimization suggested the impossibility of prosecutions in every case. Bill C-15, like the 1983 sexual-assault law, was a gender-neutral expansion of the criminal sanction designed to better protect physical integrity and to change evidentiary assumptions that children were not trustworthy. Parliament attempted to make it easier for child victims of sexual abuse to testify while not challenging the accused's ability to engage in cross-examination. There was less conflict between victims' rights and due process because the Supreme Court upheld evidentiary screens and video-taped evidence in large part because these reforms respected the accused's right to cross-examine the victim. On its own initiative, the Court reformed the hearsay rule to facilitate the prosecution of child sexual abuse and allowed historical sexual-abuse cases to proceed. Due-process decisions striking down statutory rape and vagrancy offences had the potential to result in the type of confrontations observed in chapter 5, but were largely diffused because Parliament had already intervened with less drastic, but still robust laws.

The Young Offenders Act: Due Process and Crime Control

Since the mid-1980s, youth courts, like adult courts, have become much more concerned about due process. The due-process provisions of the Young Offenders Act (YOA) attracted more public criticism than the Charter and were subject to amendments to facilitate crime control. In any event, the YOA, like the Charter, has been accompanied by increased use of punishment, with a 26 per cent increase in youth detention centre counts between 1986/7 and 1994/5 (Canadian Centre for Criminal Justice Statistics [CCJCS] 1996b: 14–16). This raised the recurring question of whether due process legitimated crime control or simply was not an effective barrier to it.

The Juvenile Delinquents Act

The Juvenile Delinquents Act (JDA) embraced a model of justice distinct from crime control and due process. Reflecting what Griffiths (1970) identified as a third 'family' model, the JDA's section 38 provided that 'the care and custody and discipline of a juvenile delinquent shall approximate as nearly as may be possible that which should be given by his parents' and that 'as far as practicable every juvenile delinquent shall be treated not as a criminal but as a misdirected and misguided child, and one needing aid, encouragement, help and assistance.' Like a parent, the state did not have to wait for an offence and could intervene if the young person was a truant, in need of training and treatment, or engaged in 'sexual immorality or any other similar form of vice' (ibid: s. 2). The wide net of control cast by the JDA was matched with a broad range of dispositions, including adjourning hearings for an indefinite period, requiring home visits by a probation officer, placing the child in a foster home 'subject to the friendly supervision of a probation officer,' or committing the child to children's aid or an industrial school (ibid: s. 20).

Due process was not required because, following the family model, it was assumed that the state acted in the youth's best interests. A disposition in the 'best interest of the child' could not be overturned because of any procedural 'informality or irregularity' (ibid: s. 17[2]). Proceedings were to be 'as informal as the circumstances permit' (ibid: s. 17[1]) and could be held in private (*B.(C.)*) 1981). Defence lawyers rarely were present because 'the juvenile-court process gave the lawyer very little to work with. Disclosure mechanisms were non-existent, the rules of evidence relaxed, and legal errors considered inconsequential' (Pearson 1991: 116). Judges were not necessarily legally trained (Bala and Kirvan 1991: 72) and their decisions could be based on confidential information not disclosed to the young person. Appeals, the driving force of the due-process model, were allowed only when 'essential in the public interest or for the due administration of justice' (JDA: s. 37).

The JDA proclaimed the caring ideology of the family model, but it often resembled a coercive crime-control assembly line (Catton 1976). In many jurisdictions, the juvenile court was 'little more than the ordinary criminal process minus most protections for the accused' (Griffiths 1970: 400–1). The Warren Court intervened out of a recognition that 'the child receives the worst of both worlds ... he gets neither the protections accorded to adults nor the solicitous care and regenerative treatment postulated for children' (*Kent* 1966: 555–6). In a case in which a juvenile was sent to industrial school for six years for making an obscene phone call, it held that juveniles enjoyed many of the same due-process rights as adults, including the right to be represented by counsel (*Gault* 1967). As Packer predicted, judicial activism and defence lawyers brought due process. Griffiths (1970: 401–4) warned, however, that something was lost in the move to due process with its assumptions of an adversarial relationship between the state and the young offender. The same individualistic approach that required respect for the rights of young people could also justify punishing them as adults so long as their rights were respected.

The Development of the Young Offenders Act

The development of the YOA had many interesting parallels to the development of the Charter discussed in chapter 1. Both were influenced by American developments; promoted by the Department of Justice in the 1960s; and the subject of provincial opposition. A 1965 report called for the repeal of status-based offences and indeterminate punishment, and the enactment of procedural protections concerning the taking of statements, pre-trial detention, the right to counsel, and appeals. Draft legislation was rejected in the 1970s because of provincial resistance and concerns that, despite due-process protections, the proposals created a 'criminal code for children' (Corrado and Markwart 1992: 148–9; Manfredi 1991: 49).

Concerns that the JDA's informal procedures and age disparities were vulnerable under the Charter (Bala 1997: 9) led to the YOA being introduced in 1981 under the twin banners of rights and responsibilities. Solicitor General Robert Kaplan argued that 'as society insists more and more on responsibility on the part of the young offender, his right to fair treatment in accordance with the principles of natural justice can no longer be left, as they have under the present law, to the discretion of those persons in authority' (Hansard, 15 Apr. 1981: 9307). Rights were secondary and restrained the growing emphasis on responsibility. Kaplan invoked crime control by arguing 'that society has a right to protection from illegal behaviour, even though committed by a minor' (ibid: 9308). He also argued that sentencing under the YOA had enough 'scope and flexibility to provide for the rights and needs of victims' by 'attempting to promote reconciliation between offender and victim' (ibid: 9309). This alluded to a non-punitive model of victims' rights that might not focus on the most serious crimes or rely on punishment. As will be seen, victims' rights, in both punitive and non-punitive forms, would influence the subsequent evolution of the YOA.

Kaplan stressed that 'the full exercise of due process under the law should be extended to young persons' (ibid: 9310). As Packer suggested, the focal point was the right to counsel, and Kaplan promised that 'under the proposed legislation, the young person would have the right to retain and instruct counsel at all stages of the proceedings ... Special safeguards would be established in order to assure proper and equitable practices in the taking of statements ... Rules of evidence and procedure would provide the opportunity to challenge the Crown's case and present a defence' (ibid). The image was a due-process obstacle course where defence lawyers could challenge the government's case at every turn. In addition, status offences would be repealed because they were 'too vague and not in keeping with modern ideas of young people having equal rights' (ibid: 9307). These new due-process rights won all-party approval,[7] with the police being the only dissenters and warning of the dangers of 'inflexible rules rendering any statement inadmissible not taken in strict conformity to the rules' and predicting that due process would 'result in clogged courts, larger fees for lawyers and less good for the accused' (Canada, JLAC, 24 Feb.1982, 64: 11). As it did in the drafting of the Charter (see chapter 1), due process won over crime control.

Due Process and the Young Offenders Act

In keeping with Packer's predictions, the right to counsel was the heart of the YOA's vision of due process. Section 56 required the police to inform young suspects that they were not obliged to say anything and that they could consult counsel and their parents. It clearly required the police to hold off obtaining statements until the suspect had a reasonable opportunity to consult counsel. It also required high waiver standards and the automatic exclusion of statements taken in violation of its enhanced right to counsel. It foreshadowed in statutory form the informational, holding-off, waiver, and exclusionary standards that the Supreme Court subsequently read into the adult system through its expansive interpretation of sections 10(b) and 24(2) of the Charter (see chapter 2). It was the harbinger of the new due process and received more criticism than the Charter.

Prior to the YOA, 'in many parts of Canada, lawyers rarely represented youths charged in juvenile court' (Bala and Kirvan 1991: 72). Section 11 of the YOA required young people to be provided with publicly funded counsel, often without inquiry as to whether their families could afford one.[8] The YOA brought more defence lawyers into youth court and gave them the ability to make due-process arguments. In British Columbia, for example, the number of young offenders represented by counsel increased from 38 per cent in 1984 to 80 per cent in 1988 (Corrado and Markwart 1992: 202). As will be seen, however, defence lawyers and due process did not help many young offenders escape punishment.

High-profile due-process decisions under the YOA created the impression that young offenders hid behind their rights. One such case involved a seventeen-year-old charged with first-degree murder in the sexual assault and killing of a three-year-old girl in Winnipeg. The police did not inform him of his right to counsel each time before they interrogated him, and as a result, incriminating statements were excluded. Even though warnings for factually guilty and street-smart seventeen-year-olds seemed 'unnecessary and frustrating to the police and society' (*J. (J.T)* 1990: 25), the Court concluded that they were required in order to protect the rights of the innocent.Nevertheless, the Court's own image of a 'worldly wise smug 17–year-old' taking advantage of his rights played into media images of teenaged murderers laughing at a system which protected their rights (*Winnipeg Free Press*, 6 Apr. 1995).

As she did in the sexual-assault cases discussed in chapter 5, Justice L'Heureux-Dubé dissented because of concerns about victims' rights and crime control. She started with a moving discussion of the three-year-old victim – her name; what she was wearing; how she was sexually assaulted; and how, when she cried, for her grandmother, her skull and neck were fractured with a cinder block. The emotional empathy that her judgment invoked for the victim also played a role in family conferences (Braithwaite and Mugford 1994), but was used here as a reason to resist the accused's due-process claims. L'Heureux-Dubé J. viewed the accused not as an abstract holder of rights, or even an unsavoury surrogate for the innocent, but as a seventeen-year-old father who carried his lawyer's card in his pocket (*J. (J.T.)* 1990: 14). She quoted parliamentarians who had objected to seventeen-year-olds being included in the YOA (ibid: 10–11) and criticized the majority for being more protective of the accused than even American courts. Adopting crime-control values, Justice L'Heureux-Dubé argued that '"interrogation in the presence of defence counsel would be an exercise in futility"' and warned that the majority's decision might strike '"a death blow"' for interrogations as a '"legitimate and proper procedure in criminal investigations"' (ibid: 18). She give weight to the prosecutor's judgment that, without the statements, the accused would be acquitted and that this would 'generate palpable disrespect for the criminal justice system and cast serious aspersion on the benefits and balances inherent in the Act' (ibid: 19–20).

On 14 September 1990, the day after the Court's judgment, the *Winnipeg Free Press* led with the story that the Supreme Court had denied the prosecutor leave to appeal a thirteen-year-old's acquittal of murdering two women, aged eighty-six and fifty-nine, during a break-in. The headline stated that the teenager had 'run around the room dancing' when informed of the Court's decision. This reinforced the image of young offenders laughing at the rights they had been granted. *J. (J.T.)* (1990)

also made the front page. The story featured a picture of the accused, now twenty-two years old, who was not dancing for joy because he was still in Prince Albert Penitentiary. The victim's grandmother expressed anguish at the thought of a new trial. 'To have to go through court once is enough for any family who has lost a loved one ... He was put away, and it was supposed to be for life' (*Winnipeg Free Press*, 14 Sep. 1990). The chief of police wondered if a young person could ever waive his rights and be successfully interrogated (*Winnipeg Free Press*, 15 Sep. 1990). Contrary to Justice L'Heureux-Dubé's fears, the accused did not go free. His statements were inadmissible, but the cinder block used to kill the victim was admissible. Later the same year, he was convicted of manslaughter and, because he had been transferred to adult court, was sentenced to twenty-two years' imprisonment (*Globe and Mail*, 27 Dec. 1990). This sentence was raised to life imprisonment in part to ensure that he was always under state control (*J.(J.T.)* 1991). Media and judicial images of laughing young offenders going free were promoted, but not realized in this case.

Cases such as *J. (J.T.)* were vulnerable to crime-control and victims'-rights criticisms, and the Justice department floated the idea of repealing section 56 of the YOA (Bala 1992: 40). As occurred with wiretaps (see chapter 2), there were proposals to replace the automatic exclusionary rule in section 56 with the minimum standards of section 24(2) of the Charter (Canada 1997: 71). Nevertheless, the YOA's robust right-to-counsel protections have so far survived relatively unscathed. This can be explained by reference to the autonomous nature of due-process discourse and the fact that public dissatisfaction with the YOA was channelled in the direction of increased punishment for the most serious offenders.

Was Due Process for Crime Control?

Decisions such as *J. (J.T.)* may have created the impression that the courts used due process to open the prison doors, but the evidence suggests otherwise. Since the enactment of the YOA, six provinces have built new prisons for young offenders, and others have converted adult facilities for use for young offenders. In most provinces, the numbers of youth detention centres expanded because sixteen- and seventeen-year-olds were for the first time not dealt with in the adult system. These teenagers received the benefit of the expanded due-process protections of the YOA, but were also sentenced more harshly. In British Columbia, for example, there was a 44 per cent increase between 1983/4 and 1986/7 in the incarceration of seventeen-year-olds (Corrado and Markwart 1988: 109–10).When only those youths who were subject to the JDA are taken into account, the proportion of custodial sentences increased in most provinces. Many of these custodial sentences were for less than three months as judges focused on the offender's responsibility for the offence and were attracted to the idea that the short, sharp shock of a brief custodial sentence would deter youth crime (Doob, Marinos, and Varma 1995: 137).

It is difficult to explain exactly why imprisonment increased under the YOA. Governments responded to public fears and were attracted to law-and-order positions. It is possible that they might have been more punitive without due process (Stuart 1996a), but it was not clear that due process actually helped keep young people out of jail. Many young people had difficulties understanding elaborate right-to-counsel warnings, and even if their statements were excluded, they, like J. (J.T.), might still be convicted on the basis of other evidence. The greater use of defence lawyers and prosecutors may have produced an adversarial approach that made it easier to send young people to prison (Corrado and Markwart 1988: 113). As discussed below, it might be the case that allowing amateurs to have a greater role through family conferencing may help make the system less punitive.

Some parts of the YOA enabled crime control even as they gave young people more rights. In 1995, young offenders were made eligible for jury trials, but only because they were also exposed to a maximum punishment of ten years' imprisonment. Status offences were abolished by the YOA, but this increased the exposure of young offenders to fingerprinting. The YOA gave young people the same rights to bail as adults, but the incidence of pre-trial detention increased, with most young offenders being detained because of fears that they would commit crimes in the future.[9] Giving youths the same rights as adults appeared to protect their rights, but it also frequently subjected them to the same crime-control measures as adults.

Although due process was not inconsistent with crime control, and at times enabled it, crime control did not need the cover of due process. It frequently justified itself in its own name. For example, the Supreme Court upheld a relatively severe sentence of two years' open custody for three break and enters by observing that the YOA's 'references to responsibility ... and to the protection of society ... suggest that a traditional criminal law approach should be taken into account in the sentencing of young offenders' (M. (J.J.) 1993: 492). This meant not only requiring a young person to take responsibility for his or her crime, but also considering that 'the sentence imposed on one member of a "swarming group" should serve to deter others in the gang' (ibid: 497). The same Court that excluded incriminating statements in *J. (J.T.)* (1990) cheerfully accepted media-induced fears of swarming teenagers and general deterrence as a legitimate goal of sentencing in youth court.[10] Due process was not hegemonic, and increased punitiveness was directly justified by appeals to crime control and victims' rights.

The YOA was the target of much public criticism and legislative amendment. Nick Bala (1994: 645) observed that 'few, if any pieces of Canadian legislation have been the subject of such sustained criticism.' The *Globe and Mail* (23 Jul. 1993) was blunter and concluded that there was 'no more reviled piece of federal legislation in this country than the *YOA* ... It seems the public anger is bottomless. It feeds on every new report of horrifying violence among our youth, and lamentably there is no end in sight to these reports.' Much of the criticism focused on the YOA's maximum penalties of imprisonment.

Punishing the Worse Cases

The YOA[11] was amended in 1992 to increase the punishment for murder from three years to five years less a day, and to provide that public protection was the primary consideration when deciding whether a young offender should be transferred to adult court. The Liberal critic George Rideout stated that he was 'pleased to see, in this legislation, that there is a movement to have public safety paramount' and criticized the government for not responding to police concerns that it was becoming too difficult to secure admissible statements from young suspects (Hansard, 30 May 1990: 12068–9). The 1992 amendments stressed the denunciation and deterrence of serious crimes and expressed concern for victims through increased punishment. Only the NDP criticized the bill for focusing exclusively on youths charged with murder. They argued that the amendments were symbolic and superficial and did not respond to the causes of youth crime, including the sexual abuse of children (ibid: 12077).

During the 1993 election campaign, all major parties (except the Bloc Québécois)[12] promised to toughen the YOA (*Globe and Mail*, 21 Oct. 1993). Public rallies to the same effect featured the families of murdered children. Following their campaign promises, the new Liberal government increased murder sentences in youth court to a maximum of ten years and made transfer to adult court presumptive for sixteen- and seventeen-year-olds charged with homicide or aggravated sexual assault. Justice Minister Allan Rock argued that bill 'addressed the very real public concerns about crimes of violence by youths in Canada' (Hansard, 6 Jun. 1994: 4872). The bill was criticized by the Bloc as a punitive measure that caved in to 'western reactionaries' (ibid: 4879), while Reform argued that the remaining restrictions on punishment were 'tragically painful for the families of the victim and perhaps ... dangerous to the community' (ibid: 4883). Public debate focused on punishing the most serious and rare offences committed by young people.

Alternatives

Most of the amendments to the YOA focused on crime control and punitive forms of victims' rights, with only occasional glimpses of a non-punitive approach to victims' rights or a recognition that the current epidemics of youth crime and child abuse might be related.

Risk and Information

While increasing punishment for the most serious offences and allowing victim impact statements in youth court, the 1995 amendments also allowed information about young offenders to be released in order to allow school officials and others to take steps to avoid the risks of serious harm. This amendment responded to a highly publicized British Columbia case in which a released young sex offender assaulted and killed a child (Bala 1997: 218), but it also reflected the growing importance of the production and distribution of risk information by criminal justice actors to other institutions (Ericson and Haggerty 1997). This amendment relied on the neo-liberal idea that individuals would have to use state-supplied information in order to protect themselves (Garland 1996). Information about offenders could create moral panics, fear, and stigmatization of offenders (Scheingold, Pershing, and Olson 1994). It could, however, perhaps also be used by school officials, child-welfare officials, and parents to take preventive and protective measures rather than relying on punishment after the fact.

Crime Prevention

The YOA's long and ambiguous list of principles was also amended in 1995 to indicate that 'crime prevention is essential to the long-term protection of society and requires addressing the underlying causes of crime by young people and developing multi-disciplinary approaches to identifying and effectively responding to children and young persons at risk of committing offending behaviour in the future' (*YOA* s.3[1][a]). Here, the concept of risk was used not as a reason for spreading fearful and stigmatizing messages about those who had committed serious offences in the past, but rather as a justification for non-punitive intervention and treatment before crimes were committed. This principle linked increased awareness of sexual and other forms of child abuse and the subsequent offending behaviour of young people. It spoke most directly, not to police and prosecutors, but to 'those who work in the health, education and social science fields' (Bala 1997: 39). Some victim advocates recognized the importance of early intervention. Priscilla de Villiers of CAVEAT, for example, noted that, in every school report card, her daughter's killer had been 'clearly identified as having severe anger problems, severe behavioural problems, uncontrollable rages etc. ... The point is that in the whole of his 32 years of life, not one person intervened' (Canada 1997: 23).

The National Crime Prevention Council (1996) prepared a series of studies describing various crime-prevention interventions targeting young people. They included pre-natal and early-child-care assistance for high-risk parents, school-based anti-bullying programs, and community programs in high-risk neighbourhoods. The famous Perry Pre-School Program demonstrated not only less offending when its young recipients became teenagers, but also less teenage pregnancy and drug use, and increased educational and work achievements. One Montreal program targeting disruptive kindergarten boys resulted in fewer self-reported delinquencies later in life (Maxfield and Spatz Widom 1996). Such programs operated on risk and surveillance concepts, but attempted to prevent crime long before it occurred. They took a more holistic approach to offending, which resisted the criminalization of politics and recognized that various forms of child abuse and neglect played a role in future offending. These initiatives were a far cry from the radical non-intervention (Schur 1973) defended by Packer and other 1960s liberals, but they were a less punitive alternative to exclusive reliance on the criminal sanction and punishment.

Family Conferences

A 1995 amendment to the YOA required the youth court to consider 'that a young person who commits an offence that does not involve serious personal injury should be held accountable to the victim and to society through non-custodial dispositions whenever appropriate' (*YOA* s.24[1.1][b]). Justice Minister Allan Rock defended keeping 'non-violent' offenders out of jail by stressing the costs of imprisonment and the value of 'restorative justice' (Hansard, 6 Jun. 1994: 4873). An appeal to restorative justice enabled politicians to defend rehabilitation without appearing to be soft on youth crime. It promised to decrease reliance on imprisonment and save money without sacrificing the offender's accountability to both the victim and society.

Family conferencing was an example of a diversion program which could hold young offenders accountable to their victims without the use of custody. These conferences provided youths with an opportunity to apologize to victims and others for their crimes and to propose a means of restitution. They relied on reintegrative shaming, and the support of both the offender's and victim's families and friends. As their name suggested, family conferences were consistent with a parental or family model of criminal justice. Unlike trials in both the crime-control and the due-process models, they should not be a 'status degradation ceremony' (Griffiths 1970: 385). They should focus on reintegration because 'when a parent punishes his child, both parent and child know that afterward they will go on living together as before' (ibid: 376).

The origins of family group conferencing were in traditional Maori forms of justice. In chapter 8, Aboriginal justice will be examined as a distinct and promising alternative to crime control and due process. Family group conferences were used most extensively in New Zealand under the 1989 Children, Young Persons and Their Families Act. (S.N.Z. 1989, no.24). This act provided for family group conferences both for child protection and for criminal proceedings. The former embraced the family-centred approach to child protection emphatically rejected by the Badgley Committee as giving insufficient attention to the criminality of child abuse (Canada 1984b). There may be some tension between the criminal justice–centred approach towards child sexual abuse discussed earlier in the chapter and less punitive forms of family conferences contemplated under the New Zealand act and the 1995 amendments to the YOA.

Section 208 of the New Zealand act encouraged alternatives to criminal proceedings 'unless the public interest requires otherwise.' Consistent with the family-centred philosophy of the entire act, any measures for dealing with offending by children should be designed 'to strengthen the family, whanau, hapu, iwi and family group ... to develop their own means of dealing with offending by their children and young persons' (ibid). Family conferences could include not only the offender's family, but also the victim. The New Zealand law provided that 'any measures for dealing with offending by children should have due regard to the interests of any victims of that offending' (ibid), and a South Australia law promoted 'concern for the needs of the victim and the need to restore harmony between the offender and the victim' (Wundersitz and Hetzel 1996: 116).

Family conferences were very different from the quick guilty plea and sentencing used in the crime-control model or the abstract legal challenges of the due-process model. Conferences last on average three hours, with much more time required for preparing the participants, who may be initially reluctant to be involved. The offender, his family, friends, and counsellors, as well as willing victims and their supporters, gather under the observation of a supervisor who may also be a police officer or social worker. Conferences were generally held in neutral settings. As in Aboriginal forms of justice, the participants often gathered in a circle (Stewart 1996: 76; Wundersitz and Hetzel 1996: 127). The circle emphasized common participation and responsibility for finding solutions, and symbolized the act of restoration which attempted to return to the victim what the offender had taken.

Consistent with YOA requirements governing diversion programs, the offender generally admitted responsibility for the offence. Victims were given an opportunity to explain how the offence affected them, and other members of the group voiced their concerns about the offender and the victim. The offender was also allowed to speak and could apologize for the offence as well as propose some plan for amends. The offender's family and friends could be in a good position to shame the offender for what he had done; to offer support and reintegration; and to provide supervision and guidance to prevent future crimes. Befitting the more informal nature, each family conference had considerable procedural autonomy, with less emphasis on speed and finality than found in either crime-control or due-process models. In New Zealand, they could be reconvened at the request of two of its members (S.N.Z. 1989, no. 25 ss.256, 270).

Family conferences could be intense, intrusive, and emotional; they were often a far cry from the abstract rationalism of due process or the bureaucratic processing of crime control. 'Voices are low; silences, particularly following the victim's statements, are important because, if victims observe genuine remorse in the young person, then they can move on from anger to forgiveness' (Stewart 1996: 78). The process may be the punishment (Feeley 1979), but more in the sense of having to confront the consequences and shame of one's action as opposed to the hassle of having to attend court. Offenders could not escape responsibility by hiding behind the legalistic arguments of their lawyers. They could, however, relate their offending behaviour to their past victimization and present circumstances. Family conferences did not rely on stark dichotomies between offenders and victims, and some youths in New Zealand were simultaneously subject to youth-justice and child-welfare conferences (Hardin 1996: 68).

Victim participation was encouraged in New Zealand by an 1994 amendment which made clear that victims should be consulted about the conference and had a right to bring their supporters. An increasing emphasis on victim participation brought increased concern about achieving restorative justice (Stewart 1996: 68). Braithwaite and Mugford (1994: 147–9) argue that victim participation was crucial both in shaming the offender for the harm caused by the crime and in allowing opportunities for restoration and reintegration. They suggested that family conferences can 'deliver victim satisfaction that the courts can never deliver.' A New Zealand study found that 60 per cent of victims who attended family group conferences were satisfied, compared with 80 per cent of other participants (Maxwell and Morris 1996: 90, 100). Victims who participated in conferences expressed satisfaction that they could understand why the offence occurred and had a voice in the ultimate disposition. When victims were not satisfied, it was often because they did not believe that the offender was sorry, and because of difficulties in obtaining reparation. Maxwell and Morris (1996: 101) concluded that it was 'unrealistic to expect that remorse for the harm caused and the healing of victims can always be achieved. That positive and constructive outcomes occur at all can be construed as a considerable achievement in contrast to the failure of criminal courts to achieve restorative goals.'

A common fear was that crime victims would be vindictive. Braithwaite and Mugford (1994: 149) argued, however, that punitive reactions were promoted by 'distance, stereotyped offenders, and a simplification of evil,' and that 'the closer people get to the complexities of particular cases, the less punitive they get.' Other research suggested that people became less punitive the more they learned about a case (Doob and Roberts 1983, 1988). Family conferences may make victims less punitive by giving them more information about the offender's background and by allowing the offender and his or her family to apologize. If victims were extremely punitive, offenders could leave and take their chances in court.

Family conferences decreased the use of courts and prisons in New

Zealand. Court appearances decreased from 63 per 1,000 young people before the 1989 New Zealand act to 16 per 1,000 after the act (Maxwell and Morris 1996: 93–4). In 1986, New Zealand had 4,000 youths imprisoned, at a cost of $206 million, but by 1991 the number and cost had decreased to fewer than 1,000 and under $113 million (Canada 1997: 50). Family conferences could not be done on the cheap, but they could save money in the long term. In 1993–4, there were 7,500 family conferences in New Zealand, and 50 full-time youth justice co-ordinators. Nevertheless, between 1991 and 1994, spending on youth justice declined from $34.5 to $27.5 million (Maxwell and Morris 1996: 102).

Unfortunately there was not much Canadian experimentation or evaluation of family conferences. A small pilot project in Winnipeg revealed that, although the offenders wanted victims to attend the conference, most victims did not attend and believed it was the judge's task to resolve the matter (Longclaws et al 1996: 198). The conferences involved Aboriginal elders, families, teachers, and, in two cases, victims seated in a 'sharing circle' (ibid). The plans devised involved probation, community service, curfews, non-association, and abstention from alcohol and weapons. Because none of the offenders was employed, restitution was not feasible (ibid: 202). Each conference lasted three to four hours, but the offenders were processed in court in about thirty minutes (ibid: 204). All the offenders were Aboriginal, and all their plans involved some cultural component. As in New Zealand and Australia, family conferences could be used in a culturally appropriate manner which incorporated different understandings of family and community.

Family conferences may be politically feasible because of their emphasis on offender responsibility and victim participation,[13] as well as the potential cost savings of decreased reliance on imprisonment. They are not necessarily appropriate for all young offenders, and the 1995 amendments of the YOA drew the line for non-punitive responses at offences involving serious personal injury. As suggested in chapter 1, punitive and non-punitive forms of victims' rights can coexist, and much will depend on the balance. Family conferences could be discredited if they were used and failed in cases of serious crime, but many of their advocates would be reluctant to conclude that they were never appropriate in cases of serious crime.

Conclusion

The images of young people in criminal justice varied dramatically. As children they were often seen as vulnerable and innocent victims of sexual abuse, while as teenagers they became criminals prepared to exploit their due-process rights. The common thread was reliance on the criminal sanction, both to protect young people from victimization and to respond to their crimes. The reliance on the criminal sanction reproduced the false crime-control assumption that the criminal law controlled crime and invited due-process challenges. For the most part, efforts to criminalize the sexual abuse of children did not encounter the same due-process obstacles as sexual assault laws discussed in chapter 5. The emphasis on the criminal sanction also contributed to the criminalization of politics. Sexual abuse was emphasized over other forms of child abuse and neglect, and not always related to broader issues concerning family structure and sexuality. Youth crime was the site of competing crime-control, due-process, and victims' rights discourses, but not often related to changes in family structure and economic and cultural opportunities.

The use of the criminal sanction increased under the YOA. Robust due-process rights did not prevent increased punishment and may have played a modest enabling role. At the same time, due process was not needed to legitimate increased punishment because crime control and victims' rights did this work much more directly. The YOA absorbed public criticism that might have otherwise been directed at the Charter and the Supreme Court of Canada for moving in a due-process direction. Instead of unsuccessful campaigns to impeach the Chief Justice (Baker 1983), there were successful campaigns to toughen the YOA in the name of both crime control and victims' rights.

Victims' rights initiatives for youth crime were not, however, uniformly punitive. The 1995 amendments to the YOA allowed the worse crimes to be punished more severely, but also pointed in the direction of early crime prevention, risk profiling, and information sharing to respond to more immediate risks. Moreover, the amendments encouraged the use of family conferences to respond to youth crime that did not result in serious personal injury. Parliament thus attempted to draw a line between punitive and non-punitive responses to youth crime. The next two chapters will similarly conclude with discussions of alternatives to crime control or punitive forms of victims's rights and due process, but only after exploring how due process and crime control have been offered as a response to the problems that various minorities and Aboriginal people faced in their interactions with criminal justice.

7

Minorities

Herbert Packer hoped that due process would promote the equality of minorities. In the 1960s, it was all too clear that African Americans required protection from the police. Ugly spectacles such as the use of attack dogs against civil-rights demonstrators had 'driven home the lesson that law enforcement unchecked by law is tyrannous' (Packer 1966: 240). To the extent that due process led to less reliance on the criminal sanction, particularly with respect to consensual crimes, this would assist 'the urban poor, and particularly those who belong to minority groups, [who] provide most of the raw material for the criminal process' (ibid: 241). Like other liberals in the 1960s, Packer believed that equality could be achieved by restraining the state.

When Packer defended due process as a response to discrimination against minorities, he focused on specific acts of police abuse. Individual cases continued to attract attention, but were supplemented in the 1980s and 1990s by knowledge about the systemic outcomes of the criminal process. Despite due-process protections, African Americans were dramatically overrepresented in American prisons. An inquiry examining systemic racism against black people in Ontario's criminal justice system also found overrepresentation (Ontario 1995). Overrepresentation analysis challenged Packer's faith that due process could achieve justice for minorities. Due process might respond to the discriminatory exercise of discretion in individual cases, but it would not affect the run-of-the-mill cases which contributed to minority overrepresentation. The danger was that it might legitimate overrepresentation as the result of a fair process.

Packer also wrote before victimization studies revealed that some minorities were disproportionately represented among the victims of crimes. African Americans were overrepresented not only in prison, but among the victims of crime. Aboriginal people in Canada were similarly overrepresented among both prisoners and victims of crime (see chapter 8). Gays and lesbians and the disabled, both groups that have become politicized since Packer's day (Cairns 1995), were disproportionately victimized by some types of crime. One could no longer assume, as Packer did, that justice for minorities could be achieved by restraining the state through due process. The rule of law and equality demanded that minorities receive the equal protection of the criminal law, but the result was often symbolic and divisive new political cases that pitted the accused's due-process claims against the equality claims of disadvantaged groups. The use of the criminal sanction in the name of the rights of minority crime victims also reproduced the questionable crime-control assumption that the criminal law controlled crime.

If due process was incapable of reducing minority overrepresentation in prison, and crime-control and punitive forms of victims' rights could not reduce minority overrepresentation among the victims of crime, the prospects for reform seemed dismal. As will be discussed in the next chapter, more progress has been made in developing Aboriginal justice as an alternative that promised to reduce both reliance on punishment and victimization. A non-punitive approach to minority crime victims would be aware of the legitimate demands for the equal protection of the law, but also recognize that the criminal sanction remained a blunt and divisive instrument. It would recognize the pitfalls of the new political case and place greater emphasis on preventive and restorative strategies.

Minorities and Due Process

Compared with the Warren Court (Graham 1970; Baker 1983), Canadian courts were slow to appreciate the implications of their due-process decisions for minorities. This was related to the lack of a tradition of seeing crime through the lens of race, and Canadian complacency about the treatment of minorities.

Investigative Stops

Richard Ericson (1982: 200–1) found that the police engaged in 'constant proactive stops' as a 'not-so-subtle way of reminding marginal people of the "order of things."' In the suburbs of Toronto in the mid-1970s, this meant targeting young '"pukers."' In Western Canada, it involved disproportionate investigative stops of Aboriginal people (see chapter 8). In Toronto in the 1990s, it meant stopping black people, particularly black males. Ontario's Commission on Systemic Racism (1995: 352–5) reported that 43 per cent of black male respondents had been stopped by the police in the previous two years as opposed to 25 per cent of white males and 19 per cent of Chinese males. This overrepresentation persisted among university graduates and older black men. The black men stopped believed that the police associated them with illegal drugs and held them to be out of order if they had expensive cars or were accompanied by white women (ibid: 356).

Police powers to engage in investigative stops were not easily amenable to judicial regulation. Due-process decisions affected only the small number of investigative stops which resulted in the discovery of incriminating evidence and prosecutions. Judicial regulation was indirect and blunt, but Canadian courts did not even bother to try. In 1990, the Supreme Court went beyond its limited exception to allow drunk-driving spot-checks (*Hufsky* 1988; see chapter 2) and authorized random stops of motorists for a wide range of traffic-safety reasons such as checking the validity of licences, insurance, and the mechanical fitness of vehicles. The majority concluded that 'the random stop is rationally connected and carefully designed to achieve safety on the highways' (*Ladouceur* 1990: 41). A four-judge minority bitterly complained that 'this case may be viewed as the last straw' because it meant 'that a police officer can stop any vehicle at any time, in any place, without having any reason to do so ... The decision may be based on any whim. Individual officers will have different reasons. Some may tend to stop younger drivers, others older cars, and so on. Indeed, as pointed out by Tarnopolsky J.A., racial considerations may be a factor too' (ibid: 27, 29). The Court continued to allow random traffic stops, but excluded drugs that were discovered when police abused their powers by making inquiries not related to traffic safety (*Mellenthin* 1992).

There were, however, few remedies for the innocent driver or pedestrian who faced the intimidating and degrading experience of being stopped and hassled by the police for no reason except perhaps the colour of his or her skin. Such a person might bring a civil action, but this was costly and, even if successful, might only result in something like $500 in damages (*Crossman* 1984). Another option was to make a complaint against the police, but in most cases such complaints were investigated by the police themselves. In one high-profile Toronto case, Audrey Smith, a black visitor from Jamaica, complained about an investigative stop that she alleged resulted in a partial strip-search on a street. Smith had to wait eight months for a board of inquiry while the police slowly investigated the case in a way they compared to 'a homicide investigation' (*Globe and Mail*, 29 Sep. 1993). The hearing before the board was disbanded because the son of one of the adjudicators, a police officer, could be called as a witness. A second hearing was stopped when the police successfully argued that one of the adjudicators could be seen to be biased because she was the president of the Congress of Black Women of Canada, Mississauga Chapter. The Toronto chapter of that organization had called Smith's detention and search an outrage and demanded the officer's suspension (*Dulmage* 1994: 363). A third hearing held that Smith's allegation was not proven by 'clear and convincing evidence' in part because her explanation about why she was in the street late at night was not accepted. Although the complaint was a non-criminal proceeding, one officer involved played the martyr by stating: 'It's been stressful on myself and my family. The kids were asking me "Are you going to jail Daddy?"' Smith's lawyer complained that the victim had been put on trial, and Smith's friend commented that all she 'ever wanted was an apology. She just wanted someone to say, "Sorry"' (*Globe and Mail*, 22 Sep. 1995).

Another high-profile complaint was made by Dwight Drummond, a Toronto television personality, who was subjected to a high-risk takedown. When a deputy police chief recommended that the officers involved face a public hearing, one police division responded by locking themselves in their station for eight hours (*Globe and Mail*, 28 Jan. 1995). Drummond's complaint was also rejected by a board of inquiry even though the police officers could not locate the person who they claimed told them she saw two black men with a gun getting into a car that was the same colour as Drummond's. One officer said he had attempted to apologize at the time, but Drummond, who had been required to lay face down in the street, described it as 'a cursory explanation' (*Globe and Mail*, 27 Sep. 1995) and not a formal apology. The Smith and Drummond cases indicated that an innocent person who had been hassled by the police and who believed that racial discrimination was a factor would have a very difficult time obtaining a remedy.

The factually guilty were sometimes more lucky. The Ontario Court of Appeal was the most active Canadian court in shaping due-process doctrine with a view to preventing discrimination against minorities.[1] In 1993, it found the stop of a young man, emerging from what had been described in a police memorandum as a 'crack house' in Toronto's Regent Park area, was an arbitrary detention contrary to section 9 of the Charter. The court was concerned that the police officer's subjective hunch 'can too easily mask discriminatory conduct based on such irrelevant factors as the detainee's sex, colour, age, ethnic origin or sexual orientation' (*Simpson* 1993: 502). The fact that the hunch was correct and cocaine was discovered in the suspect's pocket did not deter the court from excluding it as unconstitutionally obtained evidence. The Court of Appeal required police to have some objectively discernible and articulable cause to justify investigative detentions short of arrest. The case was an attempt to recognize the reality that police often stopped people when they did not intend to arrest them, and to respond to the failure of the legislature to regulate these low-visibility encounters (Young 1991, 1996). It was, however, criticized for creating, as well as regulating, police powers to engage in investigative detentions and searches (Delisle 1993). In any event, due-process decisions produced infrequent and blunt remedies for discriminatory police practices.

Bail Decisions

The Supreme Court was slow to appreciate the implications of due-process decisions for minorities. One factor was a lack of good statistics. With the exception of Aboriginal overrepresentation, there were virtually no overrepresentation data until Ontario's Commission on Systemic Racism (1995: 125) conducted its research (Roberts and Doob 1997). It found significant overrepresentation of black people among those not released after arrest or at bail hearings, especially among those facing drug charges.[2] Differences in criminal records did not explain the discrepancy, but higher unemployment among black accused played a role. These statistics suggested that black accused in Ontario were less likely to benefit from the discretionary release decisions made by police and justices in bail court.

Without the benefit of the data noted above or an intervention by a group representing the black community, the Supreme Court upheld most of the Criminal Code's bail provisions from Charter challenges. Despite acknowledging the difficulty of predicting future danger, the Court upheld denial of bail 'for the protection or safety of the public' because of the important 'objective of stopping criminal behaviour' (*Morales* 1992: 113). The Court focused on the law in the books which required a substantial likelihood of future danger and did not advert to the effects of racial stereotypes that might make black accused seem more dangerous. The Court also approved of detention when necessary to ensure the accused's attendance at trial without recognizing that routine consideration of an accused's unemployment or lack of citizenship could operate to the disadvantage of some minorities. The Supreme Court's decision upholding these grounds of detention as just causes for the denial of bail supported the argument that due process was for crime control in the sense that carefully worded legislation enabled police and judges routinely to authorize pre-trial detention while creating the appearance of fairness. The Court upheld robust pre-trial-detention powers by imagining an unsituated and raceless person that unambiguously met the criteria for detention set out in the legislation.

The Supreme Court also upheld a reverse onus that required accused charged with importing or trafficking drugs to show cause why they should be granted bail. The reverse onus was necessary because drug dealers posed a 'significant risk' (*Pearson* 1992: 146) of flight and future criminal activity. The Court acknowledged that the reverse onus would unfairly apply to '"small fry" drug dealers' (ibid) but, this time relying on the law in action, predicted that such accused would be able to satisfy the onus. Ontario's Commission on Systemic Racism (1995: 156) subsequently concluded that the reverse onus upheld as fair by the Supreme Court 'may be contributing significantly to disproportionate imprisonment of untried black accused.'

The media followed the Court by ignoring race. With headlines like 'Accused Drug Dealers Face Tougher Bail Rules' (*Montreal Gazette*, 20 Nov. 1992), the decisions were likely popular. Ontario's Commission on Systemic Racism called for Parliament to repeal the reverse onus, but this reform was not included in 1997 amendments which resurrected pre-trial detention in the 'public interest' (see chapter 3). In all likelihood, Parliament will never enact legislation that would make it look soft on accused drug dealers. In the Charter era, due-process decisions were more likely to attract a legislative reply than those which affirmed crime control or victims' rights. It also makes a difference that the African-Canadian community had less political clout than the police or feminist groups who secured legislative replies to due-process decisions (see chapters 2 and 5).

The refusal to repeal the reverse onus was politically significant, but repeal would not have been a panacea. By focusing on the reverse onus, the Ontario commission may have fallen into the trap of legalized politics, which responded to Court decisions and assumed, as Packer did, that due process would protect minorities from discrimination in the criminal process. More due process would not have addressed the complex social, cultural, and economic problems that resulted in discrimination in release decisions.

Jury Selection

Canadian courts were traditionally reluctant to admit that juries could be selected in a discriminatory manner or be capable of racial discrimination. In the early 1970s, two black accused in Ontario challenged a pool of prospective jurors because it contained no black people. The trial judge denied their claim on the basis that the sheriff had not engaged in wilful misconduct in summoning the jurors and that requiring black jurors would result in reverse discrimination (*Bradley* 1973: 40–1). Ontario's Commission on Systemic Racism (1995: 250–3) found that blacks were still underrepresented on juries and recommended that jurors no longer be required to be Canadian citizens. The Ontario Court of Appeal, however, found that the citizenship requirement was a justified restriction on the equality rights of non-citizens (*Church of Scientology* 1997), even though the Supreme Court found that the same requirement for lawyers to be unjustified discrimination (*Andrews* 1989). As was the case with the reverse onus for bail decisions, the fact that the citizenship requirement was upheld under the Charter will likely inhibit legislative reform.

If a minority accused could not have someone of the same race on the jury, then he or she might at least want to question prospective jurors about whether their verdict would be tainted by prejudice. Fearing that such questions would degenerate into an American-style jury-selection process where the accused could ask jurors almost unlimited questions in the hope of obtaining a favourable jury, Canadian courts traditionally refused to allow such questions. In one case, a judge concluded that to contemplate that jury verdicts might be influenced by racism was 'to admit to a weakness in our nation and in our community which I do not propose to acknowledge' (*Crosby* 1979: 256).

As was the case with investigative stops, the Ontario Court of Appeal was the first court to acknowledge the possibility of racism. In a case involving a black man accused of murdering a white man during a cocaine deal in Toronto, the Court of Appeal held that 'it was essential to the conduct of a fair trial' that the accused be able to ask prospective jurors whether their ability to decide the case fairly would be affected by the race of the accused and the victim (*Parks* 1993: 379). This case was decided before the Ontario commission documented black underrepresentation on juries and black overrepresentation in prison, but the court took note of systemic discrimination as measured by human-rights complaints and a report on anti-black racism in the wake of a Toronto riot after a police officer was acquitted in the shooting of a black man (ibid:

367–9). Doherty J.A. also considered 'the perceptions of those who claim to be victims of racial prejudice,' while stating that these perceptions 'cannot, necessarily, be equated with the reality of such victimization' (ibid: 369). This fitted into a victims' rights approach which paid attention to subjective perceptions and was prepared to consider the accused as a potential victim. The Court of Appeal concluded that inquiring about racial prejudice would eliminate some prejudiced jurors; encourage the remaining jurors 'to confront potential racial bias and ensure that it does not impact on their verdict,' and enhance 'the appearance of fairness in the mind of the accused' and 'many blacks [who] perceive the criminal justice system as inherently racist' (ibid: 379–80). The Court of Appeal hoped that allowing one question would legitimate the trial process as fair and non-discriminatory.

Some judges believed that the *Parks* question should be allowed only in Toronto because anti-black racism was a Toronto problem. Others believed that *Parks* had opened the door to questions about whether jurors would be prejudiced against accused charged with sexual assault or other unpopular crimes. The Ontario Court of Appeal eventually clarified that a black accused anywhere in the province could ask the question (*Wilson* 1996), but that questions directed at generic prejudice related to the crime were not allowed (*Betker* 1997). The Court of Appeal also refused to allow the *Parks* question in cases where the accused was gay (*Alli* 1996) or Vietnamese (*Ly* 1997) because of the lack of evidence of systemic discrimination against these groups. There was a danger that courts would ignore the potential of juror prejudice against accused from disadvantaged, but less studied and documented, groups.

The Court of Appeal recognized the disease of anti-black racism, but its remedy was not a cure. It only allowed a blunt question of the 'Are you a racist?' variety (Henry and Henry 1995; Roach 1995b) and disallowed questions about whether the fact that the accused was an immigrant from Jamaica and involved in illegal drugs would prejudice the jurors (*Parks* 1993: 359). Even if the *Parks* question was perfectly effective in removing jurors influenced by racist stereotypes, it affected only the small minority of cases which involved jury trials (Friedland and Roach 1997a). It remained much more difficult to suggest that a trial judge was influenced by anti-black stereotypes.[3] Jury-selection reforms affected only the high end of the justice industry. Due process in the exceptional case might legitimate crime control in the routine case.

In summary, there were real limitations to the effectiveness of *Simpson* (1993) and *Parks* (1993) in combatting racial discrimination in the criminal process, and especially in reducing minority overrepresentation in prison. *Simpson* affected only investigative stops which revealed incriminating evidence, and it forced courts to exclude evidence in those cases where police hunches and stereotypes turned out to be correct. *Parks* affected only the small minority of cases decided by juries, and only if prospective jurors honestly and correctly recognized when their deliberations would be tainted by racial stereotypes. The bail-and-juror citizenship cases suggested that courts could still ignore racial discrimination. The absence of statistical evidence of discrimination prevented some disadvantaged minorities from gaining even the limited protection offered by due-process doctrine.

From Individual Cases to Systemic Overrepresentation

At its best, due process could respond to the discriminatory exercise of discretion in individual cases. Packer had similar ambitions and did not have to respond to concerns about the disproportionate imprisonment of minorities. Like victimization studies which revealed high levels of unreported crime, overrepresentation data placed new demands on the criminal justice system. Ontario's Commission on Systemic Racism (1995: 71) stressed that black people accounted for about 3 per cent of Ontario's population, but 15 per cent of admissions to its provincial prisons. It rightly dismissed the idea that overrepresentation was a reflection of above-average criminality by blacks by arguing that neither race nor culture determined crime. More controversially, it gave short shrift (one and a half pages of analysis in a report of more than 400 pages) to the alternative thesis that black overrepresentation was related to social and economic inequality (ibid: 95–7). Rather, it focused on discriminatory enforcement as the explanation for the overrepresentation. The 'public problem' (Gusfield 1981) of black overrepresentation was located in the criminal justice system when there were social and economic factors at play which were not as amenable to visible and relatively cheap reforms.

The assumption that the criminal process should be reformed to reduce overrepresentation borrowed from employment-equity analysis (Canada 1984a; Knopff 1989). In employment equity, there was a problem if the percentage of employees of a targeted group did not match the percentage of the group in the qualified labour market. Similarly, the overrepresentation of a group in prison as compared with the population at large created an overrepresentation problem in criminal justice. Links were sometimes drawn between the overrepresentation of groups in prison and their underrepresentation among justice officials. Achieving the proper statistical measures was more difficult in criminal justice because the practices of multiple bureaucracies – the police, prosecutors, judges, and correctional officials – had to be changed. Overrepresentation analysis placed new demands on a criminal justice system that in Packer's time did not have to account for its aggregate outcomes. The ability to measure the social distribution of harms exceeded the ability to control them. (Beck 1992). Failure to reduce unreported crime or overrepresentation to zero could produce an unquenchable demand for criminal justice reform. This was not only an example of risk society, but a process of construction – a criminalization of politics, economics, demography, and culture – that attempted to use the criminal process to respond to social ills.

Due-process cures likely overemphasized the contribution of discriminatory enforcement to overrepresentation. There were real limits on how much even the most robust due-process reforms could deliver. A focus on the discriminatory effects of law and discretion was legitimate and necessary, but it also diverted attention from social, economic, and cultural factors that also contributed to overrepresentation. Just as some of the strategies examined in the previous three chapters may have overestimated the ability of the criminal law to reduce victimization, so, too, may the legal reforms examined in this section have overestimated the ability of due process to reduce overrepresentation.

Crime Control and Minorities

Since Packer's time, there was a growing recognition that some minorities were disproportionately victimized by crime. Victimization studies revealed that African Americans were overrepresented among crime victims (Elias 1993; Sampson and Lauritsen 1997), as well as among prisoners (Tonry 1995). With the exception of Aboriginal people, however, less systemic data were available in Canada (Roberts and Doob 1997). The victimization of minorities by crime was symbolized by well-publicized individual cases which inspired crime-control measures and produced new political cases pitting the due-process rights of the accused against the equality rights of minority victims.

Police Shootings

Between 1978 and 1995, sixteen black men were shot by the police in Ontario, ten of them fatally. Ontario's Commission on Systemic Racism

(1995: 377) concluded that 'the number and circumstances of police shootings in Ontario have convinced many black Ontarians that they are disproportionately vulnerable to police violence.' The most visible policy response to these shootings was unsuccessful criminal prosecutions of police officers. In a variation of the new political case, the police claimed Charter rights while the African-Canadian community demanded the equal protection of the criminal law as victims and potential victims of police violence.

Nine of the sixteen shootings resulted in criminal prosecutions, but they all ended with acquittals (Ontario 1995: 377). One reason why convictions proved impossible was the due-process nature of criminal investigations and trials. Despite being required since 1990 to 'co-operate fully'[4] with the new Special Investigations Unit (SIU) that investigated police shootings, police officers frequently refused to talk to investigators (ibid: 382). Like others accused of serious crimes, they also had an unfettered right to use peremptory challenges to keep a limited number of prospective jurors off the jury.[5] Prosecutors failed in their attempts to regulate these challenges to prevent black people and other minorities from being kept off juries in cases involving police shootings (*Lines* 1993). Canadian courts did not follow American courts in requiring prosecutors and accused to give non-discriminatory explanations for their peremptory challenges (Peterson 1993).

Once the jury was selected, the prosecutor had to establish the police officer's guilt, including the lack of any defence, beyond a reasonable doubt. As discussed in chapter 3, a murder conviction required proof that the officer subjectively knew that the victim was likely to die. Manslaughter was defined more broadly, but the Supreme Court ruled that a police officer who claimed he accidentally shot a black youth in the parking lot of a Montreal police station should not be held to a higher standard of care because of his knowledge about firearms (*Gosset* 1993). Even if the police officer acted with the necessary fault, a reasonable doubt that the officer was acting in self-defence would result in an acquittal. A claim of self-defence allowed a 'defence strategy ... [of] attacking the character of the victim. Through evidence of previous convictions, character or mental instability, the victim may be characterized as prone to violence' (Ontario 1995: 385).

Until 1993, the Criminal Code authorized the shooting of a 'fleeing felon' without regard to whether the suspect presented a danger to the police officer or others. This broad licence to kill was successfully challenged by a prosecutor in the 1993 trial of a Toronto police officer as inconsistent with the victim's right to life and security under the Charter. The police officer was charged with (and eventually acquitted of) the dangerous use of a firearm for firing six shots and wounding a nineteen-year-old black man suspected of a purse snatching. The judge held that the prosecutor had standing to act 'as the *alter ego* for the wounded suspect' (*Lines* 1993: para 43). He concluded that the 'fleeing felon' defence deprived victims and potential victims of police shootings of life and security of the person without accordance with the principles of fundamental justice because it authorized lethal force regardless of the seriousness of the offence or the threat presented by the suspect. It could not be justified as a reasonable limit under section 1 of the Charter because it could justify lethal force if necessary to stop a 'doughnut thief.' In a variation on the new political case, the prosecutor invoked the Charter rights of victims and potential victims of police violence against the accused.

The *Lines* decision restricting police powers to shoot fleeing felons was not the final word. A year later, Parliament responded with a new defence which authorized police officers to use deadly force to prevent flight if the officer 'believes on reasonable grounds that the force is necessary for the purpose of protecting the peace officer ... or any other person from imminent or future death or grievous bodily harm' (*Criminal Code*, s.25[4] am. S.C. 1994 c.12). Minister of Justice Allan Rock defended the new defence as a balance between the need expressed in *Lines* for 'a proportionate response' by the police to a fleeing felon and the need to ensure that 'police officers can continue to protect themselves and the public from serious injury or even death' (Hansard, 14 Feb. 1994: 1292–3). Rock also argued that the restricted defence responded to 'concern expressed about the present provision by minority groups across the country' (ibid). The Reform Party replied by arguing that the legislation responded to the concerns of 'certain community groups' but not the public at large (ibid: 1298) and that it forced police officers 'to weigh political implications of the use of force ...' (ibid: 1319).[6] They invoked victims' rights in the name of crime control by arguing that Parliament 'should concentrate on the victims for a change and truly make this country safe for its citizens. Taking away authority from the police is not the way to achieve this goal' (ibid: 1328). Minorities who refused to follow police orders were not seen as victims. Victims could be defined selectively, and victims' rights invoked for very different ends.

The new defence did not restrict deadly force as a response to immediate threats of death as recommended by the Ontario Task Force on Policing and Race Relations (1988: 131) and defence lawyers. Instead it also authorized deadly force to respond to the risk of future harm to others. There was little discussion in Parliament, Committee, or the media about alternatives to deadly force. The most publicized aspect of the bill was a provision allowing fisheries officers to use disabling force against fleeing foreign fishing vessels.[7] The new defence fell into the pattern observed in chapter 2 of Charter decisions provoking legislation which enabled and relegitimized police powers, even while it imposed some Charter-inspired restrictions on them.

The due-process nature of criminal investigations and trials, as well as robust defences for police use of force, made it difficult to obtain convictions when police were prosecuted for shootings (Glasbeek 1993). In the one case that resulted in a police officer being convicted, the sentence was lenient and disappointing to minorities. A police officer convicted of manslaughter in the shooting death of Aboriginal protestor Dudley George received a conditional sentence and 180 hours of community service in part because of his previous record and because he was given false intelligence that the protestors at Ipperwash had guns (*Deane* 1997). The criminal trial judged individual not collective or organizational fault.

Conflicts between the rights of minority victims and due-process claims by the accused made the law and politics of criminal justice more complex. The refusal of police officers to talk to the SIU indicated how due-process claims could conflict with claims by minority victims for the equal protection of the criminal law. The rule of law demanded that the police could be prosecuted, but it also required that they be afforded the same Charter rights as other accused. The focus on criminal prosecutions criminalized the issue of police relations with minorities and obscured the need for police reform. Acquittals legitimated police violence that, while not proven to be criminal, might still be objectionable and preventable.

Latimer *and the Disabled*

With the inclusion of mental and physical disability as a prohibited ground of discrimination in section 15 of the Charter, the disabled emerged as a minority with a constitutional identity (Cairns 1995: 51–2). In accord with an emphasis 'on achieving such advancements as accessible transportation, the right to attend main-stream schools, and access to buildings,' the disabled focused on equality rights at the time the Charter was drafted.[8] In the 1990s, however, the focus shifted to the 'right to receive equal legal protection from violence. Like many other minority groups, it is becoming clear that people with disabilities are vulnerable to violence' (*Winnipeg Free Press*, 8 Jan. 1997).

Victimization studies documented the vulnerability of the disabled to crime. A 1987 survey of women with disabilities indicated that 67 per cent had been physically or sexually assaulted as children, 33 per cent assaulted during their adult years, and 31 per cent sexually assaulted (DAWN 1987). A 1995 survey by the same organization concluded that 50.8 per cent of women with disabilities reported physical abuse, and 51.1 per cent reported emotional abuse (*Winnipeg Free Press*, 6 Feb. 1997). In *O'Connor* (1995: 57), LEAF (1996: 433) argued that the disabled were 'at least 150% as vulnerable to sexual abuse as individuals of the same age and sex who are not disabled' and convinced four judges that the equality rights of disabled sexual-assault victims should be considered when determining whether judges or the accused should have access to the victim's records. As always, high victimization rates could be constructed in different ways. The Disabled Women's Network (DAWN 1987) did not focus on the need for crime control or opposition to the accused's due-process claims, but rather on the need for assertiveness and self-defence courses to assist in prevention and recovery. High victimization rates could also be related to social, cultural, housing, and economic discrimination that left disabled people vulnerable to their care-givers. In a pattern similar to that observed with respect to women and children, however, there was an increasing emphasis on the cheaper and more controversial remedy of the criminal law.

A few weeks after the Supreme Court upheld the offence of assisted suicide in order to protect the disabled from being coerced into suicide (*Rodriguez* 1993), Robert Latimer killed his twelve-year-old daughter by running a hose from an exhaust pipe into the truck where he had placed her. He originally told authorities that his daughter had died in her sleep, but later confessed and explained that he was 'much happier for her now' because she was no longer in pain (*Latimer* 1995: 496). Tracy Latimer suffered from severe cerebral palsy and could not talk, walk, or feed herself. She was scheduled to receive extensive hip surgery to relieve pain, but the surgery itself would be painful. Although they had been divided about Sue Rodriguez's claim, groups representing the disabled were much more united on the need to have the criminal sanction applied in this very different case.

Latimer was convicted by a jury of second-degree murder and sentenced by the judge to the mandatory minimum term of life imprisonment without eligibility for parole for ten years. Many people opposed

Latimer's sentence and contributed to his defence fund. Groups representing the disabled saw the case differently. Two groups, People in Equal Participation (PEP) and Council of Canadians with Disabilities (CCD), intervened to oppose Latimer's appeal. The CCD (1995: 14–15) opposed Latimer's claim that his sentence was cruel and unusual punishment and argued that it was 'inconceivable that a court would find a violation of section 7 or 12 of the Charter because an accused argued that the race or religion of his victim mitigated the seriousness of his crime. It should likewise be inconceivable that the disability of a victim can mitigate the seriousness of a crime so as to create a violation of sections 7 and 12.' Like other groups representing the disabled, the CCD was concerned that 'the public debate and media coverage surrounding this case has demonstrated the unfortunate and bitter reality that our community places less value on the life of a disabled person than it does on the life of a nondisabled person. That reality, if left ungoverned by the applicable legal rules as stated by a trial judge, could easily lead a jury to deny the full protection of the law to persons with disabilities' (ibid: 11). Equality for the disabled demanded that the criminal sanction be applied vigorously. Latimer became another new political case which pitted the accused's due-process claims[9] against the equality rights of the victim and other potential victims.

In rejecting Latimer's appeal, the Saskatchewan Court of Appeal accepted many of the arguments noted above. The defence of necessity should not have been left to the jury because 'it is no defence for a parent to say because of a severe handicap, a child's life has such diminished value that the child should not live any longer' (*Latimer* 1995: 512). Tallis J.A. concluded that 'section 7 of the Charter was enacted for the protection and benefit of all citizens – whether healthy or handicapped' (ibid: 518). He saw the killing almost as an intentional hate crime against the disabled because it 'would never have been suggested or considered if Tracy were not handicapped ... the decision would appear to be predicated upon the diminished value assigned to the life of a handicapped child' (ibid: 519). The mandatory sentence was justified because 'it does not advance the interest of the state or society to treat such a child as a person of lesser status or dignity than others' (ibid: 512, 518–19). As will be discussed below, the Criminal Code was amended the same year to instruct courts to increase punishment motivated by hate, bias, or prejudice towards the disabled, as well as other groups protected under the Charter's equality rights. Bayda C.J.S. dissented on the basis that the sentence was not necessary to punish, deter, or rehabilitate Latimer.

Without the support of organized groups intervening in the appeal, he unorthodoxly cited letters written by individuals who believed that the life sentence was too harsh (ibid: 539). The dissent reflected the individualistic nature of due-process discourse, while the majority demonstrated how equality concerns could be used to support the imposition of punishment.

The Court of Appeal's decision was applauded by groups representing the disabled. Teresa Ducharme, the founder of PEP, commented 'I'm happy. I have no sympathy for Mr. Latimer' (*Winnipeg Free Press*, 19 Jul. 1995). The *Globe and Mail* (19 Jul. 1995) argued that, if Latimer had not been convicted, 'every disabled Canadian would be at risk,' including 30,000 severely disabled children. This assumed that the criminal law could promote equality and control risk. Shortly after Latimer's conviction, a mother in Ontario killed her disabled sixteen-year-old son and herself in a manner similar to the way Tracy Latimer was killed. The tragedy of this event, and other similar ones, could have been interpreted as demonstrating the inefficacy of the criminal sanction and the need for more expensive support for the disabled, but it only seemed to support more reliance on the criminal sanction and demands for punishment.

The Supreme Court eventually reversed Latimer's conviction and ordered a new trial because the prosecutor had engaged in 'a flagrant abuse of process and interference with the administration of justice' by having the police interview prospective jurors about their views about religion, abortion, and euthanasia (*Latimer* 1997a: 210, 200). If the *Parks* case was extended to allow the prosecutor to inquire about discriminatory views towards victims vulnerable to discrimination, it was possible that some of the questions might have been allowed in open court. The homogeneity and impartiality of juries was no longer assumed in the new political case, and the prosecutor wanted to know if prospective jurors identified with the victim or the accused.

Later that year, Latimer was again found guilty of second-degree murder, by another jury. In defiance of the mandatory life-imprisonment sentence for the crime, however, the jury recommended that he be imprisoned for one year. Essentially following the jury's recommendations, the trial judge sentenced Latimer to one year imprisonment and another year of house arrest on his farm after finding that the mandatory sentence would impose cruel and unusual punishment. He distinguished the Saskatchewan Court of Appeal's earlier decision by stressing that he found no evidence that Latimer 'killed his daughter because she was so severely disabled ... we have the rare act of homicide that was committed for caring and altruistic reasons' (*Latimer* 1997b: 343). The case was no longer portrayed as a hate crime against the disabled.

Hugh Scher, the chair of the CCD, denounced the decision as 'an outrage to Tracy Latimer's memory, and to all persons with disabilities ... People are in shock that a court would actually come out with a ruling like this in view of the tremendous risk that it places on people with a disability in Canada' (*Toronto Star*, 6 Dec. 1997). The issue was defined so that anything less than the mandatory punishment for murder devalued the lives of the disabled and placed them at risk. The Latimer case played out on the public stage as a new political case which pitted the accused's due-process claims against the equality claims of the disabled in a divisive and symbolic zero-sum confrontation.

Like women's groups, groups representing the disabled were placed in a position where they were forced to demand crime control in reaction to due-process decisions, even though they were well aware of the limited efficacy of the criminal sanction and the need for broader and more expensive economic, social, and cultural reforms. Those supporting Latimer focused more on his martyr status than on the problematic nature of his actions in the light of alternative-care and pain-management options available to his family. Latimer's vulnerability to severe punishment made him immune from the public shaming that should arguably attach to his conduct. The result of the Latimer prosecutions was a divisive but ultimately symbolic battle between due process and victims' rights. A less punitive approach would stress interventions to prevent these tragedies and reintegrative shaming for those who would treat the disabled as less-than-equal human beings.

Hate Crimes

Victimization data played a role in creating support for hate-crimes legislation. Minister of Justice Allan Rock stressed that hate-crime units of the police and 'every major group among identifiable minorities reports in recent years a troubling and significant increase in hate motivated crime.' He also cited an American study indicating that 'one in five gay men and one in ten lesbians reported being the victim of aggression and one-third of the respondents said they had received threats of violence' (Hansard, 15 Jun. 1995: 13923–4). The media played up victimization studies with headlines such as 'Hate Crimes Common,' adding that 'only a small percentage of hate-motivated crimes – perhaps one in 10 – are ever reported' (*Toronto Star*, 12 Feb. 1996). Following the same trend found in the previous two chapters, high levels of unreported crime were interpreted as demonstrating a need for stronger and more victim-sensitive criminal laws.

Enacted as part of sentencing reforms, the 1995 hate-crime law instructed judges to increase punishment if there was 'evidence that the offence was motivated by bias, prejudice, or hate based on race, national or ethnic origin, language, colour, religion, sex, age, mental or physical disability, sexual orientation, or any other similar factor' (*Criminal Code*, s.718.2 as am. S.C. 1995 c.22). The new law employed equality rights for punitive and crime-control ends. The minister of justice and EGALE both defended the law for 'sending a message' that hate crimes were unacceptable. The symbolic value of the law was stressed because it added little to the actual law of sentencing. As early as 1977, the Ontario Court of Appeal recognized that 'an assault which is racially motivated renders the offence more heinous' and deserving of a sentence which 'expresses the public's abhorrence for such conduct and their refusal to countenance it' (*Ingram* 1977: 379). A year later, the same principle was applied to a hate-motivated assault against a gay man (*Atkinson* 1978). The hate-crime law, including its controversial inclusion of sexual orientation as a prohibited ground of hate, simply codified existing sentencing principles (Shaffer 1995: 210). Parliament responded to hate crimes by making the existing common law more visible. By offering sentencing doctrine as a response to a social problem, it also promoted criminalized politics.

The symbolic nature of the legislation did not mean that it was unimportant (Edelman 1964, 1971). The legislation became a vehicle for debate about competing understandings of equality. Reform Party members and other social conservatives argued that the inclusion of sexual orientation was an example of 'special treatment,' not equality. Victim-advocacy groups also opposed the notion of hate crimes because of their belief that all victims were equal. Gay and lesbian groups, who had traditionally suffered from increased crime-control activities such as the Toronto bathhouse raids of the early 1980s (Smith 1988: 164) and the targeting of gay and lesbian pornography (Cossman et al 1997), supported the government in its attempt to send a punitive message about hate crimes. The message may not, however, succeed in reducing violence such as the unsolved murders of about thirty gay men in Montreal (Roberts 1995: 34; Peterson 1991). The educational value of the law was diluted by the vehement opposition to it.

The manner in which the government defended the legislation revealed much about the criminalization of politics. Minister of Justice

Allan Rock argued that 'Bill C-41 is a criminal law bill which amends the Criminal Code. It deals not at all with human rights, access to benefits, the right to marry or adopt. It has to do with the sentencing of people who have been proven to have committed crimes' (ibid: 13924). He stressed that it was not the government 'who has identified these groups for special treatment. It is the hoodlums and the thugs who have identified them for special treatment' (ibid: 13924, 13972). Private actors – hoodlums and thugs – were portrayed as the main opponents of equality. In turn, the government could promote equality by increasing punishment, not by providing equal benefits. When politics were criminalized, the state could be repressive, yet minimal. As had been the case with obscenity (Lacombe 1994: 105), it was less expensive for the government to rely on the criminal sanction than to make progress on questions of social, economic, or cultural equality for disadvantaged groups.

Although they will not succeed (Shaffer 1995: 218–41), hate crimes may be subject to due-process challenges. In the United States, hate-based offences were challenged as a violation of freedom of speech (Gellman 1991). As discussed in chapter 4, American courts have been less willing than their Canadian counterparts to restrict freedom of expression to protect victims from even the vilest forms of hate speech such as cross burnings (*R.A.V.* 1992). Ironically, however, the U.S. Supreme Court upheld hate crimes when they were used to punish African Americans more severely because they had attacked white people after seeing a movie portraying cross-burnings (*Mitchell* 1993). Like domestic-assault policies, hate crimes could, in the hands of police and prosecutors, be used against their intended beneficiaries.

Even if due process does not frustrate the prosecution of hate crimes, the fact that Parliament did not create a separate offence may. In a pattern that will also be observed in the next two chapters, Parliament squeezed its concerns for victims into the sentencing process by providing that hate bias was an aggravating factor when sentencing a person for an underlying offence such as assault or mischief to property. The same bill, however, also proclaimed as the fundamental principle of sentencing that punishment must be proportionate to the gravity of the offence. Parliament thus instructed judges to punish crimes such as the desecration of a synagogue more severely, while at the same time requiring that the punishment be limited by the seriousness of the crime of mischief to property (Roberts 1995: 45). Lenient sentences for hate crimes, like the fine received by Keegstra (see chapter 4), will produce understandable frustration and may dilute the symbolic and educational value of the law.

War Crimes

War-crime legislation, like hate-crime legislation, was enacted to express solidarity with the victims of the most hateful crimes. It also promised much more than it delivered. In the end, it failed to punish any war criminal or to recognize Canada's shameful role in allowing Nazi war criminals to immigrate to Canada after the Second World War (Matas 1987) after having turned away Jewish refugees before the war (Abella and Troper 1991). Following the pattern of the new political case, it produced symbolic and divisive battles between due process and victims' rights.

In an early recognition of the potential of due process to frustrate victims' rights, section 11(g) of the Charter was amended to allow the prosecution of war criminals (see chapter 1). This was a symbolic concession because the Liberal government favoured extradition of war criminals (Wagner 1984: 146) and received legal advice that the domestic prosecution of war crimes on the basis of retroactive legislation would 'fly in the face of some of the most fundamental of our legal traditions' (quoted in Matas 1987: 132; see also *Rauca* 1983: 717). Reports that Josef Mengele had entered Canada after the war led to the appointment of a public inquiry. The inquiry concluded that Mengele had not come to Canada and that many other reports of Nazi war criminals in Canada were 'grossly exaggerated' (Canada 1986: 11–13). It recommended, however, further action in more than 200 cases and warned that a 'monumental effort will be required to forge ahead' (ibid: 828). It contemplated a comprehensive approach which included strengthened extradition, denaturalization, and deportation, as well as domestic prosecutions. It recognized that 'psychologically, there would be an advantage to using the *Criminal Code* as the vehicle for the prosecution of war criminals' (ibid: 163).

The government decided to follow the 'psychologically' or symbolically appealing approach of domestic criminal prosecutions in part because of concerns about extradition to then Eastern Bloc countries. Minister of Justice Ray Hnatyshyn stressed the fairness of the 'made in Canada solution' by arguing that domestic prosecutions 'would be undertaken according to Canadian rules of evidence and in accordance with the overriding principles established in our own Canadian Charter of Rights and Freedoms' (Hansard, 12 Mar. 1987: 4078). The new legislation received all-party approval, with the opposition only adding that adequate resources for prosecutions were necessary if the hopes of survivors were not to be betrayed (ibid: 4083). The bill spent a day in committee, with the minister defending the government's decision not to strengthen extradition options. Most of the time was devoted to ensuring that the new offences were, in the new Ottawa vernacular, 'Charter-proof.'

Imre Finta, a senior gendarmerie officer in Hungary during the Second World War, was the first person prosecuted. He was accused of forcibly confining more than 8,000 Jews, robbing them, and forcing them into box cars destined for concentration camps. He was defended by Douglas Christie, who also defended Keegstra and Zundel (see chapter 4). As might be expected, the ten-month trial was controversial, and not only because it ended with a jury acquittal. As he had in Zundel's trial for denying the Holocaust, Christie attempted to exclude Jews from the jury. Because of an earlier decision that the trial judge in Zundel's trial had overreacted by denying Zundel any right to question prospective jurors, the trial judge allowed Christie to ask whether prospective jurors belonged to or supported any organization which advocated or opposed the prosecution of war crimes. The result was criticized as a 'stacked jury' because all major Jewish organizations had advocated war-crimes legislation (Matas 1994: 282). As in many other new political cases, jury selection was controversial, and the homogeneity and impartiality of prospective jurors was no longer assumed. This can be seen as the politicalization of the criminal trial, but it also reflected the criminalization of politics.

Christie invoked anti-Semitic stereotypes in cross-examining Holocaust survivors (Cotler 1995), and the trial became a 'continuation of the victimization' (Matas 1994: 295). The Supreme Court criticized Christie's conduct as 'unprofessional and prejudicial' (*Finta* 1994: 525), but also suggested that the prosecutor had been excessive in stressing the degrading treatment of victims without connecting it to the accused. The criminal trial allowed an adversarial assault on survivors and the truth of the Holocaust, but not a full examination of its nature or effects.

All of the courts that heard the case rejected Finta's arguments that the war-crimes legislation violated the Charter. Without much attention to section 11(g) of the Charter, the Supreme Court concluded that the need 'to punish those who were morally responsible for the international crime of the Second World War may certainly be considered as more important than to comply with the rather relative rule against ex post facto laws, open to so many exceptions' (*Finta* 1994: 542). As it had in *Keegstra* (1990) and *Butler* (1992), the Canadian court looked to international standards and rejected the hyper-liberalism of the American position, which rejected domestic prosecutions as inherently unfair because they were based on retroactive laws. Consistent with its tolerance of pre-charge delay in sexual-abuse cases (see chapter 6), the Court held that Finta's rights were not violated by the delay in prosecution or any evidence that had been lost in the meantime (ibid: 543). The Court also upheld provisions that made Finta guilty if he was acting in obedience to a valid law in Hungary on the basis that such a defence, would, like a defence of drunkenness to drunk driving, be inconsistent with the very purpose of the new offence. Taken on these terms, the decision could be interpreted as rejecting due-process claims that threatened the interests of victims, and some media even highlighted the Court's decision to uphold the legislation under the Charter (*Montreal Gazette*, 25 Mar. 1994).

The bottom line for most was, however, that the Court upheld Finta's acquittal and made it more difficult to prosecute similar cases in the future (*Globe and Mail*, 25 Mar.1994; *Toronto Star*, 25 Mar. 1994). The flexibility of due-process doctrine allowed the courts to uphold the legislation from Charter challenge, but also to impose serious restrictions. Prosecutors were required to prove that Finta 'knew that his acts had a factual quality that made them war crimes' (*Finta* 1994: 487). A war-crime conviction carried a special stigma that required the prosecutor to prove subjective awareness of the prohibited act (ibid: 501). Three judges argued in dissent that it was enough to prove that Finta had the fault necessary for the underlying crimes – manslaughter, kidnapping, robbery, and unlawful confinement – and that his crimes in fact, but not necessarily in his mind, constituted war crimes. The majority's position reflected the stress placed on the accused's subjective awareness in the felony-murder cases, while the minority, following the manslaughter and felony-first-degree-murder cases, stressed the actual harm that had occurred (see chapter 3). The majority also held that Finta had defences such as obedience to superior orders; that he 'had no moral choice as to whether to follow the order' (ibid: 521) and that he mistakenly believed he was following a valid law which was not manifestly unlawful. Although Finta had not testified at his trial, the Court concluded that there was an air of reality to justify putting these defences to the jury in part because of wartime hostility in Hungary towards Jews (ibid: 523). The minority predicted that these fault requirements and defences would make prosecutions and the fulfilment of Canada's international commitments 'unlikely' (ibid: 468).

The Court's decision and affirmation of an acquittal in this new political case was highly controversial. Two intervenors, the B'nai B'rith and the Canadian Holocaust Remembrance Association, supported by the federal government, applied for a rehearing and argued that the majority had 'wrongly relied on anti-Semitic Nazi propaganda' in holding that their was an air of reality to the defences. The rehearing was denied by the Court with the same 4-3 split (*Toronto Star*, 24 Jun. 1994). A second request by a coalition of Montreal synagogues representing survivors was unanimously denied (*Montreal Gazette*, 23 Jan. 1994). In the wake of the Court's affirmation of its decision, the federal government abandoned prosecutions in favour of denaturalization and deportation proceedings. The Supreme Court refused to throw out one of these cases after a federal official had inappropriately consulted judges off the record in an attempt to speed up the hearings. The Court stressed that the state was only trying to deprive the individuals of their citizenship as opposed to their liberty, and that staying proceedings would harm 'Canada's reputation as a responsible member of the community of nations' (*Tobiass* 1997: 477–8). As in *Keegstra* and *Zundel* (see chapter 4), the flexibility of due-process doctrine allowed the Court to both give and take victories to minority groups.

Summary

The victimization of minorities led to crime-control measures such as the criminal prosecution of police officers and the creation of hate and war crimes. The initial case for providing minorities with the equal benefit of the criminal sanction was almost unassailable. Discriminatory double standards in providing any state benefit, including that of crime control, were unacceptable. State inaction because a crime victim was a member of an unpopular minority was a particularly insidious and harmful form of discrimination. Nevertheless, when the actual effects of crime-control measures were examined, enthusiasm for the criminal sanction diminished. The prosecutions of police officers and war criminals resulted in acquittals, which might suggest that the accused, and even the state, did nothing wrong. When a conviction was secured, punishment was frequently perceived as excessively lenient. Criminal prosecutions did not seem to deter subsequent police shootings, killings of disabled children, or the entry of modern-day war criminals into Canada.

The use of the criminal sanction to protect minorities also promoted a criminalization of politics which diverted attention from more tangible and expensive means to increase equality, liberty, and security for disadvantaged groups. It allowed those not sympathetic to these goals to argue that the criminal process had been politicized in order to appease minorities. Crime-control measures invited due-process challenges and the symbolic and divisive battles typical of the new political case. Due-process challenges not only made it more difficult to obtain convictions, but also fractured the consensus that might have been developed around less punitive strategies. All reasonable people ought to recognize the need to support the caregivers of the disabled or Canada's shameful record with respect to war criminals, but reasonable people disagreed about the *Latimer* and *Finta* cases. As Packer well knew, the criminal sanction was a blunt and awkward instrument. The next section will explore some potentially less frustrating ways of attempting to prevent and heal the victimization of minorities by crime.

Alternatives

What follows is a preliminary discussion of an eclectic range of strategies to prevent crimes against various minorities and to achieve some measure of restorative justice after they occurred. The next chapter concludes with a discussion of Aboriginal justice, which is a more developed and holistic alternative to due-process, crime-control, and punitive forms of victims' rights.

Crime Prevention

More attention should be given to preventing the victimization of minorities rather than attempting to punish crime after it occurs. Preventive measures may be more expensive than after-the-fact criminal prosecutions. By avoiding the clashes of the new political case, however, they should command more public support.

More careful selection, training, and evaluation of police officers might help prevent discriminatory policing and police shootings. The Ontario Task Force on Race Relations and Policing (1989, 1992) stressed interventions such as employment equity, race relations, firearms training, and community relations more than crime-control interventions such as the SIU and the repeal of the 'fleeing felon' rule. Some of these were tried along with the creation of the SIU in 1990, but the task force observed in 1992 a continued failure to provide police with adequate training in the use of alternatives to firearms. Scepticism about the utility of race-relations training has been expressed (Ontario 1995: 392–405), but 'training designed to disabuse police of stereotyping which suggests that members of certain racial groups are more likely to be armed or violent than others, would seem to hold out some promise' (Stenning 1994:

I.48). More drastic preventive approaches would include disarming patrol officers.

In the context of hate crimes, prevention would mean education to encourage young people to reject the stereotypes, prejudice, and irrational fear that motivates hate crimes. Early intervention at school and home with children who demonstrate antisocial tendencies and hostility towards minorities might be more effective than the uncertain threat of punishment later in life. More resources for community living and respite for caregivers may also help prevent some crimes against the disabled. Preventive strategies might also combat fear of crime. Punitive strategies which relied on the image of the disabled as helpless victims won some public sympathy, but they also affirmed stereotypes of the disabled.

Crime prevention is also a promising approach to crimes against the elderly. Senior citizens fear crime much more than they actually suffer it, but their fears affect the quality of their lives and reflect the fact that they may have a more difficult time recovering from crime because of their physical and financial circumstances (Brillon 1987). These fears can be addressed by preventive measures such as community watch, target hardening, and consumer education to help prevent economic crime. Target hardening alone could increase the isolation of the elderly, but other preventive strategies may allow senior citizens to be engaged in the outside world. As will be discussed in the next chapter, Aboriginal people recognize that elders have much wisdom to contribute to healing and restoration after crime has occurred. In contrast, crime-control strategies construct senior citizens as passive, helpless, fearful, and punitive.

One way to prevent the disproportionate imprisonment of some minorities would be to revisit Packer's old idea of selective decriminalization. Ontario's Commission on Systemic Racism (1995: 82–3) concluded that, 'in Ontario, as in many parts of the United States, one effect of the "war on drugs", intended or not, has been the increase in imprisonment of black people' (ibid: 82–3). It recommended the use of police cautions and diversion for first offenders, but unfortunately did not explore alternative drug policies such as the decriminalization of marijuana possession or addiction-treatment programs. Although some of the commission's proposals suggested that it saw decriminalization as an important strategy to address overrepresentation, it did not defend it openly as an alternative to crime control and due process (Roach 1996d). If it can avoid the allure of crime-control and due-process remedies, an anti-racist model of criminal justice could decrease reliance on the criminal sanction.

Restorative Justice

Restorative approaches should be considered with respect to both crimes committed among minority groups and crimes committed against minorities. With respect to the former, it may be that the common ties created by shared race, age, sexual orientation, or other characteristics could facilitate reintegrative shaming (Braithwaite 1989). The relevant community may also benefit from attempting to deal with its own crime problem in its own way (Brodgen and Shearing 1993). Minority communities may be in an unique position to provide culturally appropriate dispute resolution that can keep people out of a discriminatory crime-control system. As will be discussed in the next chapter, however, suspicions that crime victims have about the ability to obtain justice in their own community should not be ignored, and restorative justice will work best where both the offender and the victim genuinely consent to its jurisdiction.

With respect to crimes committed against minorities, it might appear that a restorative approach is not warranted. Without common bonds and ties, it will be more difficult to achieve reintegrative shaming. Even here, however, there is a possibility that restorative justice can work, especially if someone close to the offenders can shame them for their discriminatory conduct and provide an example of a person who recognizes the victim's humanity and suffering. Public sympathy for minority crime victims should not be assumed, but it should not be dismissed. In Australia, companies have been shamed for exploiting Aboriginal people and senior citizens (Braithwaite 1997). The perpetrators of crimes against the vulnerable may be made more resistant to shame when they are prosecuted and can assume martyr status in their own communities.

Even if reintegrative shaming is not feasible, there are alternatives to the criminal sanction. One limited alternative is civil actions. Like criminal prosecutions, they are adversarial, focus on the past, and can put the victim on trial. Nevertheless, they can be controlled by victims, have a lower burden of proof, and can be more easily directed against organizations which can take action to prevent the harm from occurring in the future. A civil action was successful in a case where a Montreal police officer was acquitted of manslaughter in the shooting of a black man. The Supreme Court approved of the award of compensatory damages, but reversed a trial judge's award of punitive damages on the basis that the victim's family had not proven that the killing was the result of more than negligence (*Augustus* 1996: 289). The closer that civil actions or regulatory proceedings become to criminal trials, the less useful they will be in recognizing and preventing harms against minorities.

Another alternative is the coroner's inquest and other public inquiries. They have the potential to examine the causes of police shootings and other crimes against minorities and to propose means to prevent them in the future. In such forums, 'the objective must be to identify problems and to deal with them rather than to be preoccupied with "blame"' (Ontario 1995: 389). These inquiries can also focus more directly on racism than the criminal trial. A coroner's inquiry in Montreal, for example, reported that 'evidence at the inquest disclosed in some members of the Montreal Urban Community Police Department the existence of a racist attitude that is totally unacceptable. If uncorrected, it could lead to further situations endangering life' (quoted in Stenning 1994: I.2). Public inquiries can serve a cathartic function by listening to and recognizing the legitimacy of grievances. If they become concerned with individual fault, they will, like criminal trials, become embroiled in due-process challenges. The inquiry on war criminals focused on individual cases in a manner that probably is no longer acceptable (Canada 1986). Most of the individuals it examined were exonerated, and the inquiry failed to promote organizational or social accountability (Roach 1995a) for the entry of war criminals into Canada or for the anti-Semitism which explained Canada's behaviour before and after the war. A more broadly conceived inquiry could have provoked collective shame and resulted in apologies, reparations, education, and research into war crimes. The individual and collective settlements and apologies received by Japanese Canadians for their wartime internment likely produced more satisfaction than the frustrating saga of war-crimes prosecutions. Apologies, reparations, and commitments to do better in the future are the hallmarks of restorative justice. Punitive strategies frequently produce denials and due-process challenges.

The failure of the adjudication of police complaints to respond to the concerns of Audrey Smith and Dwight Drummond was discussed above. The most satisfied complainants are those whose complaints were resolved informally (Maguire and Corbett 1991). Only 10 per cent of complainants in one Ontario study wanted police officers charged or fired, and the vast majority would have been satisfied by some combination of reprimand, warning, explanation, or apology (Landau 1994: 53). Smith and Drummond might have been satisfied with a solemn, public, and sincere apology from the police officers and their superiors, especially if accompanied by tangible efforts to prevent such encounters in the future. Legalistic hearings (Martin 1993: 157) and the threat of disciplinary charges (Landau 1994: 39) encouraged officers to deny responsibility, avoid shame, and play the martyr. The dismissal of formal complaints legitimated police conduct that might not be necessary and that caused much ill will.

The success of restorative approaches frequently depends on the willingness of the victim to participate and the offender to admit guilt. Although the criminal sanction will have to be used in some cases, we should not be surprised when it makes the offender deny responsibility and employ due-process challenges. Victims will have only a limited role to play in criminal proceedings and may still be put on trial. For victims, as well as the accused, the process may be the punishment (Feeley 1979). The end result may be an acquittal, which denies victimization, or a lenient sentence, which does not met victims' expectations. A restorative approach offers offenders and victims more power over and creativity in determining the eventual outcome. It may not be appropriate with the offenders most resistant to shame or the victims most severely traumatized, but, in other cases, it may produce more constructive results than either crime control or due process.

Conclusion

Much has changed since the 1960s, when Packer and other liberals argued that due process could both reduce reliance on the criminal sanction and achieve justice for minorities. The range of minorities has increased, and groups such as the disabled, gays and lesbians, and the elderly have, like women and children, raised concerns about their victimization by crime and the inadequate response of the criminal justice system. Other minorities, particularly black people in Ontario, have raised concerns that they were targeted by the police and overrepresented in prison. Concerns about individual cases of abuses have been supplemented by better measurement of systemic overrepresentation of groups among prisoners and victims.

Canadian courts slowly started to attempt to restrain the discriminatory exercise of discretion within the criminal process. This was better than ignoring the problem, but it was insufficient. Due-process remedies such as the exclusion of evidence obtained from a discriminatory investigative stop or the *Parks* question to prospective jurors affected only a small number of cases. Requiring the state to jump higher due-process hurdles did not reduce the overrepresentation of some minorities in prison. Packer's old hope for selective decriminalization had more promise, but was not politically feasible.

Crime-control strategies such as the prosecutions of police officers and Robert Latimer, or the enactment of war- and hate-crimes legislation, failed to reduce the overrepresentation of minorities among crime victims. Relying on the criminal sanction to protect minorities created the danger of assuming that the criminal law controlled crime and of producing the symbolic and divisive struggles typical of the new political case. It also diverted attention from broader equality strategies. Crimes against minorities, like crimes against women and children, should not be isolated from their sociological, cultural, and economic contexts.

The new recognition that minorities were both vulnerable to discrimination by state actors and disproportionately victimized by some crimes created some new opportunities. It shattered Packer's assumption that equality for the disadvantaged could simply be achieved by more due process. Focusing on the disadvantages that various minorities faced both as accused and as victims created an opportunity to go beyond the traditional debate between due process and crime control, and explore alternative paths to criminal justice and more comprehensive and less punitive approaches to achieving equality for disadvantaged groups. The prevention of crime against minorities and restorative strategies when crime did occur could merge into other social, economic, and cultural reforms, and thus resist the criminalization of politics. In the next chapter, we will again see the limits of due-process, crime-control, and punitive forms of victims' rights, but also explore Aboriginal justice as a well-developed and promising alternative.

8

Aboriginal People

Aboriginal people bear the double disadvantage of being significantly overrepresented among both those imprisoned and those victimized by crime. This well-documented overrepresentation (Doob and Roberts 1997) was stressed by numerous public inquiries examining the failures of the criminal process with respect to Aboriginal people (Nova Scotia 1989; Manitoba 1991a, 1991b; Alberta 1991; Law Reform Commission of Canada [LRCC] 1991; Canada 1996b). It was also made real by individual tragedies. The wrongful conviction of Donald Marshall Jr and the shooting death of J.J. Harper generated considerable concern about how Aboriginal people were treated by police, prosecutors, defence lawyers, judges, and juries. At the same time, the murder of Helen Betty Osborne made clear that due-process reforms were not enough and that the criminal law failed to protect Aboriginal people, especially Aboriginal women. This chapter, like the previous one, critically examines due-process and crime-control strategies for reducing overrepresentation among prisoners and crime victims. Respect for the due-process rights of Aboriginal people is necessary, but it alone will not likely reduce Aboriginal overrepresentation in prison. Similarly, discriminatory double standards in crime control must be ended, but more police and prosecutions are unlikely to reduce victimization among Aboriginal people and may increase overrepresentation in prison. Packer's two models of criminal justice do not offer much hope for Aboriginal people.

Fortunately, there is an alternative with the potential to reduce both incarceration and victimization. Aboriginal justice attempts to heal both offenders and victims without reliance on punishment or adjudication of rights. Aboriginal forms of justice are diverse,[1] but, like the non-punitive model of victims' rights (see chapter 1), are often practised in circles which bring together the offender, the victim, their families, and their communities. The circle model integrates offending behaviour into larger cycles of life, family, health, nature, self-awareness, and spirituality. It resists the criminalization of politics and the labelling of offenders.

Aboriginal justice is not dominated by professionals and, unlike crime control and due process, does not place a premium on efficiency and finality. Because there is no binary verdict, the offender's past victimization and present disharmony can be recognized as the reason for an offence without denying the needs of the immediate victim or the responsibility of the offender. Unlike punitive forms of victims' rights, Aboriginal justice recognizes connections between being an offender and being a victim. The offender, as well as the immediate victim and the larger community, requires healing and restoration, and should not be seen as simply the product of the offence. The holistic approach of Aboriginal justice both promises prevention in the future and recognizes the need to address past abuses suffered by offenders and victims. Aboriginal people have been frequently and grievously harmed by the failures of due process and crime control, but their own traditions and circle healing initiatives offer the most developed and inspiring alternative to the linear processes of the due-process obstacle course and the crime-control assembly line.

Due Process and Aboriginal People

Due process could respond to individual cases of abuse and discrimination, but was not relevant in the typical case in which accused plead guilty. Increasing prison populations and Aboriginal overrepresentation in the Charter era suggested that due process was, at best, not inconsistent with increased crime control. Moreover, due process could sometimes provoke and legitimate crime control. Like young people, Aboriginal people could be given 'special' due-process rights while being punished more frequently and harshly. Finally, a romanticized vision of due process could threaten Aboriginal justice, which places less emphasis on adjudication of the accused's rights.

The Wrongful Conviction of Donald Marshall Jr

One of the main goals of due process was to guard against the risk of wrongfully convicting the innocent. In turn, the proponents of crime control argued that due process was 'haunted by the ghost of the innocent man convicted. It is an unreal dream' (*Garsson* 1923: 649). In the last decade, the ghosts of the wrongfully convicted made regular appearances. Donald Marshall Jr, a Mi'kmaq man who served eleven years for a murder he did not commit, was the first to appear, but was soon after joined by Wilson Nepoose, David Milgaard, and Guy Paul Morin.[2] These cases reminded Canadians of the fallibility of the criminal process and produced an almost desperate need to believe that the system could be fixed so that miscarriages of justice would not occur again.

A public inquiry of three judges concluded that Marshall would not have been wrongfully convicted if the police, prosecutor, defence lawyers, and judges had only 'carried out their duties in a professional and/or competent manner' (Nova Scotia 1989: 15). The actions of criminal justice professionals were criticized for not complying with due-process standards of fairness towards the accused. The prosecutor was criticized for not disclosing to the defence prior inconsistent witness statements even though there were no clear legal requirements that they be disclosed at the time of Marshall's 1971 trial (*Milgaard* 1992: 264).[3] Concern that the lack of Crown disclosure contributed to Marshall's wrongful conclusion played a role in the Supreme Court's decision in *Stinchcombe* (1990; see chapter 3) to interpret the accused's rights under section 7 of the Charter to include a right to disclosure of all relevant evidence in the prosecutor's possession.

These new rights, however, did not apply unless defence lawyers asked for disclosure, and Marshall's lawyers did not. Without vigourous and competent representation, most of the safeguards of the adversarial due-process system would fail. The inquiry criticized Marshall's lawyers for not working hard for their Aboriginal clients and not requesting disclosure or interviewing the witnesses. It concluded that 'had defence counsel taken even the most rudimentary steps an accused should be entitled to expect from his or her counsel, it is difficult to believe Marshall would have been convicted' (Nova Scotia 1989: 77). It and other inquiries (Manitoba 1991a: 102; Alberta 1991: c.3) recommended that the quality of legal representation received by Aboriginal people be improved, but it remained difficult for any accused to obtain a new trial because of ineffective assistance of counsel (Stuart 1996a: 163–4).

Another sad irony of the promise of due process was that the seventeen-year-old Marshall would probably have been better off submitting to the crime-control assembly line and pleading guilty to manslaughter. The real killer, Roy Ebsary, was eventually convicted of manslaughter and received a sentence of one year in prison (*Ebsary* 1986). Despite Marshall's proud and truthful insistence that he did not kill Sandy Seale,

Marshall's lawyers argued in their unsuccessful 1972 appeal that the judge should have left the jury with an option of manslaughter (*Marshall* 1972). This indicated another breakdown between Marshall and the lawyers who were supposed to defend him.

The Marshall inquiry criticized the trial judge for restricting the cross-examination of a young witness who had tried to recant his false testimony that he had seen Marshall stab Seale. The due-process model placed great emphasis on the accused's ability to confront and cross-examine hostile witnesses, and the inquiry concluded that Marshall would have been acquitted had his lawyer only been allowed a full cross-examination (ibid: 79). Even if the truth had been discovered on cross-examination, however, the jury, like the trial judge (Friedland and Roach 1997b: 141), might have assumed that the witness was recanting because he had been threatened by Marshall or his friends. Compliance with due-process rights would not alter negative stereotypes and suspicions about Aboriginal people.

The inquiry also noted that the jury may have interpreted Marshall's hesitant speech and discomfort at testifying 'as a negative factor and that may have influenced their ultimate disposition' (Nova Scotia 1989: 171). When Marshall testified before the inquiry in Mi'kmaq, he was a much more impressive witness. The inquiry recommended the increased use of interpreters for Aboriginal accused and witnesses. Courts were reluctant to give Aboriginal people who could speak English an interpreter and assumed that they were hesitant witnesses because they were lying (*Kent* 1986). This may change since the Supreme Court has indicated that interpreters should be provided whenever an accused with difficulties in expression requests one in good faith (*Tran* 1994).

In its 1983 decision acquitting Marshall, the Nova Scotia Court of Appeal stated that 'Marshall's evidence, old and new, if it stood alone, would hardly be capable of belief' and concluded that Marshall had been planning a robbery and had committed perjury (*Marshall* 1983). It blamed the victim by concluding that, despite his eleven years of imprisonment, 'any miscarriage of justice was more apparent than real' and was in 'large measure' caused by 'Donald Marshall's untruthfulness throughout this whole affair.' These comments were rightly criticized by the inquiry as a 'defence of the system at Marshall's expense, notwithstanding overwhelming evidence to the contrary' (Nova Scotia 1989: 120). The Court of Appeal forgot about the presumption of innocence. In doing so, it acted like an overzealous prosecutor[4] and proceeded on the assumption of guilt that pervaded the crime-control model.

The Marshall inquiry suggested that more due process in the form of Crown disclosure, cross-examination, interpreters, and respect for the presumption of innocence would have prevented Marshall's wrongful conviction. This may be true, but there remained many cracks in even a reformed due-process system. Due-process protections depended on vigorous and competent defence counsel. Aboriginal people remained vulnerable to racist stereotypes and the presumption of guilt associated with the crime-control model. The *Marshall* case boiled down to an issue of credibility between Marshall and the white witnesses who perjured themselves by telling the jury that they saw Marshall stab Seale. Many cases continued to depend on judgments about credibility which could be influenced by racial stereotypes.

Jury Selection

The jury that convicted Marshall, alone of all the actors responsible for his wrongful conviction, escaped criticism, except for a brief mention that no Aboriginal person had ever sat on a jury in Nova Scotia (ibid: 177). The failure to examine why the jury found Marshall guilty was related to the fact that it was a crime in Canada for jurors to reveal their deliberations and that there was a traditional reluctance to question the presumed impartiality of jurors. There was, however, reason to suspect whether the twelve white men who convicted Marshall were impartial. One of them, who was interviewed by the media after Marshall's innocence had been proven, denied that discrimination was involved in the guilty verdict, but explained the verdict as follows: 'with one redskin and one Negro involved – it was like two dogs in a field – you know one of them was going to kill the other ... I would expect more from a white person. We are more civilized' (*Toronto Star*, 9 Jun. 1986). Over a decade later, it remained uncertain whether an accused could ask prospective jurors whether they would be influenced by such vile and racist stereotypes associating Aboriginal and African-Canadian people with crime.

Courts in British Columbia refused to follow the *Parks* (1993) case, discussed in chapter 7. Thus Aboriginal and African-Canadian accused could not question prospective jurors about whether their deliberations would be affected by racism. The British Columbia courts readily acknowledged that some jurors might be prejudiced against Aboriginal people, but concluded that there was no evidence that such prejudices would affect their verdicts. They assumed that juries would follow judicial instructions and deliberate without prejudice (*Williams* 1994, 1996). The

British Columbia courts were wrong to discount the possibility of jurors acting on their prejudices (Roach 1995).[5] Nevertheless, they were correct that racism among jurors might not be revealed by the 'simplistic and incomplete' inquiry allowed by the *Parks* question (*Williams* 1994: 290). Such a question may have caught the anonymous racist on Marshall's jury, but it might fail to reveal deeply rooted but subtle stereotypes associating Aboriginal people and other minorities with disorder and crime (Henry and Henry 1995). It was also difficult to dispute the British Columbia Court of Appeal's observation that there was no evidence that Aboriginal overrepresentation in prison was caused by racist juries (*Williams* 1996: 229–30, 234). Most Aboriginal accused plead guilty. Juries are only available in the more serious cases, and most accused elected trial by judge alone in the hope of a quicker and more lenient disposition (Friedland and Roach 1997a: 134). Jury reform could hardly eliminate Aboriginal overrepresentation in prison, and there was a danger that it could legitimate it by creating the illusion of fair and non-racist justice. Nevertheless, attempts to control racism in the criminal process had to start somewhere and the B.C. courts rejected a necessary reform simply because it was not sufficient.

Jury selection was not simply a due-process issue affecting Aboriginal accused because of the overrepresentation of Aboriginal people as victims of serious crimes, especially homicide. Two white men charged with the murder of Helen Betty Osborne were tried by an all-white jury even though 30 per cent of the population in the judicial district of The Pas was Aboriginal (Manitoba 1991b: 86). The accused used peremptory challenges to keep six Aboriginal people off the jury (ibid: 87). Canadian courts did not follow American courts in attempting to control the discriminatory use of peremptory challenges by prosecutors and accused (Peterson 1993). Peremptories were not abolished as recommended by the Manitoba Aboriginal Justice Inquiry (Manitoba 1991a: 385). All that was required under the Charter was an equality of arms (*Bain* 1992) which provided both the accused and the prosecutor the same number of challenges. Prosecutors in cases with Aboriginal accused, and defence lawyers in cases with Aboriginal victims, could still keep Aboriginal people off the jury.

Aboriginal people were also underrepresented on juries because of high rates of non-return of jury summons, hardship excuses, language difficulties, and the distance between some of their communities and the larger centres where jury trials were held. Aboriginal participation would be increased if jury trials were held close to the community in which the crime was alleged to have occurred (Manitoba 1991a: 397). This would inch towards Aboriginal justice if only because juries 'may have some compatibility with Aboriginal cultures.'[6] Charter-based arguments concerning the right to a local jury generally failed. In one case, an elder from the remote Sandy Lake reserve accused of sexually assaulting a child unsuccessfully argued that his Charter rights would be violated if he was tried in Kenora. The victim opposed his application because she felt 'great pressure and hostility from the Sandy Lake community'(*F.(A.)* 1994: 350). The trial judge denied the accused's application because 'it would sacrifice the rights of the complainant' (ibid: 363) and any bias within a Kenora jury could be eliminated by a *Parks*-type question (ibid: 371). This was constructed as a new political case which pitted the rights of the accused against those of the victim. The victim's fears of partiality and discrimination should be taken seriously, but they also did not discredit the case for local juries in many cases where both the accused and the victim would prefer one. Community justice will work best where both the accused and the victim consent to its jurisdiction.

Reform of jury selection was necessary, but hardly sufficient. Attempts should be made not to select jurors who were influenced by the stereotypes that affected the anonymous racist on Marshall's jury, but they would not always be successful and they would run the risk of legitimating a trial process as free from racism when it might not be. Questions to reveal racism among prospective jurors, the discriminatory use of peremptory challenges, and the location of jury trials were not simple due-process issues, because they affected Aboriginal crime victims as well as Aboriginal accused.

J.J. Harper, Investigative Stops, and Over-policing

J.J. Harper was shot and killed during an investigative stop by the Winnipeg police. The police officers had been involved in a chase of a stolen car. After being informed that the suspect was in custody, Constable Cross nevertheless approached Harper and asked him for identification. Harper exercised his rights by telling Cross he did not have to tell him anything and attempted to proceed on his way. Constable Cross grabbed Harper, a struggle ensued, and Harper was fatally shot with the police officer's gun.[7] Manitoba's Aboriginal Justice Inquiry (1991b: 32) concluded that Constable Cross 'got caught up in the excitement of the chase. We believe that he decided to stop and question Harper simply because Harper was a male Aboriginal person in his path.' The inquiry concluded that Cross 'had neither reasonable nor probable grounds to believe that Harper was the suspect the police were after' (ibid: 32) and that his detention was 'inappropriate' (ibid: 38), exceeded his arrest powers under the Criminal Code, and possibly violated Harper's rights under section 9 of the Charter not to be arbitrarily detained. Constable Cross was properly trained in the relevant legal standards, but simply did not follow them.

As discussed in chapter 7, the Ontario Court of Appeal subsequently held that investigative stops must be justified by an objectively determined articulable cause, not the sort of stereotype that motivated the stop of Harper (*Simpson* 1993). The decision has been criticized for creating police powers short of arrest (Delisle 1993), but it was a genuine attempt to curb the type of encounters that resulted in Harper's death. Nevertheless, the limits of due-process decisions in reducing investigative stops should be recognized. As discussed in chapter 2, due-process standards were applied only in cases where the police discovered evidence and a prosecution was undertaken. Other remedies such as civil lawsuits and police complaints were largely illusory. In the vast majority of cases, due process did not affect the type of encounter that resulted in Harper's death.

The investigative stop and detention of Harper was part of a larger pattern of over-policing Aboriginal people. Manitoba's Aboriginal Justice Inquiry noted that 'complaints of over-policing focus on the perception that Aboriginal people are singled out for enforcement action and subjected to stereotyping by police forces. Many who appeared before us complained about being stopped on the street or on a country road and questioned about their activities' (Manitoba 1991a: 595). An earlier study found that Aboriginal people constituted 27 per cent of male arrests and 70 per cent of female arrests in Winnipeg, compared with an estimated 3 per cent of the population at the time (Bienvenue and Latif 1974). As Tim Quigley (1994: 273) has observed, over-policing of Aboriginal people can become a 'self-fulfilling prophecy.'

The Aboriginal Justice Inquiry of Manitoba (1991a: 597–600) endorsed community policing, both as part of Aboriginal self-government and because it could be more 'easily adapted to Aboriginal cultural standards than ... existing police methods' (ibid: 599). Nevertheless, community policing would place police officers in more direct contact with the community, and old crime-control habits die hard. The Territories and Saskatchewan have the most dramatic Aboriginal overrepresentation in their prisons, and they also have more police per capita than other Canadian jurisdictions (Havemann et al 1985: 22–3). Community policing could increase the over-policing of Aboriginal communities and Aboriginal overrepresentation in prisons.

Strengthened Due Process: The Anunga *Rules*

Several inquiries (Manitoba 1991a: 608; Alberta 1991: 2.56–9; LRCC 1991: 54–5) recommended the adoption of the Australian *Anunga* (1976) rules to govern interrogations of Aboriginal suspects. These rules were similar to section 56 of the Young Offenders Act (YOA) and allowed a prisoner's friend, as well as his or her counsel, to be present during interrogations. They also stressed the importance of clear cautions, full understanding by the suspect, and the use of interpreters. Like some due-process decisions examined in chapter 2, they required holding-off periods when the suspect was 'disabled by illness or drunkenness or tiredness.' The judge who promulgated these rules defended them as designed 'to remove or obviate some of the disadvantages from which Aboriginal people suffer in their dealings with the police' while noting that some may criticize them for providing special protections or for being 'unduly paternal and thereby offensive to Aboriginal people' (ibid: 415). These rules responded to concerns that Aboriginal suspects did not take the same advantage of their right to silence as other suspects. As will be seen later, truthful acknowledgments of accusations play an important role in Aboriginal justice.

It would be a mistake to place too much reliance on increased due-process protections. Evidence from Australia suggested 'that since the formal promulgation of the "Anunga Rules", there has been little improvement in police handling of Aboriginal people, in Aboriginal–police relations, or in over-incarceration' (Samuelson 1995: 189). Section 56 of the YOA (see chapter 6) and the Canadian version of *Miranda* rules (see chapter 2) did not prevent police interrogations or decrease imprisonment. Due process cannot respond to economic, social, and cultural factors that make Aboriginal people vulnerable to disproportionate imprisonment even after fair interrogations and fair trials. Special protections for specific groups may also legitimate their disproportionate imprisonment by creating the public perception that they received extraordinarily fair treatment.

From Individual Abuse to Overrepresentation

Due-process reforms may prevent some individual cases of abuse, but they will not rectify the 'shocking fact' (Manitoba 1991a: 85) of Aboriginal overrepresentation in prison. In 1995–6, Aboriginal people accounted for 16 per cent of all admissions to prisons and the majority of admissions in the Territories, Saskatchewan, and Manitoba (Canadian Centre for Criminal Justice Statistics 1996b: 30). This overrepresentation emerged as 'part of the public discourse about crime and the criminal justice system in Canada' (Roberts and Doob 1997: 481) and was defined as 'injustice personified' (Canada 1996b: 28). This confirmed the new demands placed on the criminal justice system to account for its systemic and devastating effects on disadvantaged groups.

Aboriginal overrepresentation could be explained by many factors, including the youthfulness of Aboriginal communities, high crime rates, the legacy of residential schools, and other forms of colonialism and social and economic discrimination (LaPrairie 1990, 1992).[8] The 'public problem' (Gusfield 1981) of overrepresentation was, however, attributed to discrimination in the criminal justice system (Manitoba 1991a; Alberta 1991; LRCC 1993; Canada 1996b), and Aboriginal justice was sometimes 'portrayed as a panacea for a range of community ills' (LaPrairie 1995: 529). Public discourse suppressed the possibility that even non-discriminatory criminal justice might not completely reduce overrepresentation. In other words, social, economic, and cultural injustice towards Aboriginal people might still produce overrepresentation.

There is a need to reform the existing criminal justice system to stop discrimination against Aboriginal people, and Aboriginal justice provides an inspiring and promising alternative to crime control and due process. At the same time, however, the centrality of Aboriginal justice in public discussions of Aboriginal issues (McNamara 1993) reflected the same criminalization of politics as previously observed with respect to women, children, and various minorities. Very few of the Aboriginal groups who appeared before the Joint Committee on the Constitution in 1980 and 1981 stressed criminal justice issues in their advocacy of self-government, and criminal justice frequently does not figure promeniently when self-government is negotiated. Aboriginal people who include criminal justice generally place it in its larger social and economic context and at the end of a long list of other self-government powers.[9] In contrast, governments and public inquiries frequently focused on criminal justice initiatives as opposed to broader and more holistic reforms.

Fuelled by a multiplicity of inquiries with mandates that did not extend beyond justice issues (Nova Scotia 1989; Manitoba 1991a, 1991b; Alberta 1991; LRCC 1993), criminal justice issues dominated much official discourse about Aboriginal people in the late 1980s and the 1990s. The federal Royal Commission on Aboriginal Peoples addressed social, cultural, linguistic, and economic issues as well as justice issues, but it was the exception to the rule. Just as it may have been cheaper to give women's groups victories in criminal justice matters as opposed to child care and equal pay (Lacombe 1994), so, too, may it have been cheaper to focus on criminal justice reforms as opposed to more expensive forms of social and economic justice. Aboriginal justice may be given an undue emphasis within the larger self-government project to the neglect of other related issues, including land and harvesting rights, economics, health, family relations, culture and spirituality. Because it refused to see crime as a separate issue divorced from the need for economic, social, spiritual, and cultural health, however, Aboriginal justice resists the tendency to segment justice from other issues.

Crime Control and Aboriginal People

In 1990, Carol LaPrairie argued that 'the issues of incidence of crime and offence patterns of aboriginal peoples have been largely ignored in discussions of over-representation' (p. 430). Both the Aboriginal Justice Inquiry of Manitoba (AJIM) (Manitoba 1991a: 87–96) and the Royal Commission on Aboriginal Peoples (RCAP) (Canada 1996b: 33–9) subsequently included crime in their explanations of overrepresentation. Similarly, Mary Ellen Turpel (1994: 208–9) warned that criminal justice reforms must deal with 'problems of alcohol and solvent abuse, family violence and sexual abuse, and youth crime ... and not just retreat into a pre-colonial situation.' The danger was less one of ignoring crime than of offering crime control as the solution and in so doing increasing Aboriginal overrepresentation in prisons.

One factor in the increased discussion of crime within Aboriginal communities was a growing knowledge and concern about the victimization of Aboriginal women and children. The Ontario Native Women's Association concluded that eight of ten Aboriginal women personally experienced violence, with 87 per cent of those being physically injured and 57 per cent sexually abused (Canada 1993a: 156). Both the AJIM (Manitoba 1991a: c13) and the RCAP (Canada 1996b: 269–75) specifically addressed concerns about the protection of Aboriginal women from crime. The AJIM (Manitoba 1991a: 490) also concluded that 'the question of child abuse must be addressed forcefully because, in our view, it represents the single greatest threat to the future of Aboriginal people and their societies.' Child abuse was frequently related to the legacy of sexual abuse in residential schools. Other studies indicated disproportionate Aboriginal victimization with respect to homicides (Roberts and Doob 1997: 490, 494) and personal-injury offences (LaPrairie 1995: 436).

Aboriginal overrepresentation among the victims of crime, like Aboriginal overrepresentation in prison, could be interpreted in different ways. One approach was to view victimization through feminist concerns about violence against women and children. In *O'Connor* (1995), LEAF (1996: 434) argued that 'as many as 8 out of 10 First Nations women have been sexually abused or assaulted in their lives' and that the equality rights of Aboriginal women should be considered as a ground for denying accused and judges access to the personal records of victims of sexual assault.

Unfortunately, Aboriginal crime was sometimes discussed as a veiled way of expressing hostility towards Aboriginal people and doubts about their ability to govern themselves. Some Bloc Québécois members took this approach when they objected to including the reduction of incarceration of Aboriginal offenders as a goal of sentencing.[10] Criticisms of the YOA in the West sometimes were a veiled means of being critical of Aboriginal youth.

A more constructive approach was to view disproportionate victimization by crime in the larger context of public health. Aboriginal people suffered disproportionately not only from victimization by crime, but also from accidents, disease, infant mortality, and suicide (Griffiths, Yerbury, and Weafer 1989: 125). This more holistic approach to Aboriginal well-being lent itself to more comprehensive interventions which placed less stress on criminal justice initiatives. It resisted the tendency to focus on criminal justice reforms as the main response to crime and victimization, and was more congruent with the holistic approach to healing taken by some Aboriginal people (Ross 1996; Canada 1996b). Despite the dangers that it could provide an outlet for prejudice and crime-control strategies that would increase Aboriginal overrepresentation in prison, the disproportionate victimization of Aboriginal people by both crime and other harms cannot be ignored.

The Murder of Helen Betty Osborne

In 1971, Helen Betty Osborne was abducted and, after an attempted rape, murdered. Charges were not laid until 1986, and only one of the four white men involved in her abduction was convicted of murder. The Osborne case, along with the police shooting of J.J. Harper, led to the appointment of Manitoba's Aboriginal Justice Inquiry. Harper's death symbolized a lack of due process from the police, while Osborne's death symbolized the failure of crime control. The violent deaths of both reflected a too common occurrence.

After the murder, the four white men involved in her abduction retained a defence lawyer and refused to talk to the police (Manitoba 1991b: 56–8). Even though they were not bound by the Charter and had no trouble detaining and questioning Osborne's Aboriginal friends in an intimidating manner, the police followed the defence lawyer's instructions and did not detain or question the suspects. The AJIM concluded that the police, even in the absence of reasonable grounds for an arrest, should have taken the white suspects in for questioning. 'Attendance at a detachment often will impress upon a suspect the seriousness of the situation and may cause a suspect to reassess a decision to remain silent' (Manitoba 1991b: 33). The discriminatory double standards in the way the police investigated the case suggested that Helen Betty Osborne did not receive the equal benefit and protection of crime control because she was an Aboriginal woman.

There were limits, however, to what even non-discriminatory crime control could achieve. The AJIM (Manitoba 1991b: 72, 83) concluded that one of the four suspects was so drunk that he did not have the intent to assist in the abduction and that another would have to be given immunity to testify against his accomplices. A murder conviction would be even more difficult to obtain in the Charter era because the prosecutor would have to prove subjective foresight of death and no longer have the benefit of the felony-murder rule which made those who committed or assisted in a rape guilty of murder regardless of whether they had intended to kill the victim (see chapter 3).

The AJIM also made recommendations from a victims' rights perspective. Osborne's mother was told of her daughter's death in a ten-minute conversation with the RCMP, who did not keep her informed about the investigation until an arrest was made fifteen years later. The police treated Osborne's friends harshly and no support was provided. An anonymous Crime Stopper program and financial rewards might have facilitated the investigation, but they were not used. The silence of the community was related to a general social 'indifference to the victims of crime. Unless there is a direct personal connection to victims, it is all too easy for us to disregard their plight' (Manitoba 1991b: 51). This silence was also related to a racist and sexist lack of concern about the victim. More should have been done to investigate and prosecute the murder and to respond to the suffering of its victims.

The one man convicted for her murder, Dwayne Archie Johnston, was sentenced to life imprisonment without eligibility for parole for ten years. He was granted day parole in 1995, and in protest about fifty people from Osborne's village, Norway House, marched to Winnipeg. A cousin of Osborne's complained: 'justice is not being served. If we let this go by, what message are we sending to society, that you can kill somebody and only serve 6.5 years?' (*Globe and Mail*, 14 Nov. 1995). Johnson's day parole was eventually revoked, but was restored in 1997. By that time, however, a spokesperson for the Osborne family stated that they were content with the parole 'largely because he [Johnson] apologized in meetings with the family and native leaders at the prison last December' (*Globe and Mail*, 8 Mar. 1997). Even in a case where demands for continued punishment would be very understandable, meetings between victims and offenders and apologies by offenders seemed to have played a healthy role. As will be seen, such meetings would be facilitated by Aboriginal justice.

The murder of Helen Betty Osborne was a symbol of racist and sexist violence and it stood as a shameful reminder of discriminatory double standards in extending even the limited benefits of crime control. Mary Ellen Turpel (1993: 166) has indicated a need for a broader perspective on the tragedy:

We also have to look at why this 19-year-old woman who desired a formal education had no choice but to attend high school in The Pas instead of her own community, Norway House. We have to consider why the fact that she was an Aboriginal woman made her the chosen target of an abduction, violent rape and murder by four white males. We also have to consider why the Aboriginal community in The Pas did not press for the arrest of Helen Betty Osborne's murderer(s), some of whom were brought to justice only 16 years after the offence. These dimensions to the Osborne case defy classification as 'criminal justice' problems – they reveal dysfunctional relationships between Aboriginal peoples and non-Aboriginal peoples at many levels, including among governments and citizens.

The victimization of Aboriginal people by crime cannot be isolated from broader injustices. In Osborne's case, this included a government policy that required her and others 'to move to a strange and hostile environment to continue her schooling' even after 'the smallest Manitoba communities had long had their own schools' (Manitoba 1991b: 91–2). In other cases, it would include a lack of economic and social opportunities that produced conditions conducive to alcoholism, suicide, and crime. A non-punitive approach to victims' rights should eventually blur hard-and-fast distinctions between crime and other harms.

Under-policing or Under-servicing?

At the same time as it found that over-policing led to J.J. Harper's death, the AJIM (Manitoba 1991a: 596) also found under-policing in northern areas that "would not be tolerated in southern non-Aboriginal communities of a similar size ... Aboriginal people are expected to use nonexistent telephones to call non-resident police, who are unlikely to attend within a reasonable time. Just as important, the residents of many communities complained that the police did not enforce local by-laws against the importation of alcohol to the reserve.' A study of justice in remote Cree communities in Quebec also found the paradox of Aboriginal people being over-policed with respect to minor or petty offences and under-policed with respect to more serious crimes (Brodeur 1991: 17). Could more police be the answer?

Some crime-control measures may be required in the short run. Overnight detention in lock-ups may be necessary to cope with alcohol abuse and the violence that can accompany it (Landau 1996: 10–11; Hyde 1992: 379) but not as a long-term solution. Given its accommodation of crime-control values, it should not be assumed that the Charter would prevent regulatory searches to prevent alcohol from coming into dry communities or preventive detention (see chapter 2). Some of the dangers of crime control may be avoided by the use of Aboriginal police officers, especially if they are accountable to Aboriginal communities. At the same time, Aboriginal justice spending should not continue to mimic traditional crime-control spending with the bulk of money going to policing and corrections, as opposed to crime prevention, and victim and offender services (Canada 1996b: 294).

The under-policing thesis should be approached with caution. Mary Hyde (1992: 370) has suggested that 'the dependency of native communities on police for services, not otherwise available on reserves, results in high police to population ratios, increases the likelihood of police interventions and "criminalizes" behaviour that would not otherwise be criminal if other agencies were involved.' Adding more police may only increase Aboriginal overrepresentation in prison. As Tim Quigley (1994: 274) has suggested, communities may request that a police detachment be established in their community only to find 'an almost instant "crime wave", since the police do their work by making arrests and laying charges, even if the same problems were dealt with by the community in other ways before the police were present.' Under-policing may actually be under-servicing. Aboriginal justice requires 'people like alcohol and family violence workers, traditional healers, mental health workers, sexual abuse counsellors and the like' (Ross 1994: 242) rather than the police and prosecutors who run the crime-control assembly line.

Sentencing Circles

Sentencing circles to assist trial judges in determining the appropriate sentence for Aboriginal offenders should not be confused with Aboriginal justice discussed in the next section. Like Aboriginal police forces, sentencing circles are a hybrid intervention which promise, at most, that discretion within the existing system will be influenced by the experience and wisdom of Aboriginal people.

Sentencing circles allow offenders, victims, families, elders, as well as police, lawyers, and social workers to make recommendations concerning the sentencing of Aboriginal offenders. They function on the premise that the accused has been found guilty and faces some form of punishment if the circle cannot convince the judge to accept an alternative disposition. The recommendations, if accepted by the trial judge, are implemented by court orders which are more coercive than those which would emerge from a healing circle, but less powerful because of restrictions on the court's powers, including the maximum duration of probation orders. There are also limits on the court's ability to adjourn proceedings to allow time for reflection and healing (*Taylor* 1995). The trial judge can accept recommendations that are not the product of a true consensus and involve punishment, including incarceration. One Métis probation officer who participated in a sentencing circle that recommended eighteen months' imprisonment (and was overturned by the courts as too lenient) commented that she thought it was 'a misuse of this Sentencing Circle, which is a healing process ... we're talking periods of time here' (*Morin* 1995: 142). It was not a coincidence that the existing system was most receptive to Aboriginal participation at sentencing. The same pattern was seen in chapter 7, where concerns about hate crimes were squeezed into sentencing, and continues in the next chapter, where the participation of crime victims was funnelled into sentencing. Sentencing is a flexible and secondary stage of the criminal process and can be influenced by alternative models of justice without threatening the dominance of crime control, due process, or the role of professionals.

Sentencing circles were criticized as 'small add-ons to the existing system, which stands ready with the full force of its adversarial and punishment-oriented values if the "nice" solution does not work' (Monture-

Okanee 1994: 226). At the same time, however, they introduced criminal justice professionals to an alternative model of justice, albeit in an imperfect and partial manner. Courts were temporally reconfigured from the hierarchical structure required by both crime control and due process into a circle. 'The circle significantly breaks down the dominance that traditional courtrooms accord lawyers and judges : All persons within the circle must be addressed ... The circle denies the comfort of evading difficult issues through the use of obtuse, complex technical language' (*Moses* 1992: 356–7). By not relegating the public to the back of the room and privileging judges and lawyers, the circle created an opportunity for increased participation and a wider acceptance of 'responsibility for finding an answer' (ibid: 369).

Sentencing circles allow judges to consider 'all available sanctions other than imprisonment that are reasonable in the circumstances ... with particular attention to the circumstances of aboriginal offenders' (Criminal Code, s.718.2[e]). In *Moses* (1992), a twenty-six-year-old Aboriginal accused with more than forty past convictions was required by a sentencing circle to live on a trap line, attend a two-month alcohol rehabilitation program with his brother, and live with his family in an alcohol-free home as an alternative to yet another significant period of incarceration. Nevertheless, there were limits to the ability of sentencing circles to reduce Aboriginal overrepresentation. It was not clear that sentencing discretion accounted for overrepresentation (LaPrairie 1990). Hundreds of sentencing circles were conducted (Quigley 1994), but only when the relevant Aboriginal communities had the time and resources to participate. Even then, some courts believed they 'cannot be employed in every case' because they took 'far longer than the sentencing process prescribed by the *Criminal Code*' (*Johnson* 1994: 24) and were inappropriate in serious cases that would normally result in more than two years' imprisonment (*Morin* 1995). Sentencing circles were vulnerable to crime-control concerns about denunciation and deterrence of crime[11] and due-process concerns about sentencing disparity and proportionate punishment. Serious concerns were also raised by some Aboriginal women that victims of sexual assault and domestic violence would be dominated in these informal proceedings (Canada 1996b: 271–2; Nahanee 1993).[12] Despite their potential in some individual cases, sentencing circles were unlikely to replace the quick guilty plea and sentencing hearing used to process most Aboriginal accused along the crime-control assembly line.

Sentencing circles gave criminal justice professionals a partial and imperfect glimpse of a new form of justice which provided more room for offenders, victims, their families, and their communities. There were benefits to reconfiguring the court into a circle and encouraging the offender, the victim, their families, and the community to take responsibility. At worst, however, sentencing circles appropriated the appearance of Aboriginal justice for the ends of crime control. They could encourage communities to adopt punitive ways which even then could be reversed by the courts as excessively lenient

Aboriginal Justice

Aboriginal forms of justice are diverse and defined by Aboriginal communities to meet their own circumstances. Non-Aboriginal people such as myself may have difficulty understanding Aboriginal justice, especially without decades of experience and Aboriginal teachings. Some attempt is necessary, if only because Aboriginal justice has gained official recognition and momentum. In 1994, the federal/provincial justice ministers' conference agreed that the current criminal justice system had failed Aboriginal people and 'a holistic approach including the healing process is essential in Aboriginal justice reform.' Consistent with the dual concern with restoration and prevention in a non-punitive victims' rights model, the same resolutions called for governments to 'work with Aboriginal communities on community based crime prevention /crime reduction initiatives' (as quoted in Gosse 1994: 29; see also Canada 1996b: 27–8). The official willingness to endorse Aboriginal justice was related to the manifest failure of crime control and due process to reduce Aboriginal overrepresentation among crime victims and prisoners. Expectations that Aboriginal justice would include victims and reduce costs were also factors.

The specificity and diversity of Aboriginal justice must be respected, but it provides lessons for all of us. Patricia Monture demonstrated a spirit of generosity when she wrote in a chapter for the Task Force on Federally Sentenced Women that 'we have not shared what we understand to be the truth only for the benefit of Aboriginal women or Aboriginal people, but for all Peoples' (Canada 1990: 22). In a demonstration of the potential for cross-cultural understanding, she quoted from a submission by the John Howard Society of Manitoba, which had turned to Aboriginal justice because of its 'belief that non-Native society has much to learn from Native traditions and wisdom' (ibid: 30). They had called for 'a restorative model of justice rather than a retributive one. Mediation, reparation, and reconciliation are the best methods. Solutions must come from within the local community. The focus must be on problem-solving, dialogue and mediation ... We want this to be similar to the Tribal system of justice ... a non-criminal model with the focus on the offenders with their culture and community. The victims too need their power restored and the offender needs to accept responsibility and accountability. We recommend a holistic approach' (ibid: 22). Some of the dangers in assimilating Aboriginal justice to restorative justice will be explored below, but the similarities cannot be ignored.

Judge Murray Sinclair (1994: 178) has explained that 'the primary meaning of "justice" in an Aboriginal society would be that of restoring peace and equilibrium to the community through reconciling the accused with his or her own conscience and with the individual or family that is wronged.' This definition included both restorative justice and healing. Sometimes more stress is placed on restoring harmony, sometimes more on healing. For example, the following statement stressed restorative justice: 'in the Ojibway concept of order, when a person is wronged it is understood that the wrongdoer must repair the order and harmony of the community by undoing the wrong' (Manitoba 1991a: 36). An Oji-Cree community's justice proposal stressed healing of the offender by suggesting that wrongdoing was 'a misbehaviour which requires teaching or an illness which requires healing' (Ross 1996: 5; 1992: 62). Official discussions of Aboriginal justice tended to emphasize restorative justice (Manitoba 1991a: 22; Canada 1996b: 214). With its promise of accountability and justice for victims, restorative justice may be more politically appealing than a healing vision which relies on spirituality and rehabilitation.

Unlike due process and crime control, Aboriginal justice is not dominated by professionals. Elders play an important role, but they 'do not "judge". They see the whole person and find ways (through stories, meditations, prayers, and ceremonies) of helping an individual understand the shortcomings or problems that led to anti-social acts. They focus on harmony, rehabilitation, reintegration of an offender into the family, clan and community – not on guilt' (Turpel 1993: 176). Appearing before an elder may be a daunting experience, not because of fears of punishment, but because the elder 'knows you, your family, and your community. She or he can see your faults clearly and, therefore, to meet with the Elder is to accept that any wrongdoing on your part is, in a sense, known to all. You must confront your own faults along with your virtues. This system emphasizes a willingness to accept your own lack of wisdom and to learn from the Elder. It encourages responsibility for your behaviour and reflection on how to live harmoniously in a community' (Monture-Okanee and Turpel 1992: 246).

Aboriginal justice also contemplates a role for crime victims. 'Because the purpose of law in Aboriginal society is to restore harmony within the community, not only the accused has to be considered. Other people who have been or might be affected by the offence, particularly the victim, have to be considered' (Manitoba 1991a: 36). Professors Monture-Okanee and Turpel (1992: 258) argued that 'no victims' rights movement is necessary in an Aboriginal system of justice because the victim would never be forgotten in the first place if the system was operating according to custom ... the victim is not brushed aside in the quest for punishment. It is only by focusing on the victim and offender and considering how they can heal and be reintegrated into the community that the needs of the people are served.' Victims are defined broadly to include extended family, clan members, and communities (Turpel 1993: 177). Restitution is not limited to cash payments for ascertainable losses, but includes apologies and traditional offerings (ibid: 178). One of the concerns of the Community Holistic Circle Healing Program (CHCH) in Hollow Water, Manitoba, was that the 'courtroom and process simply is not a safe place for the victim to address the victimization' (Ross 1996: 38). Aboriginal justice would not promote the adversarial cross-examination of victims which was at the centre of recent controversies over the 'rape shield' law and the counselling records of sexual-assault victims (see chapter 5). In part, this was because Aboriginal justice would make it 'safe' for the accused not to exercise his right to full answer and defence.

The offender plays a more important role than in crime control or due process. A common feature of Aboriginal-justice initiatives is 'that the offender has acknowledged responsibility for the offence' (Canada 1996b: 197). This acceptance of responsibility was very different from the custodial confessions and courtroom guilty pleas that characterized the crime-control model. Acceptance of responsibility followed from the nature of many Aboriginal languages, which focused on the fact that an accusation had been made, and Aboriginal ethics, which suggested that a 'not guilty' plea to an allegation with a factual basis was 'dishonest' (Manitoba 1991a: 22, 38; Sinclair 1994: 178). Acceptance of responsibility is a prelude to healing, not a factor mitigating punishment as in crime control or a waiver of rights as in due process.

A concern with healing made the offender's past victimization relevant, but not as an excuse. As Rupert Ross (1996: 186) explained, 'histories of victimization in offenders are never taken as excuses or justifications for what that offender has done. Rather, they are seen as forces that the offender has *given in to*, forces he or she has a responsibility to confront, deal with and resolve.' Unlike self-defence claims by battered women, the offender's experience of victimization was not squeezed into expert testimony or binary verdicts of guilty or not guilty. In summary, Aboriginal justice promised greater participation by offenders, crime victims, and the community in an attempt to restore harmony and move towards healing.

Aboriginal Justice in Relation to Other Alternatives

Linkages between Aboriginal justice and other alternatives to due process and crime control were made in the first chapter of this book and by other commentators (LaPrairie 1992; Quigley 1994; Braithwaite 1997). They were valuable in building momentum for reform, but Aboriginal justice should not be assimilated to either restorative justice or reintegrative shaming.

Aboriginal justice may place less emphasis than restorative justice on the offender and victim interacting as individuals, and more on collective responsibility as measured by the 'matrix of social and family relationships and responsibilities' (Jackson 1992: 195). Diversion programs proposed by the Gitksan and Wet'suwet'en peoples provided for the participation of not only victims and offenders, but their Houses or clans (ibid: 216). Traditions of emotional restraint may require that interactions between offenders and victims be mediated by their families. As suggested above, a stress on restorative justice rather than healing made Aboriginal justice more politically appealing, but may have raised false expectations. Some forms of Aboriginal justice may not end in a definite act of restorative justice, but focus more on the often slow and spiritual process of healing.

Aboriginal justice and John Braithwaite's influential theory of reintegrative shaming have many similarities. Both facilitate community participation and stress the need to connect offenders and victims with other individuals, families, and communities. They both do not ignore the past, but focus more on the future. Nevertheless, they are not exactly the same. Aboriginal justice may be less visibly emotional than the family conferences observed by Braithwaite and Mugford (1994). 'Indignation, hostility and angry rebuttal' may be at odds 'with the Aboriginal ethic of emotional restraint' (Turpel 1993: 174–5) in which 'great care' must 'be taken not to label things, people or events in terms of personal responses to them or to argue against anyone else's views about them' (Ross 1996: 104). Pride and a desire for healing could play a more important role than shame. Aboriginal justice may be more about taking the steps necessary to create healthy families[13] and communities into which reintegration is desirable. The healing and community-building potential of Aboriginal justice should not be ignored.

A different danger was that Aboriginal justice would be presented as a romantic return to an unrealistic past. Stanley Cohen (1985: 121) warned of the 'idealistic flaw of trying to base a social control ideology on visions derived from other societies ... the content of these visions may be historical and anthropological nonsense – underplaying the paternalism, the fixed lines of authorities and the arbitrary nature of justice ... the implicit threat of violence which often lay behind the submission to community or informal justice' (see also LaRocque 1997: 83). Cohen's criticisms, like other critiques of social control (Ericson and Baranek 1982), would have more practical bite if they presented some alternative that did not have the dangers identified. Given high rates of Aboriginal victimization and imprisonment, radical non-intervention (Schur 1973) is not an option. The issue is not social control, but whether it will be more or less punitive and more or less controlled by Aboriginal people.

Challenges from Due Process and Crime Control

Because it is a genuine alternative, Aboriginal justice is vulnerable to criticisms that it fails to respect due-process rights or take crime seriously. Debates surrounding the self-government provisions of the Charlottetown Accord (Bakan 1997: c.8) suggested that it was impossible to achieve a consensus about Aboriginal justice at the level of ideological abstraction and that the entire self-government project could be undermined by divisive and controversial debates about whether Aboriginal justice respected due-process rights or the equality rights of women. If a realistic view was taken about the ability of due process to protect liberty or the criminal sanction to control crime, however, there would be more room for accommodation.

Stated in the abstract, the conflict between due process and Aboriginal justice was great (Turpel 1990). The principle of judicial impartiality conflicts with the importance of involving elders, families, and friends (Monture-Okanee and Turpel 1992: 246); concerns about self-incrimination and legal representation conflict with the importance of personal acknowledgment of responsibility; the right to a trial in a reasonable time conflicts with the time required to achieve consensus and healing; and the principle of proportionate punishment conflicts with interventions to facilitate healing. These tensions between the liberal and individualistic values of due process and the communitarian and holistic values of Aboriginal justice should not be ignored. They are a large part of what makes Aboriginal justice a genuine alternative. Nevertheless, there are pragmatic strategies to allow due process and Aboriginal justice to coexist.

If due process could accommodate crime control and victims' rights, there is no reason why it could not also accommodate Aboriginal justice. The Charter contains plenty of interpretative flex and safety values to accommodate the aspirations of Aboriginal communities. Courts should accept limitations on Charter rights so long as Aboriginal-justice initiatives do not result in incarceration (Canada 1996b: 266). In addition, section 25 of the Charter provides that Charter rights shall not be interpreted to abrogate Aboriginal rights, including those in future land-claims agreements. Aboriginal governments could, like provincial and federal governments, be allowed to opt out of due-process rights under section 33 of the Charter for a renewable five-year period. Recourse to the override was not necessary when Parliament rejected Supreme Court decisions based on the due-process rights of accused in sexual-assault cases or replied to due-process restrictions on police powers. Aboriginal governments could be just as bold in replying to judicial decisions that were insensitive to their aspirations and values. Perhaps most important, accused could always waive their Charter rights and voluntarily participate in Aboriginal-justice initiatives.

Stated in the abstract, the conflict between Aboriginal justice and crime control is also great. Teressa Nahanee (1993: 360, 373) argued that Aboriginal women opposed the leniency of approaches 'which allow Aboriginal male sex offenders to roam free of punishment after conviction for violent offences against Aboriginal women and children.' She emphasized the need for 'punishment and deterrence of the "guilty" victimizer' (see also LaRocque 1997: 80–1). Aboriginal-justice initiatives that took on cases of serious crimes, especially sexual assaults, were vulnerable to public criticism that they did not take crime seriously enough.

Demands for crime control could, however, be accommodated. Many Aboriginal communities do not want to deal with the most serious offences as they assume more control over justice issues. The most serious crimes could be left to the crime-control professionals, but this should be done without enthusiasm or confidence and as a regrettable form of banishment. If Aboriginal justice is permanently reserved for minor offences, however, it will do little to reduce overrepresentation. More fundamentally, the assumptions of crime control should be critically examined. Punishment in the court system was often fairly lenient (Roberts 1994) and often failed to deter crime (Canada 1987, 1993a). It rarely forced offenders to take responsibility for their problems and did not guarantee the security or equality of crime victims.

Aboriginal justice has been criticized for not respecting due process and crime control. Debates around the Charlottetown Accord resembled the new political case in their symbolic and divisive nature and their frequent assumptions that punishment would control crime, and due process would guarantee liberty. At the local level, however, there remains room for pragmatic accommodations between Aboriginal justice and crime control and due process. Aboriginal communities will often not want to deal with the most serious offences, and offenders will often voluntarily participate in Aboriginal-justice initiatives.

Some Aboriginal-Justice Projects

One much-discussed Aboriginal-justice initiative is the Hollow Water Community Holistic Circle Healing Project (CHCH) used to deal with sexual abuse in Ojibway and Métis communities 200 kilometres north of Winnipeg. It was estimated that about 75 per cent of the population were victims of sexual abuse, while 35 per cent were victimizers (Ross 1994: 243). These tragically high figures suggested a significant overlap between the populations of victim and victimizer. This type of overlap was revealed in many victimization surveys (Fattah 1993; LaPrairie 1995), but was suppressed in punitive models of victims' rights which promoted dichotomies of guilty perpetrators and innocent victims.

After criminal charges were laid for sexual abuse, the accused was given five days to decide whether to plead guilty and participate in the CHCH or go through the regular court process with the option of pleading not guilty. Due process in the form of defence lawyers recommending silence and a 'not guilty' plea could be a 'barrier to healing' and a prelude to 'the second "victimization" that occurs when victims are cross-examined on the witness stand' (Ross 1996: 38). Still, most accused in Hollow Water waived their due-process rights and pleaded guilty. Rather than fighting a hard and divisive battle to eliminate the due-process option, Aboriginal justice, with its promise of non-punitive healing, could successfully compete for offenders with the due-process obstacle course. Guilty pleas also spared 'the victim the trauma of testifying in court' (Canada 1996b: 162)

274 Due Process and Victims' Rights

and could be an important first step in healing the victim as well as the offender.

An admission of guilt still exposed an offender to the possibility of incarceration, and the CHCH argued that this threat kept 'people from coming forward and taking responsibility for the hurt they are causing. It reinforces the silence, and therefore promotes, rather than breaks, the cycle of violence that exists. In reality, rather than making the community a safer place, the threat of jail places the community more at risk' (as quoted in Ross 1994: 246). This was a very different attitude towards unreported crime than that which motivated sexual-assault, sexual-abuse, and wife-assault initiatives discussed in chapters 5 and 6. Unreported crime was not related to the failings of the criminal justice to protect victims and punish offenders, but rather to the threat of punishment. Full reporting was a goal, but so that healing, not punishment, would occur. Crime control, as represented by the threat of incarceration, could impede healing. Again, however, there were grounds for pragmatic accommodations if judges deferred to the CHCH's recommendations not to imprison offenders. A successful appeal of a sentence as excessively lenient (*Morin* 1995), however, could have devastating effects on the project.

The CHCH did not fit into the adversarial roles contemplated by due-process and crime-control models. Its members did not see themselves 'as "being on the side of" the crown or the defence. The people they represent are both members of our community and the pain of both is felt in our community' (Ross 1996: 193). The offender needed the victim for forgiveness and understanding, and the victim needed the offender for recognition of the harm caused. Much time was spent with both the victim and offender (Canada 1996b: 160) and it was often important that sentencing be put off as long as possible (Ross 1996: 34). The aim was to produce a healing contract which, unlike in more individualistic forms of victim/offender reconciliation, was signed 'by a large number of people' and not just the offender and the victim (ibid: 263) The contract would last for two to three years, and the ceremony could be repeated at six-month intervals (ibid: 36). There was much more participation than contemplated under victim-impact statements (see chapter 9). In separate rounds of the circle, all participants spoke directly to the victim and the offender, and then conveyed their expectations for the future. Circles ensured procedural fairness and wide participation.

Aboriginal justice was less concerned with speed and finality than either due process or crime control, and took a longer-term perspective of time.

This may explain why the measurable results of the CHCH were not overly impressive. Of fifty-two victimizers, four had successfully completed the program by June 1995 and two had reoffended since entering the program. In addition, five others had gone to jail 'after their offences were disclosed, mainly because they refused to acknowledge what they had done' (*Globe and Mail*, 8 Apr. 1995). Victims were more likely to have completed the program, with 32 of 94 having done so, and 27 of 180 family members of victims (Canada 1996b: 166). The program appeared to do more for victims and their families than for offenders and their families.

Another Aboriginal-justice initiative was the Community Council Project run by Aboriginal Legal Services of Toronto. It operated as a diversion project for Aboriginal accused who agreed that they committed one of the offences charged and whose lawyer did not believe there was a defence on the merits. There was no formal limit on what offences could be heard, but most offences were for less serious crimes such as failing to appear, theft, prostitution, assault, mischief, and possession of stolen property (Canada 1996b: 154). As with the Hollow Water project, the offender's voluntary admission of guilt was a practical way to eliminate many theoretical tensions between Aboriginal justice and due process. Unlike in Hollow Water, the fact that most crimes diverted into this project were not serious allayed crime-control concerns.

After the acceptance of responsibility, the offender met with members of the Community Council, which consisted of volunteers from Toronto's Aboriginal community. Attendance was high, even though many of those diverted had previous convictions for not attending court. Most offenders were young and had been incarcerated in the past, and many had been involved with child-protection agencies (Moyer and Axon 1993: 51). The hearings were held in private and lasted from three-quarters of an hour to over three hours, and included personal discussions between the council volunteers and the offender. 'A Community Council hearing will look very different from a courtroom … The Council will meet wherever is necessary and appropriate … The offenders and victims who attend the Council should be made to feel welcome and to know that the Council members really do care about their situation' (Aboriginal Legal Services of Toronto [ALST] 1991). Lawyers and the media did not attend. Those who evaluated the program remarked that 'the hearing resembles a family unit; council members sit in a circle with the client and try to relate to the client's past experiences' (Moyer and Axon 1993: 65). One offender explained that 'the Council members made me more relaxed … The questions were hard, but I felt like I wanted to talk out my problems …

There was a feeling of trust and I felt that the elders understood me. They gave me a chance to speak up, which I would not have had in court' (ibid: 64–5).

The council can make a broad range of recommendations designed 'to begin the healing process necessary to reintegrate the individual into the community,' but, unlike judges, they had no coercive powers to enforce them. The Elders believed that 'while a person can be ordered to stop certain actions and to start doing other things, whether or not the person will respond is in their hands alone. It may well take time for the important messages from the Council members to reach an offender. Time in this sense could well be measured in years, not just days or months. At the same time, even if a person is not yet ready to make the changes in their life that are necessary, they may be taking steps in the right direction and those steps should be encouraged' (ALST 1991). There is more concern about helping the whole person change slowly than quickly achieving measurable and final results. Dispositions included community service related to the offender's needs, referrals to Aboriginal agencies, and maintaining contact with project staff. Only 2 per cent of cases resulted in monetary restitution, and 12 per cent in letters of apology, but more than half of the offences did not have direct victims. An evaluation found that 90 per cent of offenders complied or were in the process of complying with the council's dispositions (Moyer and Axon 1993: 52, 65–8). The council was more an example of community building than of reintegration because most of the offenders had no previous involvement with Toronto's Aboriginal community (Canada 1996b: 156).

These two programs revealed some of the promise of Aboriginal justice. They rejected dichotomies between offenders and victims while at the same time encouraging offenders to take responsibility for their crime and creating space for the immediate victims to participate. Both were based on circle models of participation, and both rejected the emphasis placed on speed and finality in both crime control and due process. Both programs, however, coexisted with due process by being premised on the offender's voluntary acceptance of responsibility. The Hollow Water project was vulnerable to crime-control criticisms that it did not impose jail time for serious offences, while the Community Council dealt mainly with less serious offences. Despite possible crime-control criticism for not punishing sexual violence, victims as opposed to offenders were more likely to have completed the Hollow Water Project. Victims played less of a role in the Toronto Community Council, which dealt with relatively minor offences. The programs were not a self-governing system of Aboriginal justice, but they provided a fuller and less distorted picture than did sentencing circles of what Aboriginal justice might be like.

Conclusion

Aboriginal people are doubly disadvantaged by their well-documented overrepresentation among both prisoners and crime victims. Equal and non-discriminatory due process was necessary to attempt to control the racist exercise of discretion in the criminal process that produced tragedies such as the wrongful conviction of Donald Marshall Jr and the death of J.J. Harper. Nevertheless, due process would not affect the routine guilty-plea cases which produced Aboriginal overrepresentation in prisons. The Helen Betty Osborne case revealed how Aboriginal people did not receive the equal and non-discriminatory benefit of crime control when they were victimized by crime. At the same time, non-discriminatory crime control would not by itself reduce the overrepresentation of Aboriginal people among the victims of crime and other harms such as suicide, accident, and premature death. Moreover, crime-control strategies such as increased policing could increase Aboriginal overrepresentation in prison.

Fortunately, Aboriginal justice holds out the promise of reducing Aboriginal overrepresentation among both prisoners and crime victims. It allows offenders to relate their crimes to their past victimization, but in a manner that facilitates healing while not denying responsibility for the offence or the suffering of the immediate victim. It also holds out the possibility of participation and healing for victims. Much public discourse about Aboriginal people in the 1990s focused on criminal justice issues, and this presented a similar risk of criminalizing broader issues as observed in other chapters with respect to women, young people, and minorities. The holistic approach of Aboriginal justice, however, better resisted attempts to criminalize broader social, economic, political, and cultural issues.

9

Crime Victims

This chapter examines the legal and political impact of crime victims who are not members of groups discussed in previous chapters. Victimization surveys suggest that in any one year almost a quarter of all Canadians are victimized by crime. Such a large, diffuse, and heterogeneous group might have less political clout than the smaller more organized groups examined in previous chapters (Roach 1993a). Nevertheless, like the groups examined in previous chapters, crime victims made their mark on criminal justice policy, particularly in relation to the punishment of offenders. Victim-advocacy groups were formed by those who had experienced the most severe crimes of violence, and they formed alliances with crime-control professionals (Elias 1986; Fattah 1989). Crime victims were constructed as the new consumers of the services, information, and punishment provided by police and prosecutors. In this sense, victims' rights legitimated crime control.

The federal government first promoted interest in crime victims (Rock 1986), but a more populist victims' movement emerged in the 1990s. It asserted victims' rights in new political cases in order to counter rights claims by the accused and the media. It also demanded better and more sensitive services from crime-control professionals and increased punishment of offenders. Every province enacted victims' bills of rights, but they were a faint and symbolic echo of the enforceable due-process and equality rights found in the Charter. Victims enjoyed less success in new political cases than the accused, the media, or disadvantaged groups, who were all attached to specific Charter rights (Cairns 1992). As in the United States, some victims' groups now demand a constitutional amendment to recognize victims' rights (Young 1997).

Most of the victories won by crime victims revolved around the punishment of offenders. Victim-impact statements were allowed in various proceedings. Victim-advocacy groups and the police campaigned vigorously for the repeal of 'faint hope' hearings, but had only qualified success in restricting such hearings. Restitution for readily ascertainable losses was available, but did not flourish as a real alternative to punishment. As with hate crimes (see chapter 7) and sentencing circles (see chapter 8), there were limits to the transformative potential of back-end reforms to the criminal process which focused on sentencing.

This chapter will conclude with a discussion of some victims' rights initiatives that could provide genuine alternatives to asserting rights and demanding crime control. Victim-compensation schemes could be expanded and revitalized to recognize the losses of all crime victims and to reject the idea that crime victims must be innocent and cooperative. Civil litigation by crime victims could also play a modest role in a nonpunitive approach to victims' rights. More fundamentally, restorative justice and crime prevention could be recognized as interventions which benefit potential and actual crime victims. Like family conferencing (see chapter 6) and Aboriginal justice (see chapter 8), victim–offender reconciliation programs (VORPs) give victims more power than they possess in even a victim-sensitive crime-control system. Unfortunately, victim-advocacy groups focused on the most serious crimes, where restorative justice may not be appropriate. A social-development approach to crime prevention could counter the criminalization of politics. The challenge of the next decade may be to have restorative justice accepted as a legitimate form of justice and to define crime prevention as an intervention which is 'tough on crime' and benefits potential victims of crime. If these developments do not occur, victims' rights may continue to compete with due-process rights and frequently be a punitive force that enables, legitimates, and relies upon crime control.

The Rise of Victims' Rights

As was the case with the groups examined in previous chapters, victimization studies documenting the risk of crime and rights claims played significant roles in the recognition of crime victims. Concerns about risks and rights were constructed to focus on criminal justice reforms, even though there were other plausible directions. There were also parallels between the evolution of victims' rights and due-process rights. Victims' bills of rights were an attempt to achieve a Charter for crime victims. Like the due-process revolution, the victims' rights movement followed American developments.

Victimization Surveys

The federal government first became interested in victims and victimization studies as part of a 'peace and security' package designed to ease public concerns about the repeal of capital punishment in 1976. The studies were originally intended as part of a crime-prevention strategy, but by 1982 focused on serving the needs of crime victims (Rock 1986: 138). Researchers in the Solicitor General's department advocated victimization studies because 'by providing data on criminal justice system functioning from the point of view of the "consumers"– those served by the system – the feedback thus provided can assist in the planning of measures to remedy the neglect often shown victims by the criminal justice system' (Evans and Leger 1979: 175). Victims were defined as the new consumers of criminal justice. The customer was always right, or at least the 'best source of information ... experts on what has happened to them, how it has affected them, and the decisions they made in response to their experiences' (Johnson 1996: 51). The personal and emotional experiences of crime victims became politically salient.

Victimization studies which revealed 'startling figures' about unreported crime helped the victims' rights movement by providing 'the ammunition of concrete data, generated by a government department, to back up rhetorical claims about the seriousness of the problem' (Maguire and Ponting 1988: 7).The first major victimization survey was conducted by Statistics Canada in 1982, and subsequent surveys in 1988 and 1993 revealed that 24 per cent of Canadians over the age of fifteen reported being victimized by a crime in the year before the survey. In 1993, 90 per cent of sexual assaults, 68 per cent of assaults, 53 per cent of robberies, 54 per cent of vandalism, 48 per cent of motor vehicle theft or attempted theft, and 32 per cent of break and enters were not reported to the police. Gartner and Doob (1994: 14) concluded that 'victims who did not report the incident to the police saw the event as one that was best dealt with another way, that was too minor to report, or that they thought that the police could not do anything about.'[1] Most crime victims served as non-punitive screens for less serious offences, and they frequently employed their own measures to respond to crime. Nevertheless, high levels of unreported crime were politically constructed as indicating an immediate need to reform the criminal justice system in order to encourage victims to report more crimes.

High levels of unreported crime suggested no one policy response. The fact that younger men, not women or the elderly, reported suffering the most crime could have depressed the 'political urgency of the social problems of victims' (Rock 1986: 333). Nevertheless, special surveys concerning crime against the elderly and violence against women were conducted. The public and politicians did not see victimization studies from the same perspective as criminologists. Underreporting of crime was equated with apathy and tolerance of crime. The political goal was to encourage full reporting, with little thought given to the inability of the system to deal with the volume of crime revealed by victimization surveys. Risk was measured and should be reduced to zero, if need be by zero-tolerance strategies that did not rely on victim cooperation. The way unreported crime was interpreted moved victims' rights in a state-centred and punitive direction, even though the same data could be interpreted as a sign that most victims did not place a priority on punishment or state intervention.

The American and Canadian Task Forces on Crime Victims

The interest in crime victims in Canada during the 1980s came mostly from governments (Rock 1986, 1988), whereas in the United States it was a populist movement. Task forces on crime victims in the early 1980s were useful reference points for the subsequent evolution of victims' rights. In the United States, the President's Task Force on Victims of Crime emphasized a punitive approach to victims' rights that frequently collided with due-process rights, while, in Canada, the Federal–Provincial Task Force on Justice for Victims of Crime took a more European approach, which placed less emphasis on punishment and opposition to due process and stressed interventions such as compensation and restitution. Since that time, however, Canadian victims' rights initiatives have moved closer to the punitive, litigious, and confrontational American model. Canadian criminal justice was Americanized not only by the due-process revolution (Lipset 1990; Bogart 1994), but by the changing politics of victims' rights.

The American task force proposed legislation to make it easier to deny bail, to privilege victim counselling records, and to abolish the exclusionary rule for search-and-seizure violations (United States 1982). Parole should be abolished, or victims should be allowed to make submissions to parole boards. A constitutional amendment should give victims a guaranteed right to be heard at all stages of judicial proceedings, including sentencing (ibid: 112). The task force also advocated 'Son of Sam' laws preventing criminals from profiting from their crimes. The crime-control orientation of the report was symbolized by its proposal that school officials be guilty of a misdemeanour if they did not report drug and violence offences to the police (ibid: 31–2). In this report, victims' rights were almost always for crime control, and there was no discussion of crime prevention or restorative justice. Victims were defined mainly by their suffering and helplessness (ibid: 11). Ignoring a substantial overlap in the population of offenders and victims, the task force portrayed offenders as cruel and evil predators compared with passive, innocent, and permanently damaged victims.

Unlike the American task force, which was composed of victims' rights advocates and members of the ideological right (including televangelist Pat Robertson), the Canadian task force was composed of bureaucrats representing the federal and provincial governments. They acknowledged that, compared with its U.S. counterpart, the Canadian victims' movement was at an 'embryonic stage.' Because of the absence of medicare and the presence of handguns, the American crime victim faced 'problems of a different magnitude' (Canada 1983: 2). They placed emphasis on the needs rather than the rights of victims because of concerns about making unenforceable promises. The Canadian report also did not oppose due-process claims (ibid: 5), which were only beginning to be made under the Charter. It did not propose 'Son of Sam' laws that would conflict with freedom-of-expression claims, and called for legislation to guarantee speedy trials (ibid: 158) that would have benefited both offenders and victims and might have helped avoid the *Askov* crisis (see chapter 3). By the 1990s, however, there was more grass-roots involvement and much more opposition to the Supreme Court's rapidly expanding due-process jurisprudence.[2]

The Canadian task force recommended Criminal Code amendments to require judges to consider restitution in all cases; to allow victim-impact statements; to require the prompt return of a victim's property; and to allow publication bans on the identity of all victims, not only victims of sexual crimes. It also recommended a surtax on fines to benefit victims (ibid: 155–7, 166). Restitution was championed not only on the basis of its benefits for victims, but also because of its contribution to the rehabilitation of the offender (ibid: 90–1). As will be seen, many of these recommendations were implemented in 1988 amendments to the Criminal Code. The task force also recommended that victims be treated with courtesy and respect by crime-control professionals and be supplied with more information about the processing of their case. Most of the provincial victims' bills of rights focused on these issues. Foreshadowing the emphasis on group rights, the task force made specific recommendations concerning the treatment of elderly victims, child victims, victims of wife and sexual assault, and Aboriginal victims. In contrast, the American task force paid little attention to the effects of victimization on disadvantaged groups.

The Canadian task force did not study restorative justice, which it inappropriately labelled 'private justice' (ibid: 13), and expressed scepticism about whether many victims would want more involvement in criminal justice (ibid: 153). It also did not present crime prevention as a victims' rights issue. It did suggest that victims would be better served by a more comprehensive insurance-based approach to compensation rather than one which required claimants to demonstrate that they were innocent victims (ibid: 99–100).

The Canadian report focused on victims' needs for services and compensation, and interventions designed for specific groups of crime victims, whereas the American report stressed punishment and the use of victims' rights to oppose due process. Subsequent developments in Canada moved in the direction of the more punitive, confrontational, and rights-driven American approach while retaining a greater emphasis on the victimization of specific groups.

Victims' Bills of Rights

The development of victims' bills of rights domestically and internationally during the last two decades (Elias 1993: 31) can be seen as a sign of a competition between the accused and the victim for rights. When pitted against due process in this manner, however, victims' right were bound to lose. The accused's due-process rights were entrenched in the constitution, and courts could enforce them by excluding evidence and staying proceedings. Even if, as in many American states, and proposed for the American Bill of Rights and the Canadian Charter (Young 1997), victims' rights were entrenched in the constitution, they would still not be as vigorously enforced by courts as due-process rights. Victims' rights generally require the state to provide information, services, and protection to crime victims, and courts remain reluctant to order governments to provide services (*Prosper* 1994; see chapter 2). Participatory rights for victims in the criminal trial could be more easily enforced, but, as discussed in chapter 3, do not guarantee recognition of victims' substantive claims.

It would be a mistake, however, to dismiss the impact of victims' bills of rights on the development of victims' policy. Victims' bills of rights could follow American trends and bring victims closer to the criminal justice system by emphasizing services and information from crime-control professionals and restrictions on due-process claims or, following international trends, they could link the treatment of crime victims to other social policies and crime prevention, and help legitimate alternatives to crime control such as restorative justice and Aboriginal justice.

The 1985 United Nations Declaration of the Basic Principles of Justice for Victims of Crimes and Abuse of Power demonstrated the progressive potential of victims' bills of rights.[3] Like other international conventions concerning the rights of women, children, racial minorities, and indigenous peoples, it contemplated positive state action and belied the argument (Petter 1986) that rights could protect only the negative liberty of the accused. It also broke down dichotomies between due-process rights and victims' rights by defining victims to include those victimized by state officials, as well as private individuals (Lamborn 1987). As suggested in chapters 7 and 8, the worst forms of state abuses, such as police shootings and gross overrepresentation of disadvantaged groups in prisons, should trigger concerns about victimization. Victims' rights initiatives that concerned themselves only with violence by private individuals were more easily dominated by the interests of crime-control professionals.

The U.N. declaration placed victim policy in the context of social policies by calling upon states 'to implement social, health, including mental health, educational, economic and specific crime prevention policies to reduce victimization and encourage assistance to victims in distress' (United Nations 1985: s.4). This not only defined crime prevention as a victims' rights issue, but resisted the criminalization of politics. The U.N. declaration also encouraged restorative justice by calling for the use of 'informal mechanisms for the resolution of disputes, including mediation, arbitration and customary justice or indigenous practices ... to facilitate conciliation and redress for victims' (ibid: A.7). Unlike domestic bills of rights, the declaration did not focus on professionally dominated criminal prosecutions which invited confrontations between due process and victims' rights. The U.N. declaration also endorsed a holistic, multidisciplinary approach to victimization by recognizing that 'victims should receive the necessary material, medical, psychological and social assistance through governmental, voluntary, community-based and indigenous means' (ibid: A.14). This recognized that crime victims needed much more than criminal justice services. The U.N. declaration endorsed the preventive, restorative, and multidisciplinary approaches to victimization associated with the non-punitive model of victims' rights identified in chapter 1.

In recognition of the U.N. declaration, Canadian governments agreed in 1988 to basic principles of justice for crime victims. These principles followed some of the U.N. principles,[4] but were more focused on criminal justice matters. Instead of crime prevention for everyone, they contemplated more limited measures 'to ensure the safety of victims and their families and to protect them from intimidation and retaliation' (Canada 1988b: s.7). The first principle was to minimize revictimization in the criminal process by treating victims with 'courtesy, compassion and with respect for their dignity and privacy' and 'the minimum of necessary inconvenience' (ibid: s.1). Victims should be treated as consumers of criminal justice, but there were fundamental limitations on their satisfaction because they did not choose to be crime victims and were exposed to an adversarial system that caused inconvenience and harm. Victims should be provided with information about criminal justice processing and be able to make their views and concerns known to criminal justice professionals 'where appropriate and consistent with criminal law and procedure' (ibid: ss.5,6). Victims were largely constructed under the 1988 principles as the passive recipients of information about a process over which they had little control. Crime control was affirmed by a final principle that 'victims should report the crime and cooperate with law enforcement authorities' even though not reporting and cooperating could be in the victim's best interest (Fenwick 1997: 320).

Manitoba was the first province to enact a victims' bill of right. The province's NDP government presented the Justice for Victims of Crime Act (S.M. 1986–7 c.28) as a means to rebalance the scales of justice that had been leaning towards the accused since the Charter (Manitoba 1986: 1962). The bill was also defended as one which 'recognizes that criminal justice is itself a service which must address and meet the special needs of victims' (ibid: 1963). Crime victims were defined as the consumers of criminal justice and the victim of the accused's due-process rights. A decade later, a (neo)-Conservative government in Ontario introduced their victims' bill of rights with remarkably similar arguments. Victims' rights was a powerful political force that captivated both the left and the right.

There were, however, some significant differences between the two bills of rights. The Manitoba legislation contemplated alternatives to criminal prosecutions by providing that victims should receive information about crime prevention and 'mediation, conciliation and informal reconciliation procedures.' This followed a similar principle in the U.N. declaration, but omitted its reference to Aboriginal justice. The legislation also created a Victims Assistance Committee composed of at least two crime victims as well as police, prosecutors, judges, and defence lawyers. Victim participation was a positive development, but the risk remained that crime victims would be dominated by crime-control professionals.

Ontario's Victims' Bill of Rights (S.O. 1995 c.6) was almost entirely oriented to crime control. There was no recognition of crime prevention or restorative justice, or that victims of crime required social services and health care. The focus was on providing victims with information about criminal investigations and prosecutions, including bail, plea bargains, court procedures, victim-impact statements, and the release or escape of the offender. Victims would be informed of (and probably frustrated with) the progress of prosecutions and punishment, but still have little real control over what happened. Victims' rights were not intended to disrupt the functioning of the crime-control system and were 'subject to the availability of resources and information, what is reasonable in the circumstances of the case, what is consistent with the law and the public interest and what is necessary to ensure that the resolution of criminal proceedings is not delayed' (ibid: s. 2[2]). Such 'Mack Truck' qualifications of due-process rights had been emphatically rejected by the joint committee that redrafted the Charter (see chapter 1). Victims' bills of rights could mimic, but not match, the Charter.

The only alternative to criminal prosecutions contemplated in the Ontario Bill of Rights was civil litigation against offenders. As will be discussed below, a less punitive and more practical approach would have facilitated civil litigation against third parties such as police or building owners who failed to take reasonable precautions to prevent crime. This, however, would have exposed crime-control professionals and corporations to liability and diverted attention away from punishing the offender through damage awards. Ontario's focus on civil litigation as compared to Manitoba's focus on social and health services also reflected a move towards privatizing victims' services, at least those not provided by police and prosecutors. As will be discussed below, most victim services were financed by surcharges on fines paid by offenders. Governments were able to increase or maintain victim services in the 1990s in part because they did not directly come out of tax revenues. Privatization occurred at a policy level as well so that crime policy became less about public policy and more about servicing and vindicating victims.

The Ontario Bill of Rights also recognized some specific groups of victims. Victims of sexual assault were given the right to be interviewed by a police officer of the same gender, and child witnesses received special protections. Civil proceedings against the accused to recover damages for domestic and sexual assaults were also encouraged. British Columbia's 1996 Victims of Crime Act (RSBC 1996, c.478 ss.2,3) also provided that victims should not be discriminated against and that the attorney general should ensure that victims whose private records were being sought had independent legal representation if they so desired. Victims' bills of rights increasingly reflected concerns about particular groups of victims and the fact that victims could be required to litigate the new political case.

Victims' bills of rights can be criticized for their symbolic nature and lack of enforcement. Even if eventually entrenched in the constitution, victims' rights would be balanced against the rights of the accused and the media, and not as vigorously enforced as those rights. Courts will continue to find it easier to exclude evidence or stay proceedings than ensure that governments provide more expensive services. Victims' bills of rights were not, however, trivial. Like the Ontario bill, they could cast victims' rights in a punitive direction or, like the U.N. declaration and parts of the Manitoba bill, they could recognize the legitimacy and need for alternatives to criminal prosecutions. Victims' bills of rights also defined crime victims as the new consumers of criminal prosecutions. Police and prosecutors could treat the new consumer politely and give them information about what was happening. Nevertheless, victims would likely remain frustrated by the lack of control over the end product and by their involuntary status as consumers of criminal justice.

Victims' Rights versus Freedom of Expression

The assertion of rights by crime victims also led to demands for 'Son of Sam' laws and extension of publication bans. These reforms focused on the most serious and sensational cases and shared the characteristics of the new political case because they pitted victims' rights against freedom-of-expression claims made by the accused and the media.

Canadian interest in 'Son of Sam' laws was another sign of the Americanization of victims' rights. New York first enacted the law because of concerns that serial killer David Berkowitz would sign a lucrative book contract. New York's first law was struck down as a violation of freedom of speech because it regulated the content of speech; applied to those not convicted of crimes; and could apply to the work of people such as Martin Luther King Jr who wrote about their civil disobedience (*Simon & Schuster*

1992). In 1994, Ontario hastily enacted its own 'Son of Sam' law to respond to fears that multiple murderer Paul Bernardo and his accomplice, Karla Homolka, would profit from their crimes. The legislation was introduced by a private member with a 25,000-signature petition, and the families of Bernardo's victims in the gallery. It was enacted after Premier Bob Rae received calls from the mothers of two girls murdered by Paul Bernardo and a fax from the head of CAVEAT. The original sponsor, noting that the victims' suffering was worse at Christmas time, told their premier that 'his actions have in fact turned the last 48 hours of this bill into a script from a Frank Capra movie, truly' (Ontario 1994: 8507). The Ontario law was even broader than the New York law that was struck down. If ever applied, it could be subject to a successful Charter challenge. 'Son of Sam' laws continued to be politically popular (*Toronto Star*, 6 Jan. 1997), but they may not be the most effective means to deter offenders and the media from exploiting sensational crimes. Public opposition to such stories may deter the reputable media, without giving the less reputable the opportunity to claim the high moral ground of defending freedom of expression in another new political case.

As discussed in chapter 3, victims intervened in Paul Bernardo's criminal trial to argue that their Charter rights would be infringed if tapes showing the sexual assault and torture of them and their daughters were shown in open court. Although recognizing that they would 'suffer tremendous psychological, emotional and mental injury' if the tapes were shown in open court, the trial judge concluded that the victims' Charter rights were not violated. In a compromise judgment, he allowed the tapes to be heard but not seen in open court. After the trial was over, the families commenced a separate civil action to argue that their Charter rights required that the judges be able to close proceedings in order 'to prevent serious harm or injustice to any person' (*French Estate* 1996: 213). They argued that serious harm should include child pornography and obscenity, and that the tapes met these definitions. This case demonstrated how victims were prepared to use civil litigation when dissatisfied with the results obtained at the criminal trial and how they were prepared to engage in political cases pitting their rights against freedom of expression.

The victims were represented by Kathleen Mahoney, who was LEAF's counsel in *Keegstra* (1990) and *Butler* (1992; see chapter 4). She called as an expert witness Catharine MacKinnon, who testified that the videotapes were pornography that devalued and dehumanized females and that the girls' murders were 'the ultimate sexual experience' (ibid: 206). The case became part of a larger debate as the victims argued that the tapes were pornography which infringed the equality rights of females and were not protected as freedom of expression. The trial judge rejected these arguments, concluding that it was not 'particularly useful in principle to categorize the videotapes as "pornographic" or "obscene" and that existing powers to protect public morals and the administration of justice could respond to any harm caused by the showing of the videotapes' (*French Estate* 1996: 209). The victims' enjoyed less success than LEAF had in *Butler* or when it defended publication bans on the identity of complainants in sexual-assault cases.[5]

The victims' other lawyer, Tim Danson, argued that the families had been treated unfairly in relation to the media and that their freedom of religion as Christians and their right to privacy had been violated. The judge dismissed these claims, concluding that it was 'unrealistic' to give automatic standing 'to all victims' (ibid: 204) and that, if religious and privacy rights were absolute, 'there would be few trials' (ibid: 212). This case stood as another example of the limited ability of adversarial and public trials to be sensitive to victims' concerns. It also demonstrated how the victims' movement encompassed claims made by equality-seeking groups and those made on a more conservative basis.

In order to gain admittance to the criminal trial and to counter rights claims by the accused and the media, crime victims asserted rights. These arguments were made in both courts and legislatures, but generally enjoyed less success than those of the accused, the media, or disadvantaged groups specifically enumerated in section 15 of the Charter. Even if victims' rights were recognized, they would be balanced against these other competing rights and not as rigorously enforced. Victims played a rights game they were bound to lose. A focus on the needs of victims (Canada 1983) may be more helpful and realistic. As will be seen, however, greater attention was paid to interventions designed to increase the punishment of offenders. Here, too, victims played a game that they did not fully win.

Victims in the Criminal Process: The Focus on Punishment

The most tangible reforms won by crime victims, such as victim-impact statements, victim fine surcharges, and the partial repeal of 'faint hope' hearings, have all revolved around the punishment of offenders. As in the field of child abuse (see chapter 6), the federal government could shape victim policy by amending its penal legislation or through its more expensive and less visible spending power. Victims' policy that focused on sentencing was partial and frequently punitive, and contributed to the criminalization of politics.

Victim-Impact Statements

Courts traditionally refused to hear from victims at sentencing for both procedural and substantive reasons. In 1982, Justice McLachlin, denied a child-sex-abuse victim's application to make representations at the offender's sentencing. In a one-page judgment, she concluded that crime victims had no standing under the Criminal Code (*Antler* 1982). A year later another judge refused to hear statements from parents of a daughter stabbed to death with a butcher knife because his 'decision must be the same whether the victim was ... a beloved daughter whose death is a tragedy that time alone can diminish or if she was alone and friendless with no one to mourn her loss' (*Robinson* 1983: 259). Concerns have frequently been expressed that victim-impact statements could create arbitrary sentencing disparities (Fletcher 1995: 200–1), but these arguments are compelling only if punishment is determined by the seriousness of the crime and not other factors such as the offender's needs for rehabilitation and deterrence, and the sometimes unwilled nature of the harm committed (Fenwick 1997: 330). Nevertheless, they echoed the popular idea that victims were too emotional and irrational to be involved in their offender's punishment.

As part of a 1988 victims' rights package, Parliament allowed victim-impact statements to be introduced at sentencing. Minister of Justice Ray Hnatyshyn stressed that they would only be in writing and 'not allow the victim ... to express any opinion on the sentence that should be imposed on the accused' (Hansard, 19 Nov. 1987: 10974). The victim's emotion would be cooled out by not being allowed to speak to the sentence and having to submit a written form. The judge was not required to consider the statement and could consider any other relevant information. If there was any dispute about the facts, the minister stressed that 'the ordinary legal principles would apply. Any facts relied upon by the Crown and challenged by the accused would have to be established on the criminal standard of proof beyond a reasonable doubt' (ibid). The victim could participate, but only in a restrained manner and at the price of possibly being put on trial (Elias 1993: 94).

Despite concerns by defence lawyers that they would increase punishment, there was no opposition to victim-impact statements in Parliament. Victim-advocacy groups, often started by parents whose children had been killed or murdered, criticized the initial definition of victims as too restrictive, and the minister introduced amendments to ensure that the 'families of homicide victims, child victims and disabled victims' could make statements (Hansard, 3 May 1988: 15085). The government refused an NDP request that victims of corporate crimes also be allowed to submit statements. Victim-impact statements as a punitive form of victims' rights worked best if the offender was perceived as an evil individual. As will be seen, however, restitution as a less punitive form of victims' rights did not need an evil offender to work and benefited corporations who suffered losses because of crime.

Despite some attention from commentators (Rubel 1986; Skurka 1993; Young 1993), victim-impact statements have not emerged as a major criminal justice issue in Canada.[6] They appeared to have been introduced in few cases, with research in British Columbia suggesting that they were obtained in only 2–6 per cent of cases and filed in court in only 1–2 per cent of all cases (Roberts 1992). Consistent with the model of victims being used for crime-control reasons, victim-impact statements were most likely to be used in cases where prosecutors believed them to be important. They were even sometimes filled out by the police, without the victim understanding that he or she was making a victim-impact statement.

Low rates of victim participation might in part be explained by an understandable reluctance by crime victims to expose their suffering to adversarial challenge. For example, a form used in Toronto to obtain victim-impact statements was almost as ominous as the right-to-counsel warnings received by the accused. The victim was warned that his or her 'participation in this program is entirely voluntary and you may withdraw this statement at any time.' The victim was then informed that the accused would receive a copy of the statement and that 'you may be required to testify as to its contents and/or produce supporting evidence, such as receipts or other documents.' The victim was then signalled that the pay-off for this exposure may not be great because 'ultimately the prosecutor will decide whether or not a given Victim Impact Statement, or any part of it, will be put before the court and the presiding Judge will determine what, if any, weight will be attached to it' (Skurka 1993: 352). Victim-impact statements in less formal proceedings, however, would be routine and less subject to professional screening and adversarial challenge.

Despite their infrequent use, victim-impact statements were politically popular. In 1992, they were made available in federal parole hearings. In the same year that it stopped financing victim-compensation schemes, this allowed the federal government to argue that the era of neglecting crime victims had ended (Hansard, 4 Nov. 1991: 4430; 12 May 1992: 10557). In 1995, the Young Offenders Act was amended to allow victim-impact statements and the Criminal Code was amended to require courts to consider victim-impact statements in the cases in which they were made available. British Columbia's 1996 Victims of Crime Act required prosecutors to give victims a reasonable opportunity to make statements before sentencing. As will be seen, victim-impact statements were also offered as a response to demands that 'faint hope' hearings be abolished.

More research needs to be done, but victim-impact statements appear to be a symbolic and punitive reform. Even in the infrequent cases in which they were introduced, the traditional reluctance of judges to base the sentencing on victims' suffering may not have changed. Crime victims were directed to put their hopes in punishment, only to be frequently disappointed. Nevertheless allowing victims to explain the impact of the crime was an important form of procedural justice that could promote closure for the victim and accountability for the offender. In less formal proceedings such as family conferences, Aboriginal justice and victim–offender reconciliation programs, victims would routinely talk about the effects of the crime on them, but not in a manner related to punishment or subject to professional screening or adversarial challenge.

'Faint Hope' Hearings

When capital punishment was abolished in 1976, Parliament provided that those convicted of first-degree murder would be ineligible for parole for twenty-five years. 'Faint hope' hearings, however, would allow murderers to apply to a jury after fifteen years' imprisonment to be declared eligible for parole. The issue lay dormant for fifteen years, but then burst onto the public scene. It pitted the police and crime victims against some of the worst murderers.

The courts were originally unsympathetic to murderers who failed at their 'faint hope' hearings and held they had no right of appeal. Relying on the same discretionary powers that it used to hear appeals by the media and crime victims, however, the Supreme Court was more creative. It ordered a new 'faint hope' hearing because the prosecutor had invited the jury to respond to the extreme violence of the murder, the suffering of the victim and her family, and the prospect that murderers might be released to kill again. In rhetoric often seen in American television shows, but rarely in Canadian courts, the prosecutor had implored the jury: 'please don't forget the victim in this case, Mary Frances McKenna. She doesn't have a chance to come before a group of people to ask for a second chance' (*Swietlinski* 1994: 459). Chief Justice Lamer stressed that it was 'completely improper' for a lawyer to ask jurors to subvert a bad law or to invite them 'to consider isolated cases in which prisoners committed murder after being released' (ibid: 462). A majority of the Court also held that victim-impact statements were generally not admissible in 'faint hope' hearings because they placed undue emphasis on retribution, denunciation, and punishment as opposed to the offender's future prospects of danger and rehabilitation. Justice Major argued that 'the victim's suffering in the years since the crime was committed does nothing to alter the nature of the offence' (ibid: 471). Press reports led with the fact that Swietlinski had stabbed McKenna 132 times, and suggested that the case, along with other due-process decisions that year (*Daviault* 1994; *Prosper* 1994; *Borden* 1994), was a sign that 'protecting the rights of the accused may not serve the public good' (*Globe and Mail*, 8 Oct. 1994). Victims of Violence and the Canadian Police Association held a joint press conference denouncing the Court (*Victoria Times Colonist*, 14 Oct. 1994). The Court protected the rights of the most unpopular criminals, and offended victims' groups and public sensibilities.

The government reversed the Court's decision by making victim-impact statements admissible in 'faint hope' hearings. Justice Minister Allan Rock explained how he had met with the wife of a murdered police officer who had described 'the anguish she felt at reliving the tragedy of her husband's death and at the whole process surrounding the 745 application. It is out of respect for that anguish, for the feeling on the part of the families of murder victims, homicide victims, that they should have some role to play in the process' (Hansard, 20 Sep. 1994: 5872). Victim-impact statements were presented as a means to allow victims to express their anguish, and the public ventilation of such understandable and intense emotions was associated with justice (Sarat 1997). The law fell into the familiar pattern of Parliament invoking victims' rights as the rationale for overruling due-process decisions, but this override was of a lesser magnitude than those discussed in chapter 5 because the Court had based its ruling on the original statutory purposes of 'faint hope' hearings, not the Charter.

Victims were, however, not satisfied. Victims of Violence argued that 'faint hope' hearings were 'an insult to victims, both those whose lives were taken and those who are left behind. It is unfortunate that the government is unable to amend the meaning of the death sentence as they have amended the meaning of the life sentence the murderer receives'

(Canada, JLAC, 29 Nov. 1994, 67: 6). Reform Party members likewise argued that 'faint hope' hearings 'bring the law into disrepute' and that they were an example of an 'irresponsible, unaccountable, bleeding-heart mentality that has ignored the rights of victims of crime, their families and society … What murderer ever gave a victim a glimmer of hope when he or she viciously tore life from the victim?' (Hansard, 20 Sep. 1994: 5881, 5884). CAVEAT joined the police in supporting a private member's bill to abolish 'faint hope' hearings. Its mover, John Nunziata, argued: 'Do not let anyone kid you that it is impossible for Clifford Olson, the Canadian version of Charles Manson, to be released' (Hansard, 19 Oct. 1994: 6933). Since the early 1980s (Rock 1986), the victims' rights movement had become more populist and less dominated by government. Petitions, lobbying by advocacy groups, and private member's bills played a role in prodding the government into action. Nevertheless, victims did not succeed in abolishing 'faint hope' hearings.

In 1996, the government returned to this controversial issue with legislation to deny 'faint hope' hearings to multiple murderers and those who could not satisfy a judicial screening process. The media focused on whether the legislation would be passed in time to block Olson's 'faint hope' hearing. Apparently immune from the public pressure in the rest of Canada, the Bloc Québécois refused to give the bill unanimous consent that would allow it to be enacted in time and argued that it was a capitulation to law-and-order sentiment.[7] The Reform Party argued that the bill was an outrage to victims and their families because it allowed some 'faint hope' hearings to still occur. While Bloc members stressed that most eligible murderers had not even applied for the hearings, Reform members stressed that most of those who had applied had been successful. Reform leader Preston Manning argued that the preservation of 'faint hope' hearings demonstrated a 'perverse set of priorities … [which] puts the rights of persons accused or convicted of crimes ahead of the rights of victims and law-abiding citizens.' For him, they were a symbol of due process as reflected 'in the Liberal inspired charter of rights and freedoms' (Hansard, 2 Oct. 1996: 5001). A Criminal Code provision that affected a small number of offenders and victims was amended twice in two years and became a primary site for symbolic battles between due process and victims' rights.

In the debates surrounding the bill, victims' rights emerged as emotional and unforgiving. Victims were portrayed as people who had 'no hope' (Hansard, 16 Sep. 1996: 4251, 4255), and 'faint hope' hearings were characterized as a cruel means of 'revictimizing the survivors' (ibid:

4244, 4255). The names of the mothers of murdered children were frequently invoked in the debates, and Sharon Rosenfeldt, Debbie Mahaffy, and Priscilla de Villiers all appeared before the committee examining the bill. John Nunziata argued that 'these mothers of victims make a compelling argument ... For them it becomes an unending funeral. To them the pain and suffering never ends ... I ask hon. members not to detach themselves from the emotion of what this is all about because it is about emotion ... Look at this through the eyes of the parents who have lost children to convicted killers' (ibid: 4255). Victims' rights were more emotional than the professionalised models of crime control or due process. The emotionalism of this debate was not, however, a necessary prelude to healing or dialogue, but 'an unending funeral' that demanded, but ultimately could not be satisfied, by punishment.

The debate was an outlet for punitive crime-control attitudes and opposition to due process. Reform Party members often argued that the state should treat the offender in the same way as the offender treated the victim. For example, Jack Ramsay argued: 'A killer does not deserve that which he denied his victim ... The glimmer of hope advocates have made a farce of our penal system by extending to murderers rights they deliberately and viciously denied their victims' (Hansard, 14 Jun. 1996: 3879). In disregard of the costs of imprisoning first-degree murderers who, in some cases, had become senior citizens in prison (*Globe and Mail*, 19 Jun. 1995), Reformers also argued that 'Canadians want section 745 abolished, killed, scrapped just like they wanted done with the GST ... Taxpayers would be saved millions and millions of dollars and murderers would be kept off the streets for at least 25 years' (Hansard, 17 Jun. 1996: 3911–12). The state could be both minimal and punitive. The Canadian Police Association criticized the bill for not responding to Canadians' fears of crime or giving 'the police forces the tools and the measures they need to bring criminals to conviction' (ibid: 3915). Increased safety and security was presented as a simple matter of turning back due process and giving the police more powers.

The new restrictions on 'faint hope' hearings were enacted,[8] but not in time to deny Olson his 'faint hope' hearing. The spectre of his hearing became a spectacle. Vigorously protested by victim-advocacy groups and the police, it ended quietly, with the jury rejecting Olson's bid in fifteen minutes and many seeing him as sick and pathetic. What was regrettably absent from the endless debates about 'faint hope' hearings was a sense of perspective. Only 80 of 314 eligible murderers at the time of Olson's hearing had bothered to apply for the hearings. None who had been released had killed again (*Globe and Mail,* 16 Aug. 1997). Even Swietlinski, who had an excellent prison record in a minimum-security institution, did not bother to pursue the Supreme Court's remedy of a new hearing because the 'faint hope' clause had become 'the ain't a hope clause' (*Globe and Mail,* 4 Jan. 1997). In an example of symbolic and punitive politics, enormous amounts of lobbying efforts and parliamentary time were devoted to the fates of a few murderers who presented relatively low risks of reoffending. Victims were allied with the police and presented as emotional and unforgiving. These forces were able to restrict, but not abolish 'faint hope' hearings.

Victim Fine Surcharges

Victim fine surcharges have not received nearly as much attention as 'faint hope' hearings, but they have played an important role in victims' policy. Surcharges of up to 15 per cent on fines under federal statutes were first introduced as part of the 1988 victims' package. Appealing to the rhetoric of restorative justice, Minister of Justice Ray Hnatyshyn argued that the surcharge 'will assist offenders in the process of accepting responsibility for their crimes by requiring them to contribute to victim services within each province as part of the debt they owe to society' (Hansard, 19 Nov. 1987: 10973). For most offenders, however, it was another government sales tax, this time one levied on their fine. Initially, there was not even any guarantee that the new funds would be spent on crime victims, and some simply went into general revenues (Hansard, 3 May 1988: 15088; Young 1993: 356). This was changed, and both federal and provincial fine surcharges were used to finance victim services and compensation schemes. This money made it easier for governments in times of fiscal restraint to expand or maintain victim services. Nevertheless, it reflected a private and punitive basis for victim services that ensured that they were not integrated or prioritized in a policy or fiscal sense with other social services. Whatever its benefits as a source of revenue, the fine surcharge was not a form of restorative justice.

Restitution

Unlike fine surcharges, restitution could achieve restorative justice by allowing offenders to make amends to their victims. In the mid-1970s, the Law Reform Commission of Canada ([LRCC] 1974c: 7–8) defended restitution as a means to respond to a victim's 'psychological need that notice be taken of the wrong done' and to treat offenders as 'responsible human beings' who could perform useful work and establish 'positive ties with family, friends and the community.' Mediation to achieve restitution would place the victim at the centre of the 'proposed settlement' and avoid the 'unrewarding and destructive' experience of the criminal trial (ibid 1974b: 9–10). This still impressive work (Jackson 1992: 178) demonstrated the progressive potential of restitution, but it was not implemented, and restitution remained a more formal process closely tied to the criminal trial.

The formal restitution provisions in the Criminal Code narrowly survived a constitutional challenge on the basis that they went beyond federal jurisdiction to enact criminal law and procedure. In *Zelensky* (1978), the accused challenged an order that, in addition to two years' imprisonment for theft from her employer, Eatons, she also provide $7,000 in stolen merchandise and $18,000 'more or less' that she stole. The Supreme Court held that restitution, especially when designed to complement punishment, was a legitimate purpose of criminal law. Nevertheless, it should be used 'with restraint and caution' and was inappropriate when there was 'any serious contest on legal and factual issues' (*Zelensky* 1978: 112–13). The restitution of $18,000 'more or less' was inappropriate because the amount stolen was in dispute and the employer had also commenced a civil action against the accused, but the restitution of the stolen property was appropriate. The Court upheld restitution as part of the criminal trial process, but indicated that it was to be used only in simple cases (Throvoldson 1988: 3).

The use of restitution by a corporate victim in *Zelensky* was typical, and organizational victims made better use of the restitution provisions than individuals (LRCC 1974c: 10; Hagan 1983). Corporate victims and middle-class offenders were the prime candidates for restitution. This raised valid distributional concerns, but should not taint the entire enterprise. There was much to be learned from the corporate sector about the most efficient and least disruptive means of preventing and recovering from crime.

As part of the 1988 package of victims' reforms, the Criminal Code was amended to allow prosecutors to seek restitution and provide for criminal-enforcement orders. Minister of Justice Ray Hnatyshyn argued that he was strengthening restitution by removing 'the onus on the victim to apply for a restitution order at the time of sentencing' (Hansard, 19 Nov. 1987: 10975). Placing 'responsibility ... upon the criminal justice system to consider the victim' was a double-edged sword. Although victims no longer had to apply, restitution would be granted only on the motion of criminal justice professionals and, following *Zelensky*, when it was readily ascertainable. Restitution, like victim fine surcharges, might become a routine part of the crime-control assembly line. The new provisions, however, were never proclaimed because of concerns about the costs of implementation. In any event, restitution was not a priority for victim-advocacy groups who focused on crimes of violence and argued that they could not be bought off with money.

The grounds for restitution were expanded in 1995 to include readily ascertainable pecuniary damages stemming from the commission of bodily harm, and temporary housing, child-care, and transportation costs incurred 'in the case of bodily harm or threat of bodily harm to the offender's spouse or child' (*Criminal Code* s.738[1][c] as am. S.C. 1995 c.22). This recognized the economic harms of wife assault, but would be of assistance only after a conviction. Restitution orders would be enforced by the victim in the same manner as a civil judgment. This would make it difficult for victims to obtain money from impecunious or defiant offenders. The amendments also contemplated that provinces could make regulations precluding restitution orders as part of probation or conditional-sentence orders. This could take away the most frequently used means to achieve restitution, as well as possibly expensive public enforcement of restitution orders. At the same time as Parliament proclaimed the provision of reparations for harm done to victims as a new purpose of sentencing, it also made it potentially more difficult for victims to obtain restitution.

The restitution provisions of the Criminal Code remained complex and underused and available only in cases of readily ascertainable damages. Restitution informally negotiated outside of court could be more promising. Something more or less representing the victim's losses and recognizing the harm done could be enough. Offenders could be encouraged or required to provide restitution as part of diversion programs and as part of their probation or conditional sentences. Voluntary restitution and/or apologies, especially when accepted by the victim, could be an important mitigating factor in sentencing. In this scenario, victims' interests would not be tied to increased punishment, and they could have the power to reduce the offender's punishment by accepting restitution and/or apologies.

Victims and Sentencing

The stakes that crime victims developed in sentencing were codified in

1995 when Parliament recognized the provision of 'reparations for harm done to victims or to the community' and the promotion of 'a sense of responsibility in offenders, and acknowledgement of the harm done to victims and the community' as new purposes of sentencing. Minister of Justice Allan Rock argued that these purposes reflected 'the importance of our recognizing the plight of victims of criminal acts' (Hansard, 20 Sep. 1994: 5871). Noting that victims had brought forward their 'message loud and clear,' his parliamentary secretary promised that the courts would 'look more to the victims and what they are suffering, the loss that they have endured' (ibid: 5915).[9] These new purposes, as well as the recognition of the legitimacy of diversion programs when the offender accepted responsibility and the needs of offenders, victims, and society were satisfied, could encourage restorative-justice measures. The new purposes, however, could be used for crime control by stressing the idea of responsibility and reparations to the community as opposed to the victim, and by reconceiving punishment as reparation to the community. Victims' rights could inspire alternatives to crime control, but they could also enable and legitimate it.

Summary

Between 1988 and 1997, victims gained a greater stake in the punishment process. Victim-impact statements were made admissible in youth and adult criminal trials and in parole and 'faint hope' hearings. Reparation to victims and recognition of the harm done to them were recognized as purposes of sentencing, along with more traditional concerns about punishment, deterrence, and rehabilitation. Nevertheless, victims often failed in their attempts to change the system. 'Faint hope' hearings were restricted, but not abolished. Restitution and victim-impact statements were infrequently used. In the end, crime victims did not enjoy the same success as women, children, and some minorities in achieving criminal justice reforms.

Alternatives

As in chapters 6, 7, and 8, the last part of this chapter examines initiatives that placed less reliance on criminal prosecutions and rights claims, and thus provided alternatives to crime control and due process. These alternatives also avoided the perils of the new political case or the criminalization of political, social, cultural, and economic issues.

Victim Compensation

Victim-compensation schemes allowed victims of violent crimes to recover some of the costs of crimes they suffered. They were originally extended only to those injured helping the police (Miers 1974), and some schemes still required a claimant to have cooperated with the police. This crime-control requirement (Burns 1992: 293) excluded the majority of victims who do not report crime to the police. Consistent with a punitive approach to victims' rights which contrasted an innocent victim with evil offenders, some provinces denied compensation to victims judged to be undeserving (Langer 1991; Sheehy 1994). Victim compensation did not rely on punishment, but could be appropriated for crime-control ends.

Although compensation schemes should not enforce images of innocent victims or engage in victim blaming, crime victims may not wish them to function solely as a needs-based form of social welfare. Shapland (1984: 144–5) concluded that victims viewed compensation 'not as mainly a matter of money or of financial assistance (charitable or otherwise) but rather as making a statement about the offence, the victim and the position that the criminal justice system was prepared to give the victims.' Compensation could provide public recognition of wrongs, and the 1983 task force recommended that victims be able to obtain hearings (Canada 1983). Nevertheless, many provinces continued to process victim-compensation applications in a bureaucratic fashion without hearings, and provided no benefits to family members.

As a form of social welfare, victim compensation was radically underinclusive and under siege. In 1992, the federal government stopped transfer payments for victim compensation, and Newfoundland and the Yukon and Northwest Territories disbanded their schemes. The remaining schemes continued to exclude claims by those who suffered property crimes and injuries from drunk driving, even if the damages could not otherwise be satisfied through insurance. John Hagan (1983: 193) found that, while half of crime victims in his study were aware of victim-compensation schemes, only 8.5 per cent actually sought compensation. In contrast, 36.6 per cent sought compensation from insurance companies. The insurance industry was more involved than the state in compensating crime victims and took an active interest in managing the risk of crime victimization (Ericson and Haggerty 1997). Like restitution, this presented distributional problems because the middle class were more likely to be compensated through insurance claims. The disadvantaged were left behind in a public system that often failed to control crime or compensate victims. Revitalized compensation schemes should allow for compensation for uninsured harm. Fine revenue, and not just surcharges, should be used to finance these schemes. New compensation schemes could also take seriously the desire of some victims and their families for public recognition of the harm that they suffered. Compensation and restitution could be creatively merged. The government could top up what offenders, because of their financial circumstances, could not pay.

Civil Litigation

Civil litigation was increasingly employed in the 1990s by survivors of incest and other forms of sexual abuse. The Supreme Court encouraged such litigation by awarding aggravated and punitive damages in a case in which a doctor had required his patient to have sex with him in exchange for painkillers (*Norberg* 1992). As under the new amendments to the Criminal Code (see chapter 5), consent was defined to recognize imbalances of powers when the accused was in a position of trust or authority. The Court also facilitated civil claims by survivors of incest by creating a presumption that, in recognition of 'post-incest syndrome,' the statute of limitations should not run until the plaintiff received therapy (*K.M.* 1992: 306). This reflected the Court's willingness to hear historical sexual-abuse claims in criminal trials (see chapter 6) and to recognize a syndrome in cases involving battered women (see chapter 5; Mosher 1994).

Although victims had more control than in public prosecutions and did not face Charter defences or the requirement of proof beyond a reasonable doubt, civil litigation remained an arduous experience, with plaintiffs being liable to have their past, including therapeutic records, discovered by defendants without the shield provided by the post-*O'Connor* amendments to the Criminal Code (*M(A) v. Ryan* 1997). The 'therapeutic jurisprudence' (Feldthusen 1993) that nevertheless developed was an example of victims going outside of the criminal process for recognition of the harms that they have suffered. Bruce Feldthusen (1993: 232) found that many lawsuits followed criminal convictions and concluded that 'a sincere apology tendered in the criminal trial might reduce the need for the plaintiff to sue an impecunious defendant in a subsequent action.' Many victims were more interested in public recognition of the wrong than in the money. In any event, civil litigation was radically underinclusive in achieving compensation for the victims of crime (Linden 1968; Hagan 1983).

Civil litigation played a modest role in crime prevention. A lawsuit or the threat of lawsuit might encourage the owners of buildings to install lighting, or private policing that might help prevent opportunistic crime. Unfortunately, Ontario's Victims' Bill of Rights only facilitated civil actions against convicted offenders who were frequently so poor as to be judgment-proof. One path-breaking lawsuit was brought by a woman who had been sexually assaulted. She argued that the Toronto police had acted negligently and in violation of her rights under sections 7 and 15 of the Charter by failing to issue warnings about a balcony rapist in the area that she lived. She alleged that the police adopted 'a policy not to warn her because of a stereotypical and, therefore, discriminatory belief that as a woman, she and others like her would become hysterical and "scare off" the attacker' and that they had 'favoured the apprehension of the criminal over her protection as a targeted rape victim' (*Jane Doe* 1990: 589). The fact that this lawsuit was successful should encourage police to issue warnings. This may increase fear, but it may also encourage potential victims to take preventive actions. The difficulty and expense of proving fault in a civil lawsuit should not, however, be underestimated. Jane Doe was required to prove that, had a warning been issued, she would have been able to prevent the sexual assault, and she had her past minutely examined in the adversarial litigation process. As with police shootings (see chapter 7), a failure to establish liability could promote complacency about police behaviour that nevertheless should be changed.

Victim–Offender Reconciliation Programs (VORPs)

Another way for crime victims to obtain compensation and recognition of the wrongs that they suffered is through VORPs, which allowed offenders to meet with their victims and attempt to make amends for their crime. Zehr (1990: 160–1) argued that 'the VORP process consists of a face-to-face encounter between victim and offender in cases which have entered the criminal justice process and the offender has admitted the offense. In these meetings, emphasis is placed upon three elements: facts, feelings, and agreement.' Although they may involve restitution, VORPs were conducted informally with the assistance of a mediator, and restoration was not necessarily based on the 'readily ascertainable' measurement of the damage done. The very act of having the offender accept responsibility and offer an apology could be more important that the tangible amends provided.

VORPs were part of a non-punitive model of victims' rights discussed in chapter 1, and they resembled family conferences discussed in chapter 6 and Aboriginal healing circles discussed in chapter 8. All three interventions brought together more participants than the crime-control assembly line or the due-process obstacle course. They did not attempt to have the state appropriate the dispute from the victim, the offender, and the community (Christie 1977). The offender, his or her family and friends, the victim, his or her family and friends, as well as others were seated together, frequently in a circle. The circle could help protect procedural fairness and equality by ensuring that everyone in the room had his or her turn to speak. It emphasized common community, not the ostracism or spectacle of the prisoner's dock or the hierarchy of the judge's raised platform and counsel tables. The circle also symbolized the act of restoration, which aspired to make both the offender and the victim whole and healthy again. The offender was obliged to recognize that a crime had been committed and had harmed the victim. The victim in turn had the power to decide whether to accept the offender's apology and plan to make amends. Family conferences, Aboriginal justice, and VORPs focused on what must be done in the future to make amends and to prevent crime, without forgetting the wrong that had occurred in the past.

Despite the greater decision-making power they promised for victims, VORPs were not championed by victim-advocacy groups. In 1988, the federal government rejected attempts to add them as a voluntary alternative to the formal restitution provisions in large part because of opposition from victims' groups (Canada 1987–8, 9: 15). Steve Sullivan of Victims of Violence criticized VORPs for blurring the distinction between victims and offenders when he argued that 'victims are not criminals and criminals are not victims' (ibid, 8: 10). His was a punitive victims' rights approach which stressed the differences between victims and offenders. He also recounted two cases in which victims, the brother of a battered wife and the father of a sexually abused child, had resorted to violence when they met the offender (ibid, 8: 18). Carol Cameron, also of Victims of Violence, argued that '99.9% [of her members] never care if they ever see that offender again and they would not choose to have a dialogue with them' (ibid, 4: 22). This punitive rejection of reintegration was echoed by another advocate, Robert Menard, when he said: 'I am very sorry, but there can be no reconciliation between a victim and his offender. I have polled my group and I can assure you that not one – not one would have wanted to be in the same room with the offender who committed the crime upon their person or property' (ibid, 8: 14). Perhaps because they were dominated by the victims of the most serious crimes, these victim-advocacy groups had very little sympathy for restorative alternatives to crime control (Scheingold, Pershing, and Olson 1994). As all too frequently occurred in public discourse about crime, concerns about the most serious crimes dwarfed the far more commonplace crimes which were much more easily amenable to VORPs.

Despite the opposition noted above, VORPs had some supporters. The Daubney Committee advocated them as a means to allow victims to regain control of their lives and to require offenders 'to "do something" for their victims and for society ... it is essential that offenders be held accountable for their behaviour' (Canada 1988a: 97). VORPs were politically feasible because they could be defended as a low-cost alternative sanction that would involve the community and victims. The hope of VORPs was that victims would be less punitive and more practical than crime-control professionals.

Unfortunately, there were not many evaluations of VORPs in Canada. The Daubney Committee cited one Manitoba study in which 90 per cent of 500 cases reached agreement, with 80 per cent of participants agreeing that they would mediate again if the need arose (ibid: 93). There was a danger that too much stress was placed on achieving agreements and that both crime victims and offenders were pressured into an agreement. The Manitoba project continued on a paltry $210,000 budget, but still conducted nearly 1,000 victim–offender mediations a year with the help of volunteer mediators. Victims reported that communicating with offenders made them less fearful, while offenders said they were made aware of the consequences of their actions on others and in some cases obtained forgiveness (*Globe and Mail*, 23 Dec. 1993). Australian studies found 'a significant minority of victims who feel worse after the conference, upset over something said or victimised by disrespect, though greatly outnumbered by victims who feel healing as a result of the conference' (Braithwaite 1997: 7). Offenders were more likely to state that they had been treated with respect and had their rights respected in conferences than in court (ibid: 20).

The best Canadian evaluation was conducted in the early 1980s on one of the first VORPs run in Kitchener, Ontario, and it was not particularly encouraging. Dittenhoffer and Ericson (1983) found that most victims were business establishments and insurance companies, not individuals. As with restitution, corporations were in a position to benefit from VORPs. This raised distributional concerns, but should not discredit the entire enterprise. The problem with the Kitchener program may have been its implementation. Volunteers were instructed not to use the word 'reconciliation,' but rather to focus on the ability of victims to have losses repaid (ibid: 332). Restorative justice should not be reduced to the instrumental issue of compensation, especially given that many victims are interested in more than money.

Concerns have also been raised that VORPs will be used only in minor cases and contribute to net-widening. (McMahon 1992: 137–40). VORPs can be more intrusive than criminal justice processing. For example, a nineteen-year-old who stole $40 worth of cosmetics agreed as part of a diversion project to attend fifteen job interviews, research the effect of a criminal record on women of her age, and spend seventy hours in community service (*Globe and Mail*, 17 Mar. 1997). Like family conferences discussed in chapter 6 or Aboriginal justice discussed in chapter 8, VORPs may intensify and disperse social control, even as they decrease the power of police, prosecutors, and judges. Although subject to abuse and excess, this new form of social control may be more acceptable if motivated by a non-punitive and integrative approach and if offenders and victims both have veto powers (Braithwaite 1989, 1997). In any event, the alternative of due process has not increased liberty, while the alternative of crime control has not prevented recidivism. VORPs may fail and sometimes be inappropriate, but, like family conferences and Aboriginal justice, they remain a real alternative.

Restorative-justice initiatives have been criticized by victim-advocacy groups and women's groups as inappropriate in cases of serious violence. Concerns have been expressed that victims will, because of inequality of bargaining power and pressure from mediators, be coerced into agreements. Family conferencing, Aboriginal justice, or VORPs could be discredited by one well-publicized failure in a case involving serious injury. As suggested in chapter 1, punitive and non-punitive approaches to victims' rights each have their place. One pragmatic solution may be to follow the example of the Young Offenders Act (see chapter 6) and articulate a clear line that requires non-punitive responses in cases that do not result in serious personal injuries. Most advocates of restorative justice (Zehr 1990; Braithwaite 1997) would oppose such a hard and fast line, and argue that these programs can work with even the most serious crimes. To ensure political survival, however, such a line may be necessary at least until restorative justice has a proven record of success and the concerns of victim-advocacy and women's groups can be addressed.

Crime Prevention

In the 1980s and 1990s, crime prevention became pervasive, especially among corporations and advantaged individuals. Sometimes encouraged by the police (Ericson and Haggerty 1997), individuals were asked to take steps to protect themselves from crime. Sacco and Johnson (1990: 85) found that 25 per cent of respondents changed activities to avoid crime; 23 per cent installed security hardware; and 3 per cent took self-defence courses. Urban residents, and especially single women, were more likely to take defensive measures, and those earning more money were more likely to install security hardware. One danger was that the disadvantaged would be left to rely on public crime control.

In the 1990s, governments began to define crime prevention as a salient issue. After examining victimization studies indicating that most crime was never reported to the police and evidence about the prohibitive costs of more prosecutions and prisons, a parliamentary committee chaired by Conservative Bob Horner concluded that 'threats to the safety and security of Canadians will not be abated by hiring more police officers and building more prisons' (Canada 1993a: 2). It recommended a community-based approach to crime prevention that included immediate opportunity reduction and longer-term social-development strategies to reduce crime. It resisted the criminalization of politics by arguing that crime was a matter not only for police and prosecutors, but for those responsible for housing, health, education, and social and economic development (ibid: 22–3).

Opportunity-reduction approaches to crime prevention were a neo-liberal approach which asked individuals to perform what were once considered exclusive governmental functions (Garland 1996). They might divert the location of crime more than prevent it. The insurance industry was in a good position to make rational and cost-effective decisions about how much money should be invested to prevent crime. Distributional concerns, however, persisted, and the least advantaged were the least amenable to the comparatively gentle control of insurance companies. Those who could not afford insurance, let alone security systems and private policing, would be forced to rely on the frequently false promise of public crime control.

Opportunity-reduction strategies also involved the police, and the Horner Committee stressed the importance of community policing. Ericson and Haggerty (1997: 157), however, criticized police attempts to 'make communities by creating a communality of fear.' Programs which simply informed people of crimes committed in their communities might only increase fear, while those which encouraged people to take practical steps to prevent crime might not. More active approaches could also combat stereotypes of crime victims and potential victims as passive and helpless. Community policing, however, presented the same problems discussed in chapter 8. Under-servicing was diagnosed as under-policing, and the police were offered as the solution to social and economic problems.

The Horner Committee also recommended social-development interventions targeting disadvantaged children at risk of committing crime in the future (Canada 1993a: 17). It heard evidence that broke down dichotomies between victims and offenders and indicated that many offenders had been the victims of child poverty and physical or sexual abuse (ibid: 10). The National Crime Prevention Council subsequently refined these recommendations with studies on preventing crime by investing in families. It outlined interventions targeting children from the prenatal stage to the teenaged years. One such intervention was the Perry Pre-School Project providing preschool programs and in home visits for children aged three to four. Children in this project had lower arrest records, as well as better education and employment, compared with a control group (National Crime Prevention Council 1996: 17). Other projects included school programs targeting bullys. A recent review of the literature found that 'early childhood interventions with socially disruptive behaviour, cognitive deficits, or parenting as an outcome generally have positive effects' (Tremblay and Craig 1995: 151). These interventions combatted the criminalization of politics observed throughout this book by blurring distinctions between offenders and victims, and relating criminal behaviour to a broad range of social, economic, educational, and cultural factors. They could, however, be criticized for increasing surveillance and risk profiling of even the youngest children. Early childhood interventions widened the net of social control, but did so in a non-punitive and integrative manner that was more promising than waiting for the child to become a teenager who could be punished.

Social-development approaches might also prevent some crimes against women, children, minorities, and Aboriginal people. The Horner Committee rejected a narrow and criminalized view of violence against women by relating the violence to women's 'lack of equality with men in social, economic and political spheres of life' (Canada 1993a: 11). This was hardly a novel insight, but one that had been frequently ignored, given the high symbolic value of criminal justice reform, the exigencies of the new political case, and the greater expense of other equality measures. Parent training and support for child care could also play some role in preventing the abuse of children. Anti-racism education and special interventions for children who displayed racist tendencies may help prevent hate crimes. Programs to reduce Aboriginal suicides might also reduce crime. Greater opportunities for disadvantaged groups might help make them less vulnerable to crime as well as to other harms.

The main obstacles to the use of social development as a form of crime prevention were the expense and the diffused political responsibility and credit for such interventions. Governments driven by fiscal concerns must be convinced that such strategies would save money in the long term. The Horner Committee also observed that government departments responsible for housing, immigration, social services, health, and education 'do not, as a general rule, perceive public safety issues and crime prevention to be components of their roles and responsibilities' (ibid: 13). As the welfare state eroded, crime prevention could become a new justification for social-welfare measures. Even the most minimal state should protect its citizens from crime.

Victim-advocacy groups expressed less scepticism about crime prevention than restorative justice. This was fortunate because crime victims were in an excellent position to speak to the need for crime prevention. Their efforts did not seem vindictive; they did not focus on the past; they did not promote a stereotype of victims as helpless or passive; and they did not result in symbolic and divisive battles with due process typical of the new political case. Women's groups, Aboriginal groups, and minority groups may, however, be concerned that crime prevention could result in victim blaming, and that opportunity reduction will not benefit those who cannot afford security systems and private policing. Much will depend on how crime prevention evolves in the future. When focused on opportunity reduction, a circle model could represent the isolation of the fortress home or the gated community, or the return of middle-class investments on insurance. When focused on social development and restorative justice, however, a circle model could represent more integrated, just, and peaceful communities.

Conclusion

Although they achieved some recognition, the rights of crime victims were more fragile than either the rights of the accused or the rights of disadvantaged groups who claimed equal protection of the criminal law. Part of the reason may be found in the Charter, which entrenched both due process and equality rights, but not the rights of crime victims. Another reason may be found in public-choice models of the legislative process. A quarter of us are victimized by crime in any year and it is impossible to organize such a large and diffuse group. The crime victims who did form groups were organized by those who experienced the worst crimes. This can help explain the focus on punitive measures such as the attempt to abolish 'faint hope' hearings and why victim-advocacy groups did not champion restorative justice or crime-prevention initiatives which addressed more typical crimes.

Crime victims have had some impact on the criminal process, but it was limited and contested. Victim-impact statements were made available, but rarely used. Victims were cooled out and the power of crime-control professionals not fundamentally disturbed. Attempts to assert the privacy rights of crime victims in sensational cases have produced political cases in which the rights of the accused and the media were pitted against victims' rights. Victims' bills of rights were enacted, but paled in comparison to enforceable Charter rights. They focused on service and information from crime-control professionals without giving victims decision-making powers. In contrast, restorative justice and crime prevention allowed victims and potential victims of crime to make decisions without being subject to adversarial due-process challenges or the false illusion that the criminal law would control crime.

10

Conclusions

The future of criminal justice will largely depend on how victims' rights evolve. The well-trodden path leads towards the criminal sanction and more victim-sensitive prosecutions as a means to protect and recognize crime victims and potential victims. Its dangers are more symbolic and divisive battles over the primacy of the rights of the accused and the victim, and the reproduction of the false assumption that the criminal law controls crime. A less-travelled, but more promising, path leads towards increased emphasis on crime prevention and restorative justice. Its dangers are disrupting the monopoly of criminal justice professionals and abandoning traditional assumptions about the criminal law. Its benefits are minimizing new political cases which pit due process against victims' rights, and providing crime victims and offenders, their families, and communities a greater role in constructively responding to crime. Both paths have their place, but the non-punitive path is in danger of being neglected and disparaged.

The Rapid Rise of Due Process and Victims' Rights

The changes over the last two decades in the way we think and talk about criminal justice have been dramatic and profound. The traditional deference to Parliament, police, and prosecutors found in the crime-control model (see chapter 1) are, like the writs of assistance, but a memory. Canadians can now outdo Americans in discussions about *Miranda* rights; exclusionary rules; and warrant, disclosure, and speedy trial requirements (see chapters 2 and 3). The due-process revolution was foreshadowed by the 1984 Young Offenders Act (see chapter 6), but, since that time, the Supreme Court has taken the due-process lead and Parliament has responded with crime-control and victims' rights legislation.

Packer's models can help us understand the rise of due process, but they cannot explain the various forces of victims' rights which made the ride bumpier and more controversial. Victimization studies revealing high levels of unreported crime, particularly sexual violence against women and children, have helped produce new demands for criminal justice reform. New laws and procedures were developed to respond to sexual and domestic violence (see chapters 5 and 6) and hate and war crimes (chapter 7), and the very notion of 'victimless' crimes was challenged by arguments that the criminal sanction was supported by the equality rights of disadvantaged groups and the risk of various harms, including insecurity and anxiety (chapter 4). Crime victims in general were constructed as the new consumers of services, information, and punishment provided by crime-control professionals. They were recognized in victims' bill of rights which matched the Charter in rights rhetoric, but not legal status (see chapter 9). Legislators took the lead with victims' rights, but courts were not oblivious to growing concerns about the rights of victims and allowed victims and other third parties to claim rights in the criminal trial (see chapter 3) and accepted limitations on various Charter rights in an attempt to recognize the harms that victims suffered (chapters 2, 3, 4, and 6).

The New Political Case: Due Process versus Victims' Rights

The rapid rise of due process and victims' rights changed the type of political case which drew headlines and critical attention. Before the 1980s, the political case was fought between the state and the individual. The state asserted its powers and claims to enforce the community's morality against the accused's claim to represent the individual and freedom. Conservatives, especially in Canada, sided with the state, while liberals, especially in the United States, sided with the individual. Herbert Packer (1968) typified the liberal approach by arguing that the state should not enforce morality and by assuming that disadvantaged groups would benefit from due process.

The political cases of the 1990s were different because they pitted due-process claims by the accused against rights claims by crime victims and groups of potential victims of crime. They challenged the assumption that the criminal trial was a bipolar affair between the state and the accused. Victims and other third parties gained a procedural and substantive stake in criminal trials by claiming that their Charter rights were violated (see chapters 3 and 4). Rights discourse was flexible enough so that rights could be invoked both as a limit on state power and as a justification for the criminal sanction. Many crimes Packer believed to be victimless and based on consensual transactions were successfully defended as necessary to protect the rights of disadvantaged groups and to honour international commitments. Women, children, and various minorities, with varying degrees of success, claimed rights to the equal protection of the criminal law. Sometimes courts upheld criminal laws from due-process challenges on the basis of the rights of crime victims and potential victims (*Keegstra* 1990; *Butler* 1992; *Levogianis* 1993; *L.(D.O.)* 1993). In other cases, due-process claims prevailed (*Seaboyer* 1991; *Daviault* 1994; *O'Connor* 1995; *Carosella* 1997; *Hess* 1990; *Heywood* 1993). In these latter cases, the Court did not have the last word, and the new political case was resolved, at least temporarily, in Parliament, which affirmed its willingness to recognize the rights of women and children as potential victims of male violence. The new political cases were high-stakes, divisive struggles about whether the rights of the accused or victims were more important. Despite the new language and the importance of recognizing victims and disadvantaged groups, the defence of the criminal sanction in the new political case reproduced the old crime-control assumption that the criminal law controlled crime.

The Criminalization of Politics

Legislative replies to due-process decisions demonstrated the pluralism of rights discourse and institutional politics, but it also reflected the legalization of politics (Mandel 1994). On any definition, politics were legalized when Parliament responded to a Supreme Court decision by simply adopting the reasoning of a dissenting judgment. The roots of legalized politics were not so much with the Charter, the Court, or even elite attraction to symbolic struggles about which rights were more important, but the broader phenomenon of criminalized politics. The criminalization of politics reflected a process in which social, economic, cultural, and political problems were addressed through criminal justice reforms. It was the process through which reformed sexual-assault laws, mandatory prosecution of spousal abuse, and criminal laws against pornography and prostitution were offered as the response to the subordination of women (see chapter 5). It was the process through which the sexual abuse of children was criminalized without much attention to why this behaviour, or other forms of child abuse or neglect, occurred within families (chapter 6). Politics were criminalized when the Special Investigation Unit, not police reform, was the response to police shootings of black men, and when the treatment of the disabled and the dying was symbolized by debates over whether the criminal sanction should be applied in the *Rodriguez* (chapter 4) and *Latimer* (chapter 7) cases. Politics was also criminalized when Aboriginal-justice initiatives dominated other aspects of self-government (chapter 8) and when concerns about crime victims were funnelled into punishment issues and not spread out through multidisciplinary attempts at preventing crime and healing and compensating crime victims (chapter 9).

Criminal justice reform would be politically appealing as a symbolic response to complex social problems even in the absence of the Charter. The Charter and due-process challenges to the criminal sanction, however, aided and abetted criminalized politics by producing legalized politics in the court and legislatures. The defensive battle to preserve the criminal sanction from Charter challenge in new political cases facilitated a loss of perspective about the limits of the criminal law. The symbolic stakes were so high that many progressive movements believed that they had no choice but to defend the criminal sanction as vital to their wider objectives. The fight to ensure the equal protection of the criminal law sometimes begged the question of what even its equal protection offered.

Was Due Process for Crime Control?

Due process threatened crime control and punitive forms of victims' rights in the new political case, but not in the routine case. The Court's enthusiastic interpretation of due-process rights did not empty the prisons. It did not even stem their growth. During the Charter's first decade, prison counts increased 50 per cent, and other forms of punishment increased 60 per cent (Canadian Centre for Criminal Justice Statistics 1996b: 14–16). Imprisonment increased under the Young Offenders Act even while offenders were granted due-process rights and portrayed as laughingly abusing their rights. The Charter might have restrained some law-and-order measures (Stuart 1996a), but the costs of imprisonment on debt-ridden governments were probably a more important restraint. In some cases, due process provoked crime control. Decisions striking down warrantless searches resulted in frequent legislative replies authorizing whatever searches the courts held to violate privacy (see chapter 2). The *Askov* crisis was exaggerated and, along with *Stinchcombe* disclosure requirements, increased the efficiency and legitimacy of plea bargaining (chapter 3). Restrictions on murder were balanced with an expansion of manslaughter (chapter 3). On occasion due process demonstrated a life of its own (Thompson 1975), but it frequently recognized and enabled crime control even as it purported to limit it (McBarnet 1981; Ericson and Baranek 1982). Due process was not inconsistent with increased crime control and in some cases provoked more efficient and legitimate crime control. It countered the worst cases of abuse, but it did not restrain the use of the criminal sanction or necessarily protect the most disadvantaged.

The critical claim that due process legitimated crime control (McBarnet 1981; Ericson and Baranek 1982; Mandel 1994) was more tenuous. Due process in Canada was not an inevitable response to a legitimation crisis (Habermas 1975). If the provinces had come on side earlier (see chapter 1), the Charter could easily have been enacted with minimal or no due-process rights or remedies. Some specific responses to due-process decisions would not have been necessary, but there is little reason to believe that the use of the criminal sanction would not have increased over the last two decades without the 'just words' (Bakan 1997) of the Charter. Due process as a legitimation tool was often indirect and ineffective. Cases such as *Askov* (1990) and *Daviault* (1994) produced a lack of public confidence, not a sense that the imposition of the criminal sanction was fair. Due-process decisions such as *Seaboyer* (1991), *Daviault* (1994), *O'Connor* (1995), and *Carosella* (1997) offended groups with enough political clout to achieve quick legislative replies. Others such as *Zundel* (1992) and *Finta* (1994) did not produce a legislative reply, but resulted in much frustration. In turn, decisions such as *Keegstra* (1990) and *Butler* (1992) which won applause from some equality seekers disappointed civil-libertarians, who played an important role in drafting the due-process provisions of the Charter. Due process was too divisive, too elite, and too controversial to legitimate the criminal sanction to the public. It was not hegemonic, but challenged at every turn by crime-control, victims' rights, and equality claims. If the criminal sanction needed to be legitimated as fair and necessary, the new pluralist and punitive politics of victims' rights did so much more directly and powerfully.

Were Victims' Rights for Crime Control?

The participation of crime victims and groups of potential crime victims was frequently channelled on the side of the prosecution and in favour of increased punishment. Victimization studies revealing high levels of unreported crimes were constructed as a reason for reforming criminal justice without consideration of how irrelevant criminal justice was for the majority of victims who did not report crime or how much the repressive capacity of the state would have to expand to deal with fuller reporting. Risks were easier to calculate than control (Beck 1992). Attempts were made to achieve zero risk through zero tolerance and reliance on the crime-control assumption that the criminal law controlled crime.

The 1983 sexual-assault reforms and the 1988 child-sexual-abuse reforms were designed to encourage reporting and make the system more sensitive to victims. These reforms increased reporting and convictions, but victims were still subject to adversarial challenges. Mandatory prosecution policies for wife assault were presented in the language of victims' rights, but they encouraged police, prosecutors, and judges to ignore the wishes of victims who did not want to cooperate in the crime-control assembly line. Victims' bills of rights offered services and information, but not enforceable rights that could inconvenience crime-control professionals. Victim participation in the criminal process was focused on interventions such as victim-impact statements and repeal of 'faint hope' hearings which attempted to increase punishment. Governments invoked their desires to protect crime victims and potential crime victims as a reason to uphold criminal laws from due-process challenges. Victims' rights were often the human, angry, and rights-bearing face of crime control.

Non-Punitive Forms of Victims' Rights

Increased concern about victims and potential victims of crimes did not, however, inevitably lead in the direction of crime control. Victimization studies revealing high levels of unreported crime could be seen as a sign of the limits of the criminal law and the need for governments, communities, and individuals to respond more creatively to the widespread incidence of crime. Corporations and advantaged individuals, with their security systems and private police, discovered the limits of traditional crime control. It was the disadvantaged who were left with the false promise of crime control and the task of defending the criminal sanction from due-process challenges. Less emphasis on the criminal sanction would minimize the symbolic and divisive battles between victims' rights and due process found in the new political case and counter the inclination to criminalize politics by throwing criminal justice reforms at complex social, political, cultural, and economic problems. Schools, families, communities, and those responsible for social services and economic opportunities, not Parliament, police, and prosecutors, should play a greater role in responding to crime.

There were glimpses of non-punitive approaches to victims' rights. Family conferences (see chapter 6), Aboriginal justice (chapter 8), and VORPs (chapter 9) all brought offenders and crime victims together to understand why the crime was committed and to work out some form of repair for the victim, rehabilitation for the offender, and reintegration with relevant communities. These interventions did not always succeed and were criticized by advocacy groups as inappropriate for the most serious crimes that dominated public discourse. Nevertheless, they offered victims more involvement and possible satisfaction than being consulted when convenient by crime-control professionals and submitting victim-impact statements in the hope that the offender would be punished more severely. They also challenged offenders by requiring them to explain their actions and make amends rather than being passively processed through the crime-control assembly line, with the lawyers doing the talking. These interventions allowed offending to be related to past victimization without excusing the crime and took a holistic and future-oriented approach to crime. Opportunity-reduction forms of crime prevention allowed victims and potential victims to regain some power that crime and fear of crime took away. Developmental forms of crime prevention countered criminalized and punitive politics by challenging unrealistic dichotomies between offenders and victims. Like restorative-justice experiments, crime prevention at times failed and was dominated by crime-control professionals (Ericson and Haggerty 1997). Nevertheless, both crime prevention and restorative justice were promising alternatives to the false promise that criminal prosecutions and punishment would control crime or that due process would increase liberty.

Packer's Models Revisited

The starting point of this book was Herbert Packer's crime-control and due-process models. These models were useful in describing the operation of the criminal justice system before the Charter (see chapter 1) and the rise of due process after the Charter (chapters 2 and 3). Even as a matter of positive description, however, Packer's models told less than half of the story. Packer could not explain why women, children, minorities, and crime victims claimed rights to the criminal sanction, and he could not comprehend the new political case which pitted due-process claims, not against the community's claims to enforce morality, but against the rights of crime victims and disadvantaged groups of potential victims. Packer's models still struck a chord, but, slowly and surely, they became as out of date as other hits of the 1960s.

Packer's models were also based on assumptions that are now empirically and normatively suspect. His crime-control model assumed that the criminal law could control crime without accounting for the fact, revealed by victimization studies, that most crime victims did not report crime to the police. He assumed that punishment was necessary to control crime, whereas it may make things worse by stigmatizing offenders and producing defiance (Braithwaite 1989; Hagan and McCarthy 1997). Packer assumed that fair treatment could be achieved only through an adversarial criminal trial in which an accused was represented by a defence lawyer. We now know that defence lawyers rarely invoke due-process rights (Feeley 1979; Ericson and Baranek 1982) and that circle-based alternatives such as restorative justice, family conferences, and Aboriginal justice can be run in a procedurally fair manner that encourages participation and deliberation (Braithwaite 1997). Packer's assumptions about the conflict between crime control and due process were challenged by, first, the American and, then, the Canadian experience, which demonstrated that a due-process revolution was not inconsistent with increased crime control. Packer assumed that due process conflicted with crime control, but new research suggests that people may be more law-abiding if they believe they are treated fairly (Tyler 1990; Braithwaite 1997). In short, fair treatment may be necessary for effective crime control, and punishment may not be necessary to control crime. Punitive approaches to victims' rights perpetuated Packer's mistakes by replicating the assumption that the criminal law controlled crime and the battle between due process and crime control (albeit reconceived as victims' rights). Non-punitive approaches, however, avoided Packer's mistakes by not relying on punishment to control crime; by treating people fairly and as responsible citizens in non-adversarial proceedings; and by seeking to reconcile the interests of offenders, victims, and their communities through restorative justice and crime prevention.

Conclusion

For better or worse, the future of criminal justice depends on victims' rights. Due process has tried its best, but has not increased liberty and may be less of a force in the future. It remains a necessary, but not a sufficient, means to protect liberty and prevent domination. Victims' rights emerged in the 1980s and 1990s as the new means to legitimate crime control, including its very shaky assumption that the criminal law controlled crime, and to counter due-process claims in the new political case. Victims' rights supported the tendency in an age of fiscal restraint and disillusionment to criminalize politics by offering criminal justice reforms as the answer to society's ills.

Nevertheless, this punitive trajectory was not uniform or inevitable. Victimization studies and concerns for victims made the system more reflexively critical of its ability to achieve safety and security. It marginalized crime-control bureaucracies' self-validating emphasis on clearance and conviction rates. High levels of unreported crime and victim dissatisfaction were constructed to create demands for criminal justice reform, but they also inspired interventions which placed less reliance on criminal prosecutions and punishment, and more emphasis on crime prevention and restorative justice.

There is irony in my optimistic conclusion that victims' rights could lead to less reliance on the criminal sanction. Thirty years ago, Herbert Packer made the very same prediction about due process, and much of this book was devoted to explaining why he was wrong. In the United States, and now in Canada, due process has proven to be consistent with increased crime control as measured by expanding prison populations. I may be repeating Packer's mistake, but in a much more obvious manner. Victims' rights could not only be consistent with increased crime control, but could enable and legitimate it much more directly than due process. My pessimistic conclusion is that victims' rights will continue as the new and improved face of crime control. New political cases will continue to be fought, and politics will continue to be criminalized.

Nevertheless, developments which included victims, but did not rely on punishment, are a cause for optimism. Corporations and the advantaged already invest in crime prevention which may not rely on state-imposed punishment. The disadvantaged must not be left to rely on the false promise of crime control and to fight new political cases in defence of a criminal sanction that unfortunately does not control crime. Developmental forms of crime prevention can resist the criminalization of politics by recognizing some of the early determinants of crime. When crime has been committed, family conferences, Aboriginal justice, and VORPs all make room for victims without relying on punishment or producing divisive and symbolic battles between victims' rights and due process.

The victims of crime cannot be ignored. In the worlds of prosecutions and punishment, they can be informed and consulted, but will have little real decision-making power. Some victims' rights will be recognized, but they will often be pitted against due-process rights. In the worlds of crime prevention and restorative justice, however, victims and potential victims of crime may find more decision-making power and less opposition. One hopes that they – all of us ultimately – can find more security and satisfaction.

Notes

1: Models of the Criminal Process

1 Throughout this book, I refer to complainants and crime victims as 'victims' for ease of narrative and not out of any intended disrespect for the presumption of innocence. I also do not intend any disrespect for those who have survived crimes or to reduce their unique and multiple identities to one of a victim. Martha Minow (1993: 1431) has aptly identified a dilemma in either recognizing or refusing to recognize victimization: 'Describing yourself as a victim has a self-fulfilling and self-perpetuating feature; and yet, failing to acknowledge or assert one's victimization leaves the harm unaddressed and the perpetrators unchallenged.' Crime victims are not homogeneous, but in this chapter some common features which make it possible to think of models based on victims' rights are stressed.

2 My use of the term 'victims' rights' is an attempt to restore agency and dignity to crime victims. Because victims have been neglected for so long and because there is a danger that the accused will have a monopoly on rights claims, it has been necessary for groups representing crime victims and potential victims to assert rights as both a rhetorical and a legal device. Nevertheless, the assertion of rights is not the whole or perhaps the most important part of recognizing and respecting crime victims. The needs of those who suffered grievously in the past are frequently more important than their rights (Ignatieff 1984; Roach 1991b). In the real world of limited resources and legalized politics, however, victims have frequently asserted their demands and needs in the language of rights. The strengths and limitations of this strategy are explored throughout this book.

3 McBarnet (1981: 6) was explicit about this when she stated: 'The vague notion of "due process" or "the law in the books" in fact collapses two quite distinct

aspects of law into one: the general principles around which the law is discussed – the rhetoric of justice– and the actual procedures and rules by which justice or legality are operationised.' Ericson (1983: 28) similarly noted that 'the model of due process in opposition to crime control is salient primarily in the discourse of the public culture. In the control culture of statutes, case law, and the work of legal agents, "due process is for crime control."'

4 The rhetoric of justice is based on an ideology of legality. Hence, McBarnet's (1979: 39) oft-quoted statement: 'Legality requires that officials be governed by law; the law is based on post hoc decisions. Legality requires each case to be judged on it own facts; the law makes previous convictions grounds for defining behaviour as an offence. Legality requires incriminating evidence as the basis for arrest and search; the law allows arrest and search in order to establish it. Legality embodies individual civil rights against public or state interests; the law makes state and the public interest a justification for ignoring civil rights.'

5 Ericson (1987: 30) writes: 'the "rights"/due process/crime control debate is more understandable in the context of the state's ideological work in the public culture concerning how it should proceed in relation to troublesome citizens than in terms of how it does proceed. It creates illusions, displacing reform talk away from social control and serving as an instrument of that control.'

6 Prison counts increased by 50 per cent between 1981/2 and 1994/5, with the greatest growth being in federal penitentiaries for those serving more than two years (CCCJS 1996b).

7 What Alan Cairns (1992, 1995) identified as 'Charter Canadians' and what Rainer Knopff and Ted Morton (1992, 1996) identified as the 'Court Party' have engaged in Charter litigation in the criminal justice field in a defensive attempt to preserve the criminal sanction from due-process challenge. They have enjoyed some success in using equality rights to defend the criminal sanction (see chapter 4), but have more frequently enjoyed success in Parliament after due-process defeats (see chapter 5) They do not act as one united party, and often at a high cost of division among their ranks and diversion of energy from other projects (Cossman et al 1997).

8 Most research has suggested that the threat of punishment does little to deter crime. When deterrence works, publicity and certainty of punishment are crucial but often cannot be sustained. The literature also suggests that imprisonment does little to rehabilitate criminals or to deter them beyond the period of incapacitation (Canada 1987: 135ff; Friedland, Trebilcock, and Roach 1990).

9 Even though the Bail Reform Act of 1972 and the Protection of Privacy Act of 1974 placed more restrictions on pre-trial detention and electronic surveil-

lance, they also enabled the state by authorizing detention and surveillance. As examined in the next chapter, legislation enacted in response to Charter restrictions on police powers shared both the restraining and the enabling features of these pre-Charter laws.

10 The federal division of powers was, however, used by the Supreme Court to protect civil liberties. For example, the Supreme Court struck down a Quebec City by-law creating an offence for distributing literature without the permission of the chief of police, with the American-educated Justice Ivan Rand writing eloquently about the dangers to freedom of speech and freedom of religion (*Saumur* 1953). Quebec responded to this early due-process decision by amending a provincial law so that it would no longer protect those such as the Jehovah Witnesses who insulted other religions (Kaplan 1989: 245; Roach, 1993b: 165). This foreshadowed the type of dialogue which emerged under the Charter between the courts protecting due-process values and legislatures acting out of a concern for crime control and victims' rights.

11 In contrast, thirty-one groups and fifteen individuals made submissions concerning equality rights; forty-two individuals and six groups made submissions concerning abortion; and twenty-five groups and sixteen individuals made submissions concerning minority language school rights (Canada 1980–1, 57: 94–5).

12 A federal/provincial task force of prosecutors in charge of producing a code of evidence recommended that judges continue to have no discretion to exclude improperly obtained evidence (Canada 1982b: 231–3). Section 26 displayed the power of crime control by rejecting law-reform proposals that judges be able to exclude improperly obtained evidence if its admission would bring the administration of justice into disrepute (Roach 1986).

13 The police and prosecutors conducted a publicity campaign that the strengthened Charter would 'Americanize' Canadian criminal law to the detriment of crime control (*Globe and Mail*, 11 Mar. 1981). They were, however, able to win over only a few disgruntled Conservative backbenchers who expressed concerns that section 24(2) would result in an American-style exclusionary rule. In an early example of victims' rights being appropriated for crime-control ends, one argued that 'this is not a time for Parliament and the courts to treat criminals as though they were a privileged class ... more tears are shed today for the criminals than are shed for the victims of crime' (Hansard, 21 Apr 1981: 9344). He also wondered whether 'the women of Canada want to protect sexual attackers to the extent that even the slightest mistake by police in following the proper investigatory and arrest procedures will exclude relevant evidence and lead to an acquittal, even if evidence of guilt is overwhelming?' (Hansard, 23 Nov 1981: 13143).

2: The Police

1 Below the Supreme Court, the police could find judicial supporters of crime control. The Ontario Court of Appeal, for example, had dismissed arguments that mandatory breathalyser tests violated the accused's rights against self-incrimination as trivial and warned that the Charter 'does not intend a transformation of our legal system or the paralysis of law enforcement' (*Altseimer* 1982: 13). In the due-process model, however, the Supreme Court had the final word, and the police were correct in predicting that the Supreme Court would be more receptive to due-process claims than would lower courts (Morton, Russell, and Withey 1992).

2 Clarkson's intoxication would have given her a good chance at manslaughter, but her husband's prior violence towards her would not have been relevant to a self-defence claim at the time (*Whynot* 1983; see chapter 5).

3 Evidence that affected the fairness of the trial could be admitted if it would have been discovered through constitutional means (*Black* 1989; *Harper* 1994; *Stillman* 1997). This reasoning had been used by the U.S. Supreme Court to chip away at their automatic exclusionary rule. The Canadian Supreme Court also admitted evidence obtained through a right-to-counsel violation because, for example, the accused behaved in a 'violent, vulgar and obnoxious' manner (*Tremblay* 1987: 567) or was too drunk to understand the warning in a drunk-driving case (*Mohl* 1989).

4 Justice McLachlin similarly argued that the logic of *Wray* 'finds no place in the Charter ... No longer is reliability determinative. The Charter has made the rights of the individual and the fairness and integrity of the judicial system paramount' (*Hebert* 1990: 36–7).

5 Despite the ability of police to obtain warrants since 1985, the Supreme Court has continued to encounter warrantless blood seizures. Due-process doctrine was not immune from the tragedies that motivated victim advocacy groups. In one case, the Court excluded the blood, but only after concluding that there was still enough evidence to try the accused for criminal negligence causing death and bodily harm (*Dersch* 1993). In another case in which a drunk, driving the wrong way and with his lights off, killed a twenty-two-year-old driver, the Court admitted the evidence in part because, 'although all cases of impaired driving causing death are tragic, the facts of this particular case are even more shocking than usual. That the offence occurred in such aggravating circumstances would surely affect the repute of the administration of justice if the evidence was excluded' (*Colarusso* 1994: 233). For the media and the Court, the decision to admit the blood sample revolved around the fact that 'the circumstances were so horrific that not allowing the evidence

would bring the administration of justice into disrepute' (*Toronto Star*, 27 Jan. 1994).

6 The Canadian Association of Police Chiefs argued that the Court's 'decisions left the police community in Canada in quite a turmoil. Many of the investigation techniques were perfectly appropriate and proper until these decisions were handed down, but suddenly they became questionable and could not be done any longer' (Canada 1993b, 4: 17). Similarly, the Canadian Police Association expressed its disappointment 'in most of the things that the Supreme Court did to us over that period of time. They closed a lot of doors for us, threw up a lot of road blocks, and in fact made our job quite difficult' (ibid, 4: 27).

7 In 1977, 1,304 wiretaps were authorized in Canada (Law Reform Commission of Canada 1986: 10), twice as many as authorized in the United States. In 1984, there were still 735 warrants issued. In 1990, during the height of the Supreme Court's activism, only 325 warrants were issued, and this number declined to 231 in 1994 (Canada 1994).

8 Evidence was excluded when a rectal search was conducted on a person arrested for unpaid parking tickets (*Greffe* 1990); when the police used unnecessary violence during the search (*Collins* 1987; *Genest* 1988); when they conducted warrantless searches in flagrant disregard of trespass laws (*Kokesch* 1990); and when they entered a person's home without even a subjective belief that they had grounds for an arrest (*Feeney* 1997).

9 Borden's lawyer praised the decision for sending 'a message to the police and to the prosecution that people's rights have to be respected – that the Charter of Rights has meaning ... If you don't have properly admissible evidence, you can't prove anything beyond a reasonable doubt – that's the law.' The prosecutor who lost the case matched due-process with crime-control concerns by arguing that 'the balance between the rights of the accused person and the rights of the community to be protected from crime is shifting very much in the wrong direction ... It's particularly disturbing ... that he should go free. That's something that's difficult to accept, if not to understand' (*Winnipeg Free Press*, 14 Oct. 1994a).

10 The bill had been fast-tracked only after the Manning family 'made a tearful appeal at a press conference for the government to pass a DNA bill quickly' (*Globe and Mail*, 21 Jun. 1995). Mr Manning told reporters that in an earlier meeting Rock had told him: 'Mr. Manning you don't have to convince me. I have a 10 year old daughter' (*Globe and Mail*, 23 Jun. 1995).

11 An opinion poll indicated that 88 per cent of Canadians favoured forcing suspects to provide DNA evidence (*Globe and Mail*, 26 Jul. 1995).

12 The reader should know that I acted as counsel for the Canadian Civil Liber-

ties Association, which intervened in the case and argued that the evidence should be excluded because of the seriousness of the violation.

3: The Criminal Trial

1 The media did report, but not on the front page, that during the crisis which bore his name Askov was more cooperative and pleaded guilty and received a six-year sentence for narcotics trafficking (*Globe and Mail*, 1 Jun. 1991)

2 Before *Askov* (1990: 487), Ontario attempted to reduce delay with directives that prosecutors provide full disclosure of their cases to the defence and engage in 'early assessment and resolution of cases, or make more accurate estimates of time requirements.'

3 Old habits die hard, and Peel experienced delay problems again in the mid-1990s. A judge in Peel warned that 'charging every conceivable criminal offence applicable to the accused's conduct rarely increases the justice done ... and not infrequently contributes to an unreasonable strain on resources' (*Globe and Mail*, 10 Feb. 1996). Another case from Peel which resulted in a two-day trial over the theft of a single newspaper was ridiculed on the front pages of the *Globe and Mail*. The defence lawyer complained that although 'this district has a reputation as "No-deal Peel,"'... this should never have gotten as far as it did.' The prosecutor, however, explained that he was not supposed to 'withdraw cases because they are putzy' (*Globe and Mail*, 6 Feb. 1997).

4 The committee's support for the monopoly and expertise of criminal justice professionals was also underlined by its recommendations that all privately commenced prosecutions be taken over by public prosecutors (Ontario 1993: 185); that a victim's desire for a prosecution did not justify one where there was no reasonable prospect of a conviction; and that a victim's reluctance to testify in open court was not a relevant factor in deciding whether to discontinue prosecutions. (ibid: 84–5).

5 Justice L'Heureux-Dubé dissented because she was concerned that appeals by third parties would delay the accused's trial or force the accused to defend proceedings at the same time against both the prosecutor and the third party (*Dagenais* 1994: 344). For her, concerns about the efficiency of the crime-control model and the bipolar orientation of the due-process model outweighed the gains of giving third parties procedural rights. Even though she was sympathetic to victims' rights in the sexual-assault and child-sexual-abuse contexts (see chapters 5 and 6), Justice L'Heureux-Dubé placed the efficiency of crime control before the recognition of the procedural rights of third parties.

6 Like many crime-control arguments that invoked victims' rights, this overstated the ability of the criminal law to respond to the harms of victimization.

The Fraser Committee (Canada 1985: 416, 531) complained that, with only about 100 to 200 pimping charges a year, 'the ability of the criminal law to deal with exploiters is much more apparent than real.'

7 Two exceptions involving statutory rape (*Hess* 1990) and war crimes (*Finta* 1994) will be discussed in chapters 6 and 7, respectively.

4: Victimless Crimes?

1 This fate of this offence as it relates to loitering by convicted sex offenders will be examined in chapter 6, as will the fate of incest, another crime that Packer (1968: 312) believed to be victimless and even 'imaginary.'

2 A mini riot in Toronto after a police officer was acquitted of shooting an African-Canadian suspect did lead to the appointment of a public inquiry to examine anti-black systemic racism (Ontario 1995; see also chapter 7).

3 Packer did not comment on the discriminatory nature of gender-specific prostitution laws and enforcement measures. The Royal Commission on the Status of Women, however, criticized the gender-specificity of the offence of being 'a common prostitute or night walker ... [who] does not give a good account of herself.' It recommended repealing this status offence and treating prostitution-related nuisances by either males or females under existing offences for disturbing the peace (Canada 1970: 369–71). Parliament instead enacted a new gender-neutral offence of soliciting 'in a public place for the purpose of prostitution' (S.C. 1972 c.13 s.13). Some courts remained reluctant to punish customers (*Dudak* 1978; Boyle and Noonan 1987), and the Criminal Code was again amended in 1982 to underline that males as well as females could be prostitutes. (S.C. 1980–2 c.125 s.11). Many feminists argued that solicitation should be decriminalized, but what they got was a criminal sanction which on its face was gender-neutral (Hansard. 4 Aug. 1982: 20039).

4 The public rhetoric occasionally slipped. When introducing the bill at the end of an evening sitting, Crosbie demonstrated both social ambivalence about prostitution and questionable wit by taunting his colleagues opposite that the House was dealing with a subject 'they will find themselves busily engaged in the next few hours.' This was greeted with the reply: 'You are the only John in the House' (Hansard, 26 Jun. 1985: 6236). Things became more serious, and the crime-control rhetoric escalated when the legislation was debated after the summer recess.

5 As discussed below, LEAF intervened in favour of hate-propaganda and obscenity offences. It also intervened in other cases to argue that the foetus was not a person protected under criminal or quasi-criminal laws. The Fraser Committee suggested that pornography was a higher priority to women's groups than prostitution, and noted that many had 'been so involved in

researching and campaigning against pornography that they simply did not have the time or resources to prepare an adequate brief on prostitution' (Canada 1985: 345). Janice Dickin McGinnis (1994: 119) has related LEAF's failure to intervene to mainstream feminism's concern about condoning prostitution as 'the ultimate degradation and violence against women.'

6 Dickin McGinnis (1994: 115) concluded that this allowed Justice Lamer to say: 'I am not falling back on the agenda of the moral morality, I am in the vanguard of the feminist movement.'

7 Both pro-life and pro-choice advocates had attempted without success to have the Charter embrace their positions. Reflecting their tendency to see the foetus as an 'innocent victim,' some pro-life advocates wanted an amendment that would prohibit abortion, but allow capital punishment. For example, Gwen Landolt of Campaign Life proposed an amendment that would provide 'the absolute right to life' for 'everyone from the moment of conception onward *who is innocent* of any crime' (Canada 1980–1, 34: 125; see also 22: 43).

8 PEP, which also intervened in Robert Latimer's appeal of his conviction for murdering his disabled daughter (see chapter 7), was reported to be composed of about forty people and supported by private donations (*Winnipeg Free Press*, 19 Jul. 1995). Its arguments, like those of the Ontario Advisory Council on the Status of Women in the prostitution cases, were useful to judges who wanted to uphold the criminal sanction in the name of victims' rights even though the group might be in a minority of those they represented.

9 In his dissent, Chief Justice Lamer similarly suggested that the majority's concerns about coercion were 'speculative' and that respect for Rodriguez's will 'may necessarily imply running the risk that the consent will have been obtained improperly' (*Rodriguez* 1993: 48). He also concluded that the law had a discriminatory effect on disabled people who required assistance in taking their lives.

10 The absence of studies did not stop Packer (1968: 318–19) from suggesting the converse – namely, that there was 'reason to believe that obscene literature acts as a substitute for rather than as a stimulus to aggressive sexual behaviour.'

11 The chair of that committee, Mark MacGuigan, defended the prohibition of degrading pornography as an attempt at 'bringing the woman's point of view into our law' (Hansard, 19 Apr. 1978: 4658).

12 The Court's statement about explicit sex resulted in a dissent by two judges who were concerned that a depiction of explicit sex on a billboard could 'be an undue exploitation of sex, because the community does not tolerate it, on the basis of its harmfulness' (*Butler* 1992: 174). It also put moralistic family-values approaches, such as those contained in the Conservative's bills and the Manitoba Court of Appeal's judgment, on the defensive. Video stores proudly

advertised that explicit sex had been legalized by the Supreme Court, and lap-dancing was legalized for a time until the Supreme Court drew the line at touching (*Mara* 1997).

13 Justice McLachlin, who wrote judgments striking down the criminal sanction in *Keegstra* (1990) and *Zundel* (1992), signed on to the *Butler* judgment uphold-ing the obscenity law. She later suggested that the more deferential standard of judicial review contemplated in *Irwin Toy Ltd.* (1989) was sometimes justi-fied in the criminal context. Although 'the criminal law is generally seen as involving a contest between the state and the accused : it also involves an allo-cation of priorities between the accused and the victim, actual or poten-tial' (*R.J.R.Macdonald Inc.* 1995: 92). Justice McLachlin's apparent rejection of criminal justice as a bipolar matter pitting the state against the accused, and recognition of criminal justice as a matter requiring a balance of the accused's rights with those of victims and potential victims of crime, is a sign of growing acceptance of the new law and politics of criminal justice.

14 Conservative John Reimer, who had once opposed an artistic defence on the grounds that pornography was a 'perversion of human sexuality' (Hansard, 3 Jun. 1986: 13910), shifted his rhetoric and defended the new legislation because it protected 'vulnerable groups from harm, such as women and chil-dren' (Hansard, 15 Jun. 1993: 20865). Old ways died hard, however, and he still maintained that 'as a personal evil pornography corrupts the morals and destroys healthy attitudes toward life for the user' (ibid: 20868).

5: Women

1 Lavallee's factum in the Supreme Court was not an argument for gender equality in self-defence law, but concentrated on technical points about the admissibility of expert evidence. There were no citations to Walker's work or the other secondary literature that figured prominently in the Court's judg-ment. LEAF (1996) did not intervene in this case or in the prostitution cases decided the same year. Thus, the vast majority of its interventions in criminal cases were on the side of the prosecutor.

2 Walker's (1979: xvi) search for a metaphor was equally imaginative. She wrote that 'it is clear that psychosocial factors bind a battered woman to her batterer just as strongly as "miracle glues" bind inanimate substances.'

3 BWS was, however, a factor in Karla Homolka's plea bargain for a twelve-year manslaughter sentence for her role in the abduction, sexual assault, and kill-ings of Leslie Mahaffy and Kristen French. One of Homolka's psychiatrists, in language that mimics Dr Shane's testimony in *Lavallee*, wrote that 'Karla's experience since her age 17 could to some degree be compared to the experi-

ences of concentration camp survivors, who as well experienced horrendous tragedies and had to go through and perform acts in order to survive' (Galligan 1996: 77). In his review of the plea bargain, Justice Galligan concluded that there was 'substantial evidence that Karla Homolka was a battered spouse to such an extent that she was completely under the control and domination of Paul Bernardo ...' (ibid: 150, 166).

4 Margaret Shaw (1993: 65) criticized the task force's emphasis on 'women's status as victims and their need to develop self-esteem' which in her view risked 'characterizing all federally sentenced women as dependant victims without any sense of self-direction or self-worth.' In my view, however, the task force's emphasis on 'creating choices' sought to empower the female inmates. Recognizing the inmates as victims risked stigmatizing them, but ignoring their victimization would have obscured real needs (Minow 1993).

5 Victimization studies since Linda MacLeod's have also been influential and controversial. Government studies in the 1980s revealed much lower figures of wife assault (Johnson 1996: 42, 45). In 1993, however, support for MacLeod's 'one in ten' figure was provided by Statistics Canada's 'Violence against Women' survey. Based on interviews with more than 12,000 women, it reported that 10 per cent of women had been victims of violence during the past year, and that 51 per cent of Canadian women had experienced at least one physical or sexual assault since the age of sixteen. This study also reported that there were thirty-eight times the number of sexual assaults as reported to the police in a year, and three times the number of wife assaults (ibid: 47, 49, 50). In the same year, the Task Force on Violence against Women reported that 98 per cent of women in its study of 420 Toronto women had reported 'some kind of sexually threatening, intrusive or assault experience some time in their lives' (Canada 1993b: 10). The methodology of victimization studies and the way their results were presented became a ground for critique, with some arguing that figures had been inflated to produce 'moral panics' (Fekete 1994; Wente 1994). The criticisms of the Statistics Canada study have been effectively rebutted (Johnson 1995: 152; Doob 1995), but the controversy over the studies underlined their importance.

6 MacLeod (1980: 63) argued that law reform was necessary to help shape 'societal attitudes and behaviour' but warned that 'a simple punitive approach does not appear to be a viable answer' and could make things worse. She also stressed the need for education, economic reforms, and transition houses. Although she followed Walker in presenting wife battering as 'an inevitable cycle' that affected even middle-class women, she explained the cycle by the failure of others to take the violence seriously.

7 'Mandatory' refers to the intent of the policies not their actual implementation by police, prosecutors, or courts.

8 In *Brown* (1992), the Alberta Court of Appeal held that the starting point for domestic-assault sentences should be the same as for any other assault, but that punishment should be increased because of the abuse of trust. This approach was codified in 1995 amendments of the Criminal Code (s.718.2[a][ii] as am. S.C. 1995 c.22). As will be seen in chapters 7–9, victims have been more frequently included in sentencing reforms than in other stages of the criminal process.

9 There was also an expectation that the less severe level of sexual assault would mainly apply to conduct 'such as touching and fondling' (*Calgary Herald*, 5 Jan. 1983). Contrary to original expectations, however, the vast majority of reported sexual assaults were treated by police and prosecutors as simple sexual assaults (Roberts and Grossman 1994: 67).

10 The maximum sentence for sexual assaults prosecuted as summary-conviction matters was increased in 1994 to eighteen months' imprisonment (S.C. 1994 c.44 s.19).

11 There was a 164 per cent increase in reported sexual assaults between 1983 and 1992. About 60 per cent of sexual-assault convictions resulted in a prison sentence, with the median sentence of 6 months and a ninetieth percentile sentence of 2 years (CCCJS 1994b: 11–15). This is significantly less severe that the average rape sentence of 4.3 years reported by Clark and Lewis (1977: 57).

12 Svend Robinson proposed an amendment that sexual history be inadmissible except to establish the identity of the person who had sexual contact with the victim on the occasion charged. He argued clearly, if inelegantly, that 'a woman is always entitled to say no. She can have sex with the entire football team if she chooses to do so, but if she wants to say no to one player, she is entitled to say no. That integrity must always be respected' (Hansard, 4 Aug. 1982: 20046).

13 The Supreme Court later rejected this clash-of-rights approach in a case involving the media's claim of freedom of expression and the accused's claims to a fair trial (*Dagenais* 1994; see chapter 3).

14 Other politicians spoke even more directly about crime victims. Edna Anderson argued that 'victims' rights advocates have long maintained that victims of crime are the forgotten persons in the criminal justice system' and that the bill is 'an excellent example of how law can effectively respond to victims of crimes without jeopardizing in any way the fundamental rights of accused persons' (Hansard, 15 Jun. 1992: 12037). Feminists resisted association with the victims' rights movement (Rock 1986, 1988), but politicians often did not.

15 Defence lawyers objected and obtained the deletion of a requirement that the accused take 'all' reasonable steps to ascertain the victim's consent. As will be seen in chapter 6, accused are required to take all reasonable steps to ascertain the age of young people when charged with statutory rape.

16 The subcommittee's recommendations concerning the law of sexual assault constituted only three of twenty-five recommendations it made. Others included the regulation of advertising; public education; gender-sensitivity training for police, prosecutors, and judges; treatment programs for violent men; and stable funding for shelters (Canada 1991).

17 Rock's statistics were probably taken from a report by the Canadian Centre for Criminal Justice Statistics (1994a) which examined alcohol and drugs as a 'risk factor' in crime. The authors presented risk information somewhat differently than the minister did. They reported that 'rates of victimization increase from 3% for partners who never drank excessively at one sitting to 11% for partners who drank excessively more than five times in the past month.' The risk professionals more clearly understood the difference between correlation and causation.

18 Pierrette Venne of the Bloc Québécois did express unease with the linkage of women and children in the preamble: 'it has really started to bug me that women are being equated with children, when it comes to victimization' (Hansard, 22 Jun. 1995: 14472). The linkage of women and children was a recurring theme in the preambles, but it presented the danger of promoting images of passive and helpless victims.

19 He also argued that 'the benefit of the doubt rests with the potential victim: the innocent bystander who gets hit by a drunk ... The due process should belong to the innocent victim' (Hansard, 22 Jun. 1995: 11046).

20 The NDP supported the bill but argued that there was a need to be both 'tough on crime and tough on the causes of crime,' including 'employment policy, educational policy, family policy, youth policy, health policy ...' (Hansard, 22 Jun. 1995: 11409).

21 Even the Addiction Research Foundation supported the bill for putting 'the public on notice than an individual must take responsibility for actions that result from the consumption of alcohol' and argued that there was no scientific basis for alcohol induced automatism (JLAC 1994, 112a: 74).

22 The outcome of this case is, however, interesting and suggests the value of alternatives to battles between due process and punitive forms of victims' rights. At his retrial, O'Connor was found guilty and sentenced to two and one-half years' imprisonment. He served about six months and was released on bail pending an appeal. O'Connor's appeal was successful on the grounds that the trial judge had erred in holding that O'Connor's exercise of authority over the complainant vitiated any issue of whether she consented to the activ-

ity (*O'Connor* 1998: 510). The case was eventually resolved by a seven-hour healing circle organized by women in the Alkali Lake Band. The circle involved the complainant, her lawyer, and her family; O'Connor, his lawyer, and his family; other complainants in the case; and community members. O'Connor apologized to the complainant, her family, and the community, and a representative of the Roman Catholic Church also apologized to those harmed by the Church's residential schools (*Lawyers' Weekly*, 10 Jul. 1998).

23 The majority repeatedly mentioned that the centre received public money (*Carosella* 1997: 295, 312), which underlined the dilemma of the dependency of feminist organizations on the state.

24 A LEAF representative defended restrictions on production to the trial judge in part on the basis that 'trial judges do not appreciate the constitutional rights of complainants; they only appreciate rights of the accused' (Canada, JLAC, 6 Mar. 1997). Justice L'Heureux-Dubé, in *Seaboyer* (1991), also expressed concerns about the ability of trial judges to make non-discriminatory decisions in the absence of legislative guidance.

6: Young People

1 In 1993, the Code was further amended to prevent the accused from personally cross-examining child witnesses; to allow support people to sit with the witnesses; and to abrogate any mandatory requirement that a jury be warned about convicting an accused on the basis of a child's evidence (Bala 1993).

2 The courts were also more inclined to allow young children to testify and to accept expert testimony about how they acted when victimized (*Marquand* 1993).

3 Justice McLachlin, however, hinted that the hearsay statement may not be necessary in a new trial because the child could testify herself and be cross-examined by the defence (*Khan* 1990: 106). Other cases have, however, allowed hearsay evidence even though the child was unable to testify or to provide a full account (Renaud 1995).

4 It also criticized judges for relying on 'the stereotypical but suspect view' that victims should make recent complaints because 'the literature suggests the reverse; victims of abuse often in fact do not disclose it, and if they do, it may not be until a substantial length of time has passed' (*W.(R.)* 1992: 145).

5 As discussed in chapter 5, note 15, a similar requirement in Bill C-49 was amended so that the accused had to take only reasonable steps, not 'all' reasonable steps, to ascertain whether a sexual-assault victim consented.

6 The new law also allowed peace bonds to be obtained prohibiting attendance at these sites if there were reasonable grounds to fear that any person would

commit a sexual offence against a child. The use of the word 'fear' was unusual in a criminal statute, but it reflected some of the concerns of the victims' rights model both in responding to fears and in attempting to prevent future victimization. These new provisions were applied after Wray Budreo, a multiple sexual offender, moved to Toronto after encountering numerous protests in other communities. There were concerns that Budreo's Charter challenges would be successful, and even calls for the Charter to be amended to provide rights for victims and prospective victims (*Globe and Mail*, 14 Apr.1995). Even though the new law did not 'not require proof of an offence, proof of a failure to meet a legal obligation, or proof of an impropriety' (*Budreo* 1996: 367), it was upheld under the Charter, except as it applied to community centres where children might not be present. Risk and reasonable fears were a basis for criminal intervention and supervision. Crime prevention was an important part of a non-punitive approach to victims' rights, but in this case was accompanied by coercion and exclusion of a notorious offender (Scheingold, Pershing, and Olson 1994).

7 There was more controversy over the requirement that sixteen- and seventeen-year-olds be dealt with under the YOA. There were concerns that a uniform age was necessary to ensure equality under the Charter. Quebec was one of the few provinces to apply the JDA to sixteen- and seventeen-year-olds. Unlike the Charter, the YOA was designed to secure Quebec's agreement. Ontario and Nova Scotia responded to the higher maximum age under the YOA by making sixteen- and seventeen-year-olds the responsibility of adult criminal courts and adult correctional ministries as opposed to family courts and child-welfare authorities (Bala 1997: 80).

8 In 1986, Parliament amended the YOA to make clear that lawyers represented young people, not their parents. The Supreme Court also decided that 'a parent is not an alternative to counsel' (*T.(E.)* 1993: 298).

9 As examined in chapter 3, the Supreme Court upheld preventive detention under the Charter, but struck down detention on public-interest grounds, which had been used to deny young offenders bail for welfare reasons, including homelessness (Doob, Marinos, and Varma 1995: 122–4).

10 The Court also demonstrated that the liberal due-process premises of the YOA had not obliterated the coercive caring promoted by the JDA by suggesting that welfare factors, such as a poor home life, could justify increased punishment (*M.(J.J.)* 1993: 495). In 1995, however, Parliament responded by providing that 'an order of custody shall not be used as a substitute for appropriate child protection, health and other social measures' (*YOA* s.24[1.1][a] as am. 1995 c.19 s.15).

11 It was first amended in 1986. In a pattern similar to that in the search-and-

seizure cases examined in chapter 2, Parliament allowed the police to obtain judicial authorization to publish the names 'of dangerous young people who are at large and a threat to community safety' (Hansard, 22 May 1986: 13533). Amendments which attempted to limit the use of open custody received little attention and the package stressed increased punishment and police powers.

12 This was an important exception. Unlike most provinces, 'Quebec maintains a youth justice system that is closely linked to the child welfare system' and diverts over half of those charged into alternative measures (Bala 1997: 9, 11). Quebec may be more resistant than the rest of Canada to American-style punitive policies. As examined in chapter 9, the Bloc Québécois also resisted attempts to repeal 'faint hope' hearings for convicted murderers.

13 Family conferences have been supported by the police in Australia and New Zealand. The National Crime Prevention Council (1996) employed tough-on-crime rhetoric to defend family conferences when it argued that they were 'tough on those who committed the offenses. They have to face their family, their relatives and their victims. They are made fully aware of the consequences of their actions and no one is pleading their case for them. The plans that the family group comes up with are not soft on the offender; they look for a penalty that really does fit the crime. They often include strong measures to make sure that the offence does not happen again.'

7: Minorities

1 In another case, the Ontario Court of Appeal held that an arrest of a black person because he met the description of a male, black, 5'8" to 5'11", with a short afro and a dark jacket did not amount to reasonable and probable cause to justify an arrest. As a result, it excluded a concealed weapon discovered on the accused (*Charley* 1993).

2 The police released 60 per cent of white people but only 30 per cent of black people facing drug charges. The courts then released 73 per cent of white people on bail, but only 56 per cent of black people (Ontario 1995: 125).

3 Anti-police stereotypes were almost another matter. The Supreme Court criticized a judge for stating that 'certainly police officers do overreact, particularly when they are dealing with non-white groups' without hearing any evidence on that issue. The majority of the Court, however, held that the judge's comments in acquitting a black youth of assaulting a police officer did not create a reasonable apprehension of bias (*S. (R.D.)*, 1997: 402).

4 *Police Services Act*, RSO 1990 c.P.15 s.113. The Police Association of Ontario warned that 'there could be a serious charter problem' with the duty to cooperate 'in the event that a charge may be imminent' (Ontario 1990: J-596).

Most minority groups were initially supportive of the SIU. Akua Benjamin of the Black Action Defence Committee argued that 'the creation of a civilian investigatory body independent of the police will not only create the factor of impartiality, it will also appear to be impartial, thus restoring the feelings of trust of police that presently do not exist in the community' (ibid: J-709).

5 The Supreme Court struck down a law that gave prosecutors many more peremptory challenges than the accused (*Bain* 1992), but Parliament simply responded by providing an equality of arms in the number of peremptory challenges. Ian Waddell of the NDP was the only member to express a concern that 'a defence or even Crown counsel could have people stand aside because they are black, Jewish, aboriginal or whatever.' He complained that the new legislation 'simply reflects the recommendations put forward 12 years ago in an environment that commonly included rulings that turned a blind eye to racism, the kind of rulings we look upon in horror today' (Hansard, 12 Jun. 1992: 11794, 11897).

6 The Reform Party initially opposed the bill as another 'legal charter based restriction on the ability of police to defend the public' (Hansard, 14 Feb. 1994: 1319). After committee hearings, however, Reform was 'satisfied that the bill responds in a reasonable manner to unfinished business of the charter argument and the ruling of the Lines case' (Hansard, 21 Apr. 1994: 3323). Even a populist party concerned about restrictions on police power could be influenced by one Charter decision of a trial judge.

7 A Bloc Québécois member from the Gaspé criticized this as a crime-control solution to a complex problem when he argued that 'using force does not allow us to get to the roots of the problem of illegal fishing' (Hansard, 14 Feb. 1994: 1295).

8 In an early example of the linkage between equality rights and the victimization of vulnerable groups, however, one representative of the disabled did express a concern about 'passive euthanasia' and attitudes which saw the disabled as '"the disposables of our society"' (Canada 1980–1: 12: 29).

9 The reader should know that I acted as counsel for the Canadian Civil Liberties Association, which applied to intervene in Latimer's case in the Supreme Court and was prepared to argue, without reference to the facts of the case, that exemptions from the mandatory sentence of life imprisonment should be possible. The issue was not argued on the appeal (*Latimer* 1997).

8: Aboriginal People

1 Family conferences, which were inspired by Maori justice and other Aboriginal practices, were examined in chapter 6.

2 This was by no means an exhaustive list. Other less-well-known innocent people wrongfully convicted include Benoit Proulx, wrongfully convicted of murder; Rejean Hinse, wrongfully convicted of robbery; Richard Norris, wrongfully convicted of sexual assault; and Norman Fox, wrongfully convicted of rape (Martin 1997).

3 In the 1987 trial of Wilson Nepoose, another Aboriginal man wrongfully convicted of murder, the prosecutor similarly failed to disclose a witness's prior inconsistent statements that could have left the jury with the impression that she was 'not credible but ... perhaps delusionary' (*Nepoose* 1992: 425).

4 Leonard Pace, the attorney general at the time of Marshall's conviction, sat as a member of the appeal panel that blamed Marshall, as opposed to the prosecutor or the lying witnesses, for the wrongful conviction. The inquiry attempted to subpoena the judges that sat on the reference to explain why Pace had been allowed to sit on an appeal despite his conflict of interest. The Supreme Court eventually decided that the principle of judicial independence protected the judges from being compelled to testify (*MacKeigan* 1989). The decision can be seen as another example of due process, here judicial independence, being pitted against victims' rights – namely, Marshall's right to a full accounting of the injustice he suffered at the hands of the Court of Appeal.

5 The reader should know that I acted as counsel for Aboriginal Legal Services of Toronto, which argued in the appeal of *Williams* to the Supreme Court that Aboriginal accused should be able to question prospective jurors about whether their deliberations would be influenced by racism.

6 Mary Ellen Turpel (1993: 177) goes on, however, to explain some important differences: 'In the Aboriginal paradigm, however, your peers are not strangers to you; their knowledge of a person is precisely why they would be relevant to restoring harmony after an anti-social act or breach of personal responsibility.'

7 As reviewed in chapter 7, police shootings of unarmed black men in Toronto and Montreal caused great controversy and resulted in many unsuccessful prosecutions. Manitoba's Aboriginal Justice Inquiry (Manitoba, 1991b: 92) followed the Ontario approach and recommended a special unit to investigate deaths and serious personal injury caused by police officers. The limits of this crime-control approach were discussed in chapter 7. In the Harper case, for example, even the inquiry, which unlike a criminal trial was not bound by a reasonable-doubt standard of liability, could not conclude what actually happened in the struggle. In part, this was because the police officers involved had in their 'effort to protect Cross and shift blame to Harper' developed an '"official version" of what happened' (ibid: 39).

8 In my view, Aboriginal overrepresentation should not be dismissed as a problem by reference to the youthfulness or high crime rates in Aboriginal communities. These factors themselves are related to larger issues such as premature mortality, under-servicing, and lack of economic and cultural opportunities.

9 Jim Sinclair of the Métis and Non Status Indians of Saskatchewan placed Aboriginal overrepresentation in prison in the following context: 'Ninety per cent of us are unemployed. Eighty per cent of us are on welfare. Sixty per cent of us are affected by alcohol and those sixty per cent affect the other people who are sober and trying to make a go of it. We have family problems. We have suicides, the highest suicide rate probably right now in the world' (Canada 1980–1: 22: 131, 29: 115).

10 Pierrette Venne argued: 'Why should Aboriginals, who make up less than 2 per cent of Canada's total population, benefit from a legal system different from that which applies to all Canadians? Why should an Aboriginal convicted of murder, rape, assault or of uttering threats not be liable to imprisonment like any other citizen of this country? Can we replace all this with a parallel justice, an ethnic justice, a cultural justice? Where would it stop? Where does this horror come from?' She went on to argue that Aboriginal people 'who claim full Canadian citizenship, who take full advantage of the generosity of our welfare state and who obtain tax exemptions and benefits' not be treated differently from other people when they commit crimes (Hansard, 20 Sep. 1994: 5876).

11 A judge who defended the use of a sentencing circle in an armed robbery case readily conceded that its sentence (which included eighteen months' imprisonment) was inappropriate in 'a retributively flavoured or ordinary sense' (*Morin* 1995: 166), but defended it as an appropriate means to achieve restorative justice. Restorative justice and rehabilitation, however, are only some of the relevant purposes and principles of sentencing.

12 Some courts attempted to respond to this concern by requiring that victims fully consent 'without coercion or pressure' and not be 'subject to battered spouse syndrome' (*Joseyounen* 1995: 439). Consent in the context of inequality was difficult to determine and very much contested.

13 In the context of domestic violence and sexual abuse, Aboriginal justice may have to contemplate the possibility that some families and some relationships should not be brought back together (Canada 1996b: 272).

9: Crime Victims

1 For unreported sexual assaults, 67 per cent of respondents said it was a personal matter; 65 per cent of respondents mentioned that they dealt with it

another way; 50 per cent said they did not want to get involved with the police; 30 per cent said that it was too minor; 29 per cent cited fear of revenge; and 28 per cent stated that police could not do anything. For unreported assaults, 64 per cent dealt with it another way; 49 per cent considered it a personal matter; 48 per cent considered it too minor; 27 per cent said the police could not do anything; and 19 per cent feared revenge. For unreported vandalism, 60 per cent of victims considered the crime too minor; 47 per cent said the police could not do anything; and 45 per cent dealt with it another way (Gartner and Doob 1994: 14).

2 In October 1994, Victims of Violence and the Canadian Police Association sponsored a widely reported news conference to argue that the Court's due-process decisions in cases such as *Borden* (1994), *Prosper* (1994; see chapter 2), and *Daviault* (1994; see chapter 5) were part of 'a pattern of offenders' rights winning over the rights of the victim and the protection of the public' (*Victoria Times Colonist*, 14 Oct. 1994). Around the same time, other stories emerged that suggested that the Supreme Court had lost touch with reality (*Globe and Mail*, 8 Oct. 1994).

3 Andre Normandeau (1983) also demonstrated this potential by proposing a 'charter for crime victims' which included not only rights to be informed of criminal justice processing and to receive reparation from the offender, but also rights to crime prevention, social services, and alternatives to the criminal justice system that would reconcile offenders and victims.

4 Governments were careful not to guarantee substantive standards so that victims only had the right to be informed of health and social services 'so that they might continue to receive the necessary medical, psychological and social assistance through existing programs and services' (Canada 1988b: s.9).

5 Following one of LEAF's (1996: 35) arguments, the Supreme Court upheld publication bans of complainants' names in sexual-assault trials. It recognized that sexual assault was 'one of the most unreported' crimes and held that the publication ban, which was mandatory at the complainant's request, was a justified restriction on freedom of expression in order to encourage victims to report sexual assaults to the police (*Canadian Newspapers* 1989: 31). This was an early example of a new political case pitting due process against victims's rights, but like those examined in chapter 6, it did not produce sustained controversy because it recognized the interests of victims.

6 The admissibility of victim-impact statements in capital cases has been a major site in the United States of struggles between due process and victims' rights. In *Booth* (1987), the U.S. Supreme Court held that the introduction of a victim-impact statement in a capital case constituted cruel and unusual punishment because victim suffering was not related to the blameworthiness of the

offender. The Court, however, soon reversed itself and allowed comments about the impact on a three-year-old boy of the murder of his mother and younger sister on the basis that the suffering of victims was foreseeable and relevant to the accused's blameworthiness (*Payne* 1991).

7 Quebec may have been more resistant to the Americanization of the Canadian victims' movement, and more willing to follow European examples of integrating victims into the prosecution process. See also chapter 6, note 12, and note 9, below.

8 They also included restrictions on victim-impact statements, which were then repealed in S.C. 1997 c.18.

9 The new sentencing bill continued to single out some groups of victims and specified that evidence that an offender abused his spouse or child or was motivated by hate or bias on a prohibited ground of discrimination was an aggravating factor in sentencing (Criminal Code, s.718.2; see chapters 5 and 7). Not everyone was impressed with the degree to which victims had been included. Pierrette Venne of the Bloc Québécois argued that the government's concerns about victims 'are expressed so timidly that we cannot take them seriously.' She argued for a more European approach, where the victim would have rights as a party to a criminal trial and be able to appeal the verdict and sentence. 'The victim should be what drives the criminal justice system and gives society the opportunity to impose just sentences on criminals in order to prevent them and their kind from making more victims' (Hansard, 20 Sep. 1994: 5876–7).

Table of Cases

References

Abella, Irving, and Harold Troper. 1991. *None Is Too Many: Canada and the Jews of Europe, 1933–1948*, 3d ed. Toronto: Lester

Aboriginal Legal Services of Toronto (ALST). 1991. 'Elders and Traditional Leaders Gathering on Birch Island – Discussion on the Community Council (Aug. 27–30, 1991.'. Toronto: ALST

Acorn, Annalise. 1991. '*R. v. Seaboyer*. Pornographic Imagination and the Springs of Relevance.' *Constitutional Forum* 2: 25

Alberta. 1991. Task Force on the Criminal Justice System and Its Impact on the Indian and Metis People of Alberta. *Justice on Trial*. Edmonton: Task Force on the Criminal Justice System and Its Impact on the Indian and Metis People of Alberta

Arcaro, Gino. 1993. *Criminal Investigations and the Formulation of Reasonable Grounds*. Toronto: Emond Montgomery

Arnella, Peter. 1983. 'Rethinking the Functions of Criminal Procedure: The Warren and Burger Courts' Competing Ideologies.' *Georgetown Law Journal* 72: 185

Ashworth, Andrew. 1994. *The Criminal Process*. Oxford: Clarendon Press

Baar, Carl. 1993. 'Criminal Court Delay and the Charter: The Use and Misuse of Social Facts in Judicial Policy Making.' *The Canadian Bar Review* 72: 305

Bakan, Joel. 1997. *Just Words: Constitutional Rights and Social Wrongs*. Toronto: University of Toronto Press

Baker, Liva. 1983. *Miranda: Crime, Law and Politics*. New York: Atheneum

Bala, Nicholas. 1993. 'Criminal Code Amendments to Increase Protection to Children and Women.' *Criminal Reports* (4th) 21: 365

– 1994. 'The 1995 *Young Offenders Act* Amendments: Compromise or Confusion.' *Ottawa Law Review* 26: 643

– 1997. *Young Offenders Law*. Concord: Irwin Law

Bala, Nicholas, and Mary-Anne Kirvan. 1991. 'The Statute: Its Principles And Provisions and Their Interpretation by the Courts.' In A. Leschied, P. Jaffe, and W. Willis, eds., *The Young Offenders Act: A Revolution in Canadian Juvenile Justice.* Toronto: University of Toronto Press

Bala, Nicholas, and Hilary McCormack. 1994. 'Accommodating the Criminal Process to Child Witnesses: *L. (D.O.)* and *Levogiannis.*' *Criminal Reports* (4th) 25: 341

Barnett, Cunliffe. 1989. 'The Glorious Decision of the S.C.C. in *R* v. *Vaillancourt.*' *Provincial Judges' Journal* 4: 14

Baum, Daniel. 1979. *Discount Justice: The Canadian Criminal Justice System.* Toronto: Burns and MacEachern

Bayefsky, Anne. 1989. *Canada's Constitution Act, 1982 and Amendments: A Documentary History.* Toronto: McGraw-Hill Ryerson

Bayley, David, and Clifford Shearing. 1996. 'The Future of Policing.' *Law and Society Review* 30: 585

Beck, Ulrich. 1992. *Risk Society: Towards a New Modernity.* London: Sage

Bianchi, Herman. 1994. *Justice as Sanctuary: Toward a New System of Crime Control.* Bloomington: Indiana University Press

Bienvenue, Rita, and A.H. Latif. 1974. 'Arrests, Dispositions, and Recidivism: A Comparison of Indians and Whites.' *Canadian Journal of Criminology* 16: 105

Blackman, Julie. 1986. 'Potential Uses for Expert Testimony: Ideas Toward the Representation of Battered Women Who Kill.' *Women's Rights Law Reporter* 9: 227

Bogart, W.A. 1994. *Courts and Country: The Limits of Litigation and the Social and Political Life of Canada.* Toronto: Oxford University Press.

Boisvert, Anne-Marie. 1996. 'Exploitation sexuelle, enseignants et présomption d'innocence.' *Criminal Reports* (4th) 48: 57

Borovoy, Alan. 1988. *When Freedoms Collide.* Toronto: Lester

Bottoms, A., and J. McClean. 1976. *Defendants in the Criminal Process.* London: Routledge

Boyle, Christine. 1981. 'Section 142 of the Criminal Code: A Trojan Horse?' *Criminal Law Quarterly* 23: 253

– 1994. 'The Role Of Equality in Criminal Law.' *Saskatchewan Law Review* 54: 203

Boyle, Christine, and Sheila Noonan. 1987. 'Gender Neutrality, Prostitution, and Pornography.' In Laurie Bell, ed., *Good Girls/Bad Girls.* Toronto: The Women's Press

Boyle, Christine, Marie Andrée Betrand, Celine Lacerte-Lamontagne, and Rebecca Shamai. 1985. *A Feminist Review of Criminal Law.* Ottawa: Minister of Supply and Services

Bradley, Craig. 1993. *The Failure of the Criminal Procedure Revolution.* Philadelphia: University of Pennsylvania Press

Braithwaite, John. 1989. *Crime, Shame and Reintegration*. Cambridge: Cambridge University Press.

– 1995. 'Inequality and Republican Criminology.' In John Hagan and Ruth Peterson, eds., *Crime and Inequality*. Stanford: Stanford University Press

– 1997. 'Restorative Justice: Assessing an Immodest Theory and a Pessimistic Theory.' University of Toronto, Faculty of Law Intensive Course Materials

Braithwaite, John, and Kathleen Daly. 1995. 'Masculinity, Violence and Communication Control.' In Mariana Valverde, Linda MacLeod, and Kirsten Johnson, eds. *Wife Assault and the Canadian Justice System*. Toronto: Centre for Criminology

Braithwaite, John, and Stephen Mugford. 1994. 'Conditions of Successful Reintegration Ceremonies: Dealing with Juvenile Offenders.' *British Journal of Criminology* 34: 139

Braithwaite, John, and Philip Pettit. 1990. *Not Just Deserts: A Republican Theory of Criminal Justice*. Oxford: Clarendon Press

Brillon, Yves. 1987. *Victimization and Fear of Crime among the Elderly*. Toronto: Butterworths

Brock, Kathy. 1992. 'Polishing the Halls of Justice: Sections 24(2) and 8 of the *Charter of Rights*.' *National Journal of Constitutional Law* 2: 266

Brodeur, Jean-Paul. 1991. *Justice for the Cree: Policing and Alternative Dispute Resolution*. Quebec: Grand Council of the Crees (of Quebec)

Brodie, Janine, Shelley Gavigan, and Jane Jenson. 1992. *The Politics of Abortion*. Toronto: Oxford University Press

Brogden, Michael, and Clifford Shearing. 1993. *Policing for a New South Africa*. London: Routledge

Bryant, A., M. Gold, H. Stevenson, and D Northrup. 1990. 'Public Attitudes toward the Exclusion of Evidence: Section 24(2) of the Canadian Charter of Rights and Freedoms.' *Canadian Bar Review* 69: 1

Burns, Peter. 1992. *Criminal Injuries Compensation*, 2d ed. Toronto: Butterworths

Burris, Carole Anne, and Peter Jaffe. 1983. 'Wife Abuse as a Crime: The Impact of Police Laying Charges.' *Canadian Journal of Criminology* 25: 309

Busby, Karen. 1994. 'LEAF and Pornography: Litigating on Equality and Sexual Representation.' *Canadian Journal of Law and Society* 9: 165

– 1996. *Discriminatory Uses of Personal Records in Sexual Violence Cases: Notes for Sexual Assault Counsellors on the Supreme Court of Canada's Decisions in R. v. O'Connor and L.L.A. v. A.B.* Ottawa: National Association of Women and the Law

Cairns, Alan. 1991. *Disruptions: Constitutional Struggles from the Charter to Meech Lake*. Toronto: McClelland & Stewart

– 1992. *Charter versus Federalism: The Dilemmas of Constitutional Reform*. Montreal: McGill-Queen"s University Press

– 1995. *Reconfigurations: Canadian Citizenship and Constitutional Change*. Toronto: McClelland & Stewart

Cairns-Way, Rosemary. 1992. 'The Charter, The Supreme Court and the Invisible Politics of Fault.' *Windsor Yearbook of Access to Justice* 12: 128

– 1994. 'The Criminalization of Stalking: An Exercise in Media Manipulation and Political Opportunism.' *McGill Law Journal* 39: 379

Calgary Herald. 1983, 5 Jan. 'New Sexual Assault Law Takes Effect.' A.16

– 1988, 9 Dec. 'Drivers Blood Sample Violation of Charter.' A-10

– 1990, 4 May. 'Battered Ruling Gets Hooray.' A.1

– 1990, 23 Nov. 'Police Handcuffed by Supreme Court.' A.3

– 1991, 8 Nov. 'Lawyer Lands Second Trial.' B.1

– 1992, 22 May. 'Supreme Court's Ruling Could Jail Man.' A.3

– 1992, 28 Aug. 'Zundel Cleared by Highest Court.' A.3

Cameron, Jamie. 1996. 'Tradition and Change under the Charter: The Adversary System, Third Party Interests and the Legitimacy of Criminal Justice in Canada.' In Jamie Cameron, ed., *The Charter's Impact on the Criminal Justice System*. Toronto: Carswell

Campbell, Robert, and Leslie Pal. 1989. *The Real Worlds of Canadian Politics: Cases in Process and Policy*. Peterborough, ON: Broadview

– 1991. *The Real Worlds of Canadian Politics: Cases in Process and Policy*, 2d ed. Peterborough, ON: Broadview

Canada. 1969. *Towards Unity: Criminal Justice and Corrections: Report*. Ottawa: Ministry of the Solicitor General.

– 1970. Royal Commission on the Status of Women in Canada. *Report of the Royal Commission on the Status of Women*. Ottawa: Information Canada

– 1972. Commission of Inquiry into the Non-Medical Use of Drugs. *Cannabis: A Report of the Commission of Inquiry into the Non-Medical Use of Drugs*. Ottawa: Information Canada

– 1979–97. JLAC. Proceedings of the Justice and Legal Affairs Committee

– 1980–1. *Special Joint Committee on the Constitution of Canada*. Ottawa: Queen's Printer

– 1981. Commission of Inquiry Concerning Certain Activities of the Royal Canadian Mounted Police. *Freedom and Security Under the Law (Second Report – Volume 2)*. Ottawa: Supply and Services

– 1982a. *The Constitution and You*. Ottawa: Supply and Services

– 1982b. Uniform Law Conference of Canada. *Report of the Federal/Provincial Task Force on the Uniform Rules of Evidence*. Toronto: Carswell

– 1982c. *Violence against Women: Report of the House Standing Committee on Health and Welfare*. Ottawa: Supply and Services

- 1983. Federal–Provincial Task Force on Justice for Victims of Crime. *Justice for Victims of Crime: Report.* Ottawa: Supply and Services
- 1984a. Commission on Equality in Employment. *Report of the Commission on Equality in Employment.* Ottawa: Supply and Services
- 1984b. Committee on Sexual Offences against Children and Youths. *Sexual Offences against Children.* Ottawa: Supply and Services
- 1984c. *Equality Now: Report of a Special Parliamentary Committee on Visible Minorities.* Ottawa: Supply and Services
- 1985. Special Committee on Pornography and Prostitution. *Report of the Special Committee on Pornography and Prostitution.* Ottawa: Supply and Services
- 1986. Commission of Inquiry on War Criminals. *Commission of Inquiry on War Criminals: Report.* Ottawa: Minister of Supply and Services
- 1987. The Canadian Sentencing Commission. *Sentencing Reform: A Canadian Approach.* Ottawa: Minister of Supply and Services
- 1988a. Standing Committee on Justice and Solicitor General. *Taking Responsibility.* Ottawa: Queen's Printer
- 1988b. Statement of Basic Principles of Justice for Crime Victims (Federal/ Provincial Secretariat)
- 1989. Department of Justice Research Section. *Street Prostitution: Assessing the Impact of the Law: Synthesis Report.* Ottawa: Minister of Supply and Services
- 1990. *Creating Choices: The Report of the Task Force on Federally Sentenced Women.* Ottawa: Correctional Service Canada
- 1991. *The War against Women: Report of the Standing Committee on Health and Welfare, Social Affairs, Seniors and the Status of Women.* Ottawa: Queen's Printer
- 1993a. *Crime Prevention in Canada: Towards a National Strategy: Report of the Standing Committee on Justice and the Solicitor General.* Ottawa: Supply and Services
- 1993b. *Final Report of the Canadian Panel on Violence against Women.* Ottawa: Minister of Supply and Services
- 1993c, Mar. House of Commons. *Legislative Committee on Bill C-109, Criminal Code, Crown Liability and Proceedings and Radiocommunication Act,* 3rd Session, 34th Parliament, Issues 1–5
- 1994. Solicitor General. *Annual Report on the Use of Electronic Surveillance.* Ottawa: Supply and Services
- 1996a. *Commission of Inquiry Into Certain Events at the Kingston Prison for Women.* Ottawa: Public Works and Government Services Canada
- 1996b. Royal Commission on Aboriginal Peoples (RCAP). *Bridging the Cultural Divide: A Report on Aboriginal People and Criminal Justice in Canada.* Ottawa: Supply and Services
- 1997. Justice and Legal Affairs Committee (JLAC). *Thirteenth Report,* Issue no. 12

Canadian Centre for Criminal Justice Statistics (CCCJS). 1994a. *Juristat* 14: 6. Ottawa: Minister of Industry (Statistics Canada)
– 1994b. *Juristat* 14: 7. Ottawa: Minister of Industry (Statistics Canada)
– 1994c. *Juristat* 14: 12. Ottawa: Minister of Industry (Statistics Canada)
– 1995. *Juristat* 15: 10. Ottawa: Minister of Industry (Statistics Canada)
– 1996a. *Adult Correctional Services in Canada 1995–96.* Ottawa: Minister of Industry (Statistics Canada)
– 1996b. *Juristat 16: 9.* Ottawa: Minister of Industry (Statistics Canada)
– 1997. *Juristat* 17: 2. Ottawa: Minister of Industry (Statistics Canada)
Carlen, P. 1976. *Magistrates' Justice.* London: Martin Robinson
Catton, Katherine. 1976. 'Models of Procedure and the Juvenile Courts.' *Criminal Law Quarterly* 18: 181
Chan, J., and Richard Ericson. 1981. *Decarceration and the Economy of Penal Reform.* Toronto: Centre of Criminology, University of Toronto
Chapman, Susan, and John McInnes. 1996. 'The Role of the Attorney-General in Constitutional Litigation: Re-Defining the Contours of Public Interest in a *Charter* Era.' In Jamie Cameron, ed., *The Charter's Impact on the Criminal Justice System.* Toronto: Carswell.
Christie, Nils. 1977. 'Conflict as Property.' *British Journal of Criminology* 17: 1
– 1986. 'The Ideal Victim.' In Ezzat Fattah, *From Crime Policy to Victim Policy.* London: Macmillan
Clark, Lorenne M.G. 1985. 'Boys Will Be Boys: Beyond the Badgley Report.' *Canadian Journal of Women and the Law* 2: 135
Clark, Lorenne M.G., and Debra J. Lewis. 1977. *Rape: The Price of Coercive Sexuality.* Toronto: Women's Educational Press
Coalition of Provincial Organizations of the Handicapped. 1993. *Factum of the Intervenor* in *Rodriguez v. British Columbia (Attorney General)* before the Supreme Court of Canada (File 23476)
Code, Michael. 1992. *Trial within a Reasonable Time.* Toronto: Carswell
Cohen, Leah, and Connie Backhouse. 1980. 'Desexualizing Rape: Dissenting View on the Proposed Amendments.' *Canadian Journal of Women's Studies,* 99
Cohen, Stanley. 1977. *Due Process of Law.* Toronto: Carswell
– 1985. *Visions of Social Control.* London: Routledge
– 1996. 'Law Reform, the *Charter* and the Future of Criminal Law.' In Jamie Cameron, ed., *The Charter's Impact on the Criminal Justice System.* Toronto: Carswell.
Corrado, Raymond R. 1993. 'Introduction.' In Joe Hudson, Joseph P. Hornick, and Barbara A. Burrows, eds., *Justice and the Young Offender in Canada.* Toronto: Thompson Educational

Corrado, Raymond R., and Alan Markwart. 1988. 'The Prices of Rights and Responsibilities: An Examination of the Impacts of the *Young Offenders Act* in British Columbia.' *Canadian Journal of Family Law* 7: 93
– 1992. 'The Evolution and Implementation of a New Era of Juvenile Justice in Canada.' In Raymond R. Corrado, Nicholas Bala, Rick Linden, and Marc Le Blanc, eds., *Juvenile Justice in Canada: A Theoretical and Analytical Assessment.* Toronto: Butterworths
Cossman, Brenda, Shannon Bell, Lise Gotell, and Becki Ross. 1997. *Bad Attitude/s on Trial: Pornography, Feminism, and the Butler Decision.* Toronto: University of Toronto Press
Cotler, Irwin. 1995. 'War Crimes and the Finta Case.' *Supreme Court Law Review* 6: 577
Cotter, Brent. 1994. 'The Provincial Perspective on the Split in Jurisdiction.' In Richard Gosse, James Youngblood Henderson, and Roger Carter, eds., *Continuing Poundmaker and Riel's Quest.* Saskatoon: Purich
Council of Canadians with Disabilities. 1995. *Factum of the Intervenors Council of Canadians with Disabilities and Saskatchewan Voice of the Handicapped* in *Her Majesty The Queen v. Robert William Latimer* before the Court of Appeal for Saskatchewan (C.A. No. 6515)
Crawford, Maria, and Rosemary Gartner. 1992. *Woman Killing: Intimate Femicide in Ontario 1974–1990.* Toronto: Women We Honour Action Committee
Damaska, Mirjan. 1973. 'Evidentiary Barriers to Conviction and Two Models of Criminal Procedure: A Comparative Study.' *University of Pennsylvania Law Review* 121: 507
– 1986. *The Faces of Justice and State Authority: A Comparative Approach to the Legal Process.* New Haven: Yale University Press
Dauvergne, Catherine. 1994. 'A Reassessment of the Effects of a Constitutional Charter of Rights and Freedoms on the Discourse of Sexual Violence in Canada.' *International Journal of the Sociology of Law* 22: 291
DAWN [Disabled Women's Network]. 1987. 'Violence against Women with Disabilities – Fact Sheet.' Reprinted in Janet Mosher, *Wife Assault – Assessing the Interventions of Law and Social Work.* Toronto: Faculty of Law, University of Toronto
Delisle, R.J. 1987. '*Collins:* An Unjustified Distinction.' *Criminal Reports* (3d) 56: 216
– 1993. 'Judicial Creation of Police Powers.' *Criminal Reports* (3d) 20: 29
Depew, Robert. 1992. 'Policing Native Communities: Some Principles and Issues in Organizational Theory.' *Canadian Journal of Criminology* 34: 461
Dershowitz, Alan. 1994. *The Abuse Excuse: And Other Cop-outs, Sob Stories and Evasions of Responsibility.* Boston: Little, Brown
Devlin, Patrick. 1959. *The Enforcement of Morals.* London: Oxford University Press
Devonshire, Reginald A. 1994. 'The Effects of the Supreme Court Charter-Based

Decisions on Policing: More Beneficial Than Detrimental?' *Criminal Reports* (4th) 31: 82

Dicey, Albert. 1959. *Introduction to the Study of the Law of the Constitution,* 10th ed. New York: St Martin's

Dickin McGinnis, Janice. 1994. 'Whores and Worthies: Feminism and Prostitution.' *Canadian Journal of Law and Society* 9: 105

Dittenhoffer, T., and Richard Ericson. 1983. 'The Victim–Offender Reconciliation Program: A Message to Correctional Reformers.' *University of Toronto Law Journal* 33: 315

Doherty, David. 1984. 'Sparing the Complainant "Spoils" The Trial.' *Criminal Reports* (3d) 40: 55

Doob, Anthony. 1995. 'Understanding Attacks on Statistics Canada's Violence Against Women Survey.' In Mariana Valverde, Linda MacLeod, and Kirsten Johnson, eds., *Wife Assault and the Canadian Justice System.* Toronto: Centre for Criminology, University of Toronto

– 1988. 'Public Attitudes towards Sentencing in Canada.' In N. Walker and M. Hough, eds., *Public Attitudes to Sentencing.* Aldershot: Gower

Doob, Anthony, Voula Marinos, and Kimberly Varma. 1995. *Youth Crime and the Youth Justice System in Canada: A Research Perspective.* Toronto: Centre of Criminology, University of Toronto

Doob, Anthony, and Julian Roberts. 1983. *Sentencing: An Analysis of the Public's View of Sentencing. A Report to the Department of Justice, Canada.* Ottawa: Department of Justice

Downs, Donald. 1996. *More Than Victims: Battered Women, the Syndrome Society and the Law* Chicago: University of Chicago Press

Drassinower, Martha, and Don Stuart. 1995. 'Nine Months of Judicial Application of the *Daviault* Defence.' *Criminal Reports* (4th) 39: 280

Dyzenhaus, David. 1991 'Obscenity and the Charter.' *Criminal Reports* 1: 367

Edelman, Murray. 1964. *The Symbolic Uses of Politics.* Chicago: University of Illinois Press

– 1971. *Politics as Symbolic Action: Mass Arousal and Quiescence.* New York: Academic

Elias, Robert. 1986. *The Politics of Victimization: Victims, Victimization, and Human Rights.* New York: Oxford University Press

– 1993. *Victims Still: The Political Manipulation of Crime Victims.* Newbury Park, CA: Sage

Elman, Bruce. 1987. '*Collins* v. *The Queen*: Further Jurisprudence on Section 24(2) of the Charter.' *Alberta Law Review* 25: 477

Erez, E. 1990. 'Victim Participation in Sentencing: Rhetoric and Reality.' *Journal of Criminal Justice* 18: 19

Erez, E. et al. 1997. 'Victim Harm Impact Statements and Victim Satisfaction with Justice.' *International Review of Victimology* 5: 37

Ericson, Richard. 1981. *Making Crime.* Toronto: Butterworths.

– 1982. *Reproducing Order: A Study of Police Patrol Work.* Toronto: University of Toronto Press

– 1983. *The Constitution of Legal Inequality.* Ottawa: Carleton University Press

– 1987. 'The State and Criminal Justice Reform.' In R.S. Ratner and John McMullan, eds., *State Control: Criminal Justice Politics in Canada.* Vancouver: University of British Columbia Press

– 1994. 'The Royal Commission on Criminal Justice System Surveillance.' In Mike McConville and Lee Bridges, eds., *Criminal Justice in Crisis.* Aldershot, U.K.: Edward Elgar

Ericson, Richard, and Patricia Baranek. 1982. *The Ordering of Justice: A Study of Accused Persons as Dependants in the Criminal Process.* Toronto: University of Toronto Press

– 1985. 'Criminal Law Reform and Two Realities of the Criminal Process.' In Anthony Doob and Edward Greenspan, eds., *Perspectives in Criminal Law.* Aurora: Canada Law Book

Ericson, Richard, and Kevin Haggerty. 1997. *Policing the Risk Society.* Toronto: University of Toronto Press

Evans, John L., and Gerald J. Leger. 1979. 'Canadian Victimization Surveys: A Discussion Paper.' *Canadian Journal of Criminology* 21: 166

Fattah, Ezzat, ed. 1989. *The Plight of Crime Victims in Modern Society.* London: Macmillan

– 1993. *Understanding Criminal Victimization.* Scarborough, ON: Prentice Hall

Feeley, Malcolm. 1973. 'Two Models of the Criminal Justice System: An Organizational Perspective.' *Law and Society Review* 7: 409

– 1979. *The Process Is the Punishment: Handling Cases in a Lower Criminal Court.* New York: Russell Sage Foundation

– 1984. *Court Reform on Trial.* New York: Basic Books

Feeley, Malcolm, and Simon John. 1992. 'The New Penology.' *British Journal of Criminology* 30: 449

Fekete, John. 1994. *Moral Panic: Biopolitics Rising,* 2d ed. Montreal: Davies

Feldthusen, Bruce. 1993. 'The Civil Action for Sexual Battery: Therapeutic Jurisprudence?' *Ottawa Law Review* 25: 203

– 1996. 'Access to the Private Therapeutic Records of Sexual Assault Complainants.' *Canadian Bar Review* 75: 537

Fenwick, Helen. 1997. 'Procedural Rights of Victims of Crime: Public or Private Ordering of the Criminal Justice Process.' *Modern Law Review* 60: 317

Fischer, Benedikt, et al. 1996. 'The New Canadian Drug Law: One Step Forward, Two Steps Backward.' *International Journal of Drug Policy* 7: 172

– 1997. 'The Battle for a New Canadian Drug Law: A Legal Basis for Harm Reduction or a New Rhetoric for Prohibition? A Chronology.' In Patricia G. Erickson, Diane M. Riley, Yuet W. Cheung, and Pat A. O'Hare, eds., *Harm Reduction: A New Direction for Drug Policies and Programs.* Toronto: University of Toronto Press

Fletcher, George. 1995. *With Justice for Some: Victims' Rights in Criminal Trials.* Reading, MA: Addison-Wellesley

Foucault, Michel. 1991. 'Politics and the Study of Discourse.' In Graham Burchell, ed., *The Foucault Effect: Studies in Governmentality: With Two Lectures and an Interview with Michel Foucault.* Chicago: University of Chicago Press

Fox, Richard G., and Maureen J. Spencer. 1972. 'The Young Offenders Bill: Destigmatizing Juvenile Delinquency?' *Criminal Law Quarterly* 14: 172

Friedland, Martin. 1965. *Detention before Trial: A Study of Criminal Cases Tried in the Toronto Magistrate's Courts.* Toronto: University of Toronto Press

– 1968. 'The Magistrates' Courts.' *Criminal Law Quarterly* 11: 52

Friedland, Martin, and Kent Roach. 1997a. 'Borderline Justice: The Use of Juries in Ontario and New York.' *Israeli Law Journal* 31: 120

– 1997b. *Cases and Materials on Criminal Law and Procedure,* 8th ed Toronto: Emond Montgomery

Friedland, Martin, Michael Trebilcock, and Kent Roach. 1990. *Regulating Traffic Safety.* Toronto: University of Toronto Press

Fudge, Judy. 1989. 'The Effects of Entrenching a Bill of Rights upon Political Discourse: Feminist Demands and Sexual Violence in Canada.' *International Journal of the Sociology of Law* 17: 445

Galaway, Burt, and Joe Hudson, eds. 1990. *Criminal Justice, Restitution and Reconciliation.* Monsey, NY: Criminal Justice Press

Galligan, Patrick. 1963. 'Advising an Arrested Client.' In Law Society of Upper Canada, *Special Lectures.* Toronto: De Boo

– 1996. *Report of the Honourable Patrick T. Galligan to Inquire Into and Report On Certain Matters Relating to Two Decisions Respecting Karla Homolka Made By Officials in the Ministry of the Attorney General.* Toronto: Queen's Printer

Garland, David. 1996 'The Limits of the Sovereign State.' *British Journal of Criminology* 36: 445

Gartner, Rosemary, and Anthony Doob. 1994. 'Trends in Criminal Victimization: 1988–1993.' *Juristat* 14 (13). Ottawa: Statistics Canada.

Gellman, S. 1991. 'Sticks and Stones Can Put You in Jail, But Can Words Increase Your Sentence? Constitutional and Policy Dilemmas of Ethnic Intimidation Laws.' *U.C.L.A. Law Review* 39: 333

Gelowitz, Mark. 1988. 'DNA Fingerprinting: What's Bred in the Blood.' In *Criminal Reports* (3d) 65: 122

Gilligan, Carol. 1982. *In a Different Voice*. Cambridge, MA: Harvard University Press.

Gilmour, Joan. 1996. 'Counselling Records: Disclosure in Sexual Assault Cases.' In Jamie Cameron, ed., *The Charter's Impact on the Criminal Justice System*. Toronto: Carswell

Glasbeek, Harry. 1993. *Police Shootings of Black People in Ontario*. Toronto: Commission on Systemic Racism in the Ontario Criminal Justice System

Glendon, Mary Ann. 1989. *A Beau Mentir Qui Vient Du Loin: The 1988 Canadian Abortion Decision in Comparative Perspective*. Toronto: University of Toronto Faculty of Law Legal Theory Workshop Series

– 1991. *Rights Talk: The Impoverishment of Political Discourse*. New York: Free Press

Globe and Mail. 1981, 11 Mar. 'The Pitfalls of Americanizing the Canadian Criminal Law.' A7

– 1981, 31 Oct. 'The Right to Get You.' A5

– 1981, 20 Nov. 'Lawyers Sceptical as Kaplan Supports More RCMP Power.' 1

– 1983, 12 Jul. 'RCMP Writs to End, Kaplan Says.' A11

– 1984, 18 Sep. 'Top Court Strikes Down Provisions for Searches Under Combines Act.' A1

– 1984, 4 Oct. 'Sparing Children from Sex Abuse.' L2

– 1985, 25 May. 'Breathalyzer Ruling Handicaps Police, Chief Says.' A1

– 1985, 1 Aug. 'Split Supreme Court Upholds Police Powers to Spot Check.' 1

– 1986, 1 Mar. 'Court Strikes Down Law Making Accused Prove Innocence.' A1

– 1986, 25 Apr. 'Murder Confession Rejected as Woman Lacked Lawyer.' A1

– 1987, 26 Jun. 'Right to Counsel Voids Confession.' A9

– 1990, 26 Jan. '"New Restriction Added to Wiretap Rules.' A4

– 1990, 3 Feb. 'Police Must Tell Accused of Right to Legal Aid.' A8

– 1990, 4 May. 'Court Widens Use of Self-Defence Plea in Battering Cases.' A1

– 1990, 1 Jun. 'Spot Checks of Motorists Legal, Court Rules.' A14

– 1990, 23 Nov. 'Top Court Urges Curb on Tactics of Police – Says Law Needed on Surveillance.' A4

– 1990, 27 Dec. 'Report Sought in Manitoba Conviction.' A9

– 1991, 20 Feb. 'Courts Continue to Throw Out Cases.' A5

– 1991, 27 Mar. '32,000 Charges Stayed Since Askov Ruling.' A10

– 1991, 1 Jun. 'Justice Swift This Time Around – Askov Pleads Guilty to Drug Charges Laid in November.' A7

– 1991, 11 Jul. 'Courts Catching Up on Backlog of Cases Created by Askov Decision.'

– 1991, 17 Jul. 'Hampton Calls for Review of Ruling in Askov Case.' A5

- 1991, 22 Aug. 'Lamer Comments Called Lame.' A5
- 1991, 24 Aug. '"Double Whammy" Predicted for Rape Victims.' A4
- 1991, 13 Dec. 'Political Battle Looms Over Sex-Assault Bill.' A6
- 1991, 26 Jul. 'Ruling Removes "Life Line" Police Say.' A1
- 1991, 25 Oct. 'Court Upholds Ad Law.' B4
- 1991, 24 Aug. 'Rape Shield Struck Down.' A1
- 1992, 28 Feb. 'Ruling Paves Way for Child-Pornography Bill, Minister Says.' A1
- 1992, 29 Feb. 'Legal Victory Bittersweet.'
- 1992, 9 Mar. 'Zundel Won't Be Charged, Police Say.' A14
- 1992, 16 Jun. 'Kiddie Porn Bill Gets Unanimous OK.'
- 1992, 29 Aug. 'Not Open Season for Zundel, Jewish Congress Says.' A9
- 1992, 28 Nov. 'Panel Says Furor Altered Paedophile.' A1
- 1992, 8 Dec. 'Judge Abruptly Ends Bishop's Sex Trial.' A1
- 1992, 19 Dec. 'Activists Hail Molester's Detention.' A10
- 1993, 23 Jul. 'Dealing with Young Criminals.' A18
- 1993, 30 Jul. 'Equality Called Key to Ending Violence.' A1
- 1993, 29 Sep. 'Strip-Search Investigation Criticized.' A16
- 1993, 1 Oct. 'Rodriguez Faces Final Weeks.' A1
- 1993, 2 Oct. 'Rodriguez Lost to Public Opinion.' A5
- 1993, 21 Oct. 'Parties Calling for Major Changes in Young Offenders Act.'
- 1993, 22 Dec. 'New Legislation Hastily Drafted.' A5
- 1993, 23 Dec. 'Victims, Offenders and Healing.' A1
- 1994, 12 Mar. 'AIDS Victim Seeks Right to Assisted Death.' A4
- 1994, 25 Mar. 'Finta's Acquittal Upheld by Court in Split Decision.' A9
- 1994, 30 Sep. 'Right to Seek Counsel Beefed Up – Breath Tests in Jeopardy.' A1
- 1994, 1 Oct. 'Killer Denied Fair Hearing.' A4
- 1994, 8 Oct. 'Supreme Court – Has the Highest Court Lost Touch with Reality? When Protecting the Rights of the Accused May Not Serve the Public Good.' D2
- 1994, 2 Nov. 'Defence of Drunkenness Sparks Plans to Change Law.' A4
- 1994, 9 Nov. '"Mercy Killing" Suspected in Death of Disabled Girl.' A1
- 1994, 25 Nov. 'Ban on Loitering Struck Down.' A1
- 1994, 26 Nov. 'The Man Who Loved Children.' D1
- 1994, 30 Nov. 'Why He's Allowed to Watch.' A18
- 1994, 8 Dec. 'Rape-Crisis Centre under Investigation for Shredding Files.' A4
- 1995, 6 Jan. 'Court Asked to Rule on Bernardo Tapes.' A7
- 1995, 28 Jan. 'Incoming Metro Police Chief Handling Disciplinary Dispute.' A10
- 1995, 25 Feb. 'Bill Rules Out Drunkenness as a Defence.' A5
- 1995, 8 Apr. 'Native Healing Helps Abuser.' A1

- 1995, 14 Apr. 'Put the Victim in the Charter of Rights.' A19
- 1995, 18 May. 'Bernardo Case Plays on People's Fears.' A1
- 1995, 19 May. 'Top Court Curbs Use of Plea Bargains.' A1
- 1995, 22 May. 'Judge Questions Shielding Accused.' A4
- 1995, 25 May. 'Compulsory DNA Samples Urged: Father of Slain Teen Wants Law to Override Suspects' Charter Rights in Certain Cases.' A1
- 1995, 31 May. 'Judge Bans Public Viewing of Graphic Bernardo Tapes.' A1
- 1995, 19 Jun. 'Murderers Costly Inmates, Good Bets for Parole.' A1
- 1995, 21 Jun. 'Rock Offers to Speed DNA Law for Mandatory Testing of Suspects in Violent Crimes Could Be Passed This Week.' A1
- 1995, 22 Jun. 'Testing DNA Testing (Editorial).' A16
- 1995, 23 Jun. 'DNA Testing Bill Passed – Law Will Force Suspects in Broad Range of Crimes to Provide Genetic Samples.' A1
- 1995a, 19 Jul. 'Justice, Mercy and Mr. Latimer.'
- 1995b, 19 Jul. 'Latimer Murder Appeal Denied.' A1
- 1995, 27 Jul. 'Families with Severely Handicapped Children in Desperate Need.'
- 1995, 22 Sep. 'Inquiry Dismisses Smith Allegations Against Police.' A7
- 1995, 27 Sep. 'Constable's Tactics Justified, Police Inquiry Board Rules.' A8
- 1995, 14 Nov. 'Osborne Killer's Parole Protested.' A14
- 1995, 15 Dec. 'Court Rules against Rape Victims.' A1
- 1996, 10 Feb. 'Duplicate Charges Delay Courts, Judges Say.' A10
- 1996, 31 May. 'New Bill Restricts Access to Records.' A1
- 1996, 3 Jun. 'Mr. Rock on Rape.' A12
- 1996, 13 Jun. 'Keep the Personal Records Out of Sexual Assault Cases.' A19
- 1996, 14 Sep. 'Bishop Given 2–1/2 Years for Assault.' A1
- 1996, 12 Dec. 'Ottawa Eyes Crime Prevention.' A1
- 1997, 4 Jan. 'Only Third of Killers Eligible Seek Parole.' A8
- 1997, 20 Jan. 'Police Back Plan to Use DNA Bank in Crime Fight.' A1
- 1997, 22 Jan. 'Prosecutors Seek Relief from Trial by Ambush.' A1
- 1997, 6 Feb. 'Plugged Peel Court in Paper Chase.' A1
- 1997, 7 Feb. 'Top Court Tosses Out Sex Case.' A1
- 1997, 14 Feb. 'Sex-Trade Activity Up, Statscan Finds.' A3
- 1997, 8 Mar. 'Osborne Killer Gets Day Parole; Statements Lead to New Probe.'
- 1997, 11 Mar. 'Olson Causes Families More Anguish.' A8
- 1997, 17 Mar. 'Minor Miscreants Avoid Court System.' A1
- 1997, 21 Mar. 'DNA Evidence Gathering Curbed.' A1
- 1997, 5 May. 'Case Sparking DNA Law Ends.' A4
- 1997, 9 Aug. 'Top Court Extends Rights of the Accused.' A1
- 1997, 16 Aug. 'Hearing for Olson a Clash of Emotions.' A1

- 1997, 22 Aug. 'Olson Bid for Early Parole Denied.' A1
- 1997, 24 Aug. 'When Things Get Awkward under the Charter of Rights.' A14
Gold, Alan D., and Michelle Fuerst. 1992. 'The Stuff That Dreams Are Made Of!
   Criminal Law and the Charter of Rights and Freedoms.' *Ottawa Law Review* 24:
   13
Gold, M., A. Bryant, M. Stevenson, and D. Northrup, eds., 1990 'Public Support
   for the Exclusion of Unconstitutionally Obtained Evidence.' *Supreme Court Law
   Review* 1: 555
Goldstein, Abraham. 1974. 'Reflections on Two Models: Inquisitorial Themes in
   American Criminal Procedure.' *Stanford Law Review* 26: 1009
Gosse Richard, 1994. 'Introduction.' In Richard Gosse, James Youngblood Hend-
   erson, and Roger Carter, eds., *Continuing Poundmaker and Riel's Quest*. Saska-
   toon: Purich
Gotell, Lise. 1997. 'Shaping *Butler*: The New Politics of Anti-Pornography.' In
   Brenda Cossman, Shannon Bell, Lise Gotell, and Becki Ross, eds.,. *Bad
   Attitude/s on Trial: Pornography, Feminism, and the Butler Decision*. Toronto:
   University of Toronto Press
Graham, Fred. 1970. *The Self Inflicted Wound*. New York: Macmillan
Grant, Alan. 1987. 'Videotaping Police Questioning: A Canadian Experiment.'
   Criminal Law Review: 375
Grant, Isabel. 1991. 'The 'Syndromization' of Women's Experience.' *University of
   British Columbia Law Review* 25: 51
- 1996a. 'Developments in Criminal Law: The 1994–95 Term.' *Supreme Court Law
   Review* 7: 203
- 1996b. 'Second Chances: Bill C-72 and the Charter.' *Osgoode Hall Law Journal*
   33: 379
Greschner, Donna. 1994. 'Book Review.' *Windsor Yearbook of Access to Justice* 14: 455
Griffiths, Curt, John F. Klein, and Simon M. Verdun-Jones. 1980. *Criminal Justice in
   Canada: An Introductory Text*. Vancouver: Butterworths
Griffiths, Curt T., J. Colin Yerbury, and Linda F. Weafer. 1989. 'Victimization of
   Canada's Natives: The Consequences of Socio-Cultural Deprivation.' In Ezzat
   A. Fattah, ed., *The Plight of Crime Victims in Modern Society*. Basingstoke:
   Macmillan
Griffiths, John. 1970. 'Ideology in Criminal Procedure or a Third "Model" of the
   Criminal Process.' *Yale Law Journal* 79: 359
Gunn, Rita, and Candice Minch. 1988. *Sexual Assault: The Dilemma of Disclosure, The
   Question of Conviction*. Winnipeg: University of Manitoba Press
Gusfield, Joseph. 1981. *The Culture of Public Problems: Drinking, Driving and the
   Symbolic Order*. Chicago: University of Chicago Press
Habermas, Jurgen. 1976. *Legitimation Crisis*. London: Heinemann

Hagan, John. 1983. *Victims before the Law: The Organizational Domination of Criminal Law.* Scarborough, ON: Butterworths

– 1991. *The Disreputable Pleasures: Crime and Deviance in Canada,* 3d ed. Toronto: McGraw-Hill Ryerson

Hagan, John, and McCarthy, William. 1997. *Mean Streets.* Oxford: Oxford University Press

Halifax Chronicle Herald. 1991, 23 Aug. 'Rape Shield Struck Down.' P1

– 1991, 26 Aug. 'Rape Victim Goes Public After "Rape Shield" Law Struck Down.' P.C15

– 1991, 6 Sep. 'Court Decision Puts Rape Victims on Trial.' B1

– 1994, 1 Oct.. 'Supreme Court Allows Drunkenness Defence in Sexual Assault Case.' D24

Hansard. Canada Debates of the House of Commons, 1979–97

Hardin, Mark. 1996. *Family Group Conferencing: Learning from the New Zealand Experience.* Washington, DC: American Bar Association

Harris, M. Kay. 1987. 'Moving Into the New Millennium: Toward a Feminist Vision of Justice.' *The Prison Journal* 67: 1

Hart, H., and Sacks, A. 1994. *The Legal Process: Basic Problems in Making and Applying the Law.* Westbury, NY: Foundation Press

Harvie, Robert, and Hamar Foster. 1990. 'Ties That Bind? The Supreme Court of Canada, American Jurisprudence, and the Revision of the Canadian Criminal Law under the Charter.' *Osgoode Hall Law Journal* 28: 729

– 1992. 'Different Drummers, Different Drums: The Supreme Court of Canada, American Jurisprudence and the Continuing Revision of Criminal Law under the Charter.' *Ottawa Law Review* 24: 39

– 1996. 'When the Constable Blunders: A Comparison of Police Interrogation in Canada and the United States.' *Seattle Law Review* 19: 497

Havemann, Paul, Keith Couse, Lori Foster, and Rae Matonovich. 1985. *Law and Order for Canada's Indigenous People.* Regina: Prairie Justice Research, University of Regina

Healy, Patrick. 1994. 'Intoxication in the Codification of the Canadian Criminal Law.' *Canadian Bar Review* 73: 515

– 1995a. 'Another Round on Intoxication.' *Criminal Reports* (4th) 33: 268

– 1995b. 'Developments in the Law of Evidence.' *Supreme Court Law Review* (2nd) 6: 369

Heidensohn, Frances. 1986. 'Models of Justice: Portia or Persephone? Some Thoughts on Equality, Fairness and Gender in the Field of Criminal Justice.' *International Journal of Sociology of Law* 14: 287

Henderson, Lynne. 1985. 'The Wrongs of Victim's Rights.' *Stanford Law Review* 37: 937

Henry, Frances, and Miriam Henry. 1995. 'A Challenge to Discriminatory Justice: The *Parks* Decision in Perspective.' *Criminal Law Quarterly* 38: 333

Hill, Casey. 1996. 'The Role of Fault under S.24(2) of the Charter.' In J. Cameron, ed., *The Charter's Impact on the Criminal Justice System.* Toronto: Carswell

Hilton, Zoe. 1989. 'One in Ten: The Struggle and Disempowerment of the Battered Women's Movement.' *Canadian Journal of Family Law* 7: 213

Holmes, Heather J. 1997. 'An Analysis of Bill C-46, Production of Records in Sexual Offence Proceedings.' *Canadian Criminal Law Review* 2: 71

Hošek, Chaviva. 1983. 'Women and the Constitutional Process.' In Keith Banting and Richard Simeon, eds, *And No One Cheered: Federalism, Democracy and the Constitution Act.* Toronto: Methuen

Howland, W.G. 1988. 'Reports on the Administration of Justice in Ontario.' *Law Society of Upper Canada Gazette* 22: 7

Hudson, Joe. 1996. *Family Group Conferencing: Perspectives on Policy and Practice.* Annadale, New South Wales: Federation Press

Hughes, Patricia. 1993. 'From a Woman's Point of View.' *University of New Brunswick Law Journal* 42: 341

Hyde, Mary. 1992. 'Servicing Indian Reserves: The Amerindian Police.' *Canadian Journal of Criminology* 34: 369

Ignatieff, Michael. 1984. *The Needs of Strangers.* London: Chatto & Windus

Inbau, Fred. 1966. 'Democratic Restraints Upon the Police.' *Journal of Criminal Law, Criminology and Police Science* 57: 265

Jackson, Michael. 1992. 'In Search of Pathways to Justice: Alternative Dispute Resolution in Aboriginal Communities.' *University of British Columbia Law Review* 26 (Special Edition): 147

Johnson, Holly. 1995. 'Response to Allegations about the Violence against Women Survey.' In Mariana Valverde, Linda MacLeod, and Kirsten Johnson, eds., *Wife Assault and the Canadian Criminal Justice System.* Toronto: Centre for Criminology

– 1996. *Dangerous Domains: Violence against Women in Canada.* Toronto: Nelson Canada

Johnson, Holly, and Karen Rodgers. 1993. 'A Statistical Overview of Women and Crime in Canada.' In Ellen Adelbery and Claudia Currie, eds., *In Conflict with the Law.* Vancouver: Press Gang

Johnson, Holly, and Vincent F. Sacco. 1995. 'Researching Violence against Women: Statistics Canada National Survey.' *Canadian Journal of Criminology* 37: 281.

Jull, Kenneth. 1987. '*Clarkson* v. *R.*: Do We Need a Legal Emergency Department?' *McGill Law Journal* 32: 359

Kaplan, William. 1989. *State and Salvation: The Jehovah's Witnesses and Their Fight for Civil Rights.* Toronto: University of Toronto Press

Katz, Lewis. 1980. 'Reflections on Search and Seizure and Illegally Seized Evidence in Canada and the United States.' *Canada–United States Law Journal* 3: 103

King, Michael. 1981. *The Framework of Criminal Justice.* London: Croom Helm

Knopff, Rainer. 1989. *Human Rights and Social Technology: The New War on Discrimination.* Ottawa: Carleton University Press

Knopff, Rainer, and Morton, F.L. 1992. 'The Supreme Court as the Vanguard of the Intelligentsia.' Occasional Paper Series, University of Calgary

– 1996. 'Canada's Court Party.' In Anthony Peacock, ed., *Rethinking the Constitution.* Toronto: Oxford University Press

Lacombe, Dany. 1994. *Blue Politics: Pornography and the Law in the Age of Feminism.* Toronto: University of Toronto Press

Lamborn, Leroy. 1987. 'The United Nations Declaration on Victims: Incorporating "Abuse of Power."' *Rutgers Law Journal* 19: 59

Landau, Tammy. 1994. *Public Complaints against the Police: A View from Complainants.* Toronto: Centre of Criminology, University of Toronto

– 1996. 'Policing and Security in Four Remote Aboriginal Communities: A Challenge to Coercive Models of Police Work.' *Canadian Journal of Criminology* 38: 1

Langer, R. 1991. 'Battered Women and the Criminal Injuries Compensation Board.' *Saskatchewan Law Review* 55: 453

LaPrairie, Carol. 1990. 'The Role of Sentencing in the Over-Representation of Aboriginal People in Correctional Institutions.' *Canadian Journal of Criminology* 32: 429

– 1992. 'Aboriginal Crime and Justice: Explaining the Present, Exploring the Future.' *Canadian Journal of Criminology* 34: 281

– 1995. 'Community Justice or Just Communities? Aboriginal Communities in Search of Justice.' *Canadian Journal of Criminology* 37: 521

LaRocque, Emma. 1997. 'Re-examining Culturally Appropriate Models in Criminal Justice.' In M. Asch, ed., *Aboriginal and Treaty Rights in Canada.* Vancouver: University of British Columbia Press

Law Reform Commission (LRCC). 1974a. *Discovery.* Ottawa: Information Canada

– 1974b. *The Principles of Sentencing and Dispositions.* Ottawa: Information Canada

– 1974c. *Restitution and Compensation – Fines (Working Papers 5 & 6).* Ottawa: Information Canada

– 1974–5. *Fourth Annual Report.* Ottawa: Information Canada

– 1975. *Limits of the Criminal Law: Obscenity a Test Case.* Ottawa: Information Canada

– 1978. *Criminal Law: Sexual Offences.* Ottawa: Minister of Supply and Services

– 1983a. *Criminal Law – Police Powers – Search and Seizure in Criminal Law Enforcement (Working Paper 30).* Ottawa: Minister of Supply and Services

- 1983b. *Writs of Assistance and Telewarrants.Report 19*. Ottawa: Supply and Services
- 1984. *Disclosure by the Prosecution*. Ottawa: Minister of Supply and Services
- 1986. *Electronic Surveillance*. Ottawa: Law Reform Commission of Canada
- 1991. *Report 34: Aboriginal Peoples and Criminal Justice*. Ottawa: Law Reform Commission of Canada

Lawyers Weekly. 1998, 10 Jul. 'Sex Charge Resolved by Native Healing Circle.' 6

LEAF (Women's Legal Education and Action Fund). 1996. *Equality and the Charter: Ten Years of Feminist Advocacy before the Supreme Court of Canada*. Toronto: Emond Montgomery

Leo, Richard. 1996. 'Inside the Interrogation Room.' *Journal of Criminal Law and Criminology* 86: 266

Lerman, Lisa. 1992. 'The Decontextualization of Domestic Violence.' *The Journal of Criminal Law and Criminology* 83: 217

Leschied, Alan, and Peter Jaffe. 1988. 'Implementing the Young Offenders Act in Ontario.' In J. Hudson, J. Hornick, and B., Burrows, eds., *Justice and the Young Offender in Canada*. Toronto: Wall & Thompson

Linden, Allen. 1968. *The Report of the Osgoode Hall Study on Compensation For Victims of Crime*. Toronto: Osgoode Hall Law School

Lipset, Seymour Martin. 1990. *Continental Divide: The Values and Institutions of the United States and Canada*. New York: Routledge

Little Bear, Leroy. 1994. 'What's Einstein Got to Do with It.' In Richard Gosse, James Youngblood Henderson, and Roger Carter, eds., *Continuing Poundmaker and Riel's Quest*. Saskatoon: Purich

Llewellyn, Karl. 1962. *Jurisprudence Realism in Theory and Practice*. Chicago: University of Chicago Press

Llewellyn, Karl, and E. Adamson Hoebel,. 1941. *The Cheyenne Way Conflict and Case Law in Primitive Jurisprudence*. Norman: University of Oklahoma Press

Longclaws, Lyle, et al. 1996. 'Piloting Family Group Conferences for Young Offenders in Winnipeg, Canada.' In Joe Hudson and Burt Galaway, eds. *Family Group Conferences: Perspectives on Policy and Practice*. Annadale, New South Wales: Federation Press

Los, Maria. 1994. 'The Struggle to Redefine Rape in the Early 1980s.' In Julian Roberts and Renate Mohr, eds., *Confronting Sexual Assault: A Decade of Legal and Social Change*. Toronto: University of Toronto Press

Lowman, John, and Brian D. MacLean, eds. 1992. *Realist Criminology: Crime Control and Policing in the 1990s*. Toronto: University of Toronto Press

Lungren, Daniel E. 1996. 'Victims and the Exclusionary Rule.' *Harvard Journal of Law and Public Policy* 19: 695

MacCrimmon, Marilyn. 1987. 'Developments in the Law of Evidence: The 1985–86 Term.' *Supreme Court Law Review* 9: 363

MacKinnon, Catharine. 1989. *Toward a Feminist Theory of the State.* Cambridge, MA: Harvard University Press.

MacLeod, Linda. 1980. *Wife Battering in Canada: The Vicious Circle.* Ottawa: Canadian Advisory Council on the Status of Women

– 1995. 'Family Group Conferencing: A Community-Based Model for Stopping Family Violence.' In Mariana Valverde, Linda MacLeod, and Kirsten Johnson, *Wife Assault and the Canadian Justice System.* Toronto: Centre for Criminology

Maguire, Mike, and C. Corbett. 1991. *A Study of the Police Complaints System.* London: HMSO

Maguire, Mike, and John Ponting, eds. 1988. *Victims of Crime: A New Deal?* Milton Keyes: Open University Press

Mahoney, Kathleen. 1992. '*R. v. Keegstra*: A Rationale for Regulating Pornography?' *McGill Law Journal* 37: 243

Mandel, Michael. 1989. *The Charter of Rights and Freedoms and the Legalization of Politics in Canada.* Toronto: Thompson Educational

– 1994. *The Charter of Rights and Freedoms and the Legalization of Politics in Canada,* rev. ed. Toronto: Thompson Educational

– 1996. 'Fundamental Justice, Repression and Social Power.' In Jamie Cameron, ed., *The Charter's Impact on the Criminal Justice System.* Toronto: Carswell

Manfredi, Christopher. 1991. 'The Young Offenders Act and Juvenile Justice in the United States: Perspectives on Recent Reform Proposals.' *Canadian Journal of Law and Society* 6: 45

– 1993. *Judicial Power and the Charter: Canada and the Paradox of Liberal Constitutionalism.* Toronto: McClelland & Stewart

Manitoba. 1986. *Legislative Debates.* Winnipeg: Queen's Printer

– Public Inquiry into the Administration of Justice and Aboriginal People. 1991a. *Report of the Aboriginal Justice Inquiry of Manitoba. Volume 1: The Justice System and Aboriginal People.* Winnipeg: Queen's Printer

– Public Inquiry into the Administration of Justice and Aboriginal People. 1991b. *Report of the Aboriginal Justice Inquiry of Manitoba. Volume 2: The Deaths of Helen Betty Osborne and John Joseph Harper.* Winnipeg: Queen's Printer

Markwart, Alan E., and Raymond R. Corrado. 1989. 'Is the Young Offenders Act More Punitive?' In Lucien A. Beaulieu, ed., *Young Offender Dispositions: Perspectives on Principle and Practice.* Toronto: Wall & Thompson

Marshall, Patricia. 1988. 'Sexual Assault, the Charter and Sentencing Reform.' *Criminal Reports* (3d) 63: 216

Martin, Dianne. 1993. 'Organizing for Change: A Community Law Response to Police Misconduct.' *Hastings Women's Law Journal* 4: 131

– 1996. 'Rising Expectations: Slippery Slope or New Horizon? The Constitutionalization of Criminal Trials in Canada.' In Jamie Cameron, ed., *The Charter's Impact on the Criminal Justice System.* Toronto: Carswell

– 1997. *Wrongful Convictions: An International Comparative Study* (prepared for the Association in Aid of the Wrongfully Convicted for submission to the inquiry into Guy Paul Morin's wrongful conviction)

Martin, Dianne, and Janet Mosher. 1995. 'Unkept Promises: Experiences of Immigrant Women with the Neo-Criminalization of Wife Abuse.' *Canadian Journal of Women and the Law* 8: 3

Martin, G.A. 1961. 'The Exclusionary Rule under Foreign Law.' *Journal of Criminal Law, Criminology and Police Science* 52: 271

Martin, Robert. 'Bill C-49: A Victory for Interest Group Politics.' *University of New Brunswick Law Journal* 42: 357

Matas, David, 1987. *Justice Delayed: Nazi War Criminals in Canada.* Toronto: Summerhill

– 1994. 'The Case of Imre Finta.' *University of New Brunswick Law Journal* 43: 281

Matsuda, Mari. 1989. 'Public Responses to Racist Speech: Considering the Victim's Story.' *Michigan Law Review* 87: 2320

Mawby, R., and S. Walklate, 1994. *Critical Victimology.* London: Sage

Maxfield, Michael, and Cathy Spatz Widom. 1996. 'The Cycle of Violence: Revisited Six Years Later.' *Archives of Paediatrics and Adolescent Medicine* 150: 390

Maxwell, Gabrielle, and Allison Morris. 1996. 'Research on Family Group Conferences with Young Offenders in New Zealand.' In Joe Hudson and Burt Galaway, eds., *Family Group Conferences: Perspectives on Policy and Practice.* Annadale, New South Wales: Federation Press

McBarnet, Doreen. 1979. 'Arrest: The Legal Context of Policing.' In S. Holdaway, ed., *The British Police.* London: Arnold

– 1981. *Conviction: Law, the State and Construction of Justice.* London: Macmillan

McConville, Mike, and John Baldwin. 1977. *Negotiated Justice.* London: Routledge

– 1981. *Courts, Prosecution, and Conviction.* Oxford: Clarendon Press

McConville, Mike, Andrew Sanders, and Roger Leng. 1991. *The Case for the Prosecution.* London: Routledge

McGillivray, Anne. 1987. 'Battered Women: Definition, Models and Prosecutorial Policy.' *Canadian Journal of Family Law* 9: 15

– 1990. 'Abused Children in the Courts: Adjusting the Scales After Bill C-15.' *Manitoba Law Journal* 19: 549

McIntyre, Sheila. 1994. 'Redefining Reformism: The Consultations That Shaped Bill C-49.' In Julian Roberts and Renate Mohr, eds., *Confronting Sexual Assault: A Decade of Legal and Social Change.* Toronto: University of Toronto Press

McMahon, Maeve. 1992. *Persistent Prison: Rethinking Decarceration as Penal Reform.* Toronto: University of Toronto Press

McNamara, Luke. 1993. *Aboriginal Peoples, the Administration of Justice, and the Autonomy Agenda: An Assessment of the Status of Criminal Justice Reform in Canada with Reference to the Prairie Region.* Winnipeg: Legal Research Institute of the University of Manitoba

Miers, D.R. 1974. 'The Ontario Criminal Injuries Compensation Scheme.' *University of Toronto Law Journal* 24: 347

Minow, Martha. 1993. 'Surviving Victim Talk.' *U.C.L.A. Law Review* 40: 1411

Monahan, Patrick, and Andrew Petter. 1987. 'Developments in Canadian Constitutional Law: The 1985–86 Term.' *Supreme Court Law Review* 9: 69

Monahan, Patrick. 1987. *Politics and the Constitution: The Charter, Federalism, and the Supreme Court of Canada.* Agincourt: Carswell.

Montreal Gazette. 1987, 19 Dec. 'Justice Well Done.' B2

– 1990, 4 May. 'Top Court Backs Battered Wife in Killing.' A1

– 1990, 1 Jun.. 'Spot Checks Needed to Stop Highway Carnage: Top Court.' B1

– 1991, 13 Jan. 'Most Back Rape Shield Law.' A6

– 1991, 1 May. 'Alcoholic Too Drunk to Be Guilty.' A1

– 1991, 23 Aug. 'Supreme Court Strikes Down Rape-Shield Law.' A1

– 1991, 10 Sep. 'A Victim's Story.' B3

– 1992, 20 Nov. 'Accused Drug Dealers Face Tougher Bail Rules.' B1

– 1994, 23 Jan. 'Top Court Rejects Synagogues' Request to Clarify Ruling in Imre Finta Case.' B1

– 1994, 25 Mar. 'Supreme Court Upholds War-Crimes Laws.' B1

– 1994, 31 Dec. 'Extreme Drunkenness Defence Ruling Sparked Furious Legal Debate.' B7

Monture-Okanee, Patricia. 1994. 'Thinking about Aboriginal Justice: Myths and Revolution.' In Richard Gosse, James Youngblood Henderson, and Roger Carter, eds., *Continuing Poundmaker and Riel's Quest.* Saskatoon: Purich

Monture-Okanee, Patricia, and Mary Ellen Turpel. 1992. 'Aboriginal Peoples and Canadian Criminal Law: Rethinking Justice. *University of British Columbia Law Review* 26 (Special Edition): 239

Moore, Kathryn. 1992. 'Police Implementation of Supreme Court of Canada Charter Decisions: An Empirical Study.' *Osgoode Hall Law Journal* 30: 547

Moore, Mark. 1995. 'Public Health and Criminal Justice Approaches to Prevention.' In Michael Tonry and David Farrington, eds., *Building a Safer Society.* Chicago: University of Chicago Press

Moran, Mayo. 1994. 'Talking about Hate Speech: A Rhetorical Analysis of American and Canadian Approaches to the Regulation of Hate Speech.' *Wisconsin Law Review*: 1425.

Morris, Ruth. 1989. Crumbling Walls: Why Prisons Fail. Oakville, ON: Mosaic

Morton, F.L. 1992a. 'The Charter Revolution and the Court Party.' *Osgoode Hall Law Journal* 30: 627

– 1992b. *Morgentaler v. Borowski: Abortion, the Charter, and the Courts.* Toronto: McClelland & Stewart

Morton, F.L., P.H. Russell, and M.J. Withey. 1992. 'The Supreme Court's First One Hundred Charter of Rights Decisions: A Statistical Analysis.' *Osgoode Hall Law Journal* 30: 1

– 1995. 'The Canadian Charter of Rights and Freedoms: A Descriptive Analysis of the First Decade.' *National Journal of Constitutional Law* 5: 1

Mosher, Janet. 1994. 'Challenging Limitation Periods: Civil Claims by Adult Survivors of Incest.' *University of Toronto Law Journal* 44: 169

Moyer, Sharon, and Lee Axon. 1993, 30 Apr. 'An Implementation Evaluation of the Native Community Council Project of the Aboriginal Legal Services of Toronto.'

Nahanee, Teressa. 1993. 'Dancing with a Gorilla: Aboriginal Women, Justice and the Charter.' In Royal Commission on Aboriginal Peoples, *Aboriginal Peoples and the Justice System: Report of the National Roundtable on Aboriginal Justice Issues.* Ottawa: Minister of Supply and Services

Nardulli, Peter. 1983 'The Societal Costs of the Exclusionary Rule.' *American Bar Foundation Research Journal:* 585

National Crime Prevention Council. 1996. *Clear Limits and Real Opportunities: The Keys to Preventing Youth Crimes.* Ottawa: NCPC

Noonan, Sheila. 1992. 'Harm Revisited: *R. v. Butler.*' *Constitutional Forum* 4: 12

Noonan, Sheila, and Christine Boyle. 1986. 'Prostitution and Pornography: Beyond Formal Equality.' *Dalhousie Law Journal* 10: 225

Normandeau, André. 1983. 'For a Canadian and International Charter of Rights for Crime Victims.' *Canadian Journal of Criminology* 25: 463

Nova Scotia. Royal Commission on the Donald Marshall, Jr, Prosecution. 1989. *Commissioner's Report.* Nova Scotia: Province of Nova Scotia

Oleskiw, Diane, and Nicole Tellier. 1997. *Submission to the Standing Committee on Bill C-46 (An Act to Amend the Criminal Code in Respect of Production of Records in Sexual Offence Proceedings).* Ottawa: National Association of Women and the Law

Olsen, Frances. 1984. 'Statutory Rape: A Feminist Critique of Rights Analysis.' *Texas Law Review* 63: 387

Ontario. 1984. Ontario Advisory Council on the Status of Women. *Pornography and Prostitution.* Toronto: Queen's Printer

– 1989. Task Force on Race Relations and Policing. *The Report of the Race Relations and Policing Task Force.* Toronto: Ministry of the Solicitor General

– 1992. Task Force on Race Relations and Policing. *The Report of the Race Relations and Policing Task Force.* Toronto: Ministry of the Solicitor General

– 1993. Attorney General's Advisory Committee on Charge Screening, Disclosure, and Resolution Discussions. *Report of the Ontario Attorney General's Advisory Committee on Charge Screening, Disclosure, and Resolution Discussions.* Toronto: Queen's Printer

– 1994. *Legislative Debates.* Toronto: Queen's Printer

– 1995. Commission on Systemic Racism in the Ontario Criminal Justice System. *Report of the Commission on Systemic Racism in the Ontario Criminal Justice System.* Toronto: Queen's Printer

Paciocco, David M. 1987. 'The Development of *Miranda*-like Doctrines under the Charter.' *Ottawa Law Review* 19: 49

– 1990. 'The Judicial Repeal of s. 24(2) and the Development of the Canadian Exclusionary Rule.' *Criminal Law Quarterly* 32: 326

– 1996a. 'Bill C-46 Should Not Survive Constitutional Challenge.' *The Sexual Offences Law Reporter* 3: 187

– 1996b. 'The Evidence of Children: Testing Rules Against What We Know.' *Queen's Law Journal* 21: 345

Packer, Herbert. 1964. 'Two Models of the Criminal Process.' *University of Pennsylvania Law Review* 113: 1

– 1966. 'The Courts, the Police and the Rest of Us.' *Journal of Criminal Law, Criminology and Police Science* 57: 238

– 1968. *The Limits of the Criminal Sanction.* Stanford, CA: Stanford University Press

– 1973. 'Criminal Code Revision.' *University of Toronto Law Journal* 23: 13

Packer, Hebert, and R. Gampell. 1959. 'Therapeutic Abortion: A Problem in Law and Medicine.' *Stanford Law Review* 11: 418

Parker, Graham. 1972. 'Copping a Plea.' *Chitty's Law Journal* 20: 310

Pearson, John. 1991. 'Legal Representation under the Young Offenders Act.' In A. Leschied, P. Jaffe, and W. Willis, eds., *The Young Offenders Act: A Revolution in Canadian Juvenile Justice.* Toronto: University of Toronto Press

People in Equal Participation Inc. 1993. *Factum of the Intervenor* in *Rodriguez v. British Columbia (Attorney General)* before the Supreme Court of Canada Court (File 23476)

Peterson, Cynthia. 1991. 'A Queer Response to Bashing: Legislating against Hate.' *Queen's Law Journal* 16: 237

– 1993. 'Institutionalized Racism: The Need for Reform of the Criminal Jury Selection Process.' *McGill Law Journal* 38: 147

Petter, Andrew. 1986. 'The Politics of the Charter.' *Supreme Court Law Review* 8: 473

Quigley, Tim. 1994. 'Some Issues in Sentencing of Aboriginal Offenders.' In Richard Gosse, James Youngblood Henderson, and Roger Carter, eds., *Continuing Poundmaker and Riel's Quest.* Saskatoon: Purich

– 1997. *Procedure in Canadian Criminal Law.* Toronto: Carswell

Ratushny, Hon. Lynn. 1997, 11 Jul. *Self Defence Review. Final Report,* submitted to Minister of Justice and Solicitor General

Razack, Sherene. 1991. *Canadian Feminism and the Law: The Women's Legal Education and Action Fund and the Pursuit of Equality.* Toronto: Second Story

Renaud, Gilles. 1995. 'A Thematic Review of "Principled Hearsay" in Child Sex Abuse Cases.' *Criminal Law Quarterly* 37: 277

– 1996. 'The Reformed Code of Criminal Restitution: Some Observations.' *The Advocate* 54: 725

Roach, Kent. 1986. 'Constitutionalizing Disrepute: Exclusion of Evidence after *Therens.*' *University of Toronto Faculty of Law Review* 44: 209

– 1990, 'Book Review.' *Canadian Bar Review* 69: 802

– 1991a. 'The Charter and the Criminal Process.' In Jane Gladstone, Richard Ericson, and Clifford Shearing, eds., *Criminology: A Reader's Guide.* Toronto: Centre of Criminology, University of Toronto

– 1991b. 'The Limits of Corrective Justice and the Potential of Equity in Constitutional Remedies.' *Arizona Law Review* 33: 859

– 1993a. 'The Problems of Public Choice.' *Osgoode Hall Law Journal* 31: 721

– 1993b. 'The Role of Litigation and the *Charter* in Interest Advocacy.' In Leslie Seidle, ed., *Equity and Community: The Charter, Interest Advocacy and Representation.* Montreal: Institute for Research and Public Policy

– 1994. *Constitutional Remedies.* Aurora, ON: Canada Law Book

– 1995a. 'Canadian Public Inquiries and Accountability.' In P. Stenning, ed., *Accountability for Criminal Justice.* Toronto: University of Toronto Press

– 1995b. 'Challenges for Cause and Racial Discrimination.' *Criminal Law Quarterly* 37: 410

– 1996a. 'The Evolving Fair Test under Section 24(2) of the Charter.' *Canadian Criminal Law Review* 1: 117

– 1996b. 'For a Victim Rights Model of Criminal Justice.' *Policy Options* 17: 1

– 1996c. 'Institutional Choice, Co-operation and Struggle in the Age of the Charter.' In Jamie Cameron, ed., *The Charter's Impact on the Criminal Justice System.* Toronto: Carswell

– 1996d. 'Systemic Racism and Criminal Justice Policy.' *Windsor Yearbook of Access to Justice* 15: 236

– 1997. 'What's New and Old about the Legal Process?' *University of Toronto Law Journal* 47: 363

Roach, Kent, and Martin Friedland. 1996. 'Borderline Justice: Policing in the Two Niagaras.' *American Journal of Criminal Law* 23: 241

Roberts, Julian. 1995. *Disproportionate Harm: Hate Crime in Canada.* Ottawa: Department of Justice

– 1996. 'Sexual Assault in Canada: Recent Statistical Trends.' *Queen's Law Journal* 21: 395

Roberts, Julian, and Anthony Doob. 1989. 'Sentencing and Public Opinion: Taking False Shadows for True Substances.' *Osgoode Hall Law Journal* 27: 491

– 1997. 'Race, Ethnicity, and Criminal Justice in Canada.' In Michael Tonry, ed., *Ethnicity, Crime, and Immigration Comparative and Cross Cultural Perspectives – Crime and Justice, v. 21.* Chicago: University of Chicago Press

Roberts, Julian, and Michelle Grossman. 1994. 'Changing Definitions of Sexual Assault: An Analysis of Police Statistics.' In Julian Roberts and Renate Mohr, eds., *Confronting Sexual Assault: A Decade of Legal and Social Change.* Toronto: University of Toronto Press

Roberts, Tim. 1992. *Assessment of the Victim Impact Statement in British Columbia.* Ottawa: Department of Justice

Rock, Paul. 1986. *A View from the Shadows: The Ministry of the Solicitor General of Canada and the Making of the Justice for Victims of Crime Initiative.* Oxford: Oxford University Press

– 1988. 'Governments, Victims and Policies in Two Countries.' *British Journal of Criminology* 28: 44

Rogers, Rix. 1990. *Reaching for Solutions.* Ottawa: Supply and Services

Romanow, Roy, John Whyte, and Howard Leeson. 1984. *Canada … Notwithstanding.* Toronto: Carswell

Rosenberg, Marc. 1996. 'The *Charter*'s Impact on the Law of Evidence in Criminal Cases.' In Jamie Cameron, ed., *The Charter's Impact on the Criminal Justice System.* Toronto: Carswell

Ross, Rupert. 1992. *Dancing with a Ghost: Exploring Indian Reality.* Markham, ON: Reed

– 1994. 'Duelling Paradigms? Western Criminal Justice Versus Aboriginal Community Healing.' In Richard Gosse, James Youngblood Henderson, and Roger Carter, eds., *Continuing Poundmaker and Riel's Quest.* Saskatoon: Purich

– 1996. *Returning to the Teachings: Exploring Aboriginal Justice.* Toronto: Penguin

Rubel, Howard C. 1986. 'Victim Participation in Sentencing Proceedings.' *Criminal Law Quarterly* 28: 226

Russell, Peter. 1983. 'The Political Purpose of the Canadian Charter of Rights and Freedoms.' *Canadian Bar Review* 61: 30

– 1987. *The Judiciary in Canada: The Third Branch of Government.* Toronto: McGraw-Hill Ryerson

– 1989. 'Book Review.' *Canadian Journal of Law and Society* 4: 190

Sacco, Vincent, and Holly Johnson. 1990. *Patterns of Criminal Victimization in Canada.* Ottawa: Supply and Services

Sampson, Robert J., and Janet L. Lauritsen. 1997. 'Racial and Ethnic Disparities in Crime and Criminal Justice in the United States.' In Michael Tonry, ed., *Ethnicity, Crime, and Immigration Comparative and Cross Cultural Perspectives – Crime and Justice, v. 21.* Chicago: University of Chicago Press

Samuelson, Les. 1995. 'Canadian Aboriginal Justice Commissions and Australia's Anunga Rules: Barking Up the Wrong Tree.' *Canadian Public Policy* 21: 187

Sanders, Andrew, and Richard Young. 1994. *Criminal Justice.* London: Butterworths

Sarat, Austin. 1997. 'Vengeance, Victims and the Identities of Law.' *Social and Legal Studies* 6: 163

Scheingold, Stuart, Jana Pershing, and Toska Olson. 1994. 'Sexual Violence, Victim Advocacy, and Republican Criminology: Washington State's Community Protection Act.' *Law and Society Review* 28: 729

Schmeiser, Douglas. 1964. *Civil Liberties in Canada.* Oxford: Oxford University Press

Schmolka, Vicki. 1992. *Is Bill C-15 Working? An Overview of the Research on the Effects of the 1988 Child Sexual Abuse Amendments.* Ottawa: Department of Justice

Schur, Edwin. 1965. *Crimes without Victims: Deviant Behavior and Public Policy.* Englewood Cliffs, NJ: Prentice-Hall

– 1973. *Radical Non-Intervention: Rethinking the Delinquency Problem.* Englewood Cliffs, NJ: Prentice-Hall

Senate of Canada. 1995. *Of Life and Death: Report of the Special Senate Committee on Euthanasia and Assisted Suicide.* Ottawa: Senate of Canada

Shaffer, Martha. 1990. '*R. v. Lavallee:* A Review Essay.' *Ottawa Law Review* 22: 607

– 1992. '*Seaboyer v. R.*: A Case Comment.' *Canadian Journal of Women and the Law* 5: 202

– 1995. 'Criminal Responses to Hate-Motivated Violence: Is Bill C-41 Tough Enough?' *McGill Law Journal* 41: 199

– 1997. 'The Battered Women's Syndrome Revisited: Some Complicating Thoughts Five Years after *R. v. Lavallee.*' *University of Toronto Law Journal* 47: 1

Shapiro, Carol. 1990. 'Is Restitution Legislation the Chameleon of the Victims' Movement?' In Burt Galloway and Joe Hudson, eds., *Criminal Justice, Restitution and Reconciliation.* Monsey, NY: Criminal Justice Press

Shapland, Joanna. 1984. 'The Victim, the Criminal Justice System and Compensation.' *British Journal of Criminology* 24: 131

Shapland, Joanna, Jan Willmore, and Peter Duff. 1985. *Victims in the Criminal Justice System.* Aldershot: Gower

Shaver, Frances. 1994. 'The Regulation of Prostitution: Avoiding the Morality Traps.' *Canadian Journal of Law and Society* 9: 123

Shaw, Margaret. 1993. 'Reforming Federal Women's Imprisonment.' In E.

Adelbery and C. Currie, eds., *In Conflict with the Law*. Vancouver: Press
Gang

Shaw, Margaret, Karen Rodgers, and Joanne Blanchette. 1992. *Paying the Price –
Federally Sentenced Women in Context No. 1992–13*. Ottawa: Ministry of the Solicitor General

Sheehy, Elizabeth. 1989. 'Canadian Judges and the Law of Rape: Should the
Charter Insulate Bias?' *Ottawa Law Review* 21: 741

– 1991. 'Feminist Argumentation Before the Supreme Court of Canada in *R. v.
Seaboyer; R. v. Gayme*. The Sound of One Hand Clapping.' *Melbourne University
Law Review* 18: 451

– 1994. 'Compensation for Women Who Have Been Raped.' In Julian V. Roberts
and Renate Mohr, eds., *Confronting Sexual Assault: A Decade of Legal and Social
Change*. Toronto: University of Toronto Press

– 1995. *The Intoxication Defence in Canada: Why Women Should Care*. Ottawa:
Canadian Advisory Council on the Status of Women

Sherman, Lawrence, and Richard Berk. 1984. 'The Specific Deterrent Effects of
Arrest for Domestic Assault.' *American Sociology Review* 49: 261

Sherman, Lawrence, J. Schmidt, P. Rogan, D. Smith, P. Gartin, E. Cohn, D. Collins, and A. Bacich. 1992. 'The Variable Effects of Arrest on Criminal Careers:
The Milwaukee Domestic Violence Experiment.' *The Journal of Criminal Law
and Criminology* 83: 137

Shilton, Elizabeth J., and Anne S. Derrick. 1991. 'Sex Equality and Sexual Assault:
In the Aftermath of *Seaboyer*.' *Windsor Yearbook of Access to Justice* 11: 107

Sinclair, Murray. 1994. 'Aboriginal People, Justice and the Law.' In Richard Gosse,
James Youngblood Henderson, and Roger Carter, eds., *Continuing Poundmaker
and Riel's Quest*. Saskatoon: Purich

Skolnick, Jerome. 1966. *Justice without Trial: Law Enforcement in Democratic Society*.
New York: John Wiley

Skurka, Steven. 1993. 'Two Scales of Justice: The Victim as Adversary.' *Criminal
Law Quarterly* 35: 334

Smart, Carol. 1989. *Feminism and the Power of Law*. New York: Routledge

Smith, George W. 1988. 'Policing the Gay Community: An Inquiry into Textually
Mediated Social Relations.' *International Journal of the Sociology of Law* 16: 163

Snider, Laureen. 1985. 'Legal Reform and Social Control: The Dangers of
Abolishing Rape.' *International Journal of the Sociology of Law* 13: 337

– 1994. 'Feminism, Punishment and the Potential of Empowerment.' *Canadian
Journal of Law and Society* 9: 75

Spohn, Cassia, and Julie Horney. 1992. *Rape Law Reform: A Grass Roots Revolution
and Its Impact*. New York: Plenum

Stenning, Philip. 1994. *Police Use of Force and Violence against Members of Visible Minority Groups in Canada*. Ottawa: Canadian Centre for Police-Race Relations

Stewart, Trish. 1996. 'Family Group Conferences with Young Offenders in New Zealand.' In Joe Hudson and Burt Galaway, eds., *Family Group Conferences: Perspectives on Policy and Practice*. Annadale, New South Wales: Federation Press

Stuart, Don. 1993. 'The Pendulum Has Been Pushed Too Far.' *University of New Brunswick Law Journal* 42: 349

– 1995. 'Parliament Should Declare a New Responsibility for Drunkenness Based on Criminal Negligence.' *Criminal Reports* (4th) 39: 289

– 1996a. *Charter Justice in Canadian Criminal Law* Toronto: Carswell

– 1996b. '*Charter* Protection against Law and Order, Victims' Rights and Equality Rhetoric.' In Jamie Cameron, ed., *The Charter's Impact on the Criminal Justice System*. Toronto: Carswell

Stubbs, Julie. 1995. '"Communitarian" Conferencing and Violence against Women: A Cautionary Note.' In Mariana Valverde, Linda MacLeod, and Kirsten Johnson, eds., *Wife Assault and the Canadian Justice System*. Toronto: Centre for Criminology

Sullivan, Terrence. 1992. *Sexual Abuse and the Rights of Children*. Toronto: University of Toronto Press

Tarnopolsky, Walter S. 1975. *The Canadian Bill of Rights*, 2d ed. Toronto: McClelland & Stewart

Taylor, Charles. 1992. *Multiculturalism and the Politics of Recognition*. Princeton, NJ: Princeton University Press

Thompson, E.P. 1975. *Whigs and Hunters*. New York: Pantheon

Thorvaldson, S. Ab. 1987. 'Restitution by Offenders in Canada: Some Legislative Issues.' *Canadian Journal of Criminology* 29: 1

Tollefson, Christopher. 1991. 'Ideologies Clashing: Corporations, Criminal Law and the Regulatory Offence.' *Osgoode Hall Law Journal* 29: 705

Tonry, Michael. 1995. *Malign Neglect: Race, Crime and Punishment in America*. New York: Oxford University Press

Toronto Star. 1981, 2 Nov. 'End Writs of Assistance.' A6

– 1984, 4 Aug. 'The Horrors of Child Abuse.' A12

– 1984, 16 Nov. 'Writs of Assistance Struck Down.' A4

– 1986, 9 Jun. 'The Tangled Trial of Donald Marshall.' A8

– 1987, 13 Dec. 'Why Constructive Murder Is Unjust.' B1

– 1987, 30 Dec. 'Law to Curb Child Sex Takes Effect This Week.' A2

– 1988, 29 Apr. 'Supreme Court Upholds Spot Checks.' A1

– 1990, 14 Apr. '"Obviously Guilty" Drug Dealer Free.' A6

– 1990, 4 May. 'Women's Groups Laud "Enlightened" Decision By Court.' A23

– 1990, 23 Aug. 'Court Ruling "Chilling" Outraged Feminists Say.' A1

- 1990a, 14 Sep. 'Murder Provision Thrown Out.' A15
- 1990b, 14 Sep. 'Turnbull Case Acquittals Upheld.' A15
- 1991, 24 Aug. 'Rape Shield Struck Down.' A1
- 1991, 9 Oct. 'Building Blitz Pledged to End Court Backlog.' A12
- 1991, 19 Dec. '2,400 Drunk Driving Cases Dropped.' A1
- 1992, 17 Feb. 'Women Urged to Fight for "No Means No" Law.' A3
- 1994, 27 Jan. 'Drunk Driver Loses Case Despite Rights Violation.' A10
- 1994, 25 Mar. 'Top Court Backs War Crimes Acquittal.' A3
- 1994, 24 Jun. 'Supreme Court Won't Reopen War Crimes Case.' A11
- 1994, 1 Oct. 'Drinking Ruled a Rape Defence – Feminists Outraged at Supreme Court Decision.' A1
- 1994, 11 Oct. 'Drunkenness Can't Be an Excuse for Rape.' A22
- 1994, 25 Nov. 'Top Court Backs Law on Paedophile Loitering.' A2
- 1995, 15 Dec. 'Court Opens Rape Records to Accused.' A3
- 1996, 12 Feb. 'Hate Crimes Common.' A1
- 1996, 31 May. 'High Court Hands Down Strict Warning to Teachers.' A3
- 1996, 3 Nov. 'Case Not Closed.' B1
- 1997, 6 Jan. 'Son of Sam Law to Be Framed.' A8.
- 1997, 14 Feb. '1 in 20 Slain Women Worked as a Prostitute.' A3
- 1997, 4 Jul. 'Community Service Ordered by Judge.' A1
- 1997, 27 Sep. 'Women Killers Stay Jailed Despite Judge's Plea.' A1
- 1997, 9 Dec. 'Judge's Decision Terrifying for the Disabled.' A6

Toronto Sun. 1990, 20 Jul. 'Peel Crooks Could Get Off – Court Cases in Peril.' 8
- 1990, 11 Nov. '$39M to Bust Court Logjam.' 3
- 1990, 20 Dec. '"Blitz" Courts Roll.' 2

Tremblay, Richard E., and Wendy M. Craig. 1995. 'Developmental Crime Prevention.' In Michael Tonry and David P. Farrington, eds., *Building a Safer Society: Strategic Approaches to Crime Prevention.* Chicago: University of Chicago Press

Tremblay, Richard E., Linda Pagani-Kurtz, Louise C. Mâsse, Frank Vitaro, and Robert O. Pihl. 1995. 'A Bimodal Preventative Intervention For Disruptive Kindergarten Boys: Its Impact Through Mid-Adolescence.' *Journal of Consulting and Clinical Psychology* 63: 560

Turpel, Mary Ellen, 1990. 'Aboriginal People and the Constitution: Interpretative Monopolies, Cultural Differences.' *Canadian Human Rights Yearbook* 6: 3
- 1993. 'On the Question of Adapting the Canadian Criminal Justice System for Aboriginal Peoples: Don't Fence Me In.' In Royal Commission on Aboriginal Peoples, *Aboriginal Peoples and the Justice System: Report of the National Roundtable on Aboriginal Justice Issues.* Ottawa: Minister of Supply and Services Canada
- 1994. 'Reflections on Thinking Concretely about Criminal Justice Reform.' In

Richard Gosse, James Youngblood Henderson, and Roger Carter, eds., *Continuing Poundmaker and Riel's Quest*. Saskatoon: Purich

Tyler, Tom. 1990. *Why People Obey the Law*. New Haven: Yale University Press

United Nations. 1985. Declaration of Basic Principles of Justice for Victims of Crime and Abuse of Power. U.N. Doc. 40/34

United States. 1982. President's Task Force on Victims of Crime. *Final Report*. Washington, DC: U.S. Government Printing Office

Vallance, Ian. 1988. 'Interest Group and the Process of Legislative Reform: Bill C-15: A Case Study.' *Queen's Law Journal* 13: 158

Valverde, Mariana, Linda MacLeod, and Kirsten Johnson, eds. 1995. *Wife Assault and the Canadian Justice System*. Toronto: Centre for Criminology, University of Toronto

Van Ness, Daniel. 1986. *Crime and Its Victims*. Downers Grove, IL: Intervarsity Press

– 1993. 'New Wine and Old Wineskins: Four Challenges of Restorative Justice.' *Criminal Law Forum* 4: 251

Van Stolk, Mary. 1972. *The Battered Child in Canada*. Toronto: McClelland & Stewart

Vancouver Sun. 1983, 13 Jan. 'The New Rape Laws.' B1

– 1985, 17 Dec. 'Rights Abuse Charged in Driver Spot Checks.' B5

– 1987, 4 Dec. 'Top Court's Ruling on Murder Provision Gives Pair New Trials.' A10

– 1987, 30 Dec. 'Tougher Sex Laws to Protect Youth.' A2

– 1991, 26 Aug. 'Rape Shield Law Brings Back Horrors.' A1

– 1992, 13 Jul. 'Jewish League Claims Keegstra Getting Away with Murder.' A4

– 1995, 25 Feb. 'Extreme Drunkenness to Be Banned as a Defence.' A10

Viau, Louise. 1996. 'L'égalité des sexes en droit criminel: un parcours sans fin?' *Canadian Criminal Law Review* 1: 89

Victoria Times Colonist. 1994, 4 Mar. 'Three Out of Four Endorse MD-Assisted Suicide, Poll Shows.'

– 1994, 14 Oct. 'Court Rulings Favor Perpetrators, Cheat Justice, Say Critics.'

– 1994, 21 Nov. 'I'm Not a Monster, Paedophile Says.'

– 1994, 25 Nov. 'Paedophile Curbs Unconstitutional, Top Court Rules.'

– 1994, 28 Nov. 'Curbs on Pedophiles Unfair? So What?'

Wagner, Charles B. 1984. 'The Passing of Legislation Allowing for Trial of Those Accused of War Crimes and Crimes Against Humanity.' *Windsor Yearbook of Access to Justice* 4: 143

Walker, Gillian. 1990. *Family Violence and the Women's Movement: The Conceptual Politics of Struggle*. Toronto: University of Toronto Press

Walker, Lenore. 1979. *The Battered Woman*. New York: Harper & Row

Weinrib, Lorraine Eisenstat. 1994. 'The Body and the Body Politic: Assisted

Suicide under the *Canadian Charter of Rights and Freedoms.*' *McGill Law Journal* 39: 618

Wente, Margaret. 1994, 26 Nov. and 3 Dec. 'A Serious Case of Statistics Abuse.' *Globe and Mail*

West, George. 1988. 'Policing the Gay Community: An Inquiry into Textually-Mediated Social Relations.' *International Journal of Sociology of* Law 16: 163

Wildsmith, Bruce. 1991. 'Getting at Racism: The Marshall Inquiry.' *Saskatchewan Law Review* 55: 97

Wilson, Larry C. 1982. *Juvenile Courts in Canada.* Toronto: Carswell

Winnipeg Free Press. 1983, 5 Jan. 'Sex Assault Laws Get Mixed Reviews.' 1

- 1985, 14 Feb. 'Illegal Blood Sample Admissible.' 1
- 1985. 24 May. 'Court Tightens Breath-Test Rules – Police Must Inform Driver of Right to Counsel, Supreme Court Says.' 1
- 1986, 1 Mar. 'High Court Strikes Down Drug Act Trafficking Section.' 1
- 1987, 5 Jun. 'Blood Sample Ruled Improper.' 8
- 1990a, 14 Sep. 'Errors Lead to Retrial.' A1
- 1990b, 14 Sep. 'Supreme Court Clears Boy, 13 in Double Killing.' A1
- 1990, 15 Sep. 'Rewrite of Juvenile Law Urged.' A3
- 1990, 5 Oct. 'Court Strikes Down Statutory Rape Law.' 10
- 1991, 30 Aug. 'Ottawa Asked to Override Rape-Shield Ruling.' 8
- 1994, 3 Oct. 'Accused Acquitted.' 1
- 1994a, 14 Oct. 'Critics Find Top Court Guilty of Neglecting Victims.'
- 1994b, 14 Oct. 'Shred Records, Profs Say.'
- 1995, 6 Apr. 'Kids Laughed in Police Car.'
- 1995, 29 Jul. 'Latimer Appeal Rejected.' A1
- 1997, 8 Jan. 'Disabled Fear for Lives as Mercy Killing Gains Acceptance.' D1
- 1997, 6 Feb. 'Disabled Vulnerable to Violence.' B2
- 1997, 11 Feb. 'Slip into Tracy Latimer's Body.'

Wolfenden, Lord. 1957. *Report of the Committee on Homosexual Offences and Prostitution.* London: HMSO

Wundersitz, Joy, and Sue Hetzel. 1996. 'Family Conferencing for Young Offenders: The South Australian Experience.' In Joe Hudson and Burt Galaway, eds., *Family Group Conferences: Perspectives on Policy and Practice.* Annadale, New South Wales: Federation Press

Young, Alan. 1991. 'All Along the Watchtower: Arbitrary Detention and the Police Function.' *Osgoode Hall Law Journal* 29: 329

- 1993. 'Two Scales of Justice: A Reply.' *Criminal Law Quarterly* 35: 355
- 1996. 'The *Charter:* the Supreme Court of Canada and the Constitutionalization of the Investigative Process.' In Jamie Cameron, ed., *The Charter's Impact on the Criminal Justice System.* Toronto: Carswell

– 1997. 'Justice for All: The Past, Present and Future of Victims' Rights in Canada' Unpublished paper preprared for CAVEAT

Zehr, Howard. 1990. *Changing Lenses*. Scottsdale: Herald

Zuber, Hon. Thomas G. 1987. *Report of the Ontario Courts Inquiry*. Toronto: Queen's Printer

Index